Convergences:
Inventories of the Present

—

Edward W. Said, General Editor

At Home in the World

Cosmopolitanism Now

Timothy Brennan

HARVARD UNIVERSITY PRESS

Cambridge, Massachusetts
London, England
1997

Printed in the United States of America

Library of Congress Cataloging-in-Publication Data

Brennan, Timothy.
At home in the world : cosmopolitanism now / Timothy Brennan.
p. cm. — (Convergences)
Includes bibliographical references and index.
ISBN 0-674-05030-4 (cloth : alk. paper).
ISBN 0-674-05031-2 (paper : alk. paper)
1. United States—Intellectual life—20th century. 2. American literature—20th century—History and criticism. 3. Popular culture—United States. 4. Civilization, Modern—American influences. 5. Arts, Modern—20th century. 6. Internationalism—History—20th century. I. Title. II. Series: Convergences (Cambridge, Mass.)
E169.12B694 1997
303.48′2—dc21 97-7299

For Ma and Pa

Contents

Acknowledgments

The early chapters of this book were written five years ago and have been revised under the withering comments of people whose perspicacity and care astounded me. There are many to thank. I hope they do not mind my mentioning them here, for in spite of the aid they gave me, some would not recognize their views in mine. As many times before, Edward Said gave me the benefit of his huge support and example. Over fifteen years, he has taught me more about *how* to do things than anyone else, even if I have not always learned his lessons.

I also depended heavily on the encouragement and advice I received while discussing my ideas with colleagues and friends who I am sure do not know how much they aided me: Keya Ganguly, Fredric Jameson, Ruth Gilmore, Peter Hitchcock, Ira Livingston, and Jonathan Scott. I cannot begin to say how much I owe to the readers who criticized the manuscript, or parts of it, at various stages: Benita Parry, Nikhil Singh, Neil Lazarus, Barbara Harlow, Khachig Tölöyan, John Beverley, H. Aram Veeser, Mary Louise Pratt, Mary Layoun, Aijaz Ahmad, Jonathan Culler, Amitava Kumar and above all, Michael Sprinker, who has been an ally and a friend at every stage.

For allowing me to present work in progress, I want to thank the various institutions where parts of this work saw the public for the first time: Oberlin College, New York University, the Institute of Culture and Society at Carnegie Mellon University, the Society for Critical Exchange at Case Western Reserve University, the "Localities" conference at Rutgers University, the Humanities Center at Wesleyan University, Wichita State University, the American Academy of Poets of the New York Public Library, Vassar College, Otterbein College, and the "City, Nation, World" conference conducted by the journal *Theory, Culture, and Society* in Berlin during the summer of 1995.

For inviting me to speak at these varied places, where I learned so much, I am indebted to Anuradha Dingwaney, Heidrun Suhr, Paul

Smith, Martha Woodmansee, George Levine, Richard Ohmann, H. Aram Veeser, Indran Amirthanayagam, Wendy Graham, Mona Narain, and Mike Featherstone. Special thanks (again) to Michael Sprinker, who allowed me to share a platform with Perry Anderson at Stony Brook in a discussion of European Union.

A particular sort of gratitude belongs to John Santos of PBS, who gave me the satisfaction of debating Dinesh D'Souza on public television. I am deeply grateful as well to the Stony Brook Foundation, which made it possible for me to do research in Cuba in the winter of 1993, and to the irrepressible Jim Murray, who with anecdotal wit and bookish love gave me access to the C. L. R. James archives in New York. Portions of Chapter 5 were originally published as "The Price of Happiness: C. L. R. James in New York, 1950" in *Between Languages and Cultures: Translation and Cross-Cultural Texts,* Anuradha Dingwaney and Carol Maier, eds., © 1995 by University of Pittsburgh Press and are reprinted by permission of the Press.

Most decisive of all in bringing the project to completion was the seminar group at the Center for the Critical Analysis of Contemporary Culture (CCACC) at Rutgers University, where as a fellow in 1993–94, I wrote about half of this book. My thanks to the seminar members and to the occasional participants, especially Richard Williams, Harriet Davidson, Martha Rosler, Bruce Robbins, Lauren Berlant, Jackson Lears, Lisa LaCourse, John Cicchino, Marcy Schwartz, James Collins, Jan Kubik, Stephen Murdock, Barbara Cooper, Phil Gregory, John Allen Douglas, and Margaret Klawunn.

Two people above all, however, deserve a special note. First, let me thank Neil Smith, whose solidarity, brilliance, and generosity affected me at every stage, often in his own home, where I lived during the writing of many of these pages. His friendship and advice over two years made everything possible, and I will always be in his debt. Second, and with particular affection, I thank Klaus Milich of Humboldt University in Berlin, where this book was completed. Chained to our desks for weeks in the hot Berlin summer of 1995, we debated ideas and phrasings on a daily basis. For giving me the use of his wonderful mind and large heart, and for giving me his very home when I needed to escape, I can say this writing would not have been the same without him.

Finally, for their love and support, my heartfelt thanks to Maggie, Molly, and Virginia, who saw me through a hard time.

Why should I say anything against these people who—like me—come home from work every day? They seem to be decent folk who live with their families, who love their children. Can we blame them for not wanting the "world" in which they feel reasonably at home to be transformed?

—Henri Lefebvre

Introduction

Several years ago I wrote about a new "cosmopolitanism" as a trend in the New York and London book markets.[1] I set out here originally to expand my remarks and deal with some of the misunderstandings they first generated by explaining better what I meant. I was eager to distinguish my sense of the term "cosmopolitanism" from those that had appeared much earlier and those that, by contrast, started to appear in the 1990s with greater frequency. As I came to understand it, the term referred not merely to the big-name novelists I first associated with it, but to the newspaper commentators, professors, and talk show hosts who admired their work and were promoting them. The term referred also to a network of academic, governmental, media, and think tank intellectuals in a variety of disciplines who had risen to prominence in the midst of an obvious, and obviously central, globalizing of experience and outlook. For that reason, a look at the concept was also a look at the structures in which the concept was being debated and, more often than not, unthinkingly used. What I eventually found myself involved in—if I can put it this way—was an "actually existing" Western aesthetics: the recurrent truths and value-laden judgments, that is, not only of literary professionals but of commentators in the media and public policy making.

My echoing of a phrase reminiscent of the cold war ("actually existing") is deliberate. Broadly speaking, a historically novel cosmopolitanism—not to be confused with either simple world traveling or the taint of being dishonorably postnational—has recently come to fruition. Without doubting the accuracy of the prognoses on global culture, one notices how in marked contrast to the past the term has become less an analytical category than a normative projection, complementing at once celebratory claims and despairing recognitions: the death of the nation-state, transculturation (rather than a merely one-sided assimilation), cultural hybridity (rather than a simplistic contrast between the foreign and the indigenous), and postmodernity (as the view that consumption is politically exciting, viable, and wholly one's own). As Mary Louise Pratt asks rhetorically: "Is the *arpillera*-maker depicting the vertical archipelago as she knows it, or as she knows the agronomists knew it, or against the way she knows the agronomists knew it?"[2] In all variants, most under attack has been the dichotomy between colonizer and colonized, though without denying inequalities as such. We have for some time now been witnessing a shift from a binary otherness to a single, internally rich and disparate plurality: a variety of levels within and sites between, rather than the lonely outposts on either side of belief's wall.

One of my aims is to take such appealing, infinitely demonstrable cultural observations and trace them alongside their implications for world citizenship in a post-perestroika age. It is right to expose the myths of authenticity at the core of claims to indigenous cultures. It is also very easy; and like its cousin, the myth of nation, the exposure tells its original formulators very little and finally, I think, misses the point. The new cosmopolitanism drifts into view as an act of avoidance if not hostility and disarticulation toward states in formation. The dichotomy and the binary almost universally deplored—as much in official policy statements and editorials as in literary theory—continues to make sense (indeed, is demanded) dialectically, not in the name of authentic, non-European culture or any other useful fiction but in the name of what this conflict over colonialism and postcolonialism has largely been about: collectivity, community, self-sufficiency.

Even as ideals like collectivity, community, and self-sufficiency have been fought for, the metropolis is largely a term equated with their absence. Trying to find them has often involved a looking back, either as a return to roots or a resistance to "progress." One has no trouble finding examples of both in a wealth of earlier movements and figures: for example, in the reformist social-contract movement of the English Chartists from the mid-nineteenth century; the idealized craftsmen communities evoked by the great English critic F. R. Leavis in his scornful depictions of media and market; or even in Ferdinand Tönnies' famous dichotomy between society and community.[3]

If we look to the future as well as the past, we are met with incompatible visions of community that still suggest binaries of an intractable sort: not three worlds, as might be expected in a discussion of colonialism, but two. In these, one knows the other and the other sees in the one only a closed book. To put the matter another way, Puerto Ricans and Liberians field a larger knowledge of the United States than North Americans do of Puerto Rico and Liberia; the socialist knows the workings of capital with excessive (often even useless) detail, whereas the organic intellectual of capital typically approaches socialism with an uncontested ignorance. Thus, for the independence leader of Guinea-Bissau, Amilcar Cabral, the dialectic of colonizer and colonized was simply not supposed to represent either a sociological explanation or a nuanced cultural model. It was itself a focus—that is, a careful exclusion. He was not lumping difference together, nor was he unaware of multiple communities with their disparate interests. He did not emphasize the disparate because it would not then, in that project, have led to more than the impossibility of doing.

Trends in book markets are not equatable with decisions made in corporate boardrooms or with speeches by a U.S. president on world order. But it is important, I think, to characterize the atmosphere in which all three are simultaneously happening. Links, on the one hand, between a humanist utopia of one-world culture and, on the other, explicit plans for the organization of a world government, have existed for a long time, and have done so precisely under the banner of cosmopolitanism. There had been murmurings of the world community of peace among the pre-Socratics and within the early Christian church, as well as among varied movements throughout the European Middle Ages. By the seventeenth century, cosmopolis came into its own as a vision of practical world government enabled by the philosophical and moral buttressing of intellectuals.

Some of its more exalted renditions arose in the Enlightenment, most notably in Kant's *Perpetual Peace: A Philosophical Essay* (1795) and his "Idea of a Universal History from a Cosmopolitan Standpoint" (1784), and again in the varied optimisms of the nineteenth century. In Anacharsis Cloots's "universal republic"—the work of a Prussian-Dutch member of the Jacobin Club in the French Revolution—and then later, in the first International Workingmen's organization founded in London in 1864, the idea had been enlisted on behalf of the wretched of the earth rather than the universally just and the classlessly enlightened. It was only in twentieth-century anticolonial movements, however, that a negative view of cosmopolitanism arose in a manner that departed from the work of cultural reactionaries like Thomas Carlyle or Oswald Spengler, whose complaint was not with foreign domination through military occupation or racialist theories, but with the impure culture of cities where "traditional values" were on the wane. The progressive view of cosmopolitanism as a dangerous thing came instead from the leaders of mass movements countering what they considered a negative utopia.

Over such a long stretch of high European history, this relatively recent pejorative sense appears almost local and idiosyncratic. I would argue it is not. Although the third-worldist sympathies of the 1960s did manage temporarily to tarnish cosmopolitanism's image, the term now arises again with the legacies of decolonization as its target. Accompanied by a phalanx of debates in several disciplines, the revival occurs at a time when there are more objective foundations for a "new world" than Kant ever knew: namely, the existence of a nation (the United States) with the individual means, the motive, and the alliances to establish the first universal law. We are finding more and more common the claim that American judges have jurisdiction everywhere—that not only does the sun never set on the American empire, there is no place it shines that is not America.

But the contemporary discourse of globalism entails the theorization of a subject—a social type—to give it scope. For the first time in cosmopolitanism's long history, this subjectivity appears as a matter of generalized autobiographical reflection (Paul Rabinow: "We are all cosmopolitans");[4] however, the theorizations today also look elsewhere, locating cosmopolitanism's features in the colonial subalterns who (it is implied) have not yet sufficiently theorized their own emergence in a common world culture. This resurrection of the semantically overdetermined term "cosmopolitan" has points of historical contact that are all heroic: etymologically, in Greece; imperially, in Dante; universally, in seventeenth-century scientific thought; and finally, in post–World War II "American Century" prophecies, of which the present rhetoric is a continuation and an attempted completion.

From earlier European projects of world government and international law—projects whose dream was not so much ethnic or intercultural unity as civic harmony—the current rhetoric of cosmopolitanism today becomes by contrast evolutionary and systemic. While it celebrates the opportunities created by unity, it wants to throw off this older utopian clothing, and through the agencies of literary theory even becomes deeply suspicious of utopia. The East-West of North-South arises at this juncture in a specific confrontation between a solidarity and a conquest: between a vision of civic harmony that continues into the present and a utopianism that is felt to have died in the United States, or more properly, arisen as heterotopia. The contrast replays that long tradition throughout the eighteenth and nineteenth centuries among European and Latin American intellectuals—many of them dissident, some of them socialist—who projected onto "America" the image of a model for world government, the world's last decent hope.

Arguments about culture in the era of the General Agreement on Tariffs and Trade (GATT), then, must speak to the unusual twist given the old relationships, for while there are many continuities with the past, there are also many novelties. The crucially related topic of structural changes within capitalism itself, for example, has typically been about stressing the ability of capital's new decentered forms to sidestep or supersede direct, class-historical confrontations. A familiar feature in recent accounts of the new capitalism is the observation that disproportion and inequality within the wealthy countries are now simply exported by expelling inferior or banned products, garbage, and toxic waste. As the North American Free Trade Agreement (NAFTA) demonstrates, jobs are being exported as well, but these exports, like the guest worker system and selective immigration laws, can just as easily be characterized as an importation of inequality that has its own sort of stablilizing function. Thus, the economic crutch that the "third world" has become for the United States is importantly different from what it had been before.

The statement, however, is both true and untrue. If dependency and world-systems theories about the reliance of the overdeveloped world on cheap labor, higher rates of exploitation, and extraction of raw materials have been plausibly countered by pointing to poor labor productivity and the weight of world trade that occurs entirely within and among corporations, it is still the case that the European countries occupy and invade. Nor have they abandoned older relationships of inequality as well as developed new ones—the new genetic robbery occurring among rare plant life in the Amazon, for example.

For that reason, although it is standard in the social sciences to distinguish between a "colonialism" that belongs to an earlier era of direct military or settler occupation and a contemporary "imperialism" or "postcolonialism" as an economic or cultural system of structural inequality, I will from time to time refer below to the present as a "colonial" era and to colonization as that which has not ended. The United States continues to invade other countries, but the invasion is not now supposed to be an invasion: rather, the nation extends its shadow, *becomes* the elsewhere, decenters itself. To what extent current theory helps the United States perform this function with relative impunity is a vital question, it seems to me.

I justify my use of economic and political observations in what is fundamentally a cultural undertaking because of the links that already exist between globalization as a concept and world culture as an outcome. When I speak of "impunity" I am referring to the fact that claims about globalism in the humanities have been met with a suspicious eagerness and even a little gullibility. In cultural theory, the transnationality of the transnational corporation has for the most part been simply assumed even as the business press greeted the idea with a good deal less solemnity: "Globalisation means having occasional board meetings in London or Paris," the *Economist* observed wryly.

We hear talk also of the mobility of capital—certainly a decisive factor in the transformation of national economies, with profound effects that are still only partly understood. But like the assertion of "postindustrial" society, mobile capital is a very problematic idea—much easier to announce than to assess. Small- and large-scale manufacture are notoriously mobile, of course, but not airports, road construction, or the multiple outlets of the service industry (fast-food restaurants, car rental businesses, hotels, hair salons). Despite important changes to the workforce, to the internal functioning of corporations, and to access to information, forecasts of economic globalization exaggerate the extent to which the old conflicts and setups have changed. Here too there are continuities concealed within proclamations of a radical break.

In inviting and morally charged language the ethos of globality has become remarkably widespread in cultural theory, and almost completely unchallenged. It is literally everywhere. And it is not the province of cultural conservatives alone seeking to establish that "America is special and entitled to a dominant place among our loyalties," the birthplace of "universal ideals to which men and women everywhere may pledge allegiance."[5] With very different intentions, cultural theory is deeply invested in globalism as well. In a recent study of world music, for example, George Lipsitz interprets an early rap video of Queen Latifah entitled "Ladies First" (1989).[6] The video shifts abruptly and covers large territory, moving from Latifah dressed ceremonially like an African queen to a line of young American Black women in modern dress (the chorus). In the course of the video, both images are punctuated by documentary footage of mass uprisings in the South African townships.

In an engaging and well-researched argument, Lipsitz shows how Latifah rejects the public discourse of conservative Black nationalism that urges women to accept subordinate places to Black men. On a somewhat different front, he also shows her countering the arguments of people like Arthur Schlesinger, Jr., who complains that minority rights movements only divide the Union and create chauvinist encampments. As a counter both to Black nationalism and Schlesinger's forced community, Lipsitz observes the sheer generosity and global solidarity of Latifah's video. It proves the likes of Schlesinger wrong, he argues. Far from exclusionary, says Lipsitz, this sort of art makes connections between American teenagers, British Black immigrants, and the rebels of the South African townships; and it does so precisely *because* it is feminist and militantly Black.[7] Its huge sense of diasporic global links is the figure of its politics, now at home in a world where such connections are not only possible but increasingly necessary. Latifah seems to be bringing into reality that very internationalism that had eluded others for so long.

The progressive thing for the cultural critic to do, in Lipsitz's view, is to demonstrate what is positive about the globalizing of representation: in this case, the common diasporic meanings exploited skillfully by Latifah in her act of tricontinental outreach. He cheers on the way she freely identifies with other subject peoples elsewhere in the diaspora, and he marks out a privileged space for that identifying in the arena of mass culture. He then accords mass culture itself a high-pitched rhetoric of "resistance" and "struggle," placing enormous hopes on efforts like Latifah's to "map out discursive and political space through the trope of the African diaspora" and to "subvert existing representations with wide circulation in mass media and popular culture."

What is so striking here is that, while much of Lipsitz's argument is true, Queen Latifah's video is American in particular and local ways. Like much other African-American cultural expression, her performance is likely to be enjoyed widely, but not necessarily accepted politically, in this case, by many Africans. Missing entirely from the analysis is a vexed and in some ways embarrassing issue: that for many people from Africa, African-American borrowings appear distant, unknowledgeable, even a little arrogant—in short, American. As penetrating as its critique of male chauvinist and racist attacks on Black women might be, the video also paradoxically domesticates the imagery of revolt in the townships and sublimates it. The local solidarities, agreements, and communiqués of the township groups that engaged in the revolts represent an anonymous labor and an organizational genius that are enlisted here on behalf of the decidedly more confined politics of rap video.

In other words, an ambiguity lies at the video's core between a solidarity and an appropriation. The sheer misunderstanding in the U.S. context of what it takes to organize a movement capable of confronting a well-armed police force permits a convivial parallelism. That parallelism empowers Black American women but it also packages South Africa as an American image-for-use. The empowerment is nevertheless important, and Lipsitz makes a good case for that, but without commenting sufficiently on its role as containment. What I am suggesting is that there is no such thing as a universal "diasporic meaning," as Lipsitz implies here. The national and ethnic dissonances within the African diaspora are exactly what the rhetoric of globalism obscures, along with (as here) its political stakes. To put it another way, the struggle represented by a career-enhancing artistic performance is just not comparable to the struggle that forced an apartheid regime to the negotiating table. One of the ways imperialism works today is to suggest that it is.

A kind of middle-class antinomianism has always been a feature of the debate on race and colonialism—from the early purveyors of the "Black Legend" of the conquistadors to Enlightenment dissidents from empire like the Abbé Raynal to the abolitionists, and on to the

European social democrats who produced the first concerted "scientific" critiques of imperialism at the turn of the century. As residents within its borders, white middle-class Americans live so close to the projection of the United States—its screen lights up so much of what they see—that it has become the backdrop of their dreaming. Any approach to the issue of literature and colonialism, one would think, would have to dwell on this projection.

Any study of what is variously being called multiculturalism, the rainbow curriculum, or postcolonial theory benefits from taking a privileged sort of U.S. experience (William Appleman Williams's "empire as a way of life") as one of its points of departure. In its present sense, postcolonial theory has more to do with the United States than Britain or, in its customary invocation, "Europe"—in spite of the vital input and leads provided by Commonwealth studies and the early work of resident colonial intellectuals there. That centrality has to do both with the geopolitical stature of the United States and its famous, highly celebrated mixedness of population, which has created a repertoire of troping and a reason for being, often by conflating the positive new alignments across borders, types, and peoples with a much less promising rhetoric of communion achieved. Such processes should be seen not only from within embattled ethnicity but from within a nonconformist mentality present in the so-called majority. This I have tried to do.

Chapter 1 explores the debates over world culture as an often surreptitious imaging of American values. I make a case for changing our criticism of the nation by looking at the way it is discussed by media intellectuals and governmental advisers rather than academic theorists, and I suggest that cultural theory misrepresents the state of that discourse. Finally, I portray the public face of the third-world writer portrayed by the North American media.

Chapter 2 attempts to set the ground for what follows by looking at methodology. It questions the frames of reference for our thinking about colonial literatures and global cultural production, and challenges three critical constants: the extolling of "complex" thinking; the ambivalent embrace of generalism; and continued support (while denying such support) for authentic racial and ethnic identities.

Chapter 3 asks what exactly the culture of the transnational corporation is, and to what degree it can be called transnational. By examining the long discourse in American politics on cosmopolitanism—especially lively after World Wars I and II—it looks at some of the homologies between current theory and that of the 1950s. I try to demonstrate how corporate management circles have employed the discourse of the humanities in their campaigns to create new global networks—campaigns based on exaggerating the extent to which these networks already exist.

Chapter 4 explores a concrete example of contemporary cosmopolitan culture: the widespread work on the hybridity of New York's Lower East Side, and the new kind of politico-erotic travel literature of the post-perestroika period that it exemplified. By looking at the travel genre of late journalistic reportage and placing cultural studies as one version of it, I explore some of the bad implications of the hostility of both toward the state-corporate nexus.

Chapter 5 turns to an extended case of Americanization in third-world cultural reception by examining the years C. L. R. James spent in New York in the early 1950s, where he wrote about (and mostly celebrated) American mass culture. Contrasting him with Ernst Bloch—whose time spent in the United States overlapped with that of James, but who vigorously rejected U.S. mass culture—I trace some of the leads James provided for contemporary cultural theory.

Chapter 6 explores the career of another cosmopolitan (like James) who in many ways refused to act like one: Alejo Carpentier. This chapter turns to the nettlesome problem that Cuba has presented to cosmopolitanism both as an independent state (at least until recently) and a mass-producer of a popular culture for export. I explore the problem through Carpentier's largely unheralded efforts to promote Cuban popular music, and through his antagonistic relationship to the European avant-gardes, whose positions form a key and very public part of contemporary critiques of indigenous culture.

As I completed this book, the critical and scholarly interest in cosmopolitanism was clearly growing. It is not hard to see why a concept that suggests an outward-looking, intercultural sensitivity is attractive when the United States is experiencing new racial tensions, immigrant anxieties, and declining living standards. Any reservations with the ethos of cosmopolitanism, one would think, should be a rather low priority when resurgent patriotism and new demands for conformity seem to characterize the national mood. As I try to argue in the following pages, I do not think we can afford to look at the matter this way. To understand the history of cosmopolitanism is to learn something about the elusiveness of imperial attitudes themselves, which are always painfully obvious in the historical record and always more or less invisible in the immediacy of now. As someone who teaches literature and the arts, I have found it hard to accept the proposition that tolerance and understanding are all that are needed for American students to learn about what is not America. Critique begins at home, and this book is, among other things, a self-critique. That, at any rate, is how I hope it will be seen.

1

Claims to Global Culture: America Abroad

> "I've never met any black writers. Are you angry and polemical or are you grim and nocturnal or are you realistic and quavering or are you indifferent and European? Those are the categories, I think," she said and neat creases delicately bracketed her wide mouth.
>
> —Dambudzo Marechera

To read Christopher Lasch's *World of Nations* (1973) is to be reminded of the persistence in American intellectual life of a futurist postnationalism.[1] Lasch catalogs its long and venerable prehistory through the age of the New England mugwumps and the early debates over the U.S. Philippine intervention at the turn of the century. He could have written the book today and suffered little from the lapse of time, challenging doctrines that sound more than familiar twenty years later: that ours is a "post-industrial" society, that American foreign policy is now "post-imperial," that radical developments in science permit visions where "technological apocalypse alternate[s] with . . . technological utopia" (xi–xii). Lasch methodically reviews the headline stories of his own cultural moment—the "counter-culture," the "political implications of ethnic particularism," canonical disputes in the "multiversity," and the "revival of cultural primitivism among the educated" (183, 190, 193). In the early years of the century, he recalls, a sort of cultural emancipation was derived from "a cosmopolitanism transcending local and even national loyalties"—the watchword of the then dominant school of sociology in the United States, "the structural-functionalism associated with Ward and Veblen, and later with the Chicago School . . . which regarded the American city as a laboratory in which the process could be studied in detail as the immigrant cultures and later the culture of Southern negroes [*sic*] visibly disintegrated in the acid of city life" (191–2).

Striking in his study is not simply the familiar ring of the cosmopolitanism he identifies from an earlier period, but his reservations about it in the 1970s. With eyes on a remarkably parallel set of ruling themes, he notes how in the United States "the revival of ethnic particularism has coincided with a new wave of enthusiasm for popular culture . . . , an enthusiasm verging on sentimentalism," and ends up fearing the "tendency to furnish cultural explanations for clearly political events" (194). In an intellectual (although not social) milieu very much like our own, his most penetrating insight—the most useful, certainly, for what I want to argue below—is that "traditional cultures" within and outside the metropolis have against all predictions survived, even as they have been underestimated or pronounced dead. It is their survival, Lasch continues, that "furnished . . . much of the resistance to industrial capitalism" (192).

Theories of cosmopolitanism enter the humanities today for the most part unaware of precursors like these. More than a description inaccurately posed as new, the term has come to stand for an existential state of political ethics—what Paul Rabinow calls "an ethos of macro-interdependencies."[2] A system of unargued values clusters around the term in which it is always understood that "complex, enfolded, inclusive, and paradoxical" truths are preferable to fixed, or even dualistic, ones.[3] "Hybridity," to take a related term, has been marshaled by many critics as an almost atmospheric slogan of multivalent ambiguity. The term's power lies in its ability to slide among its various senses, where it can allegorically act on behalf of some even as it appears to refer to others in a local and particular way. It has, first of all, a confessional meaning, involving an account of the consequences of being foreign by race or upbringing, and yet well positioned, influential, respected in certain circles precisely for one's foreignness. Combined here are disagreeable longings and displacements as well as the productive counterpoint of memory and vision such anxiety creates.

However much originally affixed to the nonwhite immigrant intellectual, hybridity thus also refers poignantly to the mixed origins of a metropolitan culture that, in spite of these mixings, is consistently portrayed as stable. Along with these meanings, however, it also indicates a political strategy of negotiation or compromise under the current system—the familiar "war of position" taken inaccurately out of Gramsci and made to serve a theoretical stance that exaggerates the politically strategic role of culture itself. The kind of corrective demanded in this use of Gramsci may stand here as a paradigm for similar demands required by the drift of cosmopolitan theory generally, which usually (as in Lasch) means recovering a specific history repressed in the excitements of a present too much with us. For it might be recalled that Gramsci—although he did say flatly that following the revolutionary crescendo of the years 1917–1921 "the war of position . . . was the only form possible in the West"—also associated the war of position with the "passive revolution" of Cavour in his writings on the risorgimento, which he felt had a "retrograde" character on Italian development as seen against Mazzini's "frontal assault."[4]

It was a matter to him, therefore, not only of infinitely variable contexts but of now forgotten emphases. He states clearly, for instance—quite out of character with the practices of "decoding" popular culture that are now implicitly defended when the "war of position" is favorably invoked—that ideological phenomena are not destroyed "as soon as they are 'realistically' explained, as if they were popular superstitions" (235). The type of thing he meant by war of position was the boycott as distinct from the labor strike (229); and, more to the point, that the concept could not be usefully applied in the colonies "where forms which elsewhere have been superseded and have become anachronistic are still in vigour" (243). In spite of the years separating Gramsci from ourselves, this continues to be true.

The doubtful benefits of "inclusion" referenced in Lasch are intimated in another way by the historian David Hollinger. He usefully points out however, that the "ascendancy of [the cosmopolitan] ideal from the mid-1910s to the mid-1960s" among American intellectuals did not always imply a defense of pluralism, since the latter was committed to the "survival and nurturing of the ethnic group as such," whereas the former had been historically opposed to the preservation of cultural differences "in parochial form."[5] Hollinger, who supports this ideal of opposing the "ethnic group as such," would seem rather embarrassing to cosmopolitanism in literary theory in that his language is so similar to that theory even while it advocates what might unkindly be called the government's race relations industry. In the spirit of the neo–melting pot theories of S. I. Hayakawa or Arthur Schlesinger, he appears to want to "manage" crisis by putting limits on tolerance for ethnicity-based self-determination.

Nevertheless, to suggest a harmony between professors of culture and governmental spokespersons would be unfair. Among other things, the "p.c." wars found the humanities as a political redoubt from which one fired shots on behalf of a democracy of access at a government and press that by contrast seemed peremptory and uncomfortably philistine. As it actually unfolds today in left cultural theory, the discourse on cosmopolitanism, moreover, is deeply humane, learned, and frankly—even belligerently—anti-imperial. These very feelings lie at the core, for example, of Arnold Krupat's persuasive appeals for "a recognition and legitimation of heterogeneity . . . as a social and cultural norm"—an appeal he logically gives the name "cosmopolitanism," understanding it as more than an "ideal." It must, in his words, "materializ[e] . . . values on the sociopolitical level, contributing to the possibility of institutionalizing what I have elsewhere called the *polyvocal polity*."[6]

In much the same vein—but in the venues of a more restricted postcolonial literary theory—Julie Newman has applauded Wole Soyinka's reply to Chinweizu, making a vital point common to our criticism. African traditional cultures, wrote Soyinka, involve advanced technology and macroeconomics, not only the cramped romanticism of Chinweizu's "language of African particulars," with its particularist demands for a "non-Western" literature defined by its pastoral imagery of orishas, yams, and grass huts.[7] It is in moments like these that the humane and thoughtful core of the cosmopolitan can be seen. Whether it is in that mode of intellectual method most closely associated with Edward Said's "wordliness"—the roaming, hungry intelligence bound neither by discipline nor dogma—or the more conjunctural moments of curricular reform on behalf of studying the world's many cultures in place of narrow, job-related specializations, the ethics of cosmopolitanism are as desirable as they are embattled.

Thus, in the former sense, Martin Bernal defends himself against the enemies of his confrontational study *Black Athena:* "My enemy is purity. What I believe in is cultural mixture. I think on the whole there is more creativity, intellectually and artistically, in societies where there are contrasts available . . . Therefore, I'm not looking for a pure Africa or a pure Europe that I'm going to elevate above all the others. What I'm interested in are zones of mixture and cultural creativity."[8] In the second, more conjunctural sense—to take one of many examples—it is a more than welcome sight to watch Edward Friedman show that conservative demands that we study "our" culture before others are "no more than a rationalization of American hegemony," and that what is needed is rather a "focus on the cosmopolitan process," that is, how, for millennia, history has merged the contributions of numerous cultures, and that for many centuries "western European civilization remained marginal to the ecumene."[9]

In each of these cases—and they are not untypical—cosmopolitanism does indeed deliver what Bruce Robbins aptly calls "an internationalist political education" evoking models of "mobile, reciprocal interconnectedness."[10] The problem with the theorization of cosmopolitanism, in other words, is not as superficial as an impertinent linkage with, say, the "American Century" theories of Walter Lippmann might suggest.

James Clifford's well-known essay "Traveling Cultures," for example, is very sensitive to the term's troubling overtones of freewheeling privilege or easily extendable coverage. After first raising the word in connection with Marcus Rediker's history of eighteenth-century merchant seamen and the "radical political culture" it reveals, he goes on to outline the risks of thinking of "cosmopolitan workers, and especially migrant labor, in metaphors of 'travel'": "The political disciplines and economic pressures that control migrant labor regimes pull very strongly against any overly sanguine view of the mobility of poor, usually non-white, people who *must* leave home in order to survive . . . [E]ven if bourgeois travelers can be 'located' on specific itineraries . . . , such constraints do not offer any simple equivalence with other immigrant and migrant laborers." By speaking of "discrepant cosmopolitanisms" he sets out to avoid an "excessive localism" as well as the "overly global vision of a capitalist or technocratic monoculture," and he responsibly points out that he is "not saying there are no locales or homes or that everyone is—or should be—traveling, or cosmopolitan, or deterritorialised. This is not nomadology." On its own grounds, there is simply nothing to add to an analysis that has so completely foreseen the probable complaints against it. As a capsule coverage of the multiple means and meanings of "dwelling-in-travel," Clifford's work is unassailable, and extraordinarily fertile.[11]

All the same, stepping outside the essay, one is struck by the enormous weaponry of scholarship and plain colloquial intelligence unleashed for an idea that is supposedly elusive and unappreciated but is actually dominant. The sheer number of critics he cites as anticipating his call (to take a partial list, Dale Eickelman, James Piscatori, Vivek Dhareshwar, Meaghan Morris, Peter Linebaugh, Mary Louise Pratt, Sara Mills, Caren Kaplan, Michael Taussig, Paul Gilroy, Kobena Mercer, and Robin Cohen) suggests nothing less than a consensus. His move, always posed as emergent, has already won a formidable following. And it has done so at the expense of studies—more plodding and more literal, surely—on the relationship of place and belonging to polity and to sovereignty.

What speaks most loudly is the essay's dedication to the trope of "travel" itself on the grounds that it is more "interesting" than the "more apparently neutral, and 'theoretical,' term . . . 'displacement.'" Actually, "travel" is the more theoretical term, and "displacement," far from being neutral, is designed precisely to force readers to remember the involuntary travel of deportation, migrations, and war. The main opposition, perhaps, is not the one Clifford sets up in his argument—not between an ethnography of conveniently manageable localities versus one (like his own) that opens up the field to an inexhaustible set of "cross-cuttings" ("historical dialogues between continuity and disruption, essence and positionality, homogeneity and differences"), although his approach more accurately characterizes the experience of the ethographic subject.[12] The argument operates on the principle that one must remain faithful at all costs to a complexity that is inherently more "interesting" and find a *"translation term"* (Clifford's emphasis) that allows the critic to talk about discrepant cosmopolitanisms as part of a single constellation that pays sincere homage to discrepancies of class, gender, and race but finds solace only in "a word of apparently general application." The problem is not what the argument does so much as what it finds unnecessary or unappealing to do: hold out a sophisticated theoretical space for a defensive nationalism that relies, inevitably, on a grounded sense of sociocultural belonging to a polity. As the great Afro-British impresario John La Rose once wrote: "All is connected."

How is it possible to divorce the near unanimity in humanistic theory of the tropes of traversing, being between, migrating, and so forth, from the climate created by the "global vision of a capitalist or technocratic monoculture"?

Criticism is attracted to the more difficult, less "easy," interpretive model. There is, in that sense, a reminder of why "cosmopolitan" was often used interchangeably with "intellectual." Raymond Williams, for example, captures this sense in describing what used to be called simply the intellectual or the bohemian but what he identifies specifically with the artistic movements of Continental modernism itself: "The experience of visual and linguistic strangeness, the broken narrative of the journey and its inevitable accompaniment of transient encounters . . . , raised to the level of universal myth this intense, singular narrative of unsettlement, homelessness, solitude and impoverished independence."[13] What is striking about the humanities at present is an attempt to rehabilitate the term "cosmopolitan" in just this sense.

Why is this happening now? In this project of rehabilitation, no one has been more direct than Paul Rabinow, who lays out a program for an ethics of modernity that urgently demands more "critical, cosmopolitan intellectuals." In an enormously inviting proposal, Rabinow (like Clifford) partakes in nothing so vulgar as the universalizing schemata of *New York Times* editorialists. His very point, in fact, is to emphasize the necessary balancing act between our "particularities of places, characters, historical trajectories, and fates" and our macro-interdependencies, always "suspicious of [the term's] imperial tendencies."[14] To depart from Rabinow's project, it would not be sufficient to catch him in the act of indifference to difference. The whole problem is much more subtle than that, more conceptual, and lies in the fissure between a perfectly defensible ethics—being against "universal truths, overly relativized preciousness"—and the practical difficulties and inappropriateness of living by such an ethic as a participant in anticolonial war.

To put this another way, his scrupulously inclusive "we"—as in the phrases "we live in-between," or "we are all cosmopolitans"—is complete as identity and incomplete as situation. Involved as he is in a valuable critique of the "dangers of high interpretive science" in the discipline of anthropology—a critique that makes the entire passage deeply attractive—he overlooks in this drama of dependency and interdependency those who do not interpret for a living, and ends by urging us all to be "suspicious of sovereign powers" (258)—a call reminiscent of Julia Kristeva's desire to be free of governments as such, and a particularly unfortunate ethic in an era of global restructuring.

Somewhat similar is Robbins's surprising claim that "there is no correct place to stand." Although much else besides, Robbins's *Secular Vocations* applauds and extends the arguments of Rabinow and Clifford. His book glosses theirs in its role as an ex post facto advocate and promoter. By definition critical and adversarial, the academic intellectual, says Robbins, chafes against professional self-interest needlessly, since for intellectuals being adversarial is unavoidable. Since intellectuals are by their very essence cosmopolitan for Robbins, "the charge of 'metropolitanism' that falls on 'celebrities' like Naipaul and Rushdie would also have to fall crushingly on the metropolitan critic who *makes* the charge, whatever his or her own political intentions and degree of celebrity."[15]

But if political institutions are irrelevant, one might ask if political positions are as well. Crucial to Robbins's view is that he thinks we all assume that "absolute homelessness is a myth" or that the "word cosmopolitan immediately evokes a privileged person," who is then, in the dominant political ethos of our time, put on the defensive for being so. But this is very far from the case. Those who challenge the unalloyed goodness of the "cosmopolitan" are working at a disadvantage, in fact. In the English language, its connotations have been relentlessly positive: "free from provincial prejudices," "not limited to one part of the world," "sophisticated, urbane, worldly." Its antonyms are pejorative in a simple denotative sense; they do not require a context to damn them.

In the *Oxford English Dictionary*, the only writers shown to use the term negatively are famous cultural conservatives such as Thomas Babington Macaulay and Thomas Carlyle, although George Bernard Shaw gives voice to its negative uses in order to show the absurdity of the position while characterizing the typical English bigot who rails against "Germans, Jews, Yankees, . . . Park Laners, [and] cosmopolitan riffraff." Like this quotation from the *OED*, most of the examples of the term's usage are drawn from the nineteenth century, although its related form "cosmopolite" finds expression, predictably, in the age of vigorous English expansionism: Hakluyt's 1598 travel and exploration narratives make telling reference to the "citizen of the one mysticall citie universall" and the "Cosmopoliticall government thereof." Looking closely, one finds many of its other usages guiltily linked to this original sense, as in John Stuart Mill's 1848 comment that capital is becoming more cosmopolitan, or in eighteenth-century meditations of De Quincey on "the formation of a great primary state-body," or in R. H. Tawney's evocative, and proto-American, description of Antwerp as a cosmopolitan city because it was a refuge for those outlawed elsewhere in Europe, and so a "home common to all nations."

How "cosmopolitan" has been used negatively in the past adds to the built-in stigma of so using it today—not only as Shaw correctly implies above, but as Rabinow suggests when he states how he wants to recuperate (and change) its meanings as earlier applied to "Christians, aristocrats, merchants, Jews, homosexuals, and intellectuals." Anyone expressing doubts about the cosmopolitanism Robbins now welcomes is in this way associated precipitously with a brand of hypocrisy (for how can intellectuals complain about the very essence of what it means to be an intellectual?) or, worse, the surly, ill-tempered, and even the bigoted—a collapsing of the varied critiques of cosmopolitanism in the past as though all were equivalent, say, to that of Oswald Spengler, who holds up a world culture paradoxically at odds with cosmopolitanism in a famous reactionary gesture of disdain for the proletarian crowds that threaten feudal virtue from the base camp of the city:

> In place of a world, there is a *city, a point* in which the whole life of broad regions is collecting while the rest dries up. In a place of a type-true people, born of and grown on the soil, there is a new sort of nomad, cohering unstably in fluid masses, the parasitical city-dweller, traditionless, utterly matter-of-fact, religionless, clever, and fruitful, deeply contemptuous of the countryman and especially of that highest form of countryman, the country gentleman. This is a very great stride towards the inorganic, towards the end—what does it signify? The world city means cosmopolitanism in place of home . . . The world city belongs not to a folk but a mob.[16]

Dick Hebdige, then, is part of a general chorus when he vilifies the anticosmopolitan stand by way of quoting Michael Antonov, a spokesman for the Union for the Spiritual Revival of the Fatherland, in an essay on the Berlin Wall: "In all spheres of the Russian peoples' life there is but one mission: to repulse the attack of rootless and cosmopolitan elements, to throw off the foreign western forms that have been foisted on the people, and to return to the immemorial origins of Russia."[17] Any student of the late nineteenth and early twentieth centuries is aware that "cosmopolitan" was a code word in Eastern Europe for the Jew, where rootlessness was a condemnation and a proof of nonbelonging precisely *there.* Linked in this sense to that sixteenth-century paranoid German Christian legend of the "Wandering Jew" Ahasuerus—condemned by Jesus for his part in the Crucifixion to wander, toiling and wretched, until the Second Coming—the term is one expression of an anti-Semitism that stretches from Luther's diatribes on the "lies of the Jews" through the Russian pogroms to the Warsaw Ghetto, and may originally have been connected to the migration of Sephardim from Spain following the infamous fifteenth-century expulsion.[18]

A North American scholar, on the other hand, is likely to recall the anti-Semitism lurking behind the term as used by Stalin, which has been much more exhaustively commented upon. He marshaled a populist anger against his opponents within the Party by labeling them "cosmopolitans," which had the connotation in its uglier side of simply Jew-as-foreigner, interloper, but also and very differently as "intellectual" in the bad sense—as fine-liver, aesthete, soft-handed trader in literary niceties. One has to take account of the fact that a separate entry is accorded this (very partial) Soviet usage in the *OED,* whereas the term's extensive use—and otherwise uniquely negative connotations—in the postwar anticolonial liberation movements is simply not mentioned. The term is actually much more complicated, even in this clearly cynical usage, than the lore surrounding Stalin suggests. It becomes all too easy to isolate anticolonial independence organizations, where "cosmopolitan" is also a term of abuse, and in a process of backwash label them "Stalinist"—a practice that I will show is not uncommon.

This Jewish link is a rather minor detour in a concept of enormous power, and it should not be overemphasized. Nevertheless, if one wants to understand it—even here, exposed in its Eastern European form—one needs to look more deeply. We might begin by recalling the Proudhonian radical and early left popular-culture activist Eugène Sue, who took on the legend in his mammoth novel *The Wandering Jew* in order to link the predicament of workingmen and all women to the famous curse delivered by Jesus on Ahasuerus.[19] Workers and women, for Sue, were left out of the salvation from misery. M. Ageyev's *Novel with Cocaine* (written between 1916 and 1919) is another interesting source, particularly in that it is not a product of Russian futurism written by a sympathizer with the revolution, but a bohemian romance indifferent to the politics of the author's country, whose social mores it registers only incidentally.[20] As a schoolchild, the hero comes more than once to the defense of the Jewish character Stein, who makes fun of himself, thus preempting the abuse his kind typically receive in these surroundings. His self-abuse, however, only begins to suggest the intricate and surprising ways in which Jews and cosmopolitans are associated with one another. In the midst of an argument, for example, one character says, "Keep out of this, Stein, will you? . . . You're the European after all, and this is an Asiatic affair" (55)—just one of several moments when Jews are called, disparagingly, "Europeans." Such acts of name-calling are repudiated by the novel, which is explicitly anti–anti-Semitic, and they are cast as those who are "envious where they would appear to be derisive" (42).

There are many points to pursue here, but the ones most relevant are these: Insofar as cosmopolitanism has an anti-Semitic charge, this predated the Soviet era despite the widespread association of this usage (as in the *OED*) with Stalin. More important, perhaps, a repulsive prejudice can, under local circumstances, exist as a distorted act of desire. Most striking to American eyes is the use of "European" as a term of rebuke. One recalls that the years in which the novel is set were ones of incipient multinational penetration into Russia and the early attempts to place the former Russian empire in its proper role as economic outpost—a role that the Russian Revolution delayed for eighty years. If a campaign *against* cosmopolitanism had been used for conservative purposes within Soviet communism, the campaign *for* cosmopolitanism played a similarly conservative ideological role in the West, with communism as its foil. Hollinger reminds us that "it was in the context of anti-Stalinism and anti-Fascism . . . that the *Partisan Review* writers drew upon the cosmopolitan ideal," referring here to Harold Rosenberg's essay "The Fall of Paris," in which the author talks about the communist and fascist perfidy involved in the fall of the capital of international culture that alone could enable "American speech to find its measure of poetry and eloquence."[21]

Whatever its merits, cosmopolitanism as a prolonged effort to argue for the expertise and political responsibility of academic professionals is a decidedly mainstream position, solidly in the conventional liberal center of the American intellectual scene. It is not today, of course, meant openly to extol a salvational Europe threatened by foreign incursions like communism, Garveyism, Islam, or ethnic particularism. In it's more recent life, the concept is intended to assert that the institutional being of American professionals allies them to non-Western cultures. That is, being an intellectual means being worldly, transnational, or cosmopolitan. To this rather self-flattering view, Barbara Herrnstein Smith's words are still a relevant riposte:

> Self-privileging operates not merely as a self-sustaining mechanism but as a productive one, generating new perceptual and conceptual articulations—new beliefs, descriptions interpretations, judgments, and justifications—even from "evidence" and "arguments" to the contrary. Since the self, even as it is transformed by its interactions with the world, also transforms how that world seems to itself, its system of self-securing is not thereby unhinged nor is it "corrected" by cosmopolitanism. Rather, in enlarging its view "from China to Peru," it may become all the more imperialistic, seeing in every horizon of difference new peripheries of its own centrality, new pathologies through which its own normality may be defined and must be asserted.[22]

Written as a lead-in to a critique of the aesthetics of Hume and Kant, these words were directed by Smith at critics whom many of those now extolling cosmopolitanism have productively fought for over a decade. There is no simplistic way they can be brought into evidence here against an argument that in so many other ways is the opposite of "imperialistic."

The issue has to do a with a missing, or displaced, third term in what appears too often as a fateful choice between two alternatives. How can one talk in this atmosphere, as Robbins does, of "future citizens of the world" without marking the reliance of such a construct on what he elsewhere calls "future world policemen"? For there is no universal programmatic interest enjoyed by intellectuals, many of whom are flagrantly unworldly in Robbins's sense, either because they are dedicated to specific national-popular cultures in spite of the barely relevant personal facts of their habits of travel or foreign residencies, or because they are that rather different thing—an internationalist.

Overlooking such distinctions Robbins alludes at one point to Rigoberta Menchu's comment that her "struggle knows no boundaries . . . , I've traveled to many places," as though Menchu represented the sort of worldliness he has been at pains to equate with cosmopolitanism.[23] It should be obvious, however, that the one category of current theory that Menchu manifestly represents is *ethnic particularism,* and it is the want of analysis on the varieties within that category—from, say, Ariel Sharon at one extreme to Ho Chi Minh at the other—that leads to many absurdities in the discourse on the nation and, as in the case of cosmopolitanism, the nation's end. To say that Menchu "knows no boundaries" would actually refer to the sort of point made by James M. Blaut about the liberation movements in general. They traditionally help "other struggles, elsewhere, as best they can."[24] One can hold on to such a nonparticularist view politically, while retaining a nationalist position. It is, in fact, the only way to do so.

Missing third terms have, by their absence, become more prominent as the discourse on cosmopolitanism has picked up steam. In a 1994 roundtable debate taking up an entire special issue of the *Boston Review,* Martha Nussbaum faced off against an impressive array of intellectuals by defending the cosmopolitan ethos against a contemporary American "patriotism."[25] Dissenting from Richard Rorty's appeal to patriotism as "shared national identity," she invokes Rabindranath Tagore's novel *The Home and the World,* endorsing the message of that novel's central drama that "patriotic pride is morally dangerous." Rorty, she charges, "substitutes a colorful idol for the substantive universal values of justice and right," for the point is to find what we all "share as both rational and mutually dependent human beings" rather than as citizens of the United States.

In this embattled forum, and as an accomplished classicist, Nussbaum wisely recounts a Western authority for her view—the Stoic philosopher Diogenes Laertius, who, when asked where he came from, responded: "I am a citizen of the world." Taking Laertius as her point of departure, she sets out an educational program that is difficult not to admire (indeed, almost all of the antagonists in the debate do so): it is not sufficient, she says, for students to learn that they are above all American citizens—they should learn "about the rest of the world in which they live, about India and Bolivia and Nigeria and Norway and their histories, problems and comparative successes"; because "our nation is appallingly ignorant of most of the rest of the world . . . , it is also, in many crucial ways, ignorant of itself."

Her appeals to an education based on "world-respect," however—so welcome in other ways—are rife with corollaries calculated to preserve the primary requisites of U.S. citizenship. There is for her always a fundamental damage done by "faction and local allegiances to the political life of a group"; we should give our first allegiance to "*no* mere form of government, no temporal power, but to the moral community made up by the humanity of all human beings" (her emphasis). Nussbaum alludes to, but never specifically examines, *our* patriotism. The reassuring veil of classical Greek and Latin legends helps this task along by beckoning "tradition" to shore up an admittedly against-the-grain view characterized by humaneness and responsibility. The debate as she sets it up pits patriotism against a cosmopolitanism displayed timelessly (and therefore alluringly) by Diogenes, Plutarch, and Tagore. And yet, key distinctions are absent. The patriotic carnival of the 1984 Los Angeles Olympics is just the same as the 1995 South African Rugby World Cup in which mostly white players embraced the new South Africa of Nelson Mandela. Both are simply "patriotism."

While many want to recognize Laertius in themselves (I do), such identifications do not rescue the term "cosmopolitan" with all of its unacknowledged historical accretions. For world respect, one might argue, is either whole or not at all. To understand and appreciate the values of all humans is to understand what Nussbaum does not: the rights of small nations—patriotism and all—including that embarrassing, but sizable, variant of socialist nationalism that is also an internationalism. A cosmopolitanism worthy of the name, in other words, would have to give space to the very nationalism that the term is invoked to counter. Such a view is simply too messy to broach in the *Boston Review* exchange. By the same token, one could argue that it is just too subtle to bicker with cosmopolitanism at a time when anti-intellectual menace and threatening demands for conformity in the United States are on the rise, and when most greet the term as meaning, colloquially, broad fellow-feeling, tolerance, and far-flung curiosity. Perhaps this is the reason for her dichotomy between nonnational emotion or concern and patriotic American identity. But the dichotomy is unacceptable, since it would mean that one is either for cosmopolitanism or against the appreciation of differences. By contrast, cosmopolitanism *is* the way in which a kind of American patriotism is today being expressed.

The truth of this claim can be traced in the rise of a field that would seem at first to meet Nussbaum's proposals for widening the scope of American education—the field of third-world (or postcolonial) literatures. In the spirit of Nussbaum's own doubts about the savoriness of sectarian allegiances, many in this field have made sure to avoid trying to recover "authentic" non-Western cultures while staking out what is distinctive to the field itself. There is general agreement, for instance, that as a distinct body of work "third-world literature" has no coherent meaning. It lacks that respect for the particular *within* the shared that Nussbaum urges us to have. At the same time, socially situated appearances have their own densities. The practice of teaching and reviewing continually shows that "third-world literature" does, in fact, exist, if only in the mind of the metropolitan reader of books. Its reality may be a phantom one, but it would be a strange sort of denial that could today deny the materiality of ideology. A U.S. media and educational apparatus of immense domestic resources has attracted writers and critics to work and to study here. They have been moved to speak about what they know best, and, inevitably, to comment on the strangeness of their new surroundings, while seeking a certain rapprochement with the American and European modes and styles that, in complicated ways, both facilitate their reception and passively mark their own earlier apprenticeships.

This process, which the university facilitates and helps oversee, has led to that very mixed product known within the university as "postcolonial studies." It is mixed because it has, on the one hand, allowed us to move beyond a fixation on bordered national literatures to one of wider scope and value. It encourages an intellectual generalism largely missing from the "specialist" biases of academic professionalization. On the other hand, it has led to a specious mastery of the whole, or a series of procrustean maneuvers to find a level of abstraction where difference is graspable. With an almost allegorical resonance in the centers of imperial power, a dialectic within the field expresses itself most acutely in cosmopolitanism. An emphasis on the world is accompanied by an emphasis on identity and the subject by calling them forth as alleviating counterpoints. In this mixture of the specific and the broad, the need, I would argue, is for the opposite: a rethinking of the indigenous in the context of an intellectual generalism.

What presents itself as a compelling possibility in this atmosphere is, then, the following: not only to supersede the would-be universal of a "U.S. point of view" by rushing to mark the margin's counternarratives but to dwell within that universal, examining its particular manias. The cultural products of North-South literary détente attain the greatest leverage and visibility now. Later, given the inevitable mechanism of streamlining and condensation, they become synecdoches of the whole, but are in important ways a similarity in difference. What is required (and faultlessly offered) in confessional accounts of non-Western experience is a constant supply of local obscurities in small enough quantities for familiarity to remain secure. Vigorously attacked at the theoretical level for its nostalgia in a global age, authenticity as ethnic belonging never quite disappears. It must now be a cultural artifact or idea that is unknown and potentially unassimilable even while the informant translates it for us with obligatory comments about the impossibility of translating it adequately.

Meanwhile, the cultural products at issue are either made here, or for here, or reminiscent of what already exists here, or (more important) of immediate and practical use here. This is one of the reasons we see such a widespread inability to imagine a psychological and moral space that is not Euro-American or whose variations on Euro-America do not pay the non-European sufficient homage. Presenting cultural products of difference entails acute discomfort. The effort to understand cultural differences is not merely a matter of historical "boning up," the learning of terms and figures or even of foreign languages, although all these things are required; it is not merely an accretive process, but a liminal one. It entails the sort of mental shift one traditionally has called "conversion."

Here, though, one might recall Edward Said's important observation in *Representations of the Intellectual* about the "unpleasant aesthetics of conversion and recantation."[26] I am using the word ironically—not as a coming into faith, nor a revelation of some unassailable truth that, suddenly beheld, is forced to become a thing to which others must subscribe. The issue is incommensurability, an absolute and cloistral division between class-historical mentalities. *This* conversion would mimic the religious metaphors of "shedding scales from the eyes" or "stepping into the light" as well as other images of psychic reorientation. Conversion would not so much mean being "inside" or "outside" the faithful as it would the unintelligibility of value in different locations of belief. And such locations have not been symmetrical.

Du Bois's *Color and Democracy*

W. E. B. Du Bois is widely recalled today for his prescient comments at the beginning of *The Souls of Black Folk* (1903) predicting that the problem of the twentieth century would be the problem of "the color line." It is rarely noted that as the century wore on, he revised that view by expanding and enriching his understanding of the problem of race. Almost nothing is said about the last decades of his life around the Communist Party—an enormously fruitful period of his mature thinking where his intellectual inquiries took him as a destination and a culmination.[27] The influence of Marxism on his writing can be seen already in his underread masterpiece of 1935, *Black Reconstruction in America, 1860–1880* (he died in Acra in 1963). Treating Du Bois's later career with dignity has, of course, been hindered by the anticommunist common sense in American intellectual life, a sense related to the difficulty of dwelling, intellectually, among the poor, the unlettered, and the forgotten for whom communism was nominally enlisted. The world of the poor is disturbing to the literary sensibility in ways that are not fully understood, and is at least as important a candidate for the distortions of "third-world" reception as are racial, historical, or linguistic differences. The socialist legacy, buried though it is in postcolonial criticism, did more to combat that inaccessibility than any other, and Du Bois's career helps to illustrate this.

It would be hard to find a writer and scholar more at the core of current postcolonial concerns than W. E. B. Du Bois. American, Harvard-trained, educated in Berlin, a moving memoirist and innovative researcher, he *invented* Black studies in this country while founding an organization (the Niagara Movement) that would later become synonymous with the integrationist antiracism of later decades. As the author in 1903 of the first American work of "cultural studies" *(The Souls of Black Folk),* his polemics against Marcus Garvey in the 1920s prefigured recent debates over "Afrocentricity" and racial "essentialism." Promethean in his output in America, he stood at the center of the Pan-African movement abroad, becoming its first secretary in 1900 in London, and active thereafter in its meetings in Paris, Lisbon, and New York. It was with little sense of disjunction that he participated in the Paris, New York, and Moscow Peace Congresses in 1949, although that action cost him his visa in 1951 when he was tried (and acquitted) of being an "unregistered foreign agent." Joining the Communist Party in 1961, he took up residence in Ghana at the invitation of the president, Kwame Nkrumah, becoming a citizen of the country in the year of his death.

Well aware that his later trajectory would harm his reputation, he retrospectively explained his development without apologies in his last autobiography, written in 1958 and 1959 (he had published two others). The decision is seen best, though, in the work he produced at the moment of making it. *Color and Democracy: Colonies and Peace* (1945)—his only book-length study of colonialism as a global phenomenon—is for that reason vital.[28] For reasons that will become clear below, the year of its composition was an important one in the development of cosmopolitanism in the aftermath of World War II under the impact of plans for a United Nations. The first chapter ("Dumbarton Oaks") analyzes the prospects of a United Nations, whose "government of men" will have "between one-fourth and one-half the inhabitants of the world [with] no part in it—no power of democratic control and scarcely an organized right of petition" (14–15).

Setting out to influence public debate over the United Nations and the postwar order, Du Bois patiently maps out what living in a colony means, and does so with a thoroughness that cedes nothing to the later writing of Frantz Fanon: "What, then, do modern colonies look like, feel like?" (19). The question itself is posed this way, in a colloquial prose, in order to help his readers think through the imperial attitudes *within* a movement generally greeted at the time as right and good. What commands our attention is not so much Du Bois's graceful presentation of necessary preliminaries having to do with resource extraction, the stealing of land, or rates of profit—but his care in pointing out how much or how little he had actual contact with "the mass of the colonial people" while doing his research. He finds most disastrous the "ruthless and ignorant destruction of their cultural patterns" (a devastation in which the Security Council members are still involved). Behind this detour-in-the-making, he concludes, is "Americanization," which "never yet meant a synthesis of what Africa, Europe, and Asia had to contribute to the new vigorous republic of the West; it meant largely the attempt to achieve a dead level of uniformity, intolerant of all variation" (72). The mandate amounted to "sneering at small nations, at 'Balkanization' and helpless Haitis, until the majority of the world's people have become ashamed of themselves." Du Bois's theoretical explanation for this dangerous arrogance on the part of the "vigorous republic" is, therefore, twofold: the race-caste system within U.S. borders that by example and the strategic power to enforce it, makes the frustration of popular rule abroad inevitable; and the exclusion of the Soviet Union, its wartime ally, from postwar decision making.

In a late chapter ("The Riddle of Russia"), Du Bois makes it clear that, for him at least, the Soviet Union was simply not an empire in the European sense. With an arguably spotty record in regard to its actual conduct in matters of national or ethnic sovereignties—its reluctance, for example, to forgo its claims to the "prisonhouse of nations" inherited from czarism—it also officially made efforts to theorize and promote an understanding of national self-determination unthinkable in the European and American empires. These efforts had been evident from the time of the remarkable congress held in Baku in the revolution's early years to the period that gave rise to the sensitive writings of Lenin on the national question. With a good deal of justification, Du Bois felt that the Soviet Union was preferable in the world's racial-colonial divide. For its own reasons perhaps, as an encircled country whose own sovereignty had repeatedly been threatened, it believed in the integrity of "small nations"—a policy that would later come to be known as "peaceful coexistence." The sustained campaigning that communist intellectuals conducted on behalf of liberation movements globally—as well as the material and military support given them by the Soviet Union—cannot simply be passed over in references to their inconsistencies or Machiavellianisms. Complex arguments over the occupation of Eastern Europe (which Du Bois could not have predicted at the time of this writing) similarly fail to address the racial-colonial division foremost in his mind.

Du Bois's argument grew so naturally from his earlier work that denying its implications today, while praising him, is a peculiar kind of mental impasse. Then again, much of the cultural work coming out of non-European countries is as ungraspable to metropolitan eyes as socialism has been, and for many of the same reasons. By "socialism," I am not referring to a specific party or movement, and I recognize how inadequate it would be to use a single word to describe the disparate realities of contemporary European social democracy, the Industrial Workers of the World, Chinese communism, and Peru's Shining Path. I am referring to a community of feeling that existed with many internal differences following the Russian Revolution—particularly the party socialisms of the Third International, their intellectual fellow travelers both within Europe and without, and the (historically related) movements of decolonization and national liberation. It is astounding that a field like postcolonial studies has so seldom alluded to these traditions, which bear on the problematics of postcoloniality not only as homologies of difference (the "other" that one can understand only after a "conversion") but as the array of movements that made the historical fact of decolonization possible. Whatever the differences in these traditions, it is still coherent, I think, to refer to them singly because of what they shared: a project of collective (or state) ownership, a belief that social classes not only existed but were in conflict, that the interests of these classes could not be negotiated in a mutually beneficial way, that specific societies were given their character by the universalization of one class's (rather than another's) interests, and that cultural policy ought to articulate the desires of the majority oppressed not only by class but by race, ethnicity, and gender.

The cultural differences between North and South, then, are contained within socialism, which throughout this century has existed in a parallel universe—in the other of two contiguous but impermeable worlds.[29] Even if North Americans were familiar with Sembène

Ousmane's Senegalese film *Guelwaar* or Valentin Kataev's Soviet novel of the 1930s *Time, Forward!*, these works would typically be misunderstood in parallel ways and for the same reasons, in part because Sembène is drawing on a Continental Marxist aesthetic refigured in African surroundings. Kataev's novel is Western, Sembène's film is not; one is traditionalist and rural, the other intensely futuristic and urban. But the sense of aesthetic joy in both is similarly conjunctural and relies on a euphoria that can be experienced only by seeking what is alien to a European market society.[30]

If anticolonialism and socialism are intertwined, so are colonialism and the cold war. The flight from tyranny toward a manifest destiny, while it is the paradigm of America's founding, is at the same time a more modern trope of postrevolutionary flight to the imperial center. A "white" immigration (as in the Russian "whites" of the early Bolshevik revolution, or in the contemporary Mexican sense of the "*guardias blancas*" of Chiapas) has fed and refed the hostilities of official U.S. thinking toward "Red" ideologies. Beginning with the European immigrants' escape from the excesses of the English Civil War and its aftermath, U.S. intellectual life has often been affected by the attraction of this polity for the world's revolutionary castoffs—whether they be the mercenaries of former wars (Nazis, the Hmong, the Shah, Ferdinand Marcos), the disillusioned inhabitants of nominal socialisms (the samizdat intellectuals, the Eastern European novelists, the comprador middle classes of Nigeria or Ghana attending U.S. schools), or a visiting professoriate and literati from England, Mexico, France, and elsewhere—an avant-garde, often with leftist reputation.

The character of thought that understands itself to be American typically combines the troping of immigration with that of the evils of the Red empire. They are also often fused, both at a deep level of signification and as a demographic and political fact—the impossibility of invoking "race," for instance, without involving oneself in the ideological defense networks of liberal theories of civil rights, voting blocs, interest groups, and ethnic communities that all used to be part of the East-West conflict. Immigration—with notable exceptions in the post-1848 German exile communities of New York, Milwaukee, and elsewhere, or in the more recent wave of Central American refugees—has traditionally fed the government's political sense of self, not only in the loose sense of supplying evidence of U.S. attractiveness as the land of freedom, but in the sense of the sheer ideological impact these communities exert as physical collectivities that bend the opinions of other, generally uninformed American communities through the suasions of "firsthand experience." Familiar testimonies of failed colonial regimes simply extend a cold-war rhetoric already in place and only rarely vary from it.

The campaigns of censure and extermination that have characterized the process of the United States' emergence as a global refuge have in the postwar period been conducted against people who either thought of themselves, or who were publicly labeled, socialist—quite apart from where they were born or what color their skin was. Intellectuals would find it harder to speak about radical democracy or new, expansive "cross-border" cultures in tones of guarded praise if they took *this* repressed story as a point of departure. We are viewing the world not only "as it is" but as recent memory depressingly reminds us it promised to be. The absence of a socialism that seemed in the late 1940s, again by the mid-1960s, and once more at the end of the 1970s to be only a matter of time screams across the landscape of a resurgent market.

This sudden plummeting into a scene of distant, perhaps impossible, prospects did not simply occur. It did not just develop out of the logic of a misbegotten dream. This scene was, to speak plainly, murdered into existence—a rather difficult gloss to add to an account of cultural emergence and contestation in the environs of a compensatory literary knowledge.[31] Had it not been for the orchestrated mass killing of leftists in Indonesia, Chile, Mozambique, Nicaragua, Colombia, Vietnam, Afghanistan, and elsewhere, the fate of world socialism would undoubtedly be very different today. It is crucial not to forget that, even at the cost of a coarseness that for many signals an intellectual failure or want of imagination. Such feelings are untouchable, as are the color of their miseries. The unromantic reality of a parallel universe shadows that of the East-West conflict, which fed into it and helped give it scope. The socialist has been seen more often than not as a beast, a bully, a psychological victim, a naif whose religious yearnings had been misdirected in a monstrous conversion. As much as the nonwhite or foreign man or woman, the socialist too has been objectifiable. But this sort of "other"—in literature, academic hiring practices, conferences on discrimination, and so on—has simply been invisible.

But the one "other" and the other are often fused in practice. A young Senegalese woman studying, say, at a U.S. commuter college will typically speak of the rituals of sharing and communal support in her country that she is dismayed to find do not exist in the United States. A Colombian graduate student confers with friends in a rapid Spanish about a New York telephone bill, contemptuously marking what to her is the signature quality of U.S. culture: the baroque methods used to cheat people under a veil of legality. Many have played with the expectation that references to a "common home" in a discussion of America will be some sort of position-taking on the issue of the world, as it were, coming *to* the United States. It is also about the United States going (or coming, depending on your point of view) to the world. Monoglot foreigners in Nebraska flash their green cards for the camera while earnest young faces from Boston or Sussex smile from the feature-story photos on enterprising Western youth now living in the Ukraine as English tutors. Black skins in Denmark, white in Senegal, not visitors but "citizens" to be, that never will be. As technical experts and humanities professors speak of deterritoriality, the term "cosmopolitanism" makes a comeback, enjoying the positive overtones it has largely always had.

The attention given globalism today is not hard to document, and the events prompting the discussion have been alarming. Wars in Panama and Iraq announce visibly what the U.S. president announces redundantly by radio as the first bombs fall on Baghdad. No mere flourish, the new order materializes even as he speaks. Thus begins a rapid finalization of agreements initiated before perestroika made them possible: the Uruguay round of the GATT accords; the U.S.–Latin American free-trade pact known as NAFTA; the Maastricht votes on European union. Next, the Rio summit on world ecology dramatizes the new reality. A U.S. president, unanimously beckoned to sign a clean-air agreement, simply says no, thereby vetoing an overwhelming number of the conference's participants. Suddenly, too, the previously misnamed United Nations ceases to be deadlocked, begins acting with military determination, but does so primarily as a surrogate for U.S. foreign policy, launching ultimatums and deploying troops in Iraq, Bosnia, and Somalia. Finally, armed liberation movements of many decades' duration are forced to negotiate in El Salvador, Mozambique, Colombia, Angola, and elsewhere.

On the cultural front, the signs are equally unmistakable. After two centuries of gradual success, world English—already the lingua franca of most business, aviation, and telecommunications—finally penetrates China. The Chinese government promotes the language now as a matter of policy, and does so in its American dialectal form through a comprehensive program (as in Japan) of importing American students who then live in the country. In Europe, with Berlin as its hub, American studies achieves a new prominence and respectability, amply funded on both sides of the Atlantic. The long struggle through UNESCO under the direction of Ireland's Sean MacBride to demand a "new information order" ignobly collapses, its purpose having been the breakup of media cartels in New York, Paris, and Moscow by forcing them under international law to share satellite and fiber-optic technologies. Just as the end of hegemony and the death of the American Century are proclaimed, new world players like Japan and Germany increase their packaging and promotion of American mass-cultural images.[32] An American cultural norm is employed for others' specific national projects rather than being imposed in an act of cultural war against established states. On the model of the comprador classes of colonialism, the ruling elites of powerful countries participate in the border transgressions as a salutary moral edification of their own citizenries.

Meanwhile, the images not only symbolize but enable the America that is projected: the quick rhythms and flattened taste of these mass-cultural forms, their sense of repetition and nondurability, of interchangeable authorship and of universal property, of linguistic informality and creativity. All of these condition audiences while serving them with an emblem for doting upon. They prepare one for life in a U.S.-type society. The world comes to America, and America to the world. And in that sort of mapping, and against that backdrop, we see the unexpected kinds of opinion-forming with which the humanities are currently involved. It may seem strange in that sense that so much caution about U.S. global designs and realizations would occupy me at the very moment that U.S. strategic power is, in the opinion of many, declining. That decline may yet prove to be true, but similar projections can be found in earlier periods, and it is not true yet.

The Public Face of the "Third-World" Writer

On the reviewers' pages—less so in the university—the meanings of non-European culture remain elusive, although their elusiveness is not necessarily noticed and is often denied in practice. When the meanings do not register, education deals with the problem in two ways: first, in the wider uses of ethnography, cleansed in many ways of its ethnocentrism by a theory-induced self-scrutiny; and second, in the institutional emergence of cultural studies—the ethnographic study of metropolitan life. Here too, however, the influences allude to a socialist legacy, muffled by the 1960s (the multicultural turn's nearest historical predecessor). The institutional tools devised to "read" the third world have in many ways already come from it; similarly, through the popularization of the cognitive category of everyday life, cultural studies can be said to have a European socialist origin. Henri Lefebvre is in this regard a key figure in his book from 1947, just as he is again, more recently, in the modalities adopted widely in colonial studies through the field of geography's theories of social "space."[33]

Under these conditions, the public stance of the writer (and critic) from the imperialized formations—negating the variety that first brought him or her into the public eye—exhibits a homogenization, although a complex one. Here is developed, passively, a set of doctrinal demands for the "third-world" writer, whose features coalesce in what then appears as an appropriate cosmopolitanism. Together, these features form a geopolitical aesthetic, first with the requisites of metropolitan assumptions in mind (or at least at hand), but then, in its full articulation, with matters of taste left untouched while it seems to reorient them. My use of the word "taste" here (and below) is, like my use of the term "third world," phenomenological. The valorized perception inherent in the idea is, as Pierre Bourdieu has argued, infinitely relative. All cultural practices and preferences in literature, painting, and music are, he argues, "linked to educational level . . . and secondarily to social origin," expressing the "generally polemical" idea that one group has of another: "The work of art is the objectification of a relationship of distinction."[34]

The cultural codes that betray one's primary links to social status are always evident in the act of appreciation, and such codes (he continues) are not limited to the field of "art": "There is no area or practice in which the [aesthetic disposition] of purifying, refining and sublimating primary needs and impulses cannot assert itself" (5). One can see the initial problem this view creates for a proper "world culture" once Bourdieu's primarily class-based observations are moved to interethnic, cross-border values where the aesthetic project is not "distinction" but commonality. I will use the word "taste," like Bourdieu, as the practice of distinction—but one in denial. The judgment of good and bad, of refined and vulgar may be sociologically groundless, but it continues to matter at the point of a socially situated perception. Revealing those sites is what matters most.

Formed in the confluence of official strategies and fresh inclusivist openings, cosmopolitanism, then, becomes a way of talking and seeing, unanchored and flexible. Its ethical postulates arise as descriptions and its implicit policies arise as ethical postulates. The intellectuals I will be looking at are differently situated in relation to contemporary globalism. The nonexilic, world-traveling writer—often an aesthete, and already attuned to the metaphysical state of transculturalism—is in many respects as old as the New World conquest. Implicit in the pirate and the *cimarron,* the type is full-blown already in the eighteenth-century French memoirist Père Labat, in the nineteenth-century Scottish journalist and traveler Lafcadio Hearn, and in the New York–based Cuban poet and revolutionist José Martí. Roving, fundamentally estranged from home, they are captivated by the attempt to depict the new sociological reality of which they are now a part. In a ghostly allusion to this past, recent writers repeat this gesture in retellings of ethnic arrival in which the transcultural is, in a sense, petrified.[35] The petrifaction of the transcultural is an important *North* American innovation in world culture.

Acting as an interlocutor for what enters metropolitan reading as a "third-world literature," cosmopolitanism also promotes a genuine aesthetic novelty. Its negotiations, which give the term "hybridity" its currency, are typically cast as the creatively tortured middle ground occupied by disparate cultural identities. Without diminishing the importance of self-definition, one notices the tendency in this discourse of belonging to deemphasize or ignore the immediately functional sense in which negotiation itself must be understood. Merged with the concept of transculturation, negotiation is also an act of muting antagonistic political objectives. Some of the features of this aesthetic novelty have been mentioned above. Cosmopolitans in this sense, for example, reject the assumptions that they are "exiles" (until now, a dominant theoretical category of twentieth-century fiction)—another term freely applied to hybridity without recognition of what is distinctive to it. On the contrary, the argument is that they represent a future world reality—a reality of world subjects. And yet, many of the contributors to, say, the genre of antityrannical independence fiction have often resisted the particular negotiations of the cosmopolitan, ones that jump too easily from failed efforts to doomed ideologies. Cosmopolitan writing, at any rate, has an epical dimension—it is about big events, not simply the painful shards of a merely personal memory. It is now the place to characterize it as writing.

1. The new cosmopolitanism has battered the Western confidence in the notion that writing from Latin America or Africa always simply follows European leads. Although the gesture is itself not new (it can be found in the Latin American vanguards of the 1920s described in Chapter 6), it has become a central feature of mainstream literary common sense for the first time. Indeed, as artistic discovery, the relations of power have reversed: U.S. and European novelists now eagerly cop the metafictional extravaganzas and the multilingual and multiracial cross-dressing of work from non-European countries. On the other hand, inasmuch as this writing makes a politics of the *present* attractive to reading publics, its now-highlighted political themes demand another and more customary sort of influence. The cosmopolitans, in other words, also model themselves on a nostalgia for "democracy" as a vision of pluralist inclusion, a diversity in unity, a global progress based on the Enlightenment, however ambivalently. In this, one sees some of that marked departure from the anticolonial legacy discussed above. Their esteem in U.S. magazines, reviews, and seminars does not come in spite of their backgrounds—the case of many prewar writers from the colonies—but precisely *because* of them. Whenever they write, the banners "India," "Latin America," or "Africa" are never out of sight. Being from "there" in this sense is primarily a kind of literary passport that identifies the artist as being from a region of underdevelopment and pain. Literary sophistication against this troubled backdrop, then, is doubly authoritative because it is proof of overcoming *that* to join *this*.

2. Today, national literary cultures like that of the United States

are better able than in the past to consider as their own, writers from foreign countries who have found recognition first in English translation. The strength and prestige of the U.S. publishing industry cannot be discounted as an important (although obviously not exclusive) recruiter, trainer, and final arbiter of literary trends: a kind of corporate literary salon. Such a setup creates new lines of influence and association. From the vantage point of the American reader, the true companions of the cosmopolitan celebrities, in fact, are less their national compatriots abroad than those who play the same roles artistically *within* the metropolis—most notably, perhaps, the Eastern European writers. All are fresh, political writers of epic events (if not writers of epics) who are critical of the West but only as those whose sympathies finally belong here. Eastern European and third-world writers are many things to the U.S. artistic community: a fund of imagery, teachers of hidden histories and traditions, responsible gadflies. But they are also creators of "literatures-of-use."

3. This new literature is characterized also by a flattening of influences—a juxtaposition of what previously had been thought to be alien cultural elements. The desired resonance of such juxtapositions is not to show (like E. M. Forster in *A Passage to India*) cultural dissonance, mutual incomprehensibility, but rather unity and complementarity. Such juxtapositions are not a matter of individual style or postmodern pastiche; they are borrowed from the meetings and mixings of distinct national and ethnic styles on American streets—Lebanese grocers speaking with Brooklyn accents, Cuban-Chinese restaurants next to Korean video stores. Unlike that of the past, the new cosmopolitanism is felt to be plebeian. The cosmopolite in this fiction is not an elitist or a jet-setter alone, but also simply the "people."

4. Cosmopolitanism displays impatience, at times even hostility, to the legacy of decolonization and is filled with parodic or dismissive references to the exalted "people" of the liberation movements. The "people" in cosmopolitan novels are not, as in Fanon, an occult presence of almost religious power; they are not the agents of historical change but the comic register of our common inadequacies, gullibilities, creativities, and desires. The vision here is deeply and warmly humanistic, and yet the people are "they" to the cosmopolitan "we" in the arena of literature. The new cosmopolitanism in fiction is inseparable from a strand of political liberalism that openly and consciously seeks to throw off what it considers to be the clichés of the

postwar rhetoric of third-world embattlement. Highly critical of imperialism, it has lost faith in independence. Indeed, its interest is in realigning our thinking away from independence toward a notion of codependence in which the point is incessantly made that the first world has borrowed also from "us." It is an assimilationism with dignity.

5. The rejection of the decolonization legacy is not at all a simply political gesture. It is also aesthetic. There is, of course, no monolithic list of features that describes the artistic outlooks of anti-imperialist intellectuals, but there are gists of ideas that the new cosmopolitanism has instinctively picked up on and now opposes. Some of these are that culture is meaningless if not considered in its "national aspect"; that culture is not an elite realm of inspiration but the means for a people to attain its own (in Fanon's words) "psycho-affective equilibrium"; that literature must guard against giving vent to the isolated intellectual's disillusionment and weariness; that irony itself is the mark of the intellectual's alienation from his or her own subject matter and that the appropriate stylistic element for historical action is impassioned sarcasm; that the language of race and ethnicity always accompanies, and often conceals, the language of class;[36] that national literary cultures go through stages; and that these stages (in ascending order) are assimilation, folklorism, combat and, finally, the stage of speaking in one's own voice. Culture is here perceived not only as a form of artistic creation but as literacy, education, and hygiene.

6. By contrast, the cosmopolitans reinforce and significantly extend already established aesthetic criteria—chief among them being complexity, subtlety, irony, and understatement. One could argue that the full reception of literature from the anticolonial legacy is impossible without a critical reappraisal of these apparently universal qualities; however, this story too is mixed, for they famously ridicule the pretensions of European art-school fiction and the American confessional novel, bringing the language of popular film, the newspapers, and international street life into a realm of literary seriousness quite different from the high/low transgressions associated with postmodernism. Politics becomes, in the technical sense, extravagant. One writes novels about writing novels—a procedure that is unique only because the experience is. Cosmopolitan writing lifts freely from such third-world genres as the jungle diary, the

prison notebook, the village joke, the scribbled clandestine note; but novelizing them with sophistication, it obviates the desire to study the genres as such.

7. In line with their ostensibly subversive and more broadly democratic efforts to claim cosmopolitanism for an international, multicultural *demos,* to be political has become a selling point. One reviles modernist detachment, bitterly attacking it as naive and parochial. On the other hand, also prevalent is the idea that artist and state are incompatible—a belief that places the writer today in a position of antagonism to one of the major tenets of the decolonization intellectual, whose involvement in a new state formation was central and defining. The goal very often is to join an impassioned political sarcasm (a situated satire) with ironic detachment, employing humor with a cosmic, celebratory pessimism.

8. The attractions of globalism, however, rest partly in the freedom to operate in more than one vein. Globalism's presence in metropolitan culture is not simply accommodating, but abrasive. Its moods allow for everything from visible and vocal advocates of the expansion of literature's boundaries to new players in a triumphal campaign to extend knowledge outside existing borders. The third-world writer who attains a certain fame plays an intermediary role, the role of ushering-in, critiquing the West, usually in acceptable ways, citing strange names, retelling hidden histories, and doing all this pedagogically.

A better sense that this process is indeed going on can be seen not only in the shift in publishers' lists (the highly acclaimed interventions of even middle-level writers like Ariel Dorfman, Sashi Tharoor, and Michael Ondaatje), the new courses, the new hirings, the new journals, and so on, but the political-correctness debate itself, which in its distinction between phony and real third-world literature makes more vivid the political stakes possessed by the issue of taste.[37] That debate allows one to discuss the issue of celebrity making in the literary field as an issue about native informants. This issue arises not only among best-selling writers, but in university hiring, in choosing insider reviewers of books, and in tokenizing speakers lists. While I am looking in this passage at the specific problem of a group of creative authors, mostly novelists, the underlying forces that produced them are at the same time generating whole strata of professors, journalists, and opinion makers who fulfill much the same function and play much the same ambivalent role. But perhaps it is in the realm of "seriousness" represented by the authors of high novels that our anxieties toward domestic hierarchies and world domination can be analyzed best. To do so meaningfully requires looking at differences as well as similarities.

Although representatives of cosmopolitan fiction can be found coming from China, Southeast Asia, the Portuguese former colonies, and the Arab world, they are relatively rare. It follows from what has been said that apart from the necessary feeling of range, or the authority that resides in being identified with a specific third-world locale, not all regions lend themselves equally to cosmopolitanism's particular allure. From the outset the role of interlocutor can be played mainly by those who write in a European language, who resist thematizing colonialism from a socialist point of view, or who avoid expressing themselves in difficult-to-assimilate genres like the oral poem, the song lyric, or the locally situated essay. In view of the number of likely candidates who clearly do not fit in with this new cosmopolitanism, however, other kinds of explanation are in order. Let me consider examples from just two areas, the Arabic and the Portuguese.

Take, for instance, Naguib Mahfouz, who seems in every way but his native tongue to be a perfect candidate for the role of Arab representative in the United States. A Nobel Prize winner who is now extensively translated into English, he was a pointed defender of Salman Rushdie following the infamous *fatwa,* and he now resides in Egypt—certainly to American minds the most Westernized Arabic country, the Camp David renegade, and the modern site of ancient cultural greatness. Or the Sudanese writer Tayeb Salih: English-educated with extensive ties abroad, a man active in public life, a high official for the BBC in Lebanon, and a writer whose most famous novel addresses (by way of revising) several European classics—*Othello,* Forster's *Passage to India,* Conrad's *Heart of Darkness*—in a style that is both complexly Freudian and self-critical. Or Etel Adnan from Lebanon, or the Mahgrebian writers Abdelkebir Khatibi, Assia Djebar, and Tahar Ben Jelloun, who all write in French, often with the moods and tastes of those steeped in the French tradition so familiar to and admired by American readers. One likely reason for ignoring these potential best-sellers is, of course, the political hostility toward the Arab world in the United States, the tireless images of "terrorism," oil dependency, and religious fanaticism. As I have been saying, however, these blunt political stances fail to give a sense of the way cultural dissonance is internalized and made invisible. When it comes to highly advanced literary traditions like the Arabic, Urdu, Bengali, or Chinese, the language problem has always been conceived of too narrowly. Translation into English is not the only difficult thing. At least as problematic is "translating" the culture itself—its sense of history, its source materials, its literary allusions and assumptions.

Many Arabic novels are either alluding to a political conflict that official American belief cannot conceive as "phantasmagoric" (the Palestinian struggle)—which, indeed, has been banished from the reviving properties of humor and metaphor in this country. By the same token, they are calling upon cultural signifiers from Sufi poetry, Koran, or secular romance *(Alf Laylah wa Laylah)* that are not a part of the common knowledge of Western readers in the same way that the largely Christian iconography of Latin America or the British imperial histories of India tend to be. If it were not for these sorts of reasons, Emile Habiby's novel *The Strange Story of Saeed the Ill-Fated Pessoptomist* could very well have been another *One Hundred Years of Solitude* for American audiences. But in addition to the impediments, there is no motive to overcome them. Because of the extensive internal networks and fully realized history of literary life in Arabic (as in Urdu and Chinese), the writing is not necessarily addressed to an English-speaking metropolis, simply because it does not have to be. Its aesthetic strategies are too independent to be pedagogical.

A different sort of problem arises with lusophone Africa and in Brazil. For the former, despite the presence of statesmen-poets like Agostinho Neto, the caustic nature of the political landscape is so forbidding as to place this writing off-limits by virtue of its "contamination" by the state. Mozambique, Angola, Guinea-Bissau are precisely that stratum of Africa that most closely resembles the Latin American and Caribbean socialist countries and movements. The most famous intellectual contributions from Brazil in the era of decolonization have both had dangerous connotations for Western sensibilities: the radical pedagogy of Paulo Freire's adult literacy writings and the birth of what would later be called liberation theology in the poor urban parishes of the Rio and São Paulo ghettos.

In Brazil's case, I am primarily talking about a division of labor. Perhaps because Portugal within the European context has for various reasons not produced literary figures of influence within the European family (being particularly distant from the Anglo-American tradition), the Portuguese literature of Brazil has no special advantages in the United States for its being a European language. While Brazil plays a decisive role culturally in recent decades in helping to form the latter's notion of the "third world" (captured in the images "rain forest," "debt" in the midst of an economic "miracle," destruction of native peoples, the "last wilderness," and so on), it artistically has not done so in literature but in music—bossa nova in the 1950s and 1960s with Frank Sinatra as interlocutor, the Western pilgrimage to the Rio Carnival, the unprecedented triumph of samba and pagode in the dance halls and music studios of the United States and Europe, and, of course, lambada as the public demonstration of third-world sexual license. All of this has unfolded in spite of such candidates as Machado de Asis before World War II, Jorge Amado as one of the most widely read and translated writers of the Latin boom, Rachel de Quieroz, and more recently, despite the intense interest of French feminism that has actively celebrated her work, Clarice Lispector.

States of Theory and the Absence of States

Although it began in the 1980s as a forum for modernist authors, "third-world literature" now clearly includes unknown, underground, even politically embattled writers of the most disparate kinds. But national belonging is not only nostalgia for types of food, scents in the sea air, or the lilt of a people's speech; it is belonging to a *polity*. If Carolyn Steedman is right in arguing that "reading literature from unfamiliar cultures often serves to reveal the convention of our own metaphoric system," this can be seen primarily as an act of political avoidance in which the international solidarities of writers who articulate the "home" of recently liberated colonial territory are confidently packaged with diasporic or postnational sensibilities.[38] The "literary," it appears, must not be about political triumphs but about loss and longing. Aesthetic reception apparently demands that alternatives be evoked as delayed hopes rather than accomplished realities. What links little-known anticolonial works like Mario de Azuela's masterpiece *Los de abajo (The Underdogs)* to socialist fiction like Sembène Ousmane's novel *Le Docker Noir (Black Docker)* is precisely the embrace of a political victory among named contestants in a class-historical confrontation. It is true that in the novel form—although not in poetry and popular song—severe limits exist to a merely celebratory sensibility. As Northrup Frye would say, no conflict, no art. Forgotten are not the novels that pay obeisant homage to new ruling elites (if there are any) but ones that imagine collective efforts to create political alternatives so that *that* conflict creates aesthetic pleasure. This is not an argument for preferring "p.c." novels to the modernist canon; nor is this a stand for realism or historicism against symbolism or psychology. It is a comment on the specific limits of inclusion into the emergent canon of third-world literature. Although not ignored, writing of the kind I have been describing has not attained a threshold of significance outside specialist circles. And the politics of that oversight is a politics of culture that must be discussed and analyzed as such.

The atmosphere enabling this narrowing of focus has occurred in a specific political context. If the primary sense of place for many former residents of colonized countries is no longer the nation, it is often a local or ethnic culture packed off into exile, jumbled together with the official cultures of the metropolis (and the cultures of other immigrants), and, where not carried on, remembered. This apparent disintegration of an older, embattled, anticolonial sense of national belonging is, however, very easy to overestimate. One tends to forget the meticulousness with which these working-class exiles to the metropolitan centers of Europe and the United States follow events in their countries of origin, visit those countries regularly, and distinguish among themselves in ways that the white majorities of Europe and the United States typically do not (a "Latino" in the United States is first of all Colombian, say, rather than Ecuadoran, just as an "Arab" is Syrian rather than Jordanian).

There is a pattern of exclusion for types of feeling and being that, against all predictions, still exist in older forms at home and abroad. U.S. and European audiences read more novels than testimonials; they see big-budget films *about* imperialist conflict *(Under Fire, The Year of Living Dangerously, Gandhi)* but not the films of formally experimental filmmakers from the countries themselves like Brazil's

Glauber Rocha or Bolivia's Jorge Sanjinés; they listen to reggae, samba, and other examples of "world music," but not to the locally influential musics that, for unexplained reasons, cannot be a part of that world: say, Algerian *chaabi,* Ecuadoran *pasillos,* or the Cuban *guateque.* This general problem of knowledge is exacerbated in quite specific and powerful ways when one is dealing with national-cultural strangeness under conditions of inequality. Learning about another culture is impossible without critically exposing one's own. For that reason, one needs to talk more frankly about the system of reviewers, professors, and commentators who take the lead in defining an always undefined taste. To begin doing so, one must look at some of the constants of the reviewers' and professors' trade. And this involves a discussion (perhaps a bluff calling is more appropriate) of the aesthetics of irony, individuality, displacement, and ambiguity—again, not in any absolute sense, but as a complaint against absolution. One needs to examine the popularized and intransigent realm of Kantian aesthetics that finds its strongest supporters today not in the philosophy departments so much as in the columns of the daily newspapers. Some of the literary forms and personalities that do not make it in the metropolis are, of course, not censored in any customary way. It is simply that they do not sell, that they are flat or pedantic, that they do not "translate" well.

According to Christopher Lehmann-Haupt, a reviewer for the *New York Times,* the norms of the public-sphere critic are explicitly anti-ideological and usually idiosyncratic—that is, they do not depend on an editorial mandate, but on the whims of personal taste.[39] But to hear Lehmann-Haupt's unguarded account of his own is to be wrenched into an understanding of the divergent protocols of individual whim in a market venue of mass readership. Pointing out that the celebrated openings for Black and third-world writing today, however great, are not as extensive as they were in the late 1960s and early 1970s, he explains that he personally has become less interested in that sort of material "for reasons that are too complicated to explain." He considers much of the work "sloppy and badly done"; Rushdie, for example, "can't write a sentence if his life depended on it." Bharati Mukherjee is "first rate," and so is Julio Cortázar, "but you can't really count him among the third world." His criteria are evanescent, the reviewer insists, and he is drawn to the offbeat, whatever else it might be. On the other hand, other considerations enter in. He generally chooses to review whatever is newsworthy (say, a book about Iraq during the Gulf War); he will go out of his way also for a great first novel, for "something that broke advance-sales records," for "what our readership would be interested in"; and there are certain writers who are *must* reviews, among whom he classifies Toni Morrison and Norman Mailer. Conjecturing on why more non-Western literature is not given the publicity of a prominent review, he answers: "It's a question of expertise. The major publishing houses are the ones we tend to review most and they are not for the most part doing third-world literature. We review them most because as a rule they have the best books."

It is important to remind ourselves that in the public culture it is mostly bewilderment that still greets declarations of third-world arrival. With the necessarily accelerated process of decay that novelty experiences in a commercial art form, the excitements of the early Rushdie interviews have not only shown their face in literary commentary but have been encased in mainstream institutional recognition. The rich promise of the tropes of political fantasy and migrancy—perhaps the two key conceptual offerings of Rushdie's translation of the Latin boom—have proliferated in a collection of inspired echoes forming the stock-in-trade of the newspaper review and the undergraduate lecture without adding anything fundamentally new to the original concepts. The scenario—if not the details—of this genre of vital storytelling had become not routine so much as emphatic about the archetypal points of contact: the suddenly unrepressed information that needed desperately to be conveyed; the unavailability of minimalist, introverted, or cool and calm expressive means; the political stories one could not escape without sublimating. What had presented itself on the eve of the canonical reform movements in the mid-1980s as the work of larger-than-life individuals—those third-world *classics* that had previously been overlooked—and what had communicated itself to a metropolitan stratum of professors, book reviewers, and publishers in the polished didacticism of well-placed promotional articles and interviews, had ceased to be monumental. It was now democratic.

What needs now to be analyzed is the ripple effects of this democratization at the lower levels and at specific points of contact: the new mammoth multicultural anthologies designed as textbooks for undergraduate teaching; the wave of highly publicized first novels by younger authors writing, often experimentally, about their own carefully nurtured marginalities in a sort of highbrow mimicry of the testimonial; the new code of authenticity that arose in assigning book reviewing to critics who by name or accent or place of birth commanded an immediate and often suspicious authority over the new literatures under review; the patterns of hiring for the new positions in the university reserved for "postcolonial" and American ethnic literatures; the arts grants explosion for painters, actors, and directors of color. While it is required by space to approach the problem of cosmopolitanism through prominent case studies, it is the massive network of agents and adherents of the larger sensibility—at times so large that it cannot easily be seen—that renders the investigation meaningful.

Large-market textbooks prepared for a postcanonical curriculum by the nation's biggest commercial publishers tend to adopt a deliberate strategy of integration, organizing under themes like "Gender and Identity" or "War and Violence" the writing of U.S. feminists, canonical figures of the nineteenth century, Arabic poets, and first-generation American immigrants writing on the theme of ethnicity.[40] Taking all of these textbooks together, it would be hard to conceive of more coverage, or to find any obvious omissions by region, gender, race, or—although the chapter subheadings predictably do not mention this—political persuasion as well. At times, the integrationist mode favors the canon and approaches a simple tokenism in its other offerings. This is the case, for example, in James Hurt's *Literature: A Contemporary Introduction,* James H. Pickering and Jeffrey D. Hoeper's simply titled *Literature,* and in Sven Birkerts's *Literature: The Evolving Canon,* which promises to teach students how "fiction, poetry, and drama have changed and expanded in a global, multicultural, and electronic environment." Demonstrating the unease of ethnic inclusion, Birkerts's publisher promotes the books' "extensive material from . . . classic authors" while hastening to point out that it is "particularly rich in authors writing from nontraditional and global perspectives."[41] At other times, without fundamentally changing the sectoralism of reference to the "classic" versus the "nontraditional," an anthology may reverse the order of its mission by stressing the non-Western literature now sanctioned by inclusion in the canon—the case of Gilbert H. Muller and John A. Williams's *Bridges: Literature across Cultures.*

In spite of this rhetoric of implicit hierarchies, several of the available anthologies are exemplary in refusing to police the "literary." One such text with a U.S. ethnic focus is Jerome Beaty and J. Paul Hunter's *New Worlds of Literature,* the best of the "American pluralism" anthologies.[42] Others in this category extend their coverage beyond the United States to the world as such, offering selections from the United States, without priority of place, next to those of Australia, Senegal, and Egypt. Here one finds the very fine anthology of Shirley Geok-Lin Lim and Norman Spencer, *One World of Literature,* and one of the more explicitly "third-world/political" anthologies, Elisabeth Young-Bruehl's *Global Cultures: A Transnational Short Fiction Reader,* which deserves more discussion.[43]

Soberly assessing a situation in which professors in traditional literary fields were transforming themselves overnight into teachers of third-world literature, the book presents itself as a training manual for such a transformation. From the pedagogical point of view, then, much rides on Young-Bruehl's presentation, which groups together its stories under five suggestive section headings: "Between Cultures: Emigrés, Refugees, Exiles"; "New Nations: National Liberations, Civil Wars, Apartheid"; "Culture Clash: Modernization, Urbanization, Westernization"; "Culture Creation: Women Writing"; and "Complex Communications." It would be difficult to find an available textbook that met better the range, in every sense of the word, of a world literature constructed outside the shelter of, say, Macmillan's paternalistic umbrella. It journeys through superb selections from West Africa and China that are, moreover, earmarked as expressing vital themes of civil war, cultural creation, and modernity; however, it then embarks on an entire section dedicated to what it calls "entrapments, fantasies" in which stories are taken from Pakistan, Egypt, Brazil, and Chile. Is there something about the experience of these vastly different places that leads to an imagination of "entrapment"? That is the implication, and it may even be true, but one does not know how to take it, especially since some of the other subheadings—"developers," "rebellions," "the circle of violence," and so on—fit more securely (and more suspiciously) within views garnered from current events as expressed in newspaper headlines, as do its subheadings "madness" and "religious visions."

Larger problems of inclusion—a point made often about worldwide anthologies—can be made here as well, and they bear specifying as a way of hinting at the sheer scale of the limits placed by publishing on the matter of scope. About sixty-five out of the eighty or so stories were originally written in English or Spanish, and of the remaining fifteen, several are in Portuguese. There is practically nothing from the French Caribbean or from francophone Africa; nothing from lusophone Africa; nothing, surprisingly, from the rich literatures of Bengal or non-English-speaking India (particularly the south); nothing from the Maghreb; almost nothing from the rich Urdu literatures of Pakistan; nothing from the patwah traditions of Jamaica, Trinidad, or Haiti; and nothing based on the oral literatures of Africa or Amerindian peoples, although much was included from the often overlooked areas of China and the Arabic-speaking world.

And there is another telling kind of oversight as well. In spite of one Vietnamese story, one story each by the Salvadoran novelist Manlio Argueta and the Palestinian novelist and poet Ghassan Kanafani, and (arguably and only in passing) threads from the work of a few others, many of the stories seemed geared precisely to expose the failures of alternatives to Westernization, even though such alternatives form a prominent and respectable theme in non-Western writing. An inordinate number of the stories shy away from the themes of revolution and anticolonial struggle, and seem to take as their motto a line from one of the stories in Part I: "Feelings are more important than ideas." Compelled to argue that her choice of selection was based on representing "ordinary people," Young-Bruehl distinguishes the quotidian from stories of "national liberation struggles," as though ordinary people did not make them. Modernization, moreover, is always presented reliably as a "stepping into the future."

A similar process can be seen in academic theory. The special issue on globalism published by *Theory, Culture, and Society* in 1990 had followed the leads of the journal *Public Culture,* whose declarations on "transnational cultures" had helped to define its image by the late 1980s.[44] Noticeable above all in this influential issue was the ineffability of globalism itself. In the appurtenances of "flows," "migrations," and technological breakthroughs, one is never given a sense of long-term plans with distinct beneficiaries. The absent agent of globalism stood more exposed in the prosaics of the social sciences. And its being absent points much more accusingly at the national and cultural fealty of the critic who can locate evolutionary trends rather than policies in this high-stakes game of global change.

In this vein, one of the contributors, Roland Robertson, rather than seeing the recent market openings of China and the collapse of the Soviet state as contributing causes, finds them added difficulties to theorization. Globalism, according to Robertson, has not happened. What might have taken place but failed to was "the imperial hegemony of a single nation or a 'grand alliance' between two or more dynasties or nations, the yielding of nationalism to the ideal of 'free trade,' . . . the worldwide triumph of a trading company." The list is startling, of course, since it describes precisely what *did* happen or is happening. Arjun Appadurai also finds it difficult to ascribe agency to these processes. In his treatment, one gets such a memorable portrait of the sheer confusion and plenitude of the new global culture that the accompanying telos of his essay is submerged by the sheer thrill of the image of multiplicity as he ranges confidently through fields in a vivid language. The operative words are significantly aesthetic: "complex, overlapping, disjunctive"—all richly positive in their connotations as signals of an order that springs, as it were, from irrepressible forces for which contempt would be anachronistic; one can only rather marvel at them. The language is carefully chosen to reflect this inertia: "refugees from Sri Lanka *find themselves* in south India," "the Hmong *are driven* to London," "international capital *shifts*" (my emphasis).

Even as a system is apparently fingered for responsibility ("international capital"), it is personified to avoid the impolitic precision of naming. The verbs attached to this personified order do not, it is true, hide behind passive constructions. But far from being clear about agency, the system—like an ambitious newcomer—is dynamic, breaking all of us as readers out of the staleness of an older equilibrium. It gets things done, and whom it acts upon and how seems primarily important only as a demonstration of variety. Thus, the forced economic migration of Sri Lankans into foreign peonage is mixed up with the politically engineered transport of former collaborators (the Hmong). The interests served in this process are not of concern to Appadurai; what draws his attention are the new configurations of cultural interflow—the great, compelling, uncertain mix-and-match of still distinct populations thrust together: "These moving groups can never afford to let their imaginations rest too long, even if they wished to" (297). Such a sentence expresses pain on its surface for the migrant's exhausted wandering, but not without an audible cheering for accompanying compensations.

The very real changes in population transfers, in geopolitical balance of forces, and in telecommunications are marshaled here as unwarranted proof that existing "center-periphery models" are obsolete. Appadurai is in a very large company when he particularizes this view to argue that cultural imperialism as such is no longer valid, asserting that the concept depends on a view of homogenization instead of the "cultural resistance" that in fact takes place. While the critical consensus repudiates the category of the "indigenous," it reinserts it by discovering in the act of consumption of Western cultural products a process of "indigenization." It is not simply a quibble to concentrate on one of Appadurai's more extreme formulations: "The central problem of today's global interactions is the tension between cultural homogenization and cultural heterogenization" (295). The *central* problem? One would have thought that the cases of Somalia, Panama, Egypt, Madagascar, and the Ukraine would summon other sorts of centralities having to do with a violent homogenization from above, as a result of more familiar types of military occupation and domestic repression. The statement speaks to the excesses, and even the absurdities, of Appadurai's larger position.

If authenticity as an assertion of ethnic or racial distinction, with consequent rights of insider knowledge, has been the target of such analyses, it has been so selectively. Posed in the caricatural purity of a culture untarnished by Western contacts, authenticity is, at all events, an easy enough candidate for caricature.[45] One wants to know, however, who actually holds the view in this purist form. More interesting is the animosity with which the "proof" is made, the intensity of the ire against national culture. National culture itself is never fully a matter of "culture," of course, but of timber rights, legal jurisdictions, and credit arrangements. Nor is the counterargument ever turned back against the authority of a critical apparatus in which authenticity in the form of hiring or publishing preferences continues to operate quietly and securely. But just as important as the selectivity of its application are the missing middle positions with which authenticity is embroiled. There is a distance between rejecting authenticity and its familiar counterpart: "There is no transcendent, privileged cultural space on which to stand that is outside capitalist reification."[46] To appreciate non-Western cultural forms—to have even a chance of understanding them—one must show this claim to be false.

Under the spotlight of this ruthless exposure of authenticity's bankruptcy as a concept, the apparatus of criticism itself can rarely be found. Achille Mbembe, for example, has quite rightly said that "filiation, in and of itself, authorizes nothing. Of itself, it bestows no immanent authority, no particular derogation."[47] But to prove that authenticity is untenable mistakes the deliberate creativity of strategy for an ontological assertion. It mistakes a modus operandi for an interpretation; it projects a failed effort at descriptive completeness or fairness onto an act of policy—the kind of confusion likely to attend an intelligentsia unwilling to look at the specific difficulties of organizing on behalf of an interest in transforming materialities. This sort of conceptual incongruity—closely related to the more general thesis of "two worlds" or incompatible epistemes—is as elusive as it is fundamental to current cultural theory. As I have been arguing, it is an extention of the point that an anticommunist political culture in the United States (classically captioned in the term "cold war" but with much more subtle contemporary manifestations among contemporary intellectuals) is a major subtext of the debates now raging over colonial theory.

This point arises full force in colonial literary theory. Robert Young, for example, contending that Marxism is a principle component of the imperialist project because of its Hegelian Eurocentrism, avers that "for orthodox Marxism there can be only one 'other' . . . into which all other oppressed groups, so-called 'minorities,' must in the last instance be subsumed."[48] In the name of resisting the Marxist critical urge to decide in advance what is best for African literature, Christopher L. Miller similarly characterizes Sembène Ousmane as a writer of "Orientalist caricature" because of his parodies of a tribal chieftain in a novel Miller calls socialist realist—as though Sembène had somehow become less African because of his allegiances.[49] For Miller, too, "ethnicity is . . . the principle obstacle to a Marxist analysis," a thesis he attempts to prove with an intemperate condemnation of Amilcar Cabral and Frantz Fanon for attempting to forge, despite their recognition of several African cultures and not just one, a "'convergence' toward 'a single national culture'" (46). He does not deny the desire of Cabral, for instance, "to respect local, ethnic cultures" but objects on principle to the labeling of any of them as "retrogressive." Such an insulting normative judgment is nothing less than the attempt to "uproot the African ethos," says Miller, in an act of "conversion and redemption."

If according to these accounts reassertions of unalloyed "tradition" are always colored by the experience of colonialism and its European taint (a truism, as I have been saying, of the discourse on authenticity), why is this particular taint of Eurocentricism in Cabral or Sembène so inauthentic? Respect for native cultures is Miller's apparent program here, but his conclusions are made inevitable by the revealing view that "it was in the name of culture and of difference that the battle for independence was fought" (45–6). What Miller ignores is what Cabral and Fanon understood very well: that their battle was over political sovereignty, with all its implications for feeding people, developing or not developing in certain directions, or debating what form of cultural hybrids the new state would nurture and protect. In each of these readings, the term "cultural imperialism" is sternly revoked. If the center/periphery model is obsolete, then so is the master/slave relationship, except insofar as it betokens mutual need, without real interest in reversal.

The recent classical statement against the concept of "cultural imperialism," however, may be that of Achille Mbembe. In order to account for postcolonial relations of power, Mbembe argues, "we must go beyond the binary categories used in standard interpretations of domination (resistance/passivity, subjection/autonomy, state/civil society, hegemony/counterhegemony, totalization/detotalization)."[50] "The basic goal" of postcolonial governments, he continues, is "the production of an imagery"; these regimes are characterized by the "grotesque and the obscene," and rather than a clear victimizer and victim, one finds the "mutual 'zombification' of both the dominant and those whom they apparently dominate. This 'zombification' means that each robbed the other of their vitality and has left them both impotent" (4–5).

Mbembe's rethinking of the would-be dichotomy between colonizer and colonized at times takes the form of a normative focus on negotiation over conflict, a framework in which one vocabulary is authorized at the expense of another and allegiances are demanded within the boundaries of that vocabulary's usage. One can thus speak about "overlapping," "pourous," "transnational," "disjunctive," and "rhizomatic" relations, but nothing so brutally bipolar as contradiction. The force of the literary, as a subtext of the position itself, is powerfully clear as well. He speaks of the "prosaics of power," the "bad taste" of the rulers, the "improvisation and indeterminacy" of the practice of power as if to say that, apart from its costs, upheaval is at least hermeneutically rich. Artistic distinction is a compensation for social disarticulation.

In this atmosphere, the critic who locates changeableness and the bewildering many-sidedness of reality in the conceptual machinery of simple war, of two sides, is seen by the proponents of hybridity as participating in little more than a "two-finger exercise." And yet one might legitimately wonder if what is so and what is hermeneutically interesting are always the same. As I examine at length below, words like "intricate" display values so transcendent in our aesthetic grasp of the real that they seem even to fall outside the provisos of Barbara Herrnstein Smith's thesis on the situatedness of all aesthetic judgment. It is truly the beyond of the beyond, like novelty and progress. And it is here, I think, that the weakness of the cosmopolitan outlook lies—in the explicit failure to see cosmopolitanism as less an expansive ethos than an expansionist policy: a move not toward complexity and variety but toward centralization and suffocating stagnation. In the Western statesman's realm, cosmopolitanism has always been a supreme compliment. To argue—as Clifford, Nussbaum, Rabinow (and, more recently, Robbins) have—that cosmopolitanism somehow has to be defended against a clumsy attack by conservative and progressive philistines alike, is to be guilty of positing the late-arriving, innovative, and minority view as though it were an oppressively general and dominant one.

The very act of developing an appropriate language and conceptual apparatus to figure globalism—the fin de siècle story of moment—has in a leftward swerve congruent with multiculturalism given an emphasis to the receiver, victim, and object of power: the women, natives, others. The objects become subjects and, in a move apparently fit for cultural analysis, discover the power they already had. At the nexus of consumption, the contemporary critic tends to find the subject transforming the product by violating its intended meanings; at the nexus of interpretation, the subject is said to manipulate the message, thereby appropriating it. Despite a revelatory language and an air of excitement, colonial theory gives the banishment of the idea of colonial victim an almost routine feel. It is as though decolonization itself were no longer necessary since liberation had occurred already at the level of the subject if only one cared to look. The formulations more often than not act as a de rigueur performative sign of maturity. The typical narrative, now glancing or emblematic, now studiously sociological or filled with data, sets out at all events to establish similar stakes, whether they are spelled out or not. These stakes lie in the categories invariably ascribed to an older narrative in need of revision: community, national state, and periphery—terms, as one can see, that reach from mere units of analysis to more powerful intimations of a highly charged ethics. What is contested as a matter of record with easily assembled evidence of cultural messiness is simultaneously drawing strength from an unarticulated euphoria for the transcultural impurity of the object. The point, as it were, lies not so much in the purported inadequacy of an always unspecified earlier position of geriatric "authenticity" as it does in the highly normative dare that someone finally challenge this welcomed polyvocality. The claim? Authentic cultures do not exist: internally cohesive and autonomous cultures are a fiction, and both the authentic and the autonomous reigned as concepts until very recently.

Remarkably unanimous is the move away from what Michael Taussig, in reference to the religion of the Putumayo of the Colombian highlands, called "two radically distinct ways of apprehending or evaluating the world of persons and things."[51] Notice, however, the shades of emphasis within this repudiation of the binary. Several not always compatible operations are at work here, although the rejected position (call it the position of struggle, of dispossession, of unresolved hostilities) is fundamentally the same. At one point, colonial theory is involved in a challenge to the idea of the passive consumer, a corollary of the center/periphery model of dependency theory; and so the force here is to reassert the "resistance" of populations that appear to be cowed or gulled in more brutish or humorless narratives. Like Mbembe, James C. Scott, in *Domination and the Arts of Resistance,* openly contests not only ideology but hegemony as well.[52] The logic of his argument is to heroize the oppressed and to cast the spokespeople for armed resistance or parliamentary strategies in the role of disrespectful paternalists, while at the same time portraying power relations as a closed circle in which resistance always complements repression. Couched in an annoying set of hints that the cultural battles of insult, playacting, memoir, or confession had never been given their due before (even though they are standard in the urban ethnographies of the nineteenth-century labor movement intellectuals), his argument suggests that in power relations there are no open ends, no ragged edges. Society is a deft and complicated perpetual-motion machine in which ruler and ruled complement each other in their antagonisms. Mbembe had written that "subaltern classes 'respond' to elite domination and manage to retain control over their own actions by reappropriating those hegemonic cultural forms that suit their purposes,"[53] and Scott agrees.

At other times, the move is more like Appadurai's implicit repudiation of the imperialist framework itself. Eager to justify her decision to read the ever familiar figures of Kipling, Burke, Forster, and (now) Rushdie as a seamless discourse on "English India," Sara Suleri, for example, declares that hers is an "attempt to break down the incipient schizophrenia of a critical discourse that seeks to represent domination and subordination as though the two were mutually exclusive terms"; she bids us not forget that the colonizer was, in the act of plundering, himself a victim of "psychic disempowerment."[54] It is, of course, revealing that a critic whose cultural capital is evenly divided between Anglo-American and Pakistani sources would assume the warrant to speak of the mutualities of colonizer and colonized, and then happily discover that there is no fundamental difference in the reading problems presented by an English novel and a South Asian one—a proposition that works better, needless to say, if one chooses Salman Rushdie rather than, say, Hasan Manto, a chronicler of partition writing in Urdu.

Another kind of problem was posed by explicitly Marxist approaches to a postcolonial theory. Despite the widely mixed (and, in the United States, mostly hostile) feelings produced by it, Aijaz Ahmad's study *In Theory* is impossible to ignore. Its attacks, as I have written elsewhere, were often deeply unwarranted.[55] Several other reviewers of his book, I think, have adequately portrayed exactly what he gets wrong about the actual positions taken in Anglo-American literary theory, as well as the mistakes he makes in his overview of U.S.

postwar politics.[56] All this being said, the book has made contributions that few appear willing to mention. Ahmad seems to me to have shown well that if the material rootedness of Marxism has been scurrilously invoked, Marx himself has not been read, and that unacknowledged material rewards have gone to intellectuals who disavow Marxism, formulate "moral" positions against racism, and espouse a radical rhetoric without connection to revolutionary movements.

Correctives to various shadings of thought within colonial studies occur widely in his book, which targets above all the role of the critic who believes that he or she is merely commenting upon a distant reality but who is in fact actually affecting it: "Very affluent people may come to believe that they have broken free of imperialism through acts of reading, writing, lecturing, and so forth. For human collectivities in the backward zones of capital, however . . . [this depends on] a revolutionary restructuring of one's nation-state."[57] This fairly typical interpolation at once intentionally embarrasses the mostly university-based reader by placing him or her in a defensive posture ("very affluent"); it demystifies the mental lucubrations of theory by suturing these to the vulgarities of class interest; and, finally, it establishes an oppositional pairing (the affluent/human collectivities) whose very obviousness enhances the point. Indeed, most of the key signposts, the factual materials, and the theoretical correctives of the first two chapters are a sort of common knowledge within the socialist community.

Ahmad's recollections of the Sino-Soviet split, his allusions to the fall of the Guevarist *foco* or the concept of Maoist encirclement, the telling contrasts between the success in the 1970s of the socialist offensive in the colonies (Angola, Vietnam, South Yemen) and the "receding of revolutionary horizons in Western Europe"—these, and much else, are relatively standard fare for anyone who participated in what might be called the new old left. Yet it is Ahmad who revived these lessons against the grain and applied them now to this very different world—stumblingly, ungenerously, even at times inaccurately, but with a core message that is useful. Against the backdrop of the cosmopolitan drift of colonial theory to which he is an exception, I would like to reconsider three of his major themes: the blight of nationalism; the emptiness of the term "third world"; and the theoretical differences that arise when dealing with Asia and with the Americas.

Understanding the nation debate as a major subtheme of cosmopolitanism demands a reconceptualization that has largely not taken place. Despite the varied contributions of writers ranging from Ernest Gellner and Eric Hobsbawm to Partha Chatterjee and Homi Bhabha, the basically taxonomic character of the discourse on the nation has gone unnoticed. One is for, another against, nationalism. Readers are told when nations originated, how they are to be defined, their importance as tropes of identity or collectivity, their future in a global economy. Added to these interests is another subset of questions: Is the nation a European invention and a result of colonization or is it indigenous and pancultural? Is it a political good or an evil when judged against the past? Ernest Renan and Lenin, Benedict Anderson and Bhabha all agree that the nation is a form of metaphysical belonging; they differ only about its origins and its uses to a practical politics. Individually, they emphasize print languages, contiguity, administrative coercions (such as passports and taxes), or simply the psychological need for a type of community in addition to other forms of belonging that would empower citizens in the face of increasing global contacts and competitions such as warfare, tourism, the World Cup, the Olympics, or beauty pageants. But the outcome of this detailed rendering of the concept is never seen actually to be helping the nation expire, even as the view that it *is* dying motivates the scholarship in the first place and is in most cases the desired outcome (although not in Anderson or Ahmad, obviously).

Reviewing approaches means reviewing the avenues of transmission. One might consider the skeptical prodding into the follies of "nationalism" by a sometime guest of the PBS program *Washington Week in Review,* Ben Wattenberg, whose book *The First Universal Nation* was adapted and played as a documentary on public television with backing from the Olin and Heritage Foundations.[58] I am suggesting that the force of the concept of the nation is more significantly embedded in television and the popular press than it is in Benedict Anderson or Ernest Gellner. The flavor of Wattenberg's handling of both the United States and the "nation" suggests the power of platitudes and their unlikely proximity to the discussion among nonspecialists. Here U.S. global influence is, with dogged circularity, called up to prove American popularity. Wattenberg expresses himself with a benign belligerence that at times seems almost to be a confession.

> We are the first universal nation. "First" as in the first one, "first" as in "number one." And "universal" within our borders and globally. In America, we now come from everywhere, becoming one people . . . vastly enriched by our pluralism. [24].

> We don't much read, watch, or listen to their [Europe's and the third world's] stuff. Is it that Americans are provincial, insular, parochial boors? More likely it is that we have a taste for just what the rest of the world now enjoys. (211)

> A new emphasis for American post–Cold War foreign policy need not be so elusive . . . In large part due to modern communications, democracy is winning the world series. The global contest will not concern whether, but what kind of, democratic values will be influential . . . In the future, the No. 1 country will be the one that is most successful in shaping the global democratic culture . . . Only Americans have the sense of mission—and gall—to engage in benign, but energetic global cultural advocacy. Hence, the doctrine of "neo–manifest destinarianism," to help form a world that is user-friendly to American values. (204)

When one immerses oneself in the nation debate as it exists among the casual readers of newspapers, one asks more significant questions about the debate's contemporary meanings. Within the United States, although the same would hold for most of Europe, the colonial diasporas have not wiped out the close attention paid by displaced peoples toward displaced polities—polities that are uninviting as they exist in their homelands, polities that have been stolen from them.

One is forced to think, in the baldest terms, about what the concept of "nation" means in the face of Wattenberg's energetic campaigning, quite apart from the abuses or comprador schemes of Uganda or Brazil, tirelessly documented in university scholarship. The crushing response that scholarship offers Wattenberg's anodyne commentary, which could serve as an illustration for precisely the dangers of the nationalist mentality, is relatively powerless in the face of the latter's emotional appeals. It therefore overlooks the equally vulgar responses they necessitate among people who are not American and who have to face such appeals constantly. Popular attractions to nationalism are incomprehensible without dwelling on the unreflective but defensible responses to this kind of cultural intimidation.

A similar problem of reconceptualization exists with the related term "third world," which Ahmad spends considerable space rejecting on the grounds of its epistemological incoherence. But is the term "third world," like the term "the West," a pamphleteer's fiction, an insufferable homogenization? The crushing familiarity of its outlines, the deadening sound of the litany of its features, do not remove it from reality. All of its differences congeal in what Teresa Hayter has called "the inexorable conversion of the dominated areas into markets for European manufactured goods and suppliers of primary commodities and raw materials for European consumption."[59] Although using the term too freely, perhaps—and without enough attention to the high-handed elitist maneuverings of the Bandung Conference—some have invoked it against the term "postcolonial" in order to remind American readers that trade debts and Rio summits still provide fuel for something like an international Popular Front, a world opinion that refuses to let the imperial order appear natural.

Ahmad's critique is interesting, however, because he concedes its "emotive power"[60] as well as the tactical wisdom of employing it within specific declarations of solidarity: "Polemic surely has a prominent place in all human discourses, especially in the discourse of politics, so the use of this term in loose, polemical contexts is altogether valid" (96). He objects only to its appropriation—the way it has been taken from its original contexts in African and Asian decolonization to arise today as an unjustified item of analysis concealing a largely first-world ignorance of local histories. He therefore identifies three distinct phases of the term (the Nehruvian, Soviet, and Maoist), arguing that only later did it attain a theoretical pretense and a subsequent imprecision that confused—for usually unstated political ends—imperialism's "international division of labor" with "the structural lack of any unified project" (16).

How, though, does one gauge the advances these corrections represent against the classical position espoused by, among others, Octavio Paz, when he assaults the term "third world" because it serves no purpose other than to create enmity toward "the West"?[61] In other words, how can we responsibly sidestep the observation that the "emotive power" of the term remains its inner strength, and that this strength is feared, fled from, and (for those reasons) ridiculed by those in Paz's "West"—and not only those who dislike the term because it suggests shabby, third-rate peoples? Few seriously contest accounts of the economic plight of underdevelopment, trade imbalances, and resources extraction. They are ritualized and repetitive, and yet there is no escaping the profound significance to culture of the brutal arithmetic of the economic indicators. The allowable discursive limits for discussing these statistics are edged off at two contradictory extremes. The term of anger ("third world"), with a theoretically mixed but at least reputable history, is avoided and condemned while the reality of the common plight is incessantly assumed and alluded to euphemistically. Metropolitan discourse is ashamed of the words but dependent on the thing's recognition. And the uses of the concept of a common horror to refer within the metropolis to what exists outside the metropolis is precisely what Ahmad's account fails to give appropriate weight.

What is the "third world" worth to the readers of American newspapers? What function does having a third world serve? What are the ways the metropolis not only steals from or builds its house upon the third world but finds it irrelevant or simply forgets it? And yet, still about raw materials, cheap labor, and strategic geographical location, the idea of the third world is immensely important to the first. It is the image of the "loser." The crucial discursive life of the term "third world" is often ignored, so it is unsurprising that some try to wish the term away even as it refuses to disappear. It is a pacifying threat, an image concocted to discipline and terrify the underpaid, the harassed, and the recently arrived. The Manichean thrust of the term "third world" is not simply a fact of official discourse to be contended with as such—with an energy of its own, outside of specialist usage or misusage. It also suggests a way of living elsewhere. As a traditional critique of capitalism, it continues to suggest that the uprooting of forms of congregation and affiliation has not completely succeeded. In this sense, the term does not merely mirror the polemical banner of the independence movements but also resists the contemptuous overtones of the "losers"; this is why the anticolonial movements, more recent guerrilla insurgencies, and the former "nonaligned" countries persisted in using the term without the reservations registered by literary theory.

As a matter of history, moreover—and one closely related to the thesis here about the New World origins of cosmopolitan rhetoric—Ahmad's conditional defense of nationalism, his dismissal of a coherent "cognitive aesthetics" of third-world literature, and his repudiation of three-worlds theory are all negatively affected by his reluctance to deal specifically with Latin America. If the United States is, as he everywhere implies, the privileged site of colonial discourse, surely this theorizing is colored by the political and demographic backwash from its favored dominions, with which it remains in close contact through an extensive network of resident intellectuals, guestworkers, and tourism—all of which have produced a distinctly New World identity. The type of cosmopolitan narrative Ahmad repudiates in the person of Salman Rushdie was, moreover, modeled explicitly on Latin American sources.

The absence presents difficulties to his thesis. Ahmad argues, for example, that "within Hispanic America, the Chilean slaughter brought to a virtual close the revolutionary dynamic unleashed by the Cuban revolution."[62] Since the point of this observation merges with another—that anticolonial nationalism had spent itself as a historical force by "about the mid-1970s" (35)—he is building a case that the scene for the reception of a narrowly textual politics in a U.S. milieu was prepared by the demoralization that came with the absence of activist struggles. This supposed demoralization, however, seems to have more to do with the resurgence of the cold war and the impending collapse of the Soviet Union than with a decline in anticolonial insurgencies, which actually inspired much of the metropolitan theorizing vicariously. In Latin America, the Sandinista victory in 1979 (six years after the Pinochet coup) generated shock waves of euphoria on a continental scale for more than a decade, not only prompting left nationalist movements in Peru, El Salvador, Colombia, and elsewhere, but (more to the point) giving a radical impetus to intellectuals and youth in the metropolitan centers.

As to Ahmad's more general proposition of decline following the Vietnamese accords in 1975, the story does not fit details like the rise of the New People's Army of the Philippines, the right-wing clerical antiimperialism of the Iranian revolution, the victory of the New Jewel movement in Granada, and the battle of Quito Carnavale in Angola between the Cuban and South African armies that led directly to the Namibian accords—all of them post-1975, and all of them (again) with resonant activist effects in the metropolis, particularly in the form of the American antiapartheid movement as well as Jesse Jackson's foreign-policy statements in the 1984 presidential elections. More decisive is the blur over that aspect of Latin American decolonization that has become a standard observation of the region's special character.[63] Formal independence occurred earlier in Latin America than in Asia or Africa, allowing it to experience at an early date both what later became known as "neocolonialism" and (as a corollary) a "nationalism" often tightly linked to the communist movement. If, for some of the same reasons, it is often contested that Latin America can properly be grouped with the third world, it might be better simply to see Latin America as that part of the third world *saturated* with Europe.

With the above exception of Ahmad, why is it, in short, that such varied thinkers from such diverse fields rush to ridicule or (in an evasive and not completely ingenuous word) "problematize" oppression? How does one gauge what they share with contemporary U.S. economic and political liberals, whose ethos they evidently share but who paradoxically seek different ends—that is, the very homogeneity that Arjun Appadurai recoils from, or that James C. Scott, Garcìa Canclini, and others deny exists when they write about "cultural resistance"? Why is it that their creative subaltern here achieves a heroism far more utopian, far more olympian in dimensions than that "working class" summoned within Marxism like a mantra to ward off periods of dismal prospects?

To answer this, one must foreground the intellectual lineage under attack. What Theodor Adorno had diagnosed as the dumbification of American mass culture—already at an advanced stage in the 1940s—is now a process under way in the third world. Under metropolitan tutelage, Adorno's diagnosis has, however, been reconverted into encouraging signs of resistance. Was Adorno so wrong? Patrician perhaps, even embarrassing in the focused limitations of his allowable pleasures, he had the advantage of describing a process of commodification that remains a languishing and sterile nightmare—vividly recounted in a variety of work from the three continents as the dislocation of community. As García Canclini justly puts it, people "make the best of what [they] have."

It is true that the futureless minions find release from the plans that crowd in on them. But these comments shouldn't obscure the courage of Adorno's willingness to call defeat by its proper name. The resistance of representation is pathetic—the tragedy of that condition Jameson sardonically called the "postmodern sublime." In popular film, these have been the themes, surely, of *Network, Brazil,* and *Kiss of the Spider Woman.* A difficult dialectic lingers behind Adorno's paternalism, one similar in many respects to the now largely discredited rhetoric of anticolonial intellectuals like Cabral, Fanon, Maurice Bishop, and others who spoke of "raising the level of the masses." Attacked as condescending or elitist, the weakness of its alternative is repressed. For in rejecting the position of intellectual leadership in order to emphasize a mass resistance that already exists, what improvement does one really find? What does one gain by an easy populism that denies that the well-off have more of everything, including cultural access—a point whose obvious corollary is that intellectuals can and do indulge in baseball games or MTV but that day laborers do not drink French wines or listen to string quartets (the theme of another kind of America film—say, Martin Ritt's *Norma Rae* or *Stanley and Iris*)? That this involves more than art appreciation only intensifies the point, it does not change it.

2

Cosmopolitanism and Method

> Phenomenology is precisely the attempt to tell not what a thought is, so much as what it feels like. It aims not at making statements about content (that being momentarily placed between parentheses), but at describing the mental operations which correspond to that content in all their temporal specificity. Its mode of proof, for the reader, consists not in logical argumentation, but rather in the shock, or the failure, of recognition.
>
> —Fredric Jameson

> It's all so complex,
> so worldly, worldly.
>
> —Otto René Castillo

Up to now I have been using terms like "complexity" and "binarism" to suggest characteristic gestures at the level of form in colonial criticism and public commentary. Formally regnant, they were also, I implied, largely untheorized. "Binarism" might seem an unlikely candidate for such a charge given the blanket attentions it has received in a variety of prominent work, although here I am referring not to its deconstructive elaborations but to the usually implicit political allegorizations that motivate its coinage and that lie behind its assumptions.

As for the other term, I am not here entering a debate on "complexity," since I am not aware that one exists, although I am suggesting that one should. After initial comments sketching out how the concepts function in actual cases, I want to explore the relationship that the emergent field of cultural studies has to postcoloniality itself, and the relation of both to what I am calling cosmopolitanism. At issue in these sections will be a number of defining methodological options that, in my opinion, derive from the critical ethics of "complexity." These options are necessarily entailed by the model of intellectual work that cosmopolitanism invokes, with its appeals to a natural empathy for heterogenity and diversity that is also, and at the same time, a veiled continuity with older and more familiar attacks on class-historical confrontations of a binary sort. Among these corollary options are "circularity" and "identity."

At the close of an essay on the framing of concepts about mass culture, Theodor Adorno once backed his way into a comment that has seemed more salient since: "We know from psychoanalysis that the reasoning, 'we know all this!' is often a defense."[1] He deals here with the formation of concepts, where beginnings are formed and possibilities delimited, and he foreshadows a point he makes later in *Minima Moralia,* where the idea of concept evolves into a related comment on style: "The writer most unwilling to make concessions to drab common sense must guard against draping ideas, in themselves banal, in the appurtenances of style."[2]

The question I would like to foreground here is this: How does the rare and unseen remain rare and unseen by being branded "obvious"? My discussion so far of the cultural dissonance evoked by a "two-worlds" model of colonial analysis can now join a rich critical literature that approaches issues of race, language, and ethnicity. That criticism's greatest present lack, I am arguing, is its previous unwillingness to examine the conditions of its own framing in Adorno's sense. A likely road, therefore, into the political aesthetics at work in the reception of "third-world" literature is itself *metacritical* just as so much of its literature is metafictional, as one can see in a variety of authors whose indeterminate canonical location, and whose anxieties of domestic allegiance, prompt extended reflections on the very "how" of explaining what they so impossibly know.

Without confronting method, it is hard to explain what ties together debates over globalism proper and talk about cosmopolitanism in the humanities. Apart from Pierre Bourdieu in *Homo Academicus* and *Outline of a Theory of Practice,* too little has been written about the matrix of codes of conduct and intellectual procedures that precede what is normally called theory.[3] How do we characterize them? Is there a way of talking about them while bracketing an engagement with them for the purpose of objectifying practice? Although they are usually not characterized this way, many of the most moving and influential acts of criticism today ask these questions, if in an unsystematic way.

More than anything else, perhaps, the appeal of Gayatri Chakravorty Spivak's work has been her anecdotal insights into the precritical assumptions of the literary professional.[4] Similarly, in *Culture and Truth: The Remaking of Social Analysis,* Renato Rosaldo cleverly locates areas for future research by looking at moments of incidental opinion-forming: "Although the official view holds that all cultures are equal, an informal filing system more often found in corridor talk than in published writings classifies cultures in quantitative terms, from a lot to a little, from rich to poor, from thick to thin, and from elaborate to simple."[5] Characterizing Javanese shadow theater as an art foregrounding the "clash of conceptual universes" (142), Rosaldo goes on to suggest the stakes of such casual value-formation. And in that gesture, perhaps, he is alluding not so much to what precedes theory as completes it. For poststructuralist theory—or what is widely and inaccurately called simply "theory"—has been exactly about identifying concepts as grounds for a precritical reorganization of the categories of knowledge. But the epistemological focus of theory—its often allusive interest in the philosophical genealogies of Husserl, Heidegger, and Nietzsche, especially—carries with it a burden of origins that is not my subject here. My own interest lies less in a primary (and in the end cognitive or originary) discursive level, since the limits of thought also reside in the conjunctural spaces of a late-twentieth-century political environment rather than in an elemental "Western metaphysics." What does a phenomenology of *that* look like?

Cultural criticism, it must be said, often works at the level of anxious political allegory. Above layers of refined close-reading and digested erudition sits a language of civil war that treats text and taste in words that borrow their energies from movements of social transformation. This is the sort of operation Fredric Jameson points to when, in a series of essays following *The Political Unconscious,* he repeatedly invokes allegory, referring to late capitalist works of the imagination as a projection into a totality that cannot be otherwise grasped in postmodernity. But here I am alluding more to that equally characteristic, although distinct, move in the earlier Jameson of "Towards a Dialectical Criticism," where he writes of the tendency of literary criticism in periods of political chill (his example is nineteenth-century Russia) to provide a haven for radical thought that can speak its mind because, to the society at large, it is "only" culture.[6]

Criticism has found much of its energy in phrases such as "libidinal economies," "long marches through the institution," "strategic essentialism," "wars of position"—all of them shadowing nothing so much as the slogans of the vanguard parties. The ransacking of those parties' vocabularies in an allegorical relocation of their stakes operates for the most part without awareness of either source or debt. Cultural study in this sense relies on leads provided by left traditions that are invoked only to be ritually rejected while being quietly "sampled" in the hip-hop sense. Coded messages underlying this allegorical translation of class war into various cultural positionings can be found in broader patterns of intellectual practice, so that what goes on furiously in acts of critical deployment plays out again, with special contextual consequences, in writing on third-world literature and popular culture.

But how does one abstract patterns from an array of detailed, thoughtful writing without simply arriving at a string of individual cases? The force of this question, made stronger by theory's recent endorsements of local knowledge, is in fact peremptory. As a question with a built-in answer, it prevents one's looking from places where broad topographies can be drawn and sketches of the whole made, for placement and orientation if not with any pretense of adequately contending with all the important details. As Lauren Berlant argues, for example, to talk about a locality is often highly abstract (it is only one example among many, after all, and always is asked to stand for so much else), whereas to speak globally is concrete—indeed, the only way to be concrete.[7] Rosaldo's book itself, for instance, even though a chain of case studies, coheres in a broader and more global vision, setting out to erase "objectivism" from anthropology—objectivism being for Rosaldo that slippage from Max Weber's "disinterestedness" into an orthodoxy. That orthodoxy he defines as "emotional disengagement, cognitive distance, and moral indifference."[8] He explains that his target in this writing—objectivism—had already been softened up for over a decade by well-entrenched (and even fashionable) criticisms of social science positivism, myths of the essential subject, and Eurocentric cultural norms. But this important move from reflection inward (by analyzing a governing concept like "objectivism") to an outward view of "interestedness"—with all of its vital associations of social positioning, political outlook, and moral engagement—did not yield a similar critique that could have been launched against objectivism's opposite—namely, in this context, heterogeneity, or what Rosaldo calls the "culturally different Other" (7). That is what now needs to be done.

It is true that in the academy, as in the literary press, cultural critics typically distrust power. But trying to see intellectual activity as more than a dispassionate inquiry or a simple adjunct of the specialist requisites of business does not necessarily address the more important problem of the critic's "interestedness." For academic appeals to intellectual generalism have had a long history after all. As a polemical slogan of recovery, "generalism" met the specialist or professionalist challenge head on, and at a very early date—for example, Max Weber's complaint about "specialists without feeling, sensualists without heart"; or, after World War II, Lionel Trilling's more recognizably modernist discomfort with the diminishing expectations of writer and thinker in consumer society when he spoke of the "generalist critic" who saw "hesitation as better than commitment, appreciation of complexity over action."[9] Trilling thereby appropriated these ideas for a left modernism whose clearest recent expression is Russell Jacoby's book *The Last Intellectuals* with its complaints about the narrow specializations of cultural theory separating the critic from the public.[10]

In spite of the similarity of these views to the very ones targeted by Rosaldo, it is nevertheless true that cultural theory by circuitous routes often finds its way to a positioning that uneasily blends with official needs even as it critically distances itself from them. Unlike the charges I criticize below, this is not a necessary circularity. It is an avoidable one. It is possible to develop a criticism that roams widely as well as deeply, associates freely, and views things from a position of generality without falling prey to "emotional disengagement" or its current, more fashionable, analogue: ambiguity and the "in-between."

Explaining the Obvious: Paul Nizan

"I would like now to complicate the issue." "Could you problematize that?" "I wonder if we couldn't dig beneath the surface." "That's just too simple." Positions might vary, but "complexity" is always the high ground. Once made, comments like these bring relief to former antagonists. Everyone can be counted on to assent to a view he or she recognizes as home. Complexity is the unassailable quality, the sign of intelligence and care, and therefore of a quiet modesty comporting with an image of solitary lucubrations.

When a consensus is so deep that it exists on the cellular level—as it does here—it is a site where the life of governing ideas begins. There is something elusive about so basic a want. Complexity has nevertheless thrown itself in the way and cut off other roads like an imposing gatekeeper. Thought comes to the real indirectly and, like a traveler to the North Pole, is unsure of his own arrival. Thinkers cannot convince themselves that anything less than an ordeal will serve, and as with a restless explorer in a sitting room following the adventure, the ordeal itself becomes the thing really desired.

Of course, reality is deceptive; it is filled with snares; it looks as if it is yielding when it turns to trickery, and for all of these reasons complexity is a welcome mark of approval for a thought worthy of its object. But there is more to the consensus than an admiration for the mirroring of the real. Very close to the surface of moments in which complexity is ritually affirmed is a demonstration of respect for serious intellectual protocols. To be scholarly one has to be "complex"—not necessarily obtuse, which is a different issue—because in one sense the activity of conferences and seminars requires problems with which to toil, interestingly, in order that they take up time and by longevity acquire importance. There is first of all the practical issue of what to *do* in a classroom, or how to establish merit in a highbrow journalistic essay. The explaining of mysteries establishes the proper distance between initiate and neophyte and generates consequent respect. There is also the broader and more long-range issue of internalizing an intellectual code of conduct that implies the social need of a cultural hermeneut: one who deciphers a social symbolism inaccessible to laypersons.

The aesthetic aspect of this problem is suggested in Fredric Jameson's pilloried essay on national allegory, where he mentions that the likes of Henry James and George Eliot offered certain "sorts of pleasures" not found in third-world fiction. Whatever questionable issues are raised by other aspects of that famous essay, he pinpoints an important pedagogical barrier to the acceptance of the very literature whose worth he is demonstrating. The pleasure of the seminar room consists in part in a lack of intellectual closure, a model of versatility, virtuosity, and play in an expressive, concrete language, rather than a proposition—blunt and final—to close discussion and do. I am speaking, in other words, of a motivated complexity outside of respect for qualities like care, circumspection, humility, perceptiveness, and sensitivity. I am speaking not on behalf of the "rough-and-ready" or a chuckleheaded common sense, or of people "with no time" to be subtle. Anti-intellectualism needs no more allies, as Margaret Randall, for example, has observed in speaking about the problems of a left rhetoric in Cuba. She describes how her son, who grew up there, explains issues to his friends sounding horribly rote and unconvincing, even though his message is one she passionately endorses. The problem she isolates, then, is "How encourage complexity while retaining the wonder?"[11]

The other half of the problem is equally nettlesome. Complexity in the sense discussed here is a self-maintaining aesthetic preference antagonistic to theories of practice—that range of subtle and (in a different sense) complex problems associated with how to bring ideas already agreed upon into the real. This comment need not be understood as a call for discarding books to organize trade unions, nor as a suggestion that study and work, reading and action, are incompatible. It is only that the common knowledge of most cultural intellectuals remains poorly understood to society as a whole. In a theoretical essay who would bother to explain today, for example, that language is no transparent vehicle of meaning, but a matrix where meanings themselves are invented, or invent themselves? that entertainments are more than outlets for enjoyment but places where social relations are reproduced? that narrative is not just a way of passing time but a structure for making "facts" intelligible?

A number of critics have blamed the isolation of intellectuals on the theoretical obscurities of their writing. In fact, expressive means are not the most important impediments. Intellectual protocols are.

To mark oneself as an intellectual worthy of notice means assuming the propositions just listed in essays geared either to original archival research or analytic novelty. Outside of pedagogical theory (where it is active, but in narrowly defined ways), very little work is dedicated to examining *how* common knowledge in one sphere can be made common in another—in what new venues, in what sort of outreach, in what kind of combination of book and act. Many of the very intellectuals of the past now influencing cultural theory had in their own times experimented with ways of bracketing intellectual novelty in the name of popular contact and dissemination. These breakthroughs in practice led, paradoxically, to breakthroughs in thought: the Raymond Williams of the postwar British adult-education movement; the Gramsci of *El Grido del popolo;* the Alexandra Kollontai of the women's section of Soviet cultural groups. To realize the surroundings that enabled their insights also required theory, but a type of theory largely unrecognized as such. While there are many professors who live admirably dual lives writing both for academic and broadly public constituencies, that activity is thought of as bipolar.

One might extend, then, Edward Said's useful summary of the four basic types of criticism—book reviewing and literary journalism, academic literary history, literary appreciation, and literary theory—to arrive at a different sort of range.[12] This would cover, say, three kinds of criticism: first, criticism dealing with the style of its own presentation—a kind of captioned thought, with its kin in philosophy; second, criticism that comments upon the social, including culture *in* society; and third, criticism about the workings and ways of the institutions in which culture is served up, delimited, and allowed to be. These might be categorized as theory, cultural studies, and the professional-political.

Left to itself, of course, the schema does not hold. What does Judith Butler do if not inscribe the gender issues of gay studies into the culture of a field known as political science? Has not Martha Woodmansee, for example, alongside her work with legal scholars debating the practical outcomes of copyright law, written movingly on eighteenth-century German poets? In practice, the conjunctural overlap of three types of criticism, instead of exemplifying the generalism I referred to above, often conceals the primarily contemplative "theory" that acts in others' names. It is hard to find any prominent critic today *not* writing about culture as politics. The problem arises with the epistemological mode of criticism spliced on to a commentary about "culture" that presents itself as political work—all three in one, supposedly, with only the first actually being prominent. It is at the crossroads that the elusive conduct of theory shields the telling gestures described below.

Either in journalism or in the academy, what the professional writer reads when she (or he) reads is more than a subject, familiar or not. She is always reading a performance by a peer—an idea, a style, a concept *she* might have had. The aficionado sees the pauses, the restraints, the choices unmade and made, and all of that comes through, if anything, more loudly than the subject. It is all about retelling for this time what others told before, although the professional cannot see creation this way. For related to complexity is the principle of novelty—a breakthrough idea at its optimal range, but usually, in light of academic modesty, a twist on an already useful knowledge. The performance of learning exceeds the learning actually passed on, and the message of that performance is always modesty, complexity, novelty. The tyranny of those values blurs vision, making the presence of the blunt and the impatient difficult to defend outside journalistic work, which is then seen as ancillary.

"But," comes the answer, "in no time more than the present has the voice of ordinary people been heard." Oral-history projects have in recent decades exploded with some of the verve and scope of the WPA years and found themselves outside the realm of simple study. Studs Terkel and Audrey Lourde are sold on the shelves of local bookstores competing with testimonial narratives, which have themselves been highly successful commercially and powerfully sanctioned within the university. It is not a question, then—at least openly—of the refinements of class crowding out the homely wisdom of the plain-speaking poor. The crossing of the divide between masses and leaders has been brewing for over a century, always accompanied in the United States by a tradition of philistine good sense found in the images of heroes like the skeptical farmer and the diffident coffeehouse savant. So broad is the cliché and so readily manipulated that the genre of challenging it is itself already broad. The humor of the country-western style, its consistent refuge in the pun, together form an argument for the homely wisdom of the unlettered and the down home, snide by turns but eager, in nonstandard English accents to demonstrate its facility with the word.

The point is not about the silence of the people or the need to cut through overspecialized jargon to let them speak for themselves. The counterpart or rival of aesthetic complexity is rather a kind of bracketing of perpetual refinements of thought. To be raw is to err; to be overfine, never. Every intellectual knows the pleasures of the rich, the full, and the profound, and favors them because others do not. What is consistently underestimated, however, is the power and wisdom of the flat, the brute, and the plain—not, as I said above, in the sense of exclusively endorsing fictional realism or of providing an apologetics for a third-world art that does not offer "those kinds of pleasures" in Jameson's sense, but as a mode of intellectual conduct. For it is a question of time very often. If one wants to do, not only say, time matters; so does persuasion, and the less time that takes, the better.

A close contact, in that sense, exists between the present moment and the 1950s, which saw one of those rare moments of unguarded intellectual renegadism when "crudeness" itself was openly endorsed—namely, in Paul Nizan, the author Sartre conceded was better than he was after reading Nizan's counterorientalist memoir *Aden, Arabie.* In one of its memorable passages, the author urges his readers to "have the courage to be crude: let us sweep the spirit of subtlety down the sewer along with the flags and the great warriors."[13] A close friend of Sartre's, companion of the bars, a name in the proper circles with old-school ties, Nizan joined the French Communist Party in 1927 and remained cantankerous and unclassifiable both within and outside of that organization until his death. By literary reputation an individualist and untamed heart, he did not fit the role of either functionary or hired pen, instead carving out a space for himself in the anonymous and beleaguered circles of the official and unofficial French left. Nizan is, in that sense, an example of self-sacrifice to the less pleasurable and more thankless world of "commitment"—one he did not popularize so much as live. And falling in a temporal sense between existential and poststructuralist heroes, he put a face on circles known today mostly by negations: the ones Sartre did not join, the ones Foucault transcended.

In his overlooked polemic *Les Chiens de garde (The Watchdogs),* Nizan pursued a critique of method. By all accounts a harsh blast, the book singled out by name now largely forgotten celebrities in French academic philosophy in order to deflate them in the eyes of a younger generation. Although the book today seems easy to dismiss as an act of transient anger, it is admirable as much for its clarity as its appetite for self-immolation. What he did not want to forget was how people think, loosely, *about* philosophy, what they expect from it, the state of mind with which they enter it—what happens, in other words, before they get to the invigorating riddles of philosophical matter itself: "One still meets so many people, so many young people, who believe that all forms of philosophical inquiry will yield benefits to the human race, because they have been convinced that this is the result of all intellectual endeavor."[14]

Nizan manages to show on every page a difficult (and obvious) art: that of grasping "the miseries of contemporary reality . . . [and] the fundamental dichotomy in consciousness" (91) of the intellectuals he considered mandarins. In *Les Chiens de garde,* the proof of this unfashionable distinction relies entirely on Nizan's earnestness—an intentional anachronism in the sophistications of existentialist France. He refuses to be chased away from pointing out the divide that exists between those who "discuss Mind and Ideas, Ethics and the Sovereign Good, Reason and Justice" and those who "fall victims to . . . misfortunes," who "bear the weight of . . . events," and who find a certain "style of philosophizing arrogant and repugnant" (14). And thus the book finds itself relieved to say: "The ideas of the rabble must be protected against the smug complacency of the professional thinker."

Nizan is capable of showing his own love for philosophy's classics. What he displays, though, is the deliberate attempt *not* to enjoy them, because of the injury enjoyment causes when it festers. He despised what he called, in a quotation that might well have come from Gramsci, "word games." The comment builds finally to a more explicit aesthetics: "Only the bourgeois have a real need for subtlety in their classifications and palpable profundity in their intellectual exercises, because they alone have something to hide—and vulgarity is a much less effective mask than subtlety and nuance" (40).

In a question related to Nizan's attack on subtlety falls the issue simply of dissipation. The passive issues, the issues of boredom and of absence, of routine and drudgery, rarely get play in such an extended way. As in Nizan, dissipation for scholars in the university would have to do with the wearing down of energies implicit in the institutional star-system. Novelty and innovation (in the restricted sense above) lie at the heart of this system, which has already been criticized elsewhere for being out of step with the democratic structures of the profession as a whole. I turn to it here only because of the obstacles it poses to a reexamination of intellectual protocols, rather than to raise more customary issues of strained departmental budgets, personal cases of injustice, or the admittedly more central (and more often commented upon) problem of the star system's commodification of theory.

As one of theory's practical frames, dissipation occurs in the sense that ideas presented in seminar papers, at conferences, or in coffee conversation (that is, unprotected ideas) can be and often are capitalized upon by those who can readily publish in the most widely read outlets without the usual one- or two-year lag time. If properly situated, one can in this way put one's own spin on ideas, thereby arresting them within the expressive form of what the academic public then sees as a remarkable mind. Building on earlier triumphs as graduate students and younger professors, or provided entry by valuable connections, some and not others receive the key grants or jobs with the smallest teaching loads and most time off. When an honorable or even brilliant book follows, what appears as proof of the original notoriety is more often than not a result of the advantages that notoriety first brought with it. Others merely get by, dissipating their energies, projecting themselves in a seemingly belated act of secondhand emulation, picking up the crumbs of invitations to contribute to low-profile anthologies or attending conferences as unpaid consultants. Eager to speak out, the previously unnoticed only ensure that the cycle continues, for they do not have the time to write up their ideas, and instead speak them, offering them in this way to the already well established who "translate" them into the language of the moment they have in notoriety helped define.

The process is, of course, a central part of any business environment, but it is significant in a realm of professional and ethical self-scrutiny where superior access and relative fairness in such matters is widely assumed. It is very similar to the process described by Tricia Rose, for example, in comments on the avenues of influence in rap music: "Although the terms dilution and theft do not capture the complexity of cultural incorporation and syncretism, this interpretation has more than a grain of truth in it. There is abundant evidence that white artists imitating Black styles have greater economic opportunity and access to larger audiences than Black innovators. Historical accounts of the genres often position these subsequently better known artists as the central figures, erasing or marginalizing the artists and contexts within which the genre developed."[15] The character of the present ideological moment makes it much more likely that this sort of point is grasped in race, but not in class; or if in class, then not in political position. Posing it this way, as a confrontation of warring parties on either side of an ideological divide, one opens oneself up to charges of an overcontestatory binarism—the theoretical stance that academic theory opposes as a matter of solemn doctrine.

By taking up this kind of charge, Barbara Herrnstein Smith has covered similar ground in *Contingencies of Value.*[16] Her effort there focused on the inescapable logic of evaluations *relative* to social grouping and situation, rather than on a specific treatment of the values promoted: "Homer, Dante, and Shakespeare do not figure significantly in the personal economies of [some] people, do not perform individual or social functions that gratify their interests . . . Other verbal artifacts (not necessarily "works of literature" or even "texts") and other objects and events (not necessarily "works of art" or even artifacts) have performed and do perform for them the various functions that Homer, Dante, and Shakespeare perform for us" (53).

My intention here is to linger over the practical meaning of what she calls the "beautiful" and the "good" that holds most sway for the "us" she identifies in the above passage. In passing, Herrnstein Smith does isolate a few examples—"utility" in Georges Bataille's theory of expenditure, for example—but she mostly occupies herself with destroying the logic of aesthetic axiology as such. As is suggested by the very adjectives one could use to commend her study ("elegant," "tightly argued," "profound"), one quality of her own work is certainly complexity. Even though she enraged many of her readers with her unanswerable portrait of prejudice against the deviants of taste, few readers could fail to see her mastery of the topic, which drove the nails only more firmly into the Kantian coffin even as it displayed the limpid logic and graceful prose of Kant's own sense of aesthetic purity.

It is very difficult and thankless to challenge both the content of a social illusion and a profession's argumentative codes at the same time. But consider a question commonly raised by documentary filmmakers: Can a politically challenging content produce a new consciousness when a film relies on the "talking heads" format of mainstream television? Without a frontal assault on form as well as ideas, there are built-in limits to transformations in thought. The values under attack are only reinscribed, now from a more moral or more widely informed vantage point. But one can target complexity as a conversation stopper—what everyone claims to have or wants to have—without entirely departing from it. What could be wrong with thinking through fully and completely, over many months or even years, a topic of importance, thereby ensuring that the problem is being seen from its many sides? And isn't this what it means to be complex? Why would one ever want to identify with the obvious?

Granted, there are also favorite narratives of intellectual achievement that contest this one and by their repetition set up a morality of the "interesting" and "important" that does not openly rely on complexity. A favorite middlebrow entertainment, for example, consists of the journalistic feature article on recent developments in physics. Here the story—as in the recent fascination with Murray Gell-Mann, for example, or with Stephen W. Hawking—concerns the fundamental simplicity of the real as revealed in a unified-field theory by oracles who do not speak in parables but make the complexities of subatomic forces plain.[17] But accounts of science, of course, rely on a public diffidence secured by technology, one that shields them from doubts about the values of their specializations. People are generally trained already to assume their own incomprehension in the face of the language of math, as well as the superior intellects of the universe's current day-keepers. Appealing to simplicity, the message is really pushing us down into humility before the mind-boggling wizardry of the scientist and his arcane cogitations, made simple for "us" but in terms that—these articles stress—can be generally appreciated without really being understood.

That Herrnstein Smith's appeal to the relativity of cultural value can still weigh so heavily means that many readers greet the view as new and dangerous. And yet the idea—in her case formulated to expose the gentilities of class along lines similar to Pierre Bourdieu in *Distinction,* although in a manner more deeply lodged within the concerns of the humanities—is not a whit less developed in that voluminous defense of comparative studies, Spengler's *Decline of the West,* where he writes: "Truths are truths only in relation to a particular mankind. Thus, my own philosophy is able to express and reflect *only* the Western (as distinct from the Classical, Indian or other) soul."[18] Those other souls referred to in Spengler's well-known reactionary complaint against cosmopolitanism, of course, are racial in his grand and generous scheme to the extent that Spengler was not shy about arguing simply that "race *is* style" (254).

The point here, at any rate, is not about his politically conservative attacks on cosmopolitanism but about style itself; and to raise it here is to marvel at the persistence of Spengler's view that culture basically is *race.* With shocking candor, Walter Benn Michaels noted as much in an essay extolling the "anti-imperialism" of various turn-of-the-century Ku Klux Klan novelists—an essay (like Michaels's, I think, willful reading of Dreiser in an early book) with a provocative cast whose urge is to demonstrate that an appropriate research look can empower any argument one happens to choose.[19]

The professional aesthetics of complexity found a comfortable home in Michaels's essay in the sense that style is often, again as in Spengler, an ideology—or as Spengler puts it, style is "the rhythm of the process of self-implementing."[20] It is important to remember that Spengler was making these suggestive comments in the context of a sweeping global-cultural synthesis, protesting at every turn the relativity of value from a perch that quietly assumed the superiority of his own. The following characteristic comment in many ways can be used today to describe Western cultural reception of non-Western literatures: "Romanticism marks the beginning of that which Goethe, with his wide vision, called world-literature—the literature of the leading world-*city,* against which a provincial literature, native to the soil but negligible, struggles everywhere with difficulty to maintain itself" (252–3, his emphasis).

Similarly, Michaels, with a thesis based on a hidden commonplace, flourishes by dint of a meticulous familiarity with out-of-the-way fiction richly presented. For his "anti-imperialism" turns out to be a much more familiar American isolationism, whose xenophobia amounts objectively to a kind of resistance against the fledgling efforts of the time to realize America's global destiny. Evidence is allowed in a sense to *be* the point, and any incoherences are easily missed by a reader who feels overwhelmed or inadequate in the face of so much knowledge. On the downside of the New Historicism, the essay amounts to facticity without coherence; historical "stuff" cherished as an object, fondled, sketched, but not explained, connected, or motivated. Altogether brilliant in its presentation, the essay is strikingly illogical and lumpy in its organization, leaping from the plots and backgrounds of the KKK fiction to an equally provocative closing movement, where research falls away, and where he unloads opinions that have been purchased, as it were, by the archival splendor of the preceding sections. His thesis is that cultural difference is always a difference rooted in race—a thesis whose routine absurdity and calculated provocation would seem appropriately naked, in Nizan's sense, were it not dressed up in so much intelligence and complexity.

What does one do, similarly, with intellectual reception in which insights are appealing precisely as artifacts of visible thinking? The massive interest in the French generation of Michel Foucault, for example, has partly to do with the intricacies of his own and others' sheer adventure of the mind—the meticulous note-taking and phenomenal rigor of his apprenticeship buried in the Bibliothèque Nationale; the refinement and internalizations of obscure theories of psychology, scientific method, philosophy, and historiography; but then, also, the personal gloss he gave them all in a protracted process of finding a voice in the context of a burning ambition to become an intellectual of Sartre's stature. It is, on the one hand, the beautiful complexity of his now personally embodied and hybrid mastery of the whole Nietzschean lineage (from Heidegger and Binswanger through Bataille and Blanchot) and, on the other, the very success he came enviably to enjoy—the lavish rewards he was given for a life of applied study—that remain an important part of the attraction.

How does one deal with the embarrassing fact that important concepts are themselves often uninteresting as expressive means—that, say, in spite of their obvious historical impact, the declarations of Patrice Lumumba and Fidel Castro are boring as works of literature? It seems relevant, for example, that the attractions of the Subaltern Studies collective—say, in Ranajit Guha's brilliant essay "Dominance without Hegemony"—have been able to recast subalternity with an excitement that for many readers is missing in the important work of Gustavo Guttiérez or Studs Terkel. How deeply is that excitement linked to expressive means—or, put more problematically, what kind of commerce exists between the theoretical grace with which subalternity has been formulated in Guha and the elusiveness of the essay's compelling descriptive power? Is indecision itself an aesthetic corollary of its power, or only an unnecessary corollary of its rethinkings of a complex problem? Rarely entertained, I think—and hardly ever defended as such on its own terms—is the attraction (rhetorically and aesthetically) of a colorless language of liberatory abstraction, a style of writing and thinking meant to excite the reader with its grandness and confidence of tone, however disappointing its grayness of terminology or linear narrative forward-drive might be. (I consider this question more fully in Chapter 5, where I discuss C. L. R. James.)

As I have been arguing, subcultures of alternative utopia throughout non-Western writing, even while being strangely inarticulate at the point of reception, are also interesting and formative. Their visions—now religious, now insurrectionary, now environmental—take on a vivid urgency in a period of enhanced designs on behalf of a universal corporate norm of exchange and self-definition. A good deal of theoretical attention has gone to the "popular" in the form of studies of subversive consumption, but the intellectual effort to *produce* an aesthetic of access for popular use has not been merely ignored but explicitly attacked. There are always resistances at the level of cultural reappropriations, of course, but they have been overemphasized and appear in sober times to be more important than they are. And this is decisive because such overemphases dovetail with efforts by corporate public relations groups to blur the distinctions between subalternity and commercial image-making. While the strategists of the boardroom may not really expect to achieve a communal sense of voluntary agreement or identification, they certainly have muscled forth the illusion that corporate success is not only a legitimate plebeian aspiration, but cool.[21]

The vitality and importance of the misunderstood art emanating from the colonized world is that it still provides models of a non-corporate popularity. Ernst Bloch—whom I look at more closely in Chapter 5—has mapped out the variety of alternative utopias from European classical times to the 1960s, a picture to which the utopian outlooks of more recent decades add nothing in either scope or degree of desperation. From an aerial view, acts of cultural resistance share perhaps a millenarian fervor that, like religion generally, revive my concern above with "concept" and "semantic dissonance" by pointing to the importance again of conversion.[22] As a matter of theory, most distinctive about the current discourse on cultural resistance is the way in which multiple, multicultural actors are collapsed together while the major historical players of a conflictual binarism are displaced from prominence. The countermovements are not at all equal in size or influence, and although Marxism is often quietly referenced in them, it appears as only one movement among many. Thus, for example, in *Culture and Imperialism* Edward Said notes in passing that while criticism has typically overlooked the centrality of imperialist thought, only a "small handful" of theoretical contributions on the cultural study of "colonial and imperial realities" have appeared until recently (he mentions Gordon Lewis, V. G. Kiernan, and Jonah Raskin), and all of them "owe a great deal to Marxist analysis and premises."[23]

To grasp the scope of the neglect is to appreciate that even here, despite Said's comment, the neglect of the Marxist contribution is mentioned (in his words) "in passing," and that the massive challenge to commonsense imperial prerogatives that the study finds shamefully absent in Europe has been lively in Marxism—and almost nowhere else in Europe—from the late nineteenth century onward. The neglect is not confined to specific writers. It is conceptual as well, and it prevents the shift back from popular consumption to intellectual production under the banner of complexity. That virtue is typically found wanting in a comment like that of the Bajan novelist George Lamming, when he writes of the "creative power of the mass"; or of Walter Rodney, when in the moving opening pages of his *History of the Guyanese Working People* he speaks of "the ordeal of free labor" and "the fashionable arithmetic of democracy."[24]

As Adorno wrote, "we know all this!" We meet the obvious again, but are forced to admit that, although obvious, such statements are not really understood. It is a curious psychological fact that those who often adopt this mode are the ones who have actually read and understood Marx. In exchange for finding disparate observations and doubts that coalesce into an astonishing philosophical unity, the strong reader of Marx often forfeits, intentionally, the ability to entertain with thought. In turn, he or she is misunderstood by those who contemptuously reject what they never quite grasped.

The cultural distance separating Lamming and Rodney from their critics, or, even more, from those who ignore them on the grounds that they are not "interesting," is at least as unbridgeable as race or nationality, but much less commented on. Their words are easily pushed aside, perhaps with feelings of regret that an accomplished novelist like Lamming and a talented historian like Rodney would mythologize a "mass" that, of course, has never been unitary nor, in its fragmentary articulations, quite so lovable as to speak of its "creativity"; or that a boastful flourish at democracy's expense should blind the authors to the horrors of its now happily defunct alternative. I am suggesting that such attitudes are made on the grounds of complexity, although they do not always explicitly mention that value.

The grandeur, after all, of Lamming and of Rodney depends on believing that there are such things as workers, after all. That proposition has been widely challenged, not only directly in the work of André Gorz, for example, but in multiple indirect ways as a strategy of silencing. The following example typifies a set of missed interventions and bungled insights concerning the matter of East and West in the cold-war sense of that ambiguous coupling (ambiguous because the East-West dichotomy is, revealingly, also an orientalist one). In early January of 1994, Harry Wu, a prisoner for nineteen years in a Chinese labor camp is interviewed on a progressive New York radio station.[25] In the story he gives, it is impossible not to see the bluntness, muscularity, and vengefulness of the Chinese government. He makes a convincing case that his jailing was less about coerced ideological conformity than the extraction of unpaid labor. In the list of goods produced for export by the detainees—everything from coal and textiles to machines tools and toys—one learns about the economic advantages of having a class of social deviants, a process that in racial terms reminds one of nothing so much as the contemporary prison farms of the American South.

The issue of *work,* one might argue, reasserts itself here in a manner reminiscent of Lamming and Rodney, and it does so in the following sense suggestive of the sort of cultural dissonance usually associated with the rhetoric of "crossing borders"—the misreading of texts and practices from nationally or ethnically foreign places in the process of "third-world" reception. The work Wu suffered in the camp was in most ways (not all) like the routine hardship of the Chinese peasant, miner, or agricultural laborer. The atrocity of the Chinese government's action for this man (and for his U.S. sympathizers) is ostensibly at the level of censorship, the jailing of dissidents. But what is implicit throughout is a simmering outrage at the elimination of the landholding and urban propertied classes, including many intellectuals, and their subsequent distribution into the ranks of the working classes. At issue, then, is a kind of class sacrilege—that he, or they, would be forced to live like that or *them.* What seems so horrible, and is horrible, seems all the more so given the supposed impropriety of the people subjected to it. This outrage stems in part from the conviction that some people and not others are appropriate subjects for enduring the "ordeal of labor." The ordeal of forced labor under miserable conditions is apparently outrageous, and visible, only at this point of transition rather than in its endemic state. What is revealed in the transition is evident only as the result of a conversion whose absence prevents understanding in the metropolitan reception of third-world cultural artifacts.

With their basis either in property or in cultural capital, such sentiments detail the impropriety of intellectuals cast by violence into the ranks of laborers—a detailing that spills over into the aesthetics of complexity. Despite shortcomings, Aijaz Ahmad's study *In Theory* succeeds in drawing attention to the cultural dissonance of class subjectivities of this type in the process of intellectual formation and position taking. As a lightning rod, it attracted a series of attacks that often illustrated in an exaggerated form the problems of method entailed by the general assumption that the lucubrations of complexity are inherently more accurate than binary confrontation in determining their object.

In dense and allusive language, Marjorie Levinson, for example, centers precisely on Ahmad's slipshod scholarship and lack of nuance by quoting Marx copiously in order to speak to Ahmad on his own terms.[26] With a powerful display of textual familiarity, she contests the operation of taking a provisional stand that involves bracketing nuance without brutalizing the opposing points in order to move the debate over to a critique of foundations. Although her critique succeeds, as others have, in demonstrating Ahmad's factual inaccuracies when characterizing specific positions in literary theory, the essay is incapable of assessing (or even of recognizing) a larger methodological point: Ahmad's clearly stated refusal to meet literary theory on its own terms and his insistence on distancing himself from it in order to express a conditional alienation from it.

Intricacy is the largest club the essay wields against Ahmad's flat stick, while it remains oblivious of the merely relative merits of intricacy consumed as better scholarship and more truth. Again, I am trying to distinguish my criticism here from that of Russell Jacoby and others who address the way theoretical jargon and obscurity separate intellectuals from the public. By contrast, I am addressing work that by most accounts is accessibly humanist in its orientations and language but that labors under an academic protocol that is, if anything, copied in the mainstream press—not at odds with it, as in Jacoby. The critic as artist is involved here in an oddly monastic form of pleasure located in gestures of deep learning, high condensations occasionally alleviated by gestures of ease and informality.

Levinson's spectacularly layered essay is as much driven by the hypertrophic need to unsheathe authoritative footnotes as it is enraged by the very quality in Ahmad's book that eludes her understanding—namely, his methodological "outward-turning," his relentless demand that a kind of literary critical scholasticism (with which Levinson obliges him repeatedly) be seen as estranged in important ways from its object. Nothing if not sharp, her essay is unable to project a sense of physical bodies, communiqués, and left-press polemics—the very things (Ahmad is saying) that make the quoting of Marxian scripture matter. Whatever one might say about Ahmad's important mischaracterizations, no one reading his work can miss that he breathes the air of men and women who planned strikes, went to prison, risked their lives, and studied not simply Marxist theory but the history of the labor movement. Levinson, by contrast, drives her points home finally with the means at her disposal—the warmly comforting combination of phrase and fellow-feeling of Wordsworth and Addison. And that difference of method, I would argue, is more important than Ahmad's discrepancies of attribution.

Above, I have deliberately overlapped race and class as mutually entangled modes of deviancy and incomprehension, and have done so to suggest the homology of such a meeting with the intertwined discourses of East-West in its cold-war sense and North-South in its postcolonial sense. If the institutional study of popular culture has traditionally (although not exclusively) turned to class, postcolonial studies have highlighted race and nation. Apart from the conceptual risks of such a de facto division of labor, a related problem exists in that the identities that might be called "cultures of persuasion" have no disciplinary home. The semantic dissonance among such cultures is neglected even though they make much of the world the way it is. They exist on the level of doing rather than being. In what is widely called cultural politics, therefore, one appropriate model should be political position or mode of organization as well as skin, accent, domicile, or dress.

Studying cultures of political persuasion is an important way of dealing with the confusion created by constructs like the "American way of life," "Black culture," or "women's writing"—phrases that can barely be uttered without a rush to qualify, extend, apologize, or backtrack. At a time when much is being written on corporate culture—widely if implicitly understood not as a taint or encroachment but as an "us" culture—a sense of identities of position would move one to think about alternatives to those massive, highly organized, disciplinary machines. The need, in other words, to preserve an area where culture can refer not only to nationality or race but to "position" or "persuasion" is greater when corporate culture passes from being a slogan of futurologists to a program with its own organic intellectual allies in sites as varied as entertainment television and the humanities classroom.

Many insightful and creative critiques of corporate cultures have been written, of course—primarily by writers trained in communications and history. In literature and cultural studies, complexity tugs one toward related ideas on a more inviting level of abstraction or celebrated provenance: the "public sphere," "mass culture," the "advertising image," the "society of the spectacle." When the issue of corporate culture is distastefully thrust into the jargons and styles of managerial experts and business apologists (and a formidably large literature exists of this type), cultural studies recoils on the grounds that the thinking is "obvious." Recoiling from the obvious, however, actually disarms the critic by creating a false notion about the state of the debate over "nation" and "globalism" as it exists among the ones most responsible for tailoring the structures that give rise to the concepts, for they do not, after all, operate in a world where academic protocols of nuance exist.

In a noisy rush to the political, cultural studies abandons literature for areas that seem more dangerously inquisitive. Who runs what on whose behalf? But even here, deep in the analysis of institutions, the critic instinctively finds his or her way to gestures of containment whose cleverness is, in a way, part of the message. One of the methodological constants of left cultural theory, in this sense, is "circularity," the demonstration of the complicity of critique in the very things it is criticizing, or of showing moments of inescapability—the reversal of roles in the drama of social good and evil.

Cultural Studies and Colonial Progress

A clear recent example of what I am calling "circularity" occurs in the richly written study of Polynesian tourism by Andrew Ross.[27] In this engaging and well-researched chapter of a larger book, Ross makes two general points: (1) campaigns for saving endangered ecosystems have generated an eco-tourism that helps destroy the environment, and (2) under neocolonial arrangements, the defense of "indigenous culture" has often propped up local, ethnically authorized satrapies and participated in myths of purity that benefit local rulers.

Ross covers massive terrain. I am concerned here only with flashes of the argument, while keeping the whole orchestrated movement of the piece in mind. Ross begins his essay with a personal tale of how "fate, jetlag, and cultural studies" brought him to a resort hotel in Fiji, where the reader now finds him witnessing a lip-synching contest that involves the impersonation of Western pop recording stars, an experience that prompts a wry meditation on "world culture." He then sets off on a long, often bitter reproach of ethnographic romanticism, particularly as it dealt with Polynesia in the cases of Captain Cook and (much later, under different circumstances) Margaret Mead. He laments that mainstream cultural narratives still use Mead's noble savages and her myths of idylls despoiled, even as recent ethnographic theory has thankfully swept those ideas away. He then moves on to a history of the Church of Jesus Christ of Latter-day Saints (LDS), along with an account of the church's paradoxical role as a preserver of "traditional" culture in Hawaii. In the closing movement, the reader is offered a more in-the-face look at one of the fruits of the LDS's business acumen and their typically Protestant attention to native cultures: a thirty-year-old ethnic theme park, the Polynesian Cultural Center, located in Oahu "just around the coast from Sunset Beach, the wet dream of world surfing culture" (43).

Very much like Appadurai and García Canclini, Ross repudiates the idea of a native who can, in fact, be lost or who needs to be recovered. Without ceding ground to a modernization narrative that would simply put the welcome mat down for invading venture capitalists, Ross nevertheless finds himself most aroused to ire by a top-heavy, nostalgic bluster over ethnic traditions endangered by the modern. There is, in other words, room in this universe for the word "exploitation," and there are passages (usually in the footnotes) that concede its relevance. But to avoid further mischief of the type minted by the conquistadors themselves—who, like some of today's most doctrinally diligent scholars protecting native rights, *knew* they were doing the natives good—Ross targets the very idea of a happier native in a preferable past. Determined to drop the scales of "nature" from eyes that need to see culturally, he draws inevitably on James Clifford's idea of "salvage ethnography," in which the Other always seems suspiciously to be in danger of disappearing at the very moment ethnography arrives to record it (a point I examine in more depth in Chapter 6). It is that sort of circularity—or rather, the consignment of others to a circular logic from which they cannot escape—that I want now to examine.

Ross's essay can be viewed as one long demolition of the arrogant zeal to preserve traditional cultures, or what Ross calls "kneejerk liberal deference to indigenous values" (24). With an appellation oddly borrowed from talk show conservatives, Ross proceeds to lay out a convincing local case describing how Indo-Fijians (indentured Indian laborers brought in the late nineteenth century) suffer under "near-apartheid rule." Far from a mere flourish, the phrase is defended in a shocking catalog of features, including an official Christian state religion, racial restrictions on land ownership rights, and "all sorts of material and political privileges" (4). The presiding government of "natives" had been established under British patronage as a "state within a state" made up of ethnic Fijians who get great mileage now out of appeals to "traditional culture," since in this context they are nothing less than fillips to a grotesque form of minority rule.

Although a casual interest may arise about why Ross rushes to elaborate this kind of reversal, about precisely why nationalism as charade is what attracts him—since he takes the trouble of conceding that the cause of tradition elsewhere has actually been rather noble, "a vehicle for justly reclaiming 'native' rights that were historically denied"—my focus here is only in part the accuracy and justice of his comments on Fiji, and much more the corollaries he draws from them. And these arise, as most interesting methodological points do, "in between." In the essay's engaging overture, for example, one gets the description of a Christmas party at a resort hotel featuring foreign guests meeting a native hotel staff who at one point entertain the assembled by staging humorous skits of tourist stereotypes (Japanese, French, and so on) and who later impersonate the rock stars and other celebrities who performed famously in the "We Are the World" video ("The Fijian Ray Charles was outstanding" [21]). Here the reader encounters an enormously complicated set of meanings, cajoled and soothed by Ross's brilliant style, but riddled with nagging questions. For example, is cosmopolitanism a part of the scene or its description?

> Once the stage show was over, the evening divided into three different spectacles. In the entertainment space, a guitar trio informally led the Fijian workers through a long medley of traditional songs, observed by only a few tourists, mostly from the hippy world traveler contingent. Meanwhile, some Fijian hipsters had joined the array of Westerners now flocking to the bar, where a dance floor and ersatz international pop music supplied the invitation to mingle. A third diversion was provided by two young Swedish women, sporting the Heidi hairdo only six weeks after Madonna had pioneered it, who had taken over the pool table and were holding the attention of hard-drinking Indo-Fijian male locals on the nondancing side of the bar. Fitfully intoxicated by each of these scenes, jetlag finally forced me to retire, but not before concluding wanly that this, surely, was "the World" that the famous music video had been incapable of rhapsodizing, here returning culturally deranged images of itself to the Western eye. (22)

Apart from the tone of bemused and omniscient witness, the passage is stunning for the way it tumbles into regions of vague double meaning. While a "Western eye" calculates the costs of cultural derangement, a (distasteful) world culture shows its real face, obliterating the more inviting illusions of indigenous life—even here, in the most isolated and far-flung outposts of an older bucolic order launched by Cook and immortalized by Paul Gaugin. The mood for the rest of the piece is set, as is its implicit thesis: the third-world subaltern, if one looks at it squarely, exists only as vestigial presence already saturated by U.S. corporate culture. There is no other world, no preserve, one can appeal to; nothing outside this overfamiliar scene. Nor does one find a refuge in parody or appropriation, which is here rather desperate and unaware, and leaves an ambiguity for the "Western eye" about who is spoofing whom. Are we to laugh at Michael Jackson or the Fijian bellhop who mimics him in the presence of Westerners? In a strange way the image systems of the metropolitan visitor (Ross, in this case) become the more authentic consciousness, the more originary culture—since "masscult" is demonstrably the common currency. To be indigenous is not so much denied possibility, it is only transferred implicitly to the visitor from America.

Or so it is, at any rate, in the luxuriantly semantic "chronotope" of the tourist hotel (to borrow again from Clifford). How different would the passage have been if set, say, in an Indo-Fijian kitchen over a stew pot in one of the *bidonvilles* mentioned elsewhere in the essay? No doubt masscult has also crept there, but not so proudly, or in such "pure" cultural forms. Aren't the highly coded exchanges in these crossroads of jet lag precisely what attracts, but also disorients, what might unkindly be called the "frequent-flyer anthropologist"? Can the state of a new world be judged from the perch of a bar stool in one of the many locales visited on the "cultural studies" speakers circuit? And how, incidentally, does the "World" of the passage's closing lines shift from being a mélange of Europeans and Fijians in common pursuit of tacky good fun to being (implicitly, but unmistakably) the Fijians alone, since only they can project "deranged images" of themselves to a "Western eye"? The scene of zany and improbable mixtures, in other words, finds its way around again to a securely modernist disenchantment, in which "they" and "I" (the "Western eye") are again securely separate, roaming on opposite sides of the bar.

Ross is well aware of most (not all) of these reservations, and they in part form his point. The images are "deranged" after all because they are undignified; the natives fail to live up to the tourist's demand for *something else,* and they altogether collapse in a display of affection for what is, after all, *bad* metropolitan culture in Ross's own terms of presentation. Leaving alone whether he misses some of the "traditional" contempt for masscult latent in such ironized performances, he stages the trauma in order to work the reader out of the clichéd responses he consciously elicits. The rest of the essay goes on to undo the standard (usually unstated) view of the typical visitor when facing the native: "You're not what you were; you've degenerated. And it is our civilization that's killing you." It is not hard for Ross to problematize this view, and he does so effectively by showing the harm in Mead's "lush romantic ode" (37), along with its legacy in current environmentalist forms of the preservation thesis. He does this in general by "complicating" the standard view with a close and informative sociology of Fiji and Hawaii: the 1987 military coup, the Tongan roots of early Polynesian invaders, *kava*-drinking ceremonies—all of the class antagonisms normally forgotten as existing within and across gender, religion, and ethnicity in these settings of supposedly dual (and only dual) antagonism between colonizer and colonized.

And yet Ross keeps returning, again and again, to the same kind of point made in a similar way—a rote patterning at odds with his vocal bid for complexity. In its various clothing, the point is based on a logic of circularity. At one moment, he wryly exposes the slogans of the tourist industry: "See paradise before it's gone announces the very industry associated with the destruction of paradise" (51), an observation that helps introduce his comments later on the Polynesian theme park. At another moment, he sums up his ongoing analysis of the ethnic Fijians' tribal council, whose members lord it over the Indo-immigrants: "The outcome of this discourse of preservation does not usually lend itself to more democratic forms of self-determination; it tends to sustain, if not reinvent, tribal and patriarchal forms of hierarchy" (89). To counter with examples where preservation played a different role (Ross himself concedes some in the footnotes) is to miss a more important issue. And that issue could be expressed in an imaginary subtitle: "Toward a Tropical Modernity." This essay is an encomium to the modern, the new, the bravely novel, in whatever deceptive packaging it might first arrive.

At the level of form, the hunt for circularity seems almost unconsciously to figure something else. It hints at a deeper commitment to the present at the expense of the past—a present with a profile drawn in icons of fallen Walls, shiny videos, and lip-synching natives. The opening movement of the essay teaches the reader that the West is, in important ways, the "World"—so let us look (he says) more soberly and optimistically at the West. While Ross finds all kinds of imperialist baggage in the sentimental hypotheses of paradise lost (wasn't Mead just repeating the motifs of Cook?), he defends the "Western way of life" against those who wrongly accuse it of devastating the South Seas:

> More often than not, the conventional binary option in these debates of Tradition versus Progress feeds off a history of thinking shaped by the "fatal impact" thesis of Western contact by which Pacific peoples were passively doomed to suffer the ravages wrought by an introduced culture based upon exploitative cash and wage economies and driven by the environmentally destructive philosophies of possessive individualism, rationalism, humanism, materialism and nationalism . . . Defined from first contact, then, as a philosophical test case of survival or extinction, the Pacific way of life still serves today as an acid test for Western anxieties about the growth and development of industrialized societies. By the same token, the Western way of life often serves as a negative model in the region, a crazy mirror for native anxieties about the future of a past partly romanticized and partly still lived. The worst legacy of this dialectic is that it perpetuates the dangerous picture of a death struggle among cultures in a region of the world that once served as the crucible for evolutionary theory. (27)

Notice how much hinges here on banishing the idyllic past. Once this is done, one can deal with "exploitative cash and wage economies" in quotation marks, as it were. The "ravages" of European contact, instead of being discussed and weighed as such, can be referenced in a belittling allusion to a supposedly absurd dialectic of a "death struggle among cultures," which is then pejoratively linked to social Darwinism. The extreme cleverness of the construct is that it renders the logical questions mute, paralyzed with fear at the lurking charges of naïveté. Namely, *were* the philosophies "environmentally destructive"? Did "possessive individualism" obliterate, like a computer virus, the delicate structure of Polynesian society as it existed before Cook? Should this legacy make one join in the opinion of those who see the Western way of life as a "negative model in the region"? Since he admits, grudgingly, that some parts of the past are "still lived" (not only romanticized), which are they?

If Ross provides in this way an exceedingly odd defense of the powerful with the warrant of soberly assessing the facts, he does so in the name of protecting native agency. He is trying to say that he, not the overdiligent promoters of the old struggles, is really defending the weak because he refuses to cast the Pacific islanders as "passive." This is, as I have noted, a maneuver found in much of culturalist theory, and it recurs constantly in Ross's essay. The "narrative of decline," he asserts, "has the effect of further empowering what is already empowered, dispossessing people of whatever agency they thought they had" (53–4). Or even more clearly: "History is best described, not by the all-or-nothing scenarios of 'fatal impact' in which colonial culture uniformly and irresistibly penetrates a defenseless native culture, but by the messy account book of cultural and economic exchange in which the institutions, rituals, and objects of both cultures are selectively appropriated, recontextualized, indigenized, and used" (28).

More or less true as it stands, this last passage illustrates exactly the need of current cultural theory for "necessary fictions." It is doubtful, for example, that the "all-or-nothing" scenario Ross mentions ever existed in this form, except polemically or perhaps in poetry. In scholarship it was always accompanied by grimmer details of the harsh conditions of forest life, preconquest intertribal warfare, or domestic forms of infighting: counteridylls that nevertheless preserved the idea of a qualitatively more profound disruption by a "dynamic" West in search of markets, tromping its big technological boots all over the countryside. What needs to be asked is what is gained by denying that the European impact was "fatal," especially when that view is supplanted by visions of a chirpy negotiation of "cultural and economic exchange." This highly weighted emphasis on "recontextualization" and "exchange" simply makes nonsense of the lopsided power the United States, France, and others hold in the region, with the Pacific as their nuclear playground.

So driven is this thinking by a souped-up "salvage ethnography" critique that it never seriously asks, simply, what happened? With routine hammering of the always ready-at-hand Rousseau, Ross has a field day with Mead's "embarrassing" narrative of the "easygoing native," more sexually in tune, freer, and (Mead would have it) a good model to copy in a country of rapacious puritanism. For a domestic project of sexual liberation at home, Mead is said to submit her ethnographic raw material to unseemly uses. But is Mead so easy to dismiss? The question remains: Was Samoan society sexually freer than Western ones, comparatively abundant, more observant of (or at least less able seriously to harm) the forests and the water? It would not be difficult to dig up an extensive body of literature by specialists on the region who made precisely this case—and although Ross's point is to cast doubt on that scholarship, surely much more evidence than he presents has to be mounted to do so.

At any rate, isn't there a distinction to be made between a problematic ideology of recovery and the data amassed, which does seem, in fact, to suggest that the disparities in sexual freedom between that kind of society and our own was real? In spite of Ross's dismissive oratory on "child of nature" myths, it seems rather clear in that writing that Samoan society was all of these things. But the power of this precritical intervention is that the other side cannot be true; no need for point-by-point refutation, no need to consider if creation myths do not largely allegorize the sad transition from labor-unintensive economies of plenty to societies of permanent surplus/scarcity, since the germ is in the bone. Ross's appeal is to the recognition of a prejudice, a utopian paternalism that his intended reading community is only too eager to grant, and that by turn leads to a slippage from one extreme to the other with no distributed middles. One apparent foundational text for Ross's line of argument—*The Country and the City*—would never have imagined that its portrait of the landed gentry's manipulation of the pastoral (a "good old days" that never existed) could be construed as saying that something like Thomas Hardy's Casterbridge never existed either, or that its different ways of meaning and having were not stamped out by liberalism's ten-league boots. A large space separates a false pastoral from the types of community possible in a pretechnocratic modernity.

On the matter of sex, Ross is particularly harsh, blaming Mead for confusing the prostitution of disempowered native women with the famous openness of Polynesians to sex with foreigners: "The fantasy of an unrestricted sexual economy among Polynesians proved crucial to the Enlightenment's ideological reworking of Arcadian myths about man in a state of nature" (35). And yet Marshall Sahlins points out that in Hawaii "women were acting in accord with the rules of sexual passion *(le'a)* that governed status and advancement" and it was only later, after Europeans had been there for a while, that sex "became a medium of commercial exchange." But what, more specifically, is the modern mélange that Ross wants to celebrate here, protecting it from rough-riding doctrines of political correctness? In one more turn to the defense-of-native-agency model, he makes the character of his modernity ever more clear:

> One of the stories about the survival of the Hawaiians is about history made under conditions entirely not of their choosing. It is a narrative of their forced integration into the world system of capitalism . . . The result of this kind of analysis—guided by dependency or world systems theory—is often to deny any degree of autonomy to indigenous cultures, and to ignore the ways in which specific groups make use of external influence to transform internal social relations . . . [In this view] museum-style preservation is the only possible response to the destructive commodity-logic of external penetration. (79)

Although strands of this argument are accurate, even helpful, Ross characteristically parodies Marxism with a gratuitous jab in the words "not of their choosing." At the end of the day, although he twists away from saying so directly, he is not resisting crude generalizations that play down "domestic class and gender conflicts." What he is really resisting is the conclusion that capitalism "integrated by force." The cumulative effect of his writing here is a "realist" defense of European contact very much of the school of John Searle—a sort of Indians-peed-in-the-stream-too school of history, that has the sea voyagers and modern buccaneers all in it together with a besmirched, "dynamically" evolving native population.

Capitalist modernity's effect on native populations can only be called a "death struggle among cultures." This may be hard to see when one feels, as Ross does, that this is "the age of cultural nationalism." So, when having a laugh at how "the stationary pictures of prelapsarian societies that were once the staple of classical anthropology have become the primary commodity of the tourist trade" (51), he contents himself with a paradox and an easy target, the tourist. What he fails to ask is why there is this intense desire for the "authentic," and why it persists in spite of the obvious inauthenticity of tourist experience—an experience that, by his own admission, eco-tourists to Hawaii consciously realize even as they pay high ticket prices for a flavor of this inauthentic premarket world. That is the more interesting question. But to ask it means to return to the nagging evidence that many people despise the capitalist modernity he portrays as inevitable and qualitatively mixed, and are willing to pay large sums of money to get an ersatz whiff of what existed before it.

In a prominent way, Ross's work suggests both the institutional reliance of cultural studies on postcolonial motifs as well as the contribution of that practice to an ethics of nonbinary "complexity." By briefly reviewing the origins of the practice, one can begin to see how its methodology reasserts, in an unlikely way, a political aesthetic most visible in Eurocentric defenses of the literary canon. I might begin by observing that cultural studies typically deals with representations more readily than the *means* of representation. One discusses differences within the intelligentsia more comfortably than differences between the intelligentsia and the socially invisible or the verbally untrained. Middle-class perspectives remain fairly secure as points of departure. A further problem may be that the various pressures that gave rise to cultural studies are not generally known in this country, and when they are considered at all are usually linked up with Stuart Hall's inaugural essays on the subject, as others have noted.[28] Hall's story describes those origins as being a combination of early left British literary criticism, American sociology, and Althusserian structuralism. It is a story filled with the names of individual thinkers and master texts that had been handed down to enterprising, offbeat students working collaboratively and across disciplines to produce new ensembles of knowledge.

This, I think, is a very misleading account of where cultural studies came from, and the account has undoubtedly done much to make people conflate the field with the textual literary theories already prominent in American universities. With the advent of structuralism in the 1950s, theory as such found itself tending toward the same intellectual feel as those sociologists (on the one hand) and those British precursors cited by Hall in his genealogy (on the other). Raymond Williams's category of "cultural materialism," for example, overlaps in many ways with that well-known effort by the philosophers in France to root cultural play in the "hard" and the "scientific" stuff of language. In Britain's case—the most well known one in the United States, and the most fetishized—activist intellectuals had been fleeing out of the Communist parties and their peripheries to reinject scholarship with a sense of the popular by firming up the study of culture, giving it a set of material parameters intelligible to sociology and to the policy-minded talk of the left political organizations. With a much more belletristic edge, French intellectuals were fully absorbed in the romance of science, although they were reclaiming its immense prestige and its systematic certitudes *for* philosophy through the vehicle of the inescapable (and systematic) structures of language itself.

All of this was unfolding in an era of Americanization, which meant primarily the massification of the public sphere by the relatively new technologies of television and computers, together with the multiple refinements in communications growing out of the use of satellites and fiber optics. Accompanying these technical developments, and ultimately more important than them, was a highly organized cultural apparatus of dissemination—an immense and new array of managers, creative specialists, and commentators who facilitated Americanization from U.S. and European bases, although both the employment of the technologies and the rise of the information classes were not, of course, restricted to the United States, and occurred on a smaller scale with less expertise elsewhere. The urge by postwar theorists for a materialism of culture, growing out of very different intellectual lineages, here converged with Americanization in an irrepressible march toward the realms of mass (that is, media) culture. This inevitable interest in communications, however, tended to play itself out in investigations of the media's semantically rich epiphenomena—their various narratives in the forms of actual programs, printed materials, and celluloid fantasies. The option was not altogether unexpected.

For, from its launching in the 1940s, media research in the United States had mostly been a combination of behavioral psychology and densely empirical surveys of media "effects" on audiences. The very groundwork of the American school of communications scholarship suggests a political outlook very hostile to the goals of the postwar cultural left: the famous statistical studies of Paul Lazarsfeld on voting decisions, for instance; Harold Lasswell's consensus thesis of American politics; and Carl Hovland's influential work on propaganda and persuasion in World War II, which he wrote at the U.S. Army's Information and Education Division and later at Yale's Attitude Change Center.[29]

Although these works continued for a time to hold sway, creating what Stuart Hall has called the "institutional hegemony of American behavioural science on a world scale" through the 1960s, its first modifications took place only from within its basic positivist methodology, in a shift of concern from "behavior change in the individual . . . [to] the larger perspectives of social groups and institutions."[30] In both cases, the links between these studies and the needs of corporations and governments to manage populations became striking, and themselves formed a crucial part of the postwar debate over mass culture. The ties of traditional communications studies to corporate needs and objectives was nowhere more obvious than in the fact that "mass culture" itself (both as a concept and as a reality) only became possible and could flourish through the very notion of "public opinion" that the empiricist scholars promoted.[31]

The muted implications of Hovland's work on wartime propaganda—that is, its unsettling links with managing minds for commercial purposes—eventually made it necessary for the North American school to develop a coherent theory of pluralism that would turn the unasked questions about unequal power and economic relations into scholarly articles about "choices" and "interest groups." When one strayed from this complacent national terrain—as one had to in the media explosion of the American Century—the effects of communications on the developing world required a quite different kind of argument, which was provided by Daniel Lerner, using the assumptions of the liberal pluralist school, in his book *The Passing of Traditional Society*. The question there was basically "how the Western ideal of press freedom could be transferred to the developing nations of the Third World."[32] Writing for UNESCO in 1964, when it was heavily directed by U.S. interests, Wilbur Schramm went even further than Lerner by making "rapid economic and social growth, spurred on by mass media, seem realistic, exciting, and relatively simple." The mass media became in this thinking almost a natural force, and a fortuitous one for the developing world: its key to "catching up" with the developed nations.

As Stuart Hall and Armand Mattelart have separately argued,

the ideology of structural functionalism was not only enabled by Americanization but also helped proliferate it in the postwar period.[33] Against it, two very different kinds of media work were then posed. One of these has come to be known as postmodernism, with its direct attachments to linguistic and literary theories, and its overall commitments to waging primarily cognitive and aesthetic warfare. The other has had far less sway in humanities circles, although one would have thought its strictly philosophical implications should have commanded more attention even if its focus on institutions did not. Within communications, broadly left critics formed what might be called a branch of "corporate-institutional" critique—people like James W. Carey, James Curran, Janet Woollacott, and Michael Gurevitch, who broke from the behavioral-consensual lineage under the impact of its confrontation with the third world, so devastatingly exposed in the varied work of scholars like Kaarle Nordenstreng, Tapio Varis, and Herbert Schiller.[34] Others in this "cultural imperialism" school included Dallas Smythe, Holly Sklar, and Stuart Ewen in North America; and in Europe, Hans Magnus Enzensberger—all more or less neglected in U.S. theoretical circles in the current rise of cultural studies.

The inexorable drift toward communications in cultural theory, in other words, had not led to methodological points of contact; a good deal of the history and the outlooks of the other disciplines remained isolated and enclosed. Nor, one suspects, was this a matter simply of resistance to the rhetorically alien worlds of another discipline. For how, then, does one account for the remarkable lack of interest in that aspect of the work of well-known literary types like Raymond Williams, Richard Hoggart, and Hall when they treat communications with the sociological clarity and completeness accorded the field within formal media research? If Nordenstreng seemed far afield, certainly Williams did not, and yet almost no one in the U.S. context has taken the latter up on his charge of studying not merely media "texts" but the interstices within which they find the light of day. In fact, not only has Williams not been followed in these leads, but his own comments on communications have been systematically ignored.

In *Communications* (1962), *Television, Technology, and Cultural Form* (1975), and *Contact: Communication and Its History* (1981), Williams went about explaining that culture is not merely (in his famous phrase) "a whole way of life" but that it is a largely abstract fabric of imminencies and possibilities that are enabled or censored out of existence by the apparatuses of communication. It is usually forgotten that the second part of the two-part project that began with *Culture and Society* (and that launched Williams's career in England) was *The Long Revolution,* published in 1960—an intensive empirical study of the rise of the British newspaper, the news-reading public, and the effects of both on the class identities and allegiances of British literary intellectuals.

Similarly, Richard Hoggart, a professor of literature, founded the Centre for Contemporary Cultural Studies at Birmingham (CCCS) in 1964 by first setting it up within the existing structures of an English department; and this, despite the fact that its first funded project was "a study of social change through an examination of the popular press, 1930–4."[35] Playing off of the energies generated by his own book *The Uses of Literacy*—a study of the transformation of traditional working-class "everyday life" in the 1950s—Hoggart left the Centre in 1970 to become assistant director-general at UNESCO; he wrote an important critical study of the British press that appeared in 1967 *(Your Sunday Paper),* and he oversaw projects dedicated to examining the complementary relationship between literary taste and the media, as in the multivolumed work he inspired and contributed to, *Literary Taste, Culture, and Mass Communications.*[36]

In this respect, it is significant that the founders of the CCCS were not at all sure at first whether to call it a school of "cultural" studies or "communications" studies. This ambivalence is evident in the Centre's next director, Stuart Hall, who apart from being the intellectual guide of the school from 1968 to 1979 was also the one assigned to cover problems of the media. The author of very early articles like "The Social Eye of the *Picture Post,*" Hall has written several sociological overviews of the British postwar period that see it very consciously through the spectrum of debates occurring within communications studies at least until the mid-1980s, when the theoretical tendencies I am examining in this chapter moved him away from communications to analyses of "representation" and "identity."[37]

I spend time relating this history to stress the missed options in our present understanding of cultural studies. What seems in many respects to be an arrival also has aspects of a retreat. In a variety of poststructuralist studies on "techno-culture" and the "hyperreal" in which the theory and communication lineages at last confidently meet, key technical terms are borrowed from American sociology in a strategy of co-optation.[38] The motives of many of these studies is indirectly to do battle with functionalist positivism. And yet a certain debt is paid to the public fascination with science wherein the incantations of the technical are marshaled forth to locate ideological "effects" in what amounts finally to a sedentary rapture. Despite departures in style and repertoire of influences, postmodern cultural studies shares with the market research approach to communications a decisive celebration of the "new" in which the turn to the media has crowded out that third element of media critique enlivened from the start by third-world problematics—that found, for example, in the work of Schiller, Enzensberger, and, above all, Michele and Armand Mattelart.[39]

The only way now to reclaim the media as an object of analysis that can present itself to the public as previously unforeseen (and therefore urgent to look at) is to vie with the language of the various "posts" for passion and cleverness of phrase. This kind of impediment once again raises the issues of middle-class points of departure and scholars' own fleeting self-recognition as information managers. In that sense, the methodological target of functionalism represents a misconception and an unresolved tension. For "function," although it may well conjure up nightmares of audience surveys, positivist data, and bureaucratic dread-speak, also alludes precisely to "functionaries"—that is, those working for the ones who now hold power, the ones who have the privilege of worrying about policy. With a similar line of argument, Jim McGuigan, Simon Frith, and Jon Savage have quite rightly contested contemporary cultural studies' "cheerful populism, by academics' new-found respect for sales figures, by the theoretical pursuit of the joys of consumption."[40] They go on to underline some of the points I am making here by observing that "the great failing of our age is the idea, received wisdom from right to left, upmarket and downmarket, that to be popular you have to be populist" (116).

In that way, analyses within cultural studies have opted for a philosophy of a very narrow stripe. When efforts have been made to expand or complement these analyses with reference to the relevant work of Schiller or Noam Chomsky, those thinkers are automatically discarded as existing in the dutiful, upright, and utterly predictable world of correct political practice, where the object of the game is merely to compile data on various injustices, conspiracies, and acts of greed. One assumes that the information in question may vary from page to page but that the kind of point made is always the same. There is no philosophical meat to the work. It is, in short, already known. But it is no such thing and has been insufficiently analyzed, particularly in its more naked colonial forms. It is widely unappreciated, for example, that a deliberate splicing of literary theory with a "cultural materialist" approach to the media was evident in Latin America at roughly the same time as the birth and growth of the CCCS.

The work of Michele and Armand Mattelart, which elucidates these Latin American sources, is easy to miss today, since it is widely associated with a spent era.[41] Most critics of popular culture are familiar with Armand's early study cowritten with Ariel Dorfman, *How to Read Donald Duck,* and are loosely acquainted with the fact that he wrote a few other critiques of corporate culture. But despite a recent translation of the Mattelarts' *Penser les medias* by the University of Minnesota Press, U.S. critics for the most part do not have an accurate idea of how extensive and ongoing their work has been, or how directly relevant to the positions of the theorist-as-manager. The role played on their thinking by long-term engagements in Latin America has been similarly overlooked. Occasionally, as in the little-known writing of Michael Chanan, Armand's later work received some attention, as it did in Edward Said's book *Covering Islam.* But both of these cases were also essentially 1970s products, giving to Mattelart now the unmistakable look of the bargain basement in a time of cyberpunk, hacking, and the hyperreal. With people like Jean Baudrillard now guiding the readers of popular culture into the inevitable terrains of the media, this other tradition needs to be recovered.

Taken as a whole and as they arise in widely different contemporary writers, the tendencies of contemporary cultural studies are these: The Althusserian concept of "overdetermination," of course, is an important point of departure, although it is here pushed well beyond the semi-autonomy of the superstructure to suggest that primary determinations reside principally in ideas, values, and emotions. A second point of departure is the wholesale adoption of the fieldwork paradigm of anthropology in which the objective is to explain what an artifact or practice "means." What is more, culturalism brings with it a set of oddly dogmatic corollaries, which derive not merely (as one would expect) from the discursive politics of poststructuralism, but from certain latent themes in the CCCS and even in Williams. These are (1) that the primary impediment to understanding culture has been the "base-superstructure" model of Marxism; (2) that attempts to give economics or material interests priority in matters of culture are always a form of "economism" in which (as Richard Johnson puts it) the effort to go for the "brutally obvious determinations" fails to give adequate weight to the "social life of subjective forms"; and finally, and most important, (3) that culture is the arena in which the most important political battles today take place—a doctrine, one might say, borrowing a phrase from Williams, of "cultural revolution."[42]

The difficulty with the first of these charges is that not one of the cultural theorists presently read as Marxist (among them, Alexandra Kollontai, Georg Lukacs, Walter Benjamin, Jean-Paul Sartre) were ever guilty of this dichotomy, and often—as is the case with Henri Lefebvre's seminal and pioneering theorization of "everyday life" written as early as 1947—exposing this dichotomy was precisely the point that they themselves were making against the second-order writers within the party organizations: "We may note that the concept of *socio-economic formation* has almost disappeared from Marxist writing, to be replaced by the simplified scheme: *"economic base—political superstructure."*[43] It can be seen that Lefebvre's point here is to remind people what Marx originally wrote rather than to point to some still uncharted future. The widely acknowledged centrality to cultural studies of the construct "everyday life" had, moreover, found its origins not in Lefebvre, but in early Soviet cultural debates (as *"byt"*). Lefebvre had been able usefully to revive it through an unprejudiced relationship to socialist traditions.

In any event, the process of complaint and rectification has been obscured to a degree that strains one's confidence in their sincerity. Cultural studies, after all, is now targeting a calcified or mechanistic mode of analysis that had much more to do with forces hostile to Marxist theory: the canonical strictures of higher education, for example; the atomization of disciplinary knowledge in the university along the lines of business specialization; and the careerist pragmatism instilled in researchers working under commercial and industrial constraints. Activist intellectuals, many of them now nameless, have done more than anyone to combat these forces and pave the way for the present freedoms. And the simple fact is that the crusade against base-superstructure simplifications had been a central tenet within Marxism almost from the time of Marx himself.

The point, perhaps, is not precedence so much as the conditions and objectives of those who presented the extraordinary idea of studying culture as a totality. It is odd that Gramsci—by all accounts a central forerunner of the field—has been thought central *in spite of* rather than because of his membership in the Communist Party and (what is rarely seen) his being an early European commentator on cultural imperialism as a Sardinian suffering under the domestic colonial prejudices of Northern Italy. Gramsci is a brilliant confirmation of the point I am making, but in many ways he only carries on the kind of work initiated by early Bolsheviks like Leon Trotsky in his articles from the early 1920s in *Pravda,* later assembled under the title *Problems of Everyday Life;* or in Alexandra Kollontai's early book *Marxism and Sexual Revolution.*[44]

With respect to the latter two charges, it is in part the lack of attention given the imperially informed lineage of communications studies outlined above that permits a certain methodological impertinence. Assaulting the "obvious" in a simplistic and schematic way, theory discovers in the invitingly messier term "culture" an object that is nevertheless shorn of the complications of "material interest." With Williams as warrant (although he himself is rarely guilty of the conflation), culture simply *becomes* the material world.

In spite of years of self-questioning—beginning perhaps in 1957 with Northrup Frye's admission that critics had no discipline of their own—there is a sense in which the cultural critic's mulling over the limitations of his or her theoretical practice has limits of its own. What career does to vision, what the perks and payments of those from newsrooms and faculty luncheon halls do to the limits of questioning, is typically not asked. The cultural critic, progressive by inclination, has the job of finding a place within a rebellious respectability. The search creates tensions that express themselves in the need for arguments that can be countered. The "monolithic" and the "univocal," for example, must continually be found, although they rarely can be, in order to demonstrate one's subtlety, complexity, and dialogism.

And so one sees the creation of an entire list of necessary fictions: the charge of "Occidentalism," for example, leveled equally against

Afrocentricity (where the charge has some merit) and third-world critics of imperialism; or the idea, supposedly from Marxism, that only class matters; or the proposition, supposedly from needlessly arcane left intellectuals, that writing accessible to popular audiences dilutes the mission of theory. None of these charges can be adequately documented except in marginal cases, and so they typically are not. As I have been arguing, the most important "revisions" entailed by these necessary fictions lie in targeted concepts like the binarism of colonizer and colonized, and the base-superstructure model from Marxism, where one sees unwoven the tightly knit anxieties of the cultural critic.

To take one example—although it is a completely standard, almost rote sentiment—a recent well-known theorist asserts that "Marxism's ambition to unify isolated working-class struggles into a mass movement of the proletariat has hampered its ability to provide articulations for new and emerging political positions . . . in addition to its perceived inability to seriously theorize the subalternity of women."[45] This is, first of all, simply untrue, and could only be uttered by someone who had never experienced or seriously studied the political climate of Europe between the wars, when the working class was much more visible as an organized site of dual power and counter-hegemony in all aspects of social life.

The emphasis on a working class, however, did not have to do with a blunt, universalizing (and, by implication, white and male) fetishizing of laborers but with a recognition of means. European and male prejudices clearly played a part in the formulations, of course, but the focus on a transgender, transethnic unity of a sector defined by its relationship to production was an effort at theorizing what seemed with good justification to be the sole practical agency for transformation.

But well beyond this, the extensive counterevidence to the claim makes one wonder about the diligence of the effort. To see how intensely "personal life"—and women's rights—was a vital issue in the early Soviet Union, one might look at any number of sources that suggest that far from repressing the categories of gender, race, and nationality, early communism promoted and theorized them. Abram Room's film *Bed and Sofa* (1927), for example, is an exploration of sexual politics and communal living that would remind most of the relaxed sexuality and cool domesticities of Greenwich Village, although with the immeasurable background joy of a socialism in power. And this is not an isolated example. The invaluable recent research on early Soviet women's organizations by Wendy Goldman and the insights into the concept of "cultural revolution" in Soviet futurist theater by Katerina Clark have both demonstrated the immense, and defining, contributions made by Continental socialism to the present practice of cultural studies and minority rights.[46] That lineage had been carried on in the postwar cultural work of C. L. R. James (as I describe in more detail in Chapter 5) and the interwar theory of Karl Korsch, who like Lefebvre (but earlier) was staking out *for* socialism the very critique now associated with its avoidance, as he complained of tendencies in materialist theory to fall into the "error" of believing that "reality pertained only to the economic phenomena" while "forms of consciousness" were "lost in pure 'ideology.'"[47]

The leftist culture critic wages battle between poles of feeling that do not present themselves as polar: anger and ambition. Recent studies of sex-work, for instance, dig down into the everyday surroundings of women's second-class treatment and document their refusal to be victims while the authors of such studies find their way to a promising combination of shock and denunciation. Unproclaimed from the start in these projects, but felt in every word, is a sick-and-tired attitude in which cobwebby old scholarship must be fled from in order to arrive at something more relevant. But there is already a respectable tradition of such writing in what used to be called counterplanning on the shop floor—a study of microstrategies of resistance in the workplace such as working to rule, slowdowns, and industrial sabotage. A serious study of such precursors would help supply the self-criticism they eventually generated. The shortcomings of microresistance were found in the fact that none of these actions led to anything but themselves, always staking out a space of dignity on others' terms. At what point, then, did a declaration against socially specific gender oppression become an argument that surviving was itself an act of battle? At what point did the good intentions of the researcher conspire to produce this necessary fiction—the prostitute as rebel—in an act of reading into events a narrative that should be true, but really isn't?

In debates over the end of the public sphere, one finds additional fictions that help tie social readings of culture to literary critical tropes. Intellectuals, it is argued, are just too obscure, too intellectual, which leads to the paradox of complexity again, but from another direction. As a matter of scholarly style, the system of evaluation here in many ways contradicts the assumptions outlined above. The charge is that intellectuals do not know how to speak to the public and end up handing over power to cultural conservatives who do. Popularized again recently by Russell Jacoby, the argument is raised at predictable intervals in a variety of venues, and always as a revelation.

Again, if there is some truth in this charge at the level of political organization, the literary counterevidence is so close at hand that the point of interest continues to be the need to proclaim it. While there are difficulties with his thesis even as a description of a tendency within literary theory of the last few decades—for there has been throughout, I would argue, a steady flow of academic critics acutely aware of the need to speak plainly and powerfully in mass venues—it is the strongest part of Jacoby's argument. The fact is that through the agency of a number of casual journalists, innovative artists, and authors, the ideas of Barthes, Foucault, and Lacan have entered the culture in the form of theatrical productions, museum notes on photography exhibits, satirical novels, and even MTV commentary. In assessing theory's inaccessibility, Jacoby and his successors do not give sufficient attention to the hostility that exists toward the ideas themselves as distinct from their presentation. And if some of the subsequent attempts to rectify the overspecializations of theory legitimately escaped Jacoby given the time his study was written, more recent champions of the cause have failed to reckon with those who set out to make recent positions within the humanities more broadly known and did so with a respect for theory often conveniently missing in the harshest critics of obscurity.[48]

Especially in the last five years or so, journals like *Transition, Lingua Franca,* and *Culturefront: A Magazine of the Humanities,* composed in a lively prose with full-color layouts, have risen up with conspicuous desire to be popular. It is difficult to see how one could underplay the crossover designs of contemporary masscult theorists or forget about concerted efforts, stemming from the "p.c." wars, to make the curricular changes in the university more broadly understood.[49] Because of the campaigning of its recent presidents, the Modern Language Association now hires a public relations firm to influence government and press on its behalf. What hidden cause prods the critic into this eternal return to an unnecessary confession? Apart from plain censorship, what stymies progressive intellectuals is harder to name, more internal to their practice, and so more invisible than the failure to employ a ready-at-hand populism.

As I have been arguing, the problem is not so much accessibility through a change of expressive means as it is a contestatory (rather than market-driven) accessibility. That demands a reconceptualization of the system of status and rewards that separates intellectuals from the "people" lying beyond the word "public." Methodologically, the problem here lies with the notion of complexity as political position instead of as scholarly armature—a notion whose avoidance of binaries relies on problematizing the "crude" oppositions of an older left narrative. Some of the assumptions of multiculturalism's politics of identity illustrate this avoidance—above all, as I argue below, when they are popularly presented.

Anna Deveare Smith, or Authenticity

A spotlight in the New York Public Theater shines down on the hard-edged, youthful face of Anna Deveare Smith, winner of a keenly competitive Obie Award. Her play *Fires in the Mirror: Crown Heights, Brooklyn, and Other Identities* opened in June of 1992, the time of the Los Angeles riots. By the following April, the play was picked up by *American Playhouse,* thereby reaching a national television audience. John Leonard in *New York* magazine echoed the praise of other print media: "the astonishing Smith . . . her surpassing generosity . . . a loving mimic . . . a chameleon and an exorcist."[50] In June of 1993 her new work, *Twilight: Los Angeles, 1992*—similar in form to *Fires in the Mirror* but based on the Los Angeles uprising rather than the Crown Heights "riots"—opened to ovations at the Mark Taper Forum. The reviewer for the *New York Times* remarked: "In her new show, Anna Deveare Smith captures Los Angeles."[51] Not long afterward, she landed roles in the Hollywood films *Dave* and *Philadelphia,* and in late July, appeared on the Arsenio Hall show.

Both versatile and honest, Smith had taken audiences through a series of impressions based on personal interviews with real people, in shows (as she put it) "built around a specific controversial and timely event."[52] The found quality of the characters was a feature that kept ringing through the favorable reviews. Composed of short mimicries of actual, often anonymous or little-known Black and Jewish New Yorkers reacting to the Crown Heights events, the theater playbill came equipped with a rundown of the events themselves: Yosef Lifsh, a Hasidic man, kills a recent Caribbean immigrant, seven-year-old Gavin Cato, when his car jumps the curb in Brooklyn. A visiting Australian Jew, Yankel Rosenbaum, is later stabbed and dies in the hospital. Occupied by police for three days, Crown Heights is riven by marches and recriminations.

Although the subject matter was timely and the performance was impeccable, Smith had launched a success that was still in many ways wildly improbable. That heightening of the real in the current-events mind slot was, it is true, not unlike Hollywood in its docudrama mode. Nor were rising stars unheard of from the environs of "serious" theater of the off-Broadway type.[53] Others from the Public Theater milieu had been trying this sort of thing for years. Eric Bogosian, for example, had created a series of savage character-monologues on white America—embittered suburbanites flipping burgers by the poolside, gloomy Pearl Jam fans—and had himself found success in feature film.[54]

Theatrically, the Smith piece had relied on impersonations, often of well-known people, even though by her own admission she is not really an impersonator in the usual sense of the term. "It's a matter of me having an ear that's microscopic enough to hear a person's individuality in a moment . . . I just try to find that distinct moment and do exactly what they did. Character appears in language."[55] But even more unlikely was this: before each performance, she faced the audience dressed in a cardigan sweater to explain, out of character, the genesis of the work as well as the stakes involved in the politics of subjectivity. As a Stanford theater professor, in other words, she was not only playing multiple roles, trying on other people's genders and races (twenty-five roles in *Fires in the Mirror* alone), but opening each performance with a classroom primer on literary critical theories of identity. What achieved massive public acclaim was not simply an off-Broadway play. It was a sort of highbrow bohemian theater for readers of Judith Butler and bell hooks.

Given the nature of the material and the origins of its artist, one has to look at the way in which identity is publicly coded as distinct from the way it is academically theorized. Smith in a way allows both to be seen at once. According to the theoretical underpinnings of *Fires in the Mirror* as highlighted in the lecture she gives to open each performance, the audience is meant to see in the counterpoint of Hasidic Jew and Afro-Caribbean American (1) that identity is fluid, or at least flexible, and that it appears natural but is always much more a pastiche of learned or chosen behaviors and manners; (2) that supposedly known identities of racial or ethnic groups as a whole are at once fictive and surprisingly (and depressingly) confirming of our expectations—that is, there is enormous diversity within each group in such a way as to defy our first impressions, but there is also an elusive continuity with those impressions, perhaps imposed by the consignment of a given individual to a group; (3) that hostilities toward others are often the result simply of ignorance, that the play is designed to provide information about how Blacks or Jews see things, *really* see things, expressing themselves in unguarded moments in their revealing accents; and (4) that there has been a lot of wrongdoing on both sides and that the injuries are largely the result of being locked into an ethnic identity that has been predefined. Against conflict (although about it) and for ambiguity, it stands against the essentialisms that enable racial and ethnic othering: famously, Blacks and Jews, who in a final intimation of circularity bring the virus of essentialism back in the form of an unseemly conflict between themselves.

Here, then, is an example of how the theoretical issue of identity played out in a practical, nonacademic milieu by way of artistically documenting poverty, justice, and the law. Although part of a more general eagerness to hear the stories of minority intellectuals in education, media, and the arts, Smith's play did not simply arrive to fill a base commercial need in the wake of the Rodney King beating. It cannot be said to be in the least opportunist in that way. The Crown Heights play was only the latest in a series of plays Smith developed after 1990 under the running title *On the Road: A Search for American Character.* The echoes in that cover title of both a conventional image of "migrancy" as well as a well-known Beat novel suggests something, perhaps coincidentally, of the return to the weak and confused counterculture of the 1960s, as though we could again experience shock in talking about race frankly, and as though Smith were to contemporary crowds what Lenny Bruce was to his.

It was crucial, in other words, that this play was performed by a Black woman. Equally important however, was that she was not just a Black woman or Stanford professor, but one who could identify with and ventriloquize for American Jews unflinchingly. A successful production demanded someone who could embody the hope of Black-Jewish reconciliation in an honest forum or cast agents of familiar, everyday conflicts as villains, heroes, or something in between—someone with that kind of courage to speak plainly in tough times. She had both to understand Jews and to represent Blacks. These subterranean virtues of empathy for one group and physical embodiment of another were not themselves theatrical. I am not talking here, in other words, about the magic of "try-on" identities in a dramatic theatrical closure, as in Peter Weiss's *Marat/Sade*, for example. The virtues of empathy and representation, unparallel and not interchangeable, had here to be found only in the social subtext of the critical praise with which the play was greeted. They were not in themselves mentionable; they were separate from, and subversive of, the drama enacted because they implied an incongruity of ethnic experience at odds with the message of negotiation within the play.

The truth of this play is deeply mixed, and like other recent triumphs in the ethnic arts it contains ideas of extraordinary democratic and critical force. But along with them came a certain timidity: a large sign reading "this far, and no further." In this way the play also creaks with untold stories. What are the implications, for example, of understanding Jews and "representing" Blacks? In the milieu of the Public Theater, one wonders how adequately she can capture the meaning of rap artists, community activists, and James Brown—all of whom she portrays. What prevents her, ultimately, is not that she is an intellectual, speaks well, or is an artist—although those identities are never separable from her aura in the act of impersonation, and are deeply linked to the play's actual message for the audiences that attended. What prevents her is the impossibility of representation in that context, before *that* audience. If part of her declarations is that, although Black, she cannot, it is a point her audience cannot in practice grasp.

Comments like these underscore the notion that identity in the real drama of the social is much messier than even Smith is able to make it, not so much because of the complexity of cross-cultural communication, but because of the ideological strictures against naming the more obvious antagonisms depicted in the performance and implicit in the performance itself. One has to begin with its context—an Ansbacher Hall filled with many more white faces than

Black ones, and reviewers who are overwhelmingly white journalists. Implicit in the structure of the play, for example, is balance. By race, the characters impersonated arrive in the following exact pattern as reprinted in the program (although not, of course, with their races cited as here): Black, Jew, Jew, Jew, Black, Black, Jew, Black, Black, Black, Jew, Black, Jew . . . and so on. Numerically scrupulous, the play was, in a sense, contextually careless, for the opinions to be played to and the judgments to be wrestled with were largely white and, in sizable numbers, Jewish as well. Nor could balance be very appropriate, obviously, in accounting for the realities of Crown Heights, where Blacks are by most knowledgeable accounts the target of incessant police abuse and where the Hasidim, although victims of a citywide verbal abuse and anti-Semitism, have the ear of city hall and a great deal of appreciable local autonomy.

None of that sort of reality, however, enters the drama. And therefore as Smith wends her way from A. M. Bernstein to Angela Davis, understanding is extended to the people who articulate rage, but not to those organizing themselves in ways the Ansbacher audience is unprepared to consume as theater. By the end, one notices that fully four prominent African-Americans have come up for treatment—Ntozake Shange, Angela Davis, Leonard Jeffries, and the Reverend Al Sharpton—even though only Sharpton was associated with the events. The rest of the characters, Black and White, were unknown preschool teachers, graphic artists, churchgoers, or anonymous young men. Prominent personalities—especially ones who are controversial precisely because they are prominently Black—are more vulnerable in an impersonation than are the anonymous (however much they are given names, ages, and a phantom reality as interviewees). There was, for example, no Elie Wiesel, no Saul Bellow, no (*New York Times* op-ed columnist) A. M. Rosenthal to balance the well-prepared sense of extremity in the caricatures of the tabloid villains, Jeffries and Sharpton.

Identity is a crucial weapon of self-definition in social struggle, but here it appears as a more restricted set of personal choices, fulfillments, and self-consciousness. As such, it raises the issue of even how "Jewish" are the play's Jews. Centering on the Hasidim allows many of the professionals in the audience to say "that's me" when there is talk of the Holocaust but "that's them" when the play deals with the orthodoxies of Hasidic dress and eating practices. In other words, the entire production is calculated as an entertainment of a particularly restricted sort—an act of defusing fears as performed from the sensible perch of evenhanded reflection—strictly from the outside, perhaps, but led by an insider.

For the very reason that identity politics has arisen on behalf of women and minorities assuming authority, it is not easy to point out the snags in its current articulation without appearing to oppose that authority. But the effort has to be made, because this mechanism of progressive change often works against itself. This is particularly true when it comes to white ethnicity, in which many of the desperate resources of identity politics in Black American culture have a much greater warrant. I would like to close this chapter with one particularly charged site of identity politics in practice—one, like Smith's, based less on theories of subjectivity than on what forms those theories have taken publicly and practically.

It is often only a name that links one by an untrustworthy filiation called "blood" to a family lore and a genealogical tree. Outside the arena of one's own dreams that filiation may have little foundation—although it might lead (as it often does) to marrying within one's group and perhaps to a pilgrimage to the home country upon graduating from college. All of this might only add shading and textual relief to a different kind of authority one may have from years in the library studying a group or a people; but identity usually confers authority in a presumptive flash where being precedes essence. There is nothing so unneedful of proof, so immediately assumed, as the camaraderies of race and ethnicity. Such presumptions, however, are by their nature unbalanced. The stakes for white ethnics can no longer be thought comparable to those for people of color, in spite of the brilliant reminders found in recent research on those racially suspect late arrivals from nonapproved parts of Europe who, in the lynchings of Jews and Italians up through the early twentieth-century, learned how hard it was to be considered white in various parts of America.[56]

As a problem, filiative authority meets the study of third-world literature in minority hiring practices in the university, where it is marshaled by administrators and English faculties to redress biases in a setting of institutional racism. Despite the obvious impetus given minority hiring by the rising interest in American "ethnic" and non-

Western literatures, as well as the related but somewhat different rise of "postcolonial theory," these hiring trends are in many ways affected negatively by their association with these emerging fields.[57] Both a paradox and a reversal accompany such a situation: the defense of teaching non-Western literatures is widely perceived as being made in the language of civil rights (inclusion, equality of representation) rather than on the grounds of what those literatures offer a humanist knowledge pushing beyond European provincialism. At the same time, and paradoxically, affirmative action as social redress no longer defends itself in the language of civil rights but stands as a peculiar manifestation of an assumed specialized knowledge. Black scholars are sought to teach Black literature. In addition to being a form of liberal racism, this process ensures a low hiring cap; it marginalizes and diminishes the value of what is taught by making it appear particular and special; and it loudly proclaims to white students that this is not their field.

One can take the position that affirmative action does not go far enough at the same time that he or she argues that there is racism underlying its present practice—and not at all in the sense of the Allen Bakke court decision of the 1970s arguing that whites are, as whites, being discriminated against. The point is rather that the process may ultimately *diminish* the numbers of minorities hired even as it discriminates against younger professors—white and Black—on the basis of creed. And it is this link between the racism of skin and the, often combined, discrimination against political positioning, that brings the issue into the larger problem of cosmopolitanism.

Many academics are now familiar with the kind of situation in which an African scholar, say, arrives in this country having done his or her research on Hegel and then, upon arrival, is asked by the university to fill an opening in African-American literature; or with the situation of a young modernist with a Latino name recently graduated from Harvard who upon arriving to teach a course on Arnold Bennett is discreetly encouraged by his new colleagues to teach a course on Latin American literature. In Renato Rosaldo's sense of the most salient and revealing discussions of the academy being "corridor talk," one is also familiar with the off-the-cuff comments of hiring committees who refer to the colonial slot as the "exotic" position, by which they mean exotic not as in *does* but exotic as in *is*.

Is there any merit to the assumption that people from the former colonies, or those related by birth to those who were or are, have a special insight into the teaching of colonial literatures? The answer must be a guarded yes, for there is a certain range of codes and idioms that they alone will grasp from past experience. But it is also the case that the American-born, European-descended white student will have an experiential advantage in many of the codes and idioms relevant to postcolonial studies, not only because imperialism is a two-sided relationship, but because "postcolonialism" has become a field indelibly marked by American academic and publishing opportunities as a matter of sheer numbers and imperial centrality. In other words, it is precisely from the vantage point of renegacy from the white mainstream, from a certain willed noninvolvement in the ambiguous privileges of racial or class birthright, that many insights into imperialism can best be found.

Unlike in postcolonial studies, the matter is more complicated in African-American studies given the domestic tradition of historical exclusion of Blacks from positions of authority. Here, apart from the largely specious issue of the authenticity of specialist knowledge is the practical one of teaching by example, of visibly embodying as a matter of silent instruction, the attainment of a status to which the students can then aspire. Added to this is the matter of confidence that a Black student feels when getting advice and counseling from someone who knows something personally about racial exclusion. African-American studies must, in that sense—at least in the United States—be set apart. Administrators at many universities have decided, at any rate, that it is much better for their school's image of seriousness and respectability to have nonwhite professors as the ones teaching postcolonial topics. In addition to scholarly excellence, authenticity becomes an issue in this field in a way it does not, say, for Midwestern American Lutherans who teach Saint Augustine or for heterosexual southern women who teach Melville. If it is defensible in some cases that that be so, the theoretical justifications are self-contradictory and unbalanced, and they obscure the actual criteria at work.

Indeed, the point can be taken still further. For a certain kind of scholarly projection across the minefields of identity is quite common, but it is unquestioned (as it should be unquestioned) on the grounds of original and rightful place.[58] Minority scholars from one race or nationality are usually not challenged for speaking about another—a condition that is only possible under liberal racism. This situation typically does not raise the charge of portable ethnicity, nor should it. But if that is so, what then is won and lost in acceding to such an idea when it comes to white professors? It is the experience of some white students at job interviews to meet the white professor who cocks his or her head and asks archly, "So how did *you* get interested in *that?*" as if to say, it is not yours; or, on the other side of the equation, there is the new Black candidate who meets the white professor in the halls of his university who talks impulsively about Toni Morrison. In the current American framework, to be a white postcolonial scholar is to be embroiled in a suspicious wannabe-ism, a troublemaking attitude that attaches itself vicariously to Black culture as a synecdoche for disruption—a renegadism that all in all is felt to be rather crude intellectually, too political, and racially impertinent.

When administrators provide special incentives to departments to hire minorities and subsequently permit them to hire new faculty members through a dean's initiative without using up a job slot that has been given the department for general use, the "third-world" positions are usually the slots in which the hiring is done. Hiring committees observe that the pool of minority candidates who come to them are already heavily concentrated in these fields: African-American literature, postcolonial theory, and, increasingly, American ethnic literatures. This is true, but the very attitudes and policies discussed here ensure the outcome, and they protract it. A minority graduate student may specialize in these fields out of a personal commitment or elaboration of an embattled identity. But graduate school is about professionalization, whose only logical end point is a job. The current practice tells the minority student very clearly what his or her proper intellectual scope ought to be, what job he or she will be most highly rewarded to fill; and it tells white graduate students to enter at their own risk. In this way, filiative authority ensures a pattern of research segregation within the humanities departments.

Furthermore, because the third-world position is typically filled as a surplus offering by administrators eager to avoid the embarrassing demographics of their institution's racial composition, the intellectual prejudices already existing toward non-Western literatures are fortified—those prejudices being that they lack interest as literatures, are methodologically strident, or are crudely autobiographical. The equation between hiring Black, on the one hand, and filling the third-world slot, on the other, facilitates the designs of departments to replicate themselves. If three openings occur in one year, for example, this setup makes it likely that two of them will go to so-called traditional candidates in so-called traditional fields. Because faculties in their majority do not understand or are contemptuous of curricular reform, they find it easier to promote discrimination in the very act of a highly restricted affirmative action by virtue of ignorance of the *field.*

Just as non-Western literatures are bracketed in the very process of their widespread inclusion—recuperated into studies of European influence or, more likely, into American pluralism—new minority hirees are often expected in this atmosphere to fill the role of friendly informant: not, as any specialist is asked to do, about a field, but about a race or a third-world locale. This, of course, insults the scholar's training by making professional expertise a matter of being; yet it also asks the scholar to represent the Black poor or rural multitudes who through a complex process of social pressures made minority hiring an issue in the first place. Affirmative action, then, turns out to be about cultures of persuasion as well as filiation, although it is almost never recognized as such, and there are no public or legal grounds on which to make such a case.

The protocols of emergence for new fields like postcoloniality and cultural studies, I have been arguing, block the radical break they announce in the act of entering. They do so because the framing of their questions flees from the class-historical conflicts prohibited, as a matter of decorum, in American institutional settings. Identity politics has provided a way to promote a real but limited rejoinder to earlier forms of exclusion, but has also substituted itself for a theory that would bring together class, race, and political position in a continuity with movements of the colonial past.

By selectively ignoring parts of that past—I have mentioned early Soviet cultural theory, the work of specific (and often slighted) anticolonial intellectuals, and corporate-institutional critiques of the media—cultural theory has been paradoxically less new and more crude than many of the positions it originally marked out as having those qualities. Its methodology allegorizes a series of related rhetorical tropes—complexity, circularity, and identity—by implicitly making them the preferred weapons of a one-sided battle against binary thinking.

3

The Culture of the Transnational Corporation

> People with global mindsets trust process rather than structure to deal with the unexpected . . . People with global mindsets value diversity, multicultural teamwork, and play, as the basic form within which they accomplish their professional, personal, and organizational objectives . . . People with global mindsets see the world as a balance of contradictory forces that are to be appreciated, pondered and *managed.*
>
> —Stephen H. Rhinesmith

> Management will increasingly be the discipline and the practice through which the "humanities" will again acquire recognition, impact, and relevance.
>
> —Peter F. Drucker

> I was an internationalist before anyone was.
>
> —Ted Turner

Very little has been written about the place the cultural critic occupies in the American economy at the moment of a widely proclaimed globalism. When work of that sort has appeared, the functionalism of the role has often been denied in a recuperation of images of the traditional intellectual, who may not be cast, as he or she once was, as a disinterested seeker of truth, but who retains in some accounts an unlikely aura of disinterestedness, especially in conservative returns to criticism as literary appreciation (à la Frank Lentricchia).

What follows is a tentative attempt to outline some of the unforeseen uses of cultural theory in the worlds of business and public policy. In an era of globalist campaigning, that function not surprisingly entails theorizing the nation, and the patterns that theorizing has taken remind one of nothing so much as a joke related by Freud.

Freud tells the story of a man who complains to his neighbor for returning a kettle in a damaged state. Seeing the accusation coming, the neighbor is well armed: "I never borrowed a kettle from B. at all," he says. "Secondly, the kettle had a hole it already when I got it from him; and thirdly, I gave him back the kettle undamaged."[1] Arguments that allegiance to the nation-state is disastrous and that the nation-state no longer exists are often found together. In fact, they belong together.

Investigating what he calls the "ethics of post-sovereignty," Michael J. Shapiro, for example, struggles with these very antagonisms. Noting ambiguously that "political boundaries [have] become increasingly ambiguous," he is forced to concede that "the geopolitical map of states . . . still dominates how things are valued, actions are interpreted, and persons are assigned identities."[2] If Shapiro sees the staying power of the existing geopolitical map, others see its imminent redrawing, although not without lamenting the staying power of nations as such. "Instability Threatens Much of World at Year's Close," screams a *Miami Herald* headline over a region-by-region synopsis of ethnic mayhem, an article that takes up six full-length columns.[3] Replicating the *Herald*'s frightful list of local rebellions in a pan-global setting, the *New York Times* portrays the grim tasks of Washington in the coming era: "As Ethnic Wars Multiply, U.S. Struggles to Meet the Challenge."[4] Meanwhile, Robert Reich, secretary of labor in the first Clinton administration, shows no concern for this chorus of alarm: he presents a more bucolic and evolutionary scenario of a postnational reality guided with imperfect benevolence by new forms of trade and labor organization.[5]

More spritely reflections on what might be called "globality" (to give a sense of globalism's light and colorful packaging) represent a different genre within this larger trend, but a crucial one for hammering into a hard common sense what is most dubious in the commentary. In an essay by Pico Iyer for *Time* magazine, the same wobbling between one nation and one world persists. Using a novelist's license, Iyer crafts a type of writing on the globality theme without spontaneity, every sentence a variation, colorfully wrapped, of an optimism that sounds oddly like a threat. "All the world's a rainbow coalition," says Iyer in a typical formulation, as though taking the high drama and sincerity of Salman Rushdie's essays of a decade ago and transforming them into something glibber and more formulaic. "Values," he continues, "travel at the speed of fax . . . a common multiculturalism links us all—call it Planet Hollywood, Planet Reebok or the United Colors of Benetton . . . the global village is defined, as we know, by an international youth culture that takes its cues from American pop culture . . . as national borders fall, tribal alliances and new manmade divisions rise up . . . the transnational future is upon us . . . America may still, if only symbolically, be a model for the world."[6] One is reminded, disconcertingly, of Stuart Hall's memorable lament that in postmodernism "the world dreams itself to be American,"[7] which perhaps should more accurately read: "The world, in poverty, wants to partake in what it dreams, wrongly, to be American."

It is with a sense of this skywriter visibility of globality that maverick entrepreneur Ted Turner in the epigraph above recalls the role of CNN in covering events at once local and distant by outpost governments in times of emergency, often relying on local footage and native broadcasters. CNN, he contends, has been nothing less than a force for world peace: experimenting with a new global news style, the network prompted Middle East peace conferences with its stunning coverage of the Persian Gulf War. The "cross-border wars" of places like Northern Ireland were much more numerous before CNN began broadcasting, according to Turner. It was against the stream of the foreign-policy gurus that he set about establishing world unity before "globalism" positioned itself as the campaign slogan of the American bourgeoisie. Says Turner frankly: "I want to be a knight in shining armor. Martin Luther King and Gandhi are my heroes."[8]

This racy op-ed sort of globalism, as well as the more technicist discourse now inundating the fields of political science, anthropology, and international affairs, bears directly on the nation debate in academic culturalist circles, as Masao Miyoshi has perceptively pointed out in an essay that urges cultural criticism to consider corporations as assiduously as it has personal identities.[9] But just as Turner's use of the word "internationalist" deliberately puns on the socialist movement, so has terminological cross-dressing characterized the debate on cosmopolitanism, where the interchangeability of terms has concealed important differences. An initial task, then, in launching the argument I develop below is to distinguish among terms like "global," "worldly," "international," and "cosmopolitan," which in ensemble have concealed a slippage among the sites of formulation, each with their own intended ends and self-identities. In academic cultural theory, it is customary to associate the urbane, the worldly and the transnational (three distinct concepts) with the single governing term "cosmopolitan" and then to claim these associations as recent and defining. But devised primarily to stand against the valorization of specialist intellectuals narrowly confined to academic disciplines or floating in a realm of ideas without material consequences, "worldly"—in Edward Said's famous coinage—was a way of pointing to a form of reading and thinking that roamed widely, made broad connections, but never lost its sense of immediate correspondence to a conjunctural politics.[10] Although angrily opposed to religious and ethnic exclusions, blind patriotic allegiances, and single-minded solidarities, Said has also, of course, spent a good deal of time immortalizing the anticolonial intellectuals who were historically antagonistic to cosmopolitanism in the sense outlined in Chapter 1.[11]

Terminological slippage of the type described here implies forms of commerce between critics from distinct terminological worlds; and although several critics imply that intellectuals have come to see themselves as "transnational" only recently, that view has been a standard of European thought for centuries. Cultural narratives are part of a social matrix shared by policy making, media opinion forming, and literary theory; they blend in a single, not entirely seamless texture of ideas and opinions while undergirding, coloring, modulating, even at times directing those ideas and opinions. In analyzing the positions shared by academic trends in studies of "professionalism" and in "cultural studies," one wonders if there are not analogues today to the beguiling liberality combined with confidence in the justice of European mastery found safely in nineteenth-century writers by a host of commentators. The conflation of terms like "worldly" and "global" is, I would argue, one of them.

Indeed, there are recent aspects of the debate that give the term "postcolonial" real meaning as a description of the present. As I remarked above, the logic of international rule has been widely perceived as moving from the occupation of foreign territories (or their control from afar) to the generalization of "here." Beyond implying sophisticated forms of cultural dissemination and persuasion, this proposition underscores a civic aspect of the nation debate that has become unfashionable and that has a small voice in the current theories—namely, the issue of sovereignty. The stakes of a phrase like the new "transnational subject" cannot be understood without exploring such a concept. Culture and sovereignty coalesce over the claim—found widely in global theorizing—that metropolitan societies possess an immanent allure at odds with the injustices required to keep them running.

The testimony of immigrant communities themselves, however, suggests that they are very often not drawn to "America" so much as to a wage setting. The feelings expressed in the lyrics of the song "Jaula de Oro" ("The Gilded Cage") by the Mexican *norteño* band Los Tigres del Norte are typical in this respect.

> My life is here in the United States.
> Ten years have already gone by.
> Having made the crossing by river, my papers are still not in
> order
> And I'm still illegal.
> I brought my wife and children over very young
> from my beloved Mexico that they have already forgotten,
> but that I will never forget
> even though I can't return.
>
> In order to earn some money, I am like a prisoner
> in this huge country
> When I remember Mexico I'm at the point of tears
> And although this is a cage of gold,
> It hasn't stopped being a prison.[12]

The constantly new crop of involuntary immigrants into metropolitan national settings dramatizes not the evanescence of borders (Shapiro's "post-sovereignty") but their absolute liminality and fixedness. And if the song offers evidence of a mixed reality—for the mother and the children have forgotten the home country—the speaker's view is the one most often denied in practice.

It is not so much the involuntary or coercive aspect of displacement that is forgotten but the one-sidedness of the conclusions drawn about the felt community of the nation. An overwhelming number of accounts look to reigning politico-emotive mythologies—ideological rituals of invented history and ethnic exclusion—while failing to analyze the reality of a simpler, more knifelike communal sense based upon the passport, the green card, and the open-ended residency permit. Since nationhood as residency in a wage setting plays almost no role in current theory, a simplistic coupling of formally cosmopolitan experience and transnational identity is facilitated.

Under what pretext does one feel a part of a collective with people who are, after all, strangers, but who also call themselves American? The answer need not always be found in complex cultural processes of ethnic or religious binding, which remain crucial aspects of identity and longing in a sense quite separate from a properly national affiliation. Another form of binding (and identity) is civic. Nationals vote in the same elections, pay taxes to the same authority, and stand in the same lines at international airports—even those who by look, origin, or personal identity are only whites with accents, "Asians," "Venezuelans," or "Senegalese." The massive community of illegals in Europe and the United States could not be more cosmopolitan, objectively, but they have no use for a theory of "migrancy" that finesses their limits to belonging on the grounds not of culture but of law. Moreover, between the legals and the illegals stand sizable outpost communities of temporary residents that affect the cultural life of the nation and are affected by it, but for whom observations of transculturation are misplaced.

The point is not to deny the importance of the immaterial pull of nationalism arising at lively conjunctures of need for war or sacrifice, when organic intellectuals of government (often literary intellectuals) serve up romanticized masculinist tales of national virtue or heroic origin (tales that it has become almost de rigueur to "expose" as fictional!). There is an important and soberly material sense of citizenship having to do simply with one's *papers*. It is in the end at least as important and lasting as cultural affiliation, and the only one resilient enough to withstand the strain on myths of the nation-family that arise when wealthy capitalist countries are, as Louise Bennett once put it, "colonized in reverse" by nonwhite people who flock to lands for which they often have no abiding love, no intention of joining, no lasting attachment, but which offer them, temporarily, the hope for a living wage. This immensely important aspect of the debate is not so much overlooked as ignored, perhaps because it does not invite the appealing subtlety of cultural analysis possible in discussions of intricate social allegories involving gendered or racial identities.

Although I discussed the debates over globalism within the academic disciplines of geography, anthropology, and cultural studies in an earlier chapter, one of my purposes below is to follow the meandering paths of the globalism debate through the public sphere—the journals of the policy experts, the editorial pages, and the corporate managerial training manuals—rather than through the seminal theories most recently cited in debates over the nation, theories glossed, in turn, by a staggering number of metacommentaries and now obligatory allusions.[13] Doing so brings one to see parallels between the present and the 1950s, when the urgency of an emergent global culture (and polity) was as strong as it is today. Naturally, the conditions of capital mobility, the absence of significant noncapitalist sectors of the world economy, and decades of tinkering with more flexible and decentered forms of corporate organization, have made globalism seem more real than in the 1950s. There has been accordingly, a free-fall consensus that capital is directed now by transnational corporations for whom national allegiances no longer bind and are not even coherent. It is remarkable, however, that this point has been made without seriously asking what, in fact, *is* the cultural life of the transnational corporation. First, a few distinctions.

If the Nation Is Dead, Why Doesn't Henry Kissinger Know it?

There can be no theorizing nationalism without theorizing globalism, and there can be no talk of globalism without Americanization. In the evidence mounted to show the preventable tragedies of ethnic identity mobilized on behalf of state power, the parties are both familiar and (as presented) interchangeable: Tutsi and Hutu in Rwanda; Shiite and Druse in yesterday's Beirut; Croat, Serb, and Muslim in today's Sarajevo. Invoking these conflicts has made transnationalism seem almost like a solution. This is the conclusion, at any rate, of Robert Kaplan's essay "The Coming Anarchy: How Scarcity, Crime, Overpopulation, Tribalism, and Disease Are Rapidly Destroying the Social Fabric of Our Planet," which portrays a disintegration of third-world order so pathetically complete that the world itself can only be seen as divided radically between "the healthy, well fed, and pampered by technology" and the "poor, nasty, brutish, and short."[14]

Perhaps testing conservative waters for the depths of a reemergent positivist racism, Kaplan's extreme and often shocking formulations are entirely at odds with mainstream humanities discourse. In fact, they deliberately contest the latter's studied worldliness: "Western religion is undermined by animist beliefs not suitable to a moral society," "loose family structures are largely responsible for . . . the explosion of the HIV virus [in Africa]," the Ivory Coast suffers from the departing "talents of a French expatriate community," West Africa is "one never-ending shanty-town," the state is a "purely Western concept," ours is a "crowded planet of skinhead Cossacks and *juju* warriors, influenced by the worst refuse of Western pop culture" (46, 54, 48, 59, 62).

The neo-Victorian tinge of the essay helps to sketch out only one of several scenarios enabled by the thesis, based on Martin Van Creveld's *Transformation of War* and shared by a majority of culturalist theorists, that "the period of nation-states and, therefore, of state conflict is now ending" (73). For Kaplan, as state power fades, cultures are "thrown back on their own strengths" (74). It is not that the end of the perilous journey will not be a "racially hybrid, globalized man" (74), but that we first must pass through an era of "large-scale border upheaval" fueled by "religious perversity" and other nonstate forces with the intermediate results being "environmentally induced praetorian regimes" and a vast suburbanization of the wealthy and intelligent in various security zones. Utterly out of step in most ways with the message of most postnation academic theorizing, Kaplan's vision represents one of the more salient forms that the cultural argument can take.

Decoupled in this way from the viability of nationhood, theory can choose between prognoses of disintegration—as in Kaplan—or of celebration of the cultural differences implied by new global citizenship, and it can do so without fundamental disagreement about the fate of polities as such. Entering the terrain of culture from the latter perspective remains crucial, of course, to contest from a position of knowledge and experience Kaplan's rhetoric of fear and loathing. Indeed, an essay like "The Coming Anarchy" might be cited as evidence for the decisively political character of academic cultural work. But again, with attention to the civic aspects of the nation debate, it is still precipitous to concede the argument's pretexts. Let me summon, then, two pairings from the recent news: first, "Marcos" (the nom de guerre of the *subcommandante* of the Zapatistas in Chiapas) and Carlos Salinas de Gortari (the former president of Mexico); and second, Sinn Fein's Gerry Adams and Ian Paisley of the Ulster Protestants.

Theory is confronted with an unseemly dilemma when it notes that sententious slogans such as "rising sectoralism," "ethnic bloodletting," or "small-scale border skirmishes" do not begin to capture the effects of the stand-ins here for nationalism and internationalism. If the Chiapas uprising had been—as the Zapatistas themselves made clear it was—a rebellion against NAFTA, then a large minority of the Irish Republic (as well as the leadership of Sinn Fein) had distinguished itself for opposing Ireland's entry into the European Community as provided for in the Maastricht accords of 1991, and had done so at a time when being against NAFTA and Maastricht was perceived by nearly everyone as being quaint and picturesque but unrealistic; whereas Salinas staked his presidency on the acceptance of NAFTA, and Paisley's Orange support in Parliament proved decisive for John Major in getting Maastricht accepted in England.

Granted, in Chiapas the permeability of borders across the Mayan regions extending from the eastern Mexican states of Chiapas and the Yucatán into Huehuetenango and the western highlands of Guatemala suggests some of that postnation theorizing that deals in "localities." Thus, some have speculated (wrongly, as it turns out) that the Zapatistas themselves may only have been Guatemalan regulars from the Guerrilla Army of the Poor who had filtered westward across the border. And the ethnic composition of the insurrectionists, being almost entirely but not quite entirely Mayan Quiché, does seem to favor popular readings of the future that see shifting, monadic identities with little respect for older patterns of orderly campaigning as citizens within tidy national frameworks. Other points can also be conceded to the current discourse on the nation. Ulster suggests the anachronism or insufficiency of borders—not only the one separating the Six Counties from the South, but the one separating England from the Republic. For the war has been carried to the gates of Heathrow Airport and Regent Street shopping centers by Dublin Gastarbeiter flowing freely across the Irish Sea.

What cannot be lost is the insistence of Marcos and Adams on negotiation with a domestic state in which a principal demand had been an opting out of, or a stepping back from, "inevitable" international frameworks that both perceived to be inimical to their interests and, however late the date, avoidable. Too much is conceded to a specious futurology that speaks at times, and paradoxically, in the nineteenth-century manner of inevitable logics, evolutionary necessities, and organic developments. All of these are supposedly moving everyone toward a world of interlinked corporate headquarters giving orders in the lingua franca of English above figurehead states that have been fully integrated into business decision making and decisively decoupled from national formations. In this fantasy, parliament gives way to the boardroom without any of the present pretenses of electoral gaming; passports are thrown away in one vast free-flight zone; national peculiarities are relegated to the curios of carnivals, gift shops, and ethnic-pride parades.

Telescoping of this sort—which overlooks, among other things, the noncooperation of campesinos in San Cristóbal de las Casas—helps to enact what it pretends to comment on. Assessments of the present always lead to a kind of future. Thus, postnational theorizing, prognoses of an emergent globalism, the insistence that the transnational corporations have relegated state decision making to subsidiary issues, although extreme and inaccurate, do encourage these very outcomes. At the very moment that the ethnographers of metropolitan masscult, the students of professionalism, or the theorists of the intellectual have made a convincing case for the role that imaginative and ideological forms play in the exercise of power, they have stopped short of casting the glance homeward by neglecting to look at how their cultural and aesthetic work dovetails with more explicitly governmental analysts arguing, and celebrating, an "inevitable" globality.

Some of these—Ben J. Wattenberg of the American Enterprise Institute, or emeritus historian Theodore H. Von Laue, for example—write of "supply-side demographics" and the "liberating discipline of globalism" in a breezy style. With much more thought, the cultural critic is in some ways only "riffing" on policy talk or (conversely) supplying it with raw material. The close parallels between emphases in journals like *Transition* and *Public Culture,* on the one hand, and *Foreign Affairs,* on the other, are remarkable and depressing. But although less interesting hermeneutically, and conducted in the roughest and most empirically naive think tank jargon, the middlebrow analyses are more valuable than highbrow theory as registers of the moods shaping those who actually have power. The value of studying Von Laue's *World Revolution of Westernization* or Wattenberg's *First Universal Nation* can be seen by mulling over their painful Malthusianisms, their encomiums to American culture as the world's "common property," or their neolib bragging for multiculturalism.[15]

If complexity is a constant virtue of the essay as a form of displaced art, the graduate student turns without exception to Homi Bhabha's anthology *Nation and Narration,* or Andrew Parker et al.'s *Nationalism and Sexualities,* or Etienne Balibar and Immanuel Wallerstein's *Race, Nation, Class: Ambiguous Identities.*[16] Far too vulgar or vicious to be interesting enough to criticize, selections like Kaplan's essay "The Coming Anarchy" give a necessary and largely underestimated sense of the discursive environment by combining dressed-up environmentalist positions of a brutally frank Hobbesian tinge with assumptions shared (in this sense only) by the left academy: "The world . . . has been moving during the course of this century from nation-state conflict to ideological conflict to, finally, cultural conflict"[17]—Kaplan's favorable summary of an argument by Samuel P. Huntington of Harvard's Olin Institute for Strategic Studies.

The examples I have considered so far illustrate the diversity within globalization theories, which do not all ignore the civic. Some of the most notable even deny the postnational framework of its premises. Francis Fukuyama's famous thesis, which talks about the end of history as (to quote Perry Anderson's summary) a "tying of liberal democracy and capitalist prosperity . . . in an emphatic terminal knot," indicates rather clearly that in the U.S. State Department, at least (where Fukuyama is based), the projection is for the continued viability of the nation-state and for the functioning of a post-perestroika order within the traditional bounds of individual governments that preside over bordered territories, advance domestic agendas, and maintain a separate ledger for domestic economic and political plans and priorities.[18]

It might be counterargued that what is wrong with Fukuyama's vision is that this posited homogeneity of goals, this community of outlook that appears so convincing when one views the world as an inventory of individual nation-states, is precisely the illusion. For the goal or outlook is now potentially common because the effective polity is now potentially singular. Instead of the fall of the Soviet state being a matter that convinced governments of the unitary road of conduct, one sees instead an opening for former Soviet rivals to cap the conflict by imposing their global rule. In other words, one goal (or "end") is projected because one government is foreseen. The place to look for counterproofs to Fukuyama's thesis of a "common normative commitment to free markets and free elections" is therefore no longer in various governments' policies, but in the subgovernmental programs of emergent political oppositions, which continue to express the conflicts of the recent past in an incomparably weaker, more diffuse way.

While hinting at this, Perry Anderson's important essay on Fukuyama ("The Ends of History") fails to appreciate its surreptitious return to a projected (rather than actual) globalism in the course of an argument about the nation-state. His admiration for Fukuyama's "[in]comparable synthesis—at once so deep in ontological premise and so close to the surface of global politics" includes a questioning of the thesis of potential third-world enrichment that underlies Fukuyama's citing of the Korean and Taiwanese models. Nevertheless, Anderson accepts Fukuyama's terms of formal democracy with an inexplicable ease before registering some rapid reservations in the essay's closing movement.

Perhaps more telling is Anderson's difficulty in challenging the gradual bloating of the definition of "ends" themselves—the very mark, on one level, of his essay's brilliance in that the force of his dismissal of the "superficial" responses to Fukuyama locates itself in describing how this term has been misunderstood by Fukuyama's critics. That is, as Anderson points out, Fukuyama does not pretend to say all conflict is over, but only that it can occur uniquely within the framework of liberal capitalism. By progressively stretching the very meaning of democracy and capitalism (which social-democratic responses to Fukuyama have rightly observed consist of mixed societies) and by tinkering again and again with the actual range and severity of conflicts allowable within Fukuyama's thesis, one is simply left with a world picture very similar to the customary one. In spite of Anderson's impressive synthesis of ambitious historical philosophies over two centuries in three languages, one finds more accurate in the end Eduardo Galeano's casual remarks that Western triumphalism after "the Fall" was "a funeral for the wrong corpse."[19]

In his 1994 book *Diplomacy,* Henry Kissinger also departs from postnation thinking as he cautions against premature celebration following the fall of the Berlin Wall. After gravely citing the short-lived international orders created by the Peace of Westphalia (1648) and the Congress of Vienna (1815), he concludes, conservatively but wisely, that world "order will have to emerge much as it did in past centuries: from a reconciliation and balancing of competing national interests."[20] Kissinger chides America for its wishful thinking, for its "habit of rejecting history" (27) by "extol[ling] the image of a universal man living by universal maxims" (806). Explicitly contradicting the globalism enthusiasts, he reasons that the collapse of the cold-war Other "frees nations to pursue foreign policies based increasingly on their immediate national interest" (833)—a Bismarckian call, typical of Kissinger, not to cloak acts of state in idealistic sentimentalism but rather to make them guiltlessly. What Kissinger might have added is that even in relatively controlled regional formations such as the European Community, despite the Brussels-based commission and other G-12 bodies designed for intervening in what previously had been protected domestic spheres (the European Parliament and Court of Justice), supranationality has not been achieved: union persists as a federated body of preexisting states until such time as the European Monetary Union transforms the region into a quasi nation under German sway, given the strength of the deutsche mark. How can something that is still so obviously here be projected everywhere, in a reflex futurism, as already gone or about to go?

In spite of the more cautious but not altogether dissenting contributions of Fukuyama and Kissinger, postnation theorizing dominates thinking among politicians and cultural analysts. Robert Reich's book *The Work of Nations: Preparing Ourselves for Twenty-First Century Capitalism* takes the rhetoric of national obsolescence to a height unreached elsewhere in pop-political commentary. More than anyone else, he brings the cultural and the civic into a natural union. The book rises to a crescendo where, joining diverse company, Reich concludes: "The cosmopolitan man or woman with a sense of global citizenship is able to maintain appropriate perspective on world problems and possibilities.

Devoid of strong patriotic impulse, the global symbolic analyst is likely to resist zero-sum solutions," interpreting world events more responsibly than "citizens whose frame of reference is narrower."[21] With the effulgence of a self-help manual, Reich counsels laypersons on the facts of economic life, warning them against revitalizing "abstract entities" like "America" (as a coherent and distinct nation) by calling them "a form of vestigial thought" (77). To encourage such idealisms, he warns, only prevents Americans from realizing that prosperity in the future lies with individuals who negotiate their skills and insights directly in the international marketplace. The unskilled production-line and service workers, hoping to cash in their loyalty to an "American" company of choice, will fall by the way.

Much of this tough love does, in fact, sketch out the choices that will likely be available to out-of-work Silicon Valley managers and underpaid high-school teachers in the decades ahead. But the book is in many ways an ultimatum posing as an oracle. Effective when it spells out the "internationalism" of the commodity—often "designed-in-Denmark-manufactured-in-Singapore-from-California-pine"—and also when explaining that the traditional image of the corporation with a single head office and its own factories and labor force is a cartoon, the book nevertheless mythifies what it attempts to demystify. Its account of how, in the 1950s, Americans made a devil's bargain by allowing the large corporations to have their way in exchange for prosperity elides the mechanism through which this bargain was supposedly arrived at, thus displacing responsibility in a specious charge of balance. In a striking rhetorical move, Reich enlists explicitly cultural figures both to enhance the look of this narrow future and to finesse the stakes in bringing it about. Again and again, he stresses that the new economy is not about vulgar "things," not about carnal operatives lifting boxes or turning screws, not about physical buildings on large lots, but about "skills," "insights," "ideas," "speed," "versatility."

The transnational corporation (TNC) for Reich appears at times not to exist at all except in the minds of clever men and women who planned it or hired lawyers to draw up the relevant papers. More to the point are his specific claims about the transnationality of the TNC. Their apocalyptic mood is unmistakable:

> Underneath all is changing. America's core corporation no longer plans production of a large volume of goods and services; it no

> longer owns or invests in a vast array of factories, machinery, laboratories, warehouses, and other tangible assets; it no longer employs armies of production workers and middle-level managers; it no longer serves as gateway to the American middle class. In fact, the core corporation is no longer even American. It is increasingly a facade behind which teams an array of decentralized groups and subgroups continuously contracting similar diffuse working units all over the world (81).

Of course, the factories continue being staffed, the warehouses fill up and empty in a flurry of sweat, the ledgers (now computerized) list numbers representing sales of goods that are, one notices, tangible. That factories and warehouses are now "out-contracted" and that the TNC can benefit from their bottom-line productions without having to suffer the burden of ownership or overlordship—that is really the case, although not Reich's point. He prefers the language of "decentralization," which lies at the heart of the claims of globalism: "[The corporation is] a weblike combination of all of these groups plus some outside investors" (101).

The persistently national character of the transnational corporation itself, of course, has been grossly understated here. Reich's work is less an analysis than a blueprint for a strategy of labor discipline amenable to recent U.S. administrations. There are, first of all, the primary issues of organizational functioning to consider. Global corporations continue to rely heavily on domestic state structures in areas ranging from selective tariffs (which persist in spite of the GATT accords), bans on trade to sensitive political regions, military and financial threats against foreign-trade competitors, the creation of highly policed free-market zones, and extensive subsidizing in the form of technologies acquired and refined through public funding that are later delivered free for industry to exploit (particularly in the aerospace, biotech, and communications fields).[22]

In regard to some of these matters in her ongoing research on what she calls the "global city," Saskia Sassen goes so far as to remark that "there is no global economy *out there*... It is embedded in processes, in institutions, in structures, in markets that are somehow located within national sovereign territories."[23] Second, one finds undiminished the jealous defense of the concept of restrictive citizenship. Without that the domestic differentiations in wage levels, environmental controls, and social and legal protections (however much they are now being harmonized downward) would not be tenable. There is more than an anachronistic carryover at work in the wording of U.S. passport applications, where filers are asked to swear, under penalty of imprisonment, that they have not "made an affirmation or other formal declaration of allegiance to a foreign state; entered or served in the armed forces of a foreign state; accepted or performed the duties of an office, post, or employment under the Government of a foreign state or political subdivision thereof; made a formal renunciation of nationality," and so on.[24] One prophet of capitalist rationality, Peter Drucker, similarly points out that "patriotism is not enough. There has to be citizenship as well . . . To restore citizenship is a central requirement of the post-capitalist polity" (the term "post-capitalist" is his slogan for transnationalist).[25]

If only in much clearer language, Reich's scenario reinvents in classical form the pattern in cultural studies whereby centralization is described enthusiastically as diversification.[26] The process he recounts as a modern evolution of structures and techniques has been, in fact, a process of national governments, infiltrated by hired representatives (often elected ones), unleashing a hasty series of deregulations and privatization schemes. "Restructuring" remains the preferred euphemism for what is actually a series of mergers, recapitalization, leveraged buyouts, and strategic alliances. In this sense, I am not talking about the nation versus some other more international form of "decentered" governing, but only larger, vastly more powerful nations, now with vague accountability and an urge to rationalize difference—what Drucker is frank enough to call the process from "the nation-state to the megastate" (113).

As Europe plods in the direction of Germano-Europa, the United States similarly experiments in the hemisphere of Monroe. The cross-border incursion has, post-perestroika, increasingly been pushed into a much heightened violation of sovereignty by the application of domestic U.S. law over territories outside its boundaries. Characterizing the new capitalism, many point to its export of problems to the third world, which then performs the economic function of receptacle for various metropolitan disasters. Jobs are one of these exports, of course, but the guestworker system and selective immigration laws (or, more commonly, practices in violation of existing laws) are also a less often acknowledged *importation* of jobs as well. America, as I said above, does not only occupy or invade an "elsewhere" for geopolitical advantage. It generalizes "here" in the sense that liberal media analysts mean when writing that now "*where* one is has less to do with what one knows and experiences."[27] Extending its shadow, empire now becomes the elsewhere. This is, perhaps, the principle meaning of decentering.

With implications for the rhetoric of multiculturalism in another context, the appetite for "becoming the Other" (to use a deliberately grandiose phrase) had been theorized by Walter Lippmann already in the years after World War I, when, as D. Steven Blum has noted, he postulated that "there was no longer any neat demarcation between domestic American politics and international affairs . . . the United States, whether in war or at peace, was . . . inextricably tied to the international order, irreversibly enmeshed in the Great Society."[28]

What Kissinger scoldingly called "Wilsonianism"—the view that "America is possessed of an exceptional nature expressed in unrivaled virtue and unrivaled power . . . so confident of its strength and the virtue of its aims that it could envision fighting for its values on a worldwide basis," describes the measures taken since 1989 to enact Woodrow Wilson's dream of universal collective security.[29] But just as Wilson privately understood, the security is less collective than American, as is demonstrated by a series of recent actions in which a vast U.S. legal net has been flung over citizens abroad, acting out a world citizenship repudiated widely outside the United States.

On June 15, 1992, the U.S. Supreme Court handed down a decision claiming that the United States may (in the words of an editorial) "kidnap foreigners in their own countries and, over their countries' protests, drag them here for criminal trial"—a decision stemming from the case of a Mexican gynecologist, Dr. Humberto Alvarez Machaín, whom a federal grand jury thought complicit in the torture and murder of Enrique Camarena Salazar, an employee of the U.S. Drug Enforcement Agency.[30] Alvarez Machaín had been seized by Mexican bounty hunters in Guadalajara who, working under direction of U.S. agents, handed him over to authorities at the border against the furious objections of the Mexican government.

Even more celebrated and more flagrant was the abduction of Manuel Noriega, whose trial brought the following directions from U.S. District Court Judge William Hoeveler to the jury: "The fact that the defendant is Panamanian and not a U.S. citizen is irrelevant, . . . as is the question of whether or not American courts have jurisdiction over a foreign head of state."[31] Distinct as both these cases are from traditional extradition arrangements, they are also becoming the law of the global land. Even before the watershed Supreme Court ruling on the new *ius romanorum* of American legality, the *New York Times* was agitating that the Pan American 103 bombing suspects be "kidnapped abroad, which is permitted under American law in terrorism cases."[32] It has long been the practice of the United States' closest Mideast ally, Israel, to abduct foreign nationals for trial or assassinate them. Examples include that of Sheik Abdul Karim Obeid, a Shiite spiritual leader imprisoned in 1989, and the murders of Palestine Liberation Organization official Kalil al-Wazir in Tunis and Sheik Abbas Musawi, a leader of the Lebanese Party of God.[33]

While debates over the nation have battled their way through questions of origin, definition, and cultural creation, most critics have failed to reconceptualize the debates' terms. One discusses whether or not the idea of the modern nation-state in its many shades originated in Europe; whether the nation amounts to a common language, common history, or contiguous territory; whether or not developments such as print-capitalism and the decline of religion spawned new forms of imagined community. In this still important terrain, and from very different quarters, lie a series of doubts about the continued viability of the state system—entailing, as it did, forms of continued national-popular fealty, legal obligations, and symbolic pride. But the issue of sovereignty makes many of these preferences moot, even though they range from positions of hostility toward the "tyrannies" of states in general, the pathologies of ethnic exclusion, or (quite differently) the restrictively bourgeois character of the national project. The "illusion" of sovereignty has played a central role in left critiques of nationalism, prominently in Hobsbawm, but definitively in Immanuel Wallerstein, where all states are said to serve the interests of a hegemonic world system.

Given the high-handedness of the U.S. legal system in the above cases, forming an opposition to the antinationalist mood is perhaps too easy; it becomes much harder when one enters the arena of the "universal human rights" endorsed by Secretary of State Warren Christopher at the Vienna Conference on Human Rights in June of

1993. This endorsement—despite the widely known unwillingness of the United States to embrace the original Universal Declaration passed by the United Nations General Assembly in 1948 (for its wording guaranteeing employment, health care, and unionization rights)—is connected to the globalization of U.S. domestic law. Thus, shortly after the Vienna Conference, a *New York Times* editorial called for the establishment of a "permanent international criminal court" to try world-class outlaws such as General Mohammed Farah Aidid of Somalia, to weed out "ethnic cleansers" and "terrorists, hijackers, and smugglers of drugs, wildlife and other contraband" since the World Court does not deal with individuals.[34] Were it always a case of State Department evasions, one would not need to pause over the response of progressive journalists who, looking forward to the Vienna Conference, enthusiastically supported moves to make rape a war crime in the aftermath of the Bosnian outrages, and who ambitiously remarked that "U.S. women could really shape things there."[35]

With the very arrogation of the right to be the final arbiter of policy in Iraq, Japan, Chile, South Africa, and elsewhere, U.S. imperialism loosens its hold on the imagination of "America." It is, we have all learned, the European refuge, on the one hand; on the other, an Indian "reservation." It is a land where almost everyone is from somewhere else, mixing together under conditions of relative opportunity; but, at the same time, an anonymous, top-heavy polity that is rapidly assuming an ideological conformity with the help of media saturation. Accounting for these kinds of contradictions is very hard for an official myth to bear—hence the uneasiness of the p.c. wars in deciding how to present the myth to tomorrow's citizenry.

Among its many outcomes, the pattern of U.S. military intervention leads to an influx of immigrants who can survive either by refusing to join America (even as they live and work here) or by identifying with an increasingly incoherent U.S. national mythology. Traditional citizenship remains crucial, since without a stable sense of America the domestic government cannot marshal support for its foreign interventions, collect the tax revenues required to develop its weaponry, or explain poor economic performance on unfair Japanese trade practices, Arab oil cartels, and the "invasion" of illegal aliens stealing "our" jobs. The significance of books like Reich's is that they seek an alternative to these defensive nationalist postures without abandoning the goal of competitive national advantage; and they thus sit comfortably with an older rhetoric of unassimilated foreigners that routinely emanates from the U.S. Senate and various conservative think tanks.

Julia Kristeva as George Orwell: The 1950s in the 1990s

Going to the library shelves today in an effort to trace out the idea of a new world order, one is struck by the concentration of books in two decades—the 1950s and the 1990s. It is with these two decades that the current terms of the nation debate especially belong, for their perspectives (and even their very wording) are immensely similar. Popularized by former president George Bush's memorable speech during the American bombing of Baghdad, the phrase "new world order" had been in use for some time. It achieved a slightly ironic ring as a taunt to the measures taken by the G-77 (or so-called late-developing) countries in the 1970s who had been arguing for a "new international economic order," an argument that itself popularized the term "transnational corporation."

Thus Richard Falk, under the auspices of the Institute for World Order, in 1975 dedicated a lengthy section of his *Study of Future Worlds* to the project of "Designing a New World Order." Like Kissinger's *Diplomacy,* the book takes stock of earlier systems of world order, from the Peace of Westphalia ("constituted *exclusively* by the governments of sovereign states") through the openings provided by the aftermath of world war in the 1920s and the 1950s, when a more properly "transnational" logic began to emerge.[36] In the typically judicious language of the genre, Saul H. Mendlovitz suggests in his 1975 anthology *On the Creation of Just World Order: Preferred Worlds for the 1990s* the deliberate planning for a world, now unfolding, and on schedule, *in* the 1990s! His language preempts a good deal of what arrives as novel in the speculations following the post-*festum* era after 1989: "We are no nearer a world government than we were a century ago, but we are much nearer a world culture. Today, there are more independent governments in the world, fewer empires, and a wider distribution of formal jurisdiction on the international scene . . . Certain tastes in music, films, sports, and magazines have become almost global."[37]

It was the early 1920s when Walter Lippmann fought to reeducate American policy-makers, urging them to prepare themselves for the "complex interdependency of modern mass societies," abjuring their "isolationism, parochialism, and xenophobia" to embrace what he called, simply, "cosmopolitanism." Lippmann thereby suggests the explicit parallels between the term and the extraordinarily massive world-government theorizing among liberal intellectuals at moments of U.S. benevolent ascendency. Such advocacy was not simply "a sociological description of the epoch" but "an ideal of enlightened conduct."[38] According to D. Steven Blum, Lippmann's cosmopolitanism "had to do with habits of mind, with an intellectual outlook or way of seeing the world" that were intimately tied in his own way of thinking, rather than with a chauvinist attempt to extend by force a U.S. jurisdiction. Lippmann believed he was opposing that. Instead his work fit in the lineage of liberal futurology that entailed "cooperation to foster disarmament and to outlaw war internationally" (105). Although eager to foment renewed interest in the lost catholicity of outlook of the American nineteenth century, and although predictably wary of the scourge of collectivism that he believed always led in practice to totalitarianism, Lippmann couched his endorsement of free-market economics in his later writing as an enlightened response to the narrow "containment" thinking of the cold war—an approach he thought immature and overly bellicose.

The dry ironies launched by cultural studies and by critics of salvage ethnography may have merit inasmuch as they expose scholars who are busy tracking a "source" they are convinced they will find, but never do. But these ironies are almost never reversible. This striking mixture of prophecy as the *present*—a sign of longing as much as civilizational confidence—characterized the "world law" sort of cosmopolitanism at a very early date: "The argument which [H. G.] Wells made for a World State in 1901 was, in essence, the same argument which he continued to make for it throughout the rest of his life. The world state is inevitable, he said; indeed, in some respects it already is here . . . National lines and national barriers already show signs of becoming obsolete . . . 'Whatever we may say to the contrary, trade is cosmopolitan and largely defies customs barriers.'"[39] In a pattern of maniacal relapses and recoveries throughout European history, globalism keeps promising to arrive, always seems, in fact, to be just around the corner if not already here, but which continues to find its reality only in an unfulfilled desire against a backdrop of preparations for future war.

If Lippmann looked forward to globalism's cosmopolitan mood, and Richard Falk discovered its measured passions in the form of a revival, the 1950s themselves saw various unblushing proclamations that, in the words of G. A. Borgese's *Foundations of the World Republic* (1953), "the age of nations has ended."[40] Practical attempts to popularize the idea of world government in the days of a fledgling United Nations were the province of journals such as *World Government News,* the "Monthly Report of Progress Toward World Federation," whose articles sought, among other things, to demonstrate the emergence of a single "world culture." The January 1950 issue contains an essay entitled "Myth Information: Writers' Board Show Hits Belief That Sovereignty Can Keep Peace"—an account of an evening of entertainment featuring "a star-studded list of authors and participants headed by Oscar Hammerstein II, as director, and Clifton Fadiman, as master of ceremonies" performing before "probably one of the most powerful groups of opinion-makers ever to come together" in "a swiftly-paced show that must have effectively shattered the myth of national sovereignty in the minds of most of the audience."[41] The clinching moment seems to have been a gag involving Eddie Albert, who, pretending to be an electrician, asked curious questions of Fadiman about world government while fiddling with the microphone.

As with Borgese, however, this particular enthusiasm for a globalism under America's inclusive umbrella was often expressed in the rather different forum of intellectual history—extended reconsiderations of earlier thought on the "universal reasonable standards of government." Such was the project, for example, of Walter Schiffer's book *The Legal Community of Mankind* (1954), which set out from the unity of Western Christendom in the late Middle Ages to trace out the momentous genealogy of the idea through Grotius, Samuel Pufendorf, Christian Wolff, nineteenth-century positivist theories of international law, and more modern ideals of collective security. Concerned, as many in the period were, with the timidities and idealism of the United Nations, Schiffer follows a worn path when he testifies to the impossibility of achieving peace and security "without fundamentally altering the political structures of the world," and in the end he rejects "the United Nations idea" since "the world can become a legal community in the same sense as a state only if it is organized like a state, and . . . the independence of supposedly subordinate groups is an obstacle to the complete legal unity of the world."[42] The full flavor of the eternal return may be captured best, however, by reviewing Edward Meade Earle's instructive collection *Nationalism and Internationalism* (1950), which draws for support on H. G. Wells's campaigning for a world state, glowingly endorses the need for a federated Europe, and rails against "cultural nationalism," the term revived today as an unwanted ethnic particularism. As Jackson Lears has pointed out in a penetrating essay, the era "eerily anticipates our current cultural situation" in which a populist euphoria among literary intellectuals for what the time called "bad taste" was "picked up, popularized, and mass marketed by corporate elites."[43] Pushing the parallelism further, Lears goes on to describe how "a hegemonic historical bloc was formed by the groups often characterized as a 'new class' of salaried managers, administrators, academics, technicians, and journalists—people who manipulated symbols rather than made things." In Irving Howe's words in 1953, writes Lears, "established power and the dominant intellectual tendencies [came] together in harmony" around the issue of consumption (50). Having reached then, as Francis Fukuyama tells us we have reached now, the "final stage of economic growth," people discovered what the "new" anthropology today rediscovers: that (according to W. W. Rostow) "for the intellectual, consumption constituted the last frontier, the last opportunity to exercise some influence on society" (46). Subversive consumption is already present as a concept in the 1950s.

Within literary politics, an extended case for the evils of nationalism in this period could be found in George Orwell, who did much more than simply set the stage for an important feature of postwar literature (including, for Orwell, the literatures of India, not only Europe); he helped direct it, and his argument became paradigmatic. As an ex-Etonian and former member of the colonial police in Burma, he understood that the type of Englishman and Scot who came to Burma did not constitute a "natural aristocracy" who would govern with "justice and mercy," and yet was quick to point out that "the nationalism of defeated peoples is necessarily revengeful and shortsighted."[44] We are used to seeing Orwell's discussion of nationalism as part of his early rejection of the imperial swagger, but not as the formulation of a way of thought that has become widespread in the postwar period. This is perhaps why Bernard Crick in his biography underplays it when he mentions Orwell's distinction between patriotism and nationalism: "It is typical that he makes this distinction, which is of extraordinary importance, briefly and almost in passing, neither elaborating it theoretically nor exploring its implications."[45] But Crick is not accurate here. "Notes on Nationalism," which Orwell wrote for the journal *Polemic* in 1945 (and which Crick revealingly refers to as "one of his finest essays"), is a sustained theoretical attack on the various ideologies that threatened English identity—ideologies that include third-world nationalism, but are not limited to it.

Despite his intense disdain for the brutalities of British imperial practice in essays like "Marrakech" and "Not Counting Niggers," the sudden issue of England's very survival as an independent country during the war led Orwell as a premature globalist of the Kissinger (rather than the Pico Iyer) stripe to respect the defensive bulwark that patriotism could provide, and to want to "deflate vulgar patriotism before stating a case for a kind of common sense, populist patriotism" that could be found even in such unlikely figures as Winston Churchill.[46] He distinguished between "*patriotism,* as love of one's own native land (so that anyone who grows into that love can be a patriot), and *nationalism,* as a claim to natural superiority over others," so that "states must naturally consist of one nation and seek to exclude others."[47] There have been other and more eloquent critics of empire. But Orwell is exceptional here in at least two senses: First, as a director of the BBC's India Section during the war and as a practicing novelist, Orwell wrote authoritatively about the problems of language and literature in the struggle for national-cultural domination. He did so specifically within the context of Anglo-Indian relations on the eve of Indian independence. Second, as a convert to "populist patriotism" following the war, Orwell became an articulate spokesperson for the "English soul," the creation of which he conceived in terms of deliberate cultural practices by conscious "propagandists." These sides of Orwell's work have not been given the attention they deserve.

Orwell made his observations from a position of special authority. As Raymond Williams points out, "theoretically a member of the ruling class, and sharing its insistent myth and ideology of 'England,' he and men like him were in practice on the outer edge of the system." This led to a "double vision, rooted in the simultaneous positions of dominator and dominated."[48] It is the particular contribution of Orwell not only to have defined a prevalent colonial attitude within England when its imperial status was declining but to have argued within England that novels can be instruments in global power conflicts: "The growth, especially during the last few years, of an English-language Indian literature is a strange phenomenon, and it will have its effect on the post-war world, if not on the outcome of the war itself." In this respect, it is significant that he originally intended the famous essay "The Lion and the Unicorn" to be a massive, three-decker novel. According to an autobiographical note in 1940, he mentions planning the work as "a long novel in three parts," probably combining the third-world color of *Burmese Days,* the British stereotypes of *Coming Up for Air,* and the stark international projections of *1984* (not yet written).[49]

Continually remarking on the "invisible chain" and the "emotional unity" that bind together the British nation—particularly in his almost forgotten postwar book *The English People* (1947)—Orwell talks about the "family resemblance" between Cockney, Yorkshireman, and Scot, and about the weakening of British morale caused by the left-wing intelligentsia's lack of patriotism; but he refuses to allow the former corners of the empire a similar exuberance: "The basic fact about nearly all Indian intellectuals is that they don't expect independence, can't imagine it and at heart don't want it."[50] Orwell wrote these words even though he supported the independence of India and even during the war when his efforts were directed through his work at the BBC to keeping India in an English frame of mind—to using (in his own words) "the English language as a weapon of war."[51]

The topic consistently troubles him throughout 1945, not only in the form of disgust with the ugliness of foreign conquest, as in the earlier essays, but theoretically, as he muses over an unmanageably vast truth about the era opened up by the war. The nation is "mystical," he says; it is "a subtle network of compromise"; he doubts whether national cultures can really exist, or whether forty-five million people can be a unit. And as he wonders, he struggles to invent a patriotic sentiment acceptable to the critically minded and to the minorities within Britain. Although he finally resigns his position at the head of the BBC's English-language Indian program in September of 1943, he does so only because he feels no one in India is listening, and because his is a "hopeless task." The most strikingly contradictory conclusions from this way of thinking inevitably followed in the form of his reassertion of English as "the worldwide *lingua franca*"—a very clear and conscious preference for an enlightened linguistic imperialism, shared by the popular "basic English" schemes of I. A. Richards, C. K. Ogden, and Orwell himself.[52]

It is in this light that his attacks on nationalism in 1945 have to be judged. The significant thing here is that Orwell equates the national liberation struggles on the horizon with a broader tendency of political fanaticism and dishonesty, and an accompanying corruption of literary taste. It is in much the same spirit that Friedrich Meinecke in *Cosmopolitanism and the National State* (1963) rejects the idea that the two elements of his title are mutually exclusive. He goes on to show through an analysis of Germany from the Seven Years' War to Bismarck that the "cosmopolitan ideal" emboldened German nationalism, as is suggested by the selfishly altruistic slogan "It is un-German to be merely German."[53]

Punctuated by historical moments of metropolitan opportunity, this scholarly lineage is where much of the current work on globalism came from, although it is often difficult to see it as belonging in this company once shorn of its self-conscious contemporaneity. Julia Kristeva's *Strangers to Ourselves,* for example, cited for its novel insights by Dick Hebdige and other recent critics, recounts the history of the cosmopolitan ideal in Europe in terms not fundamentally different from Schiffer, Borgese, and Lippmann. In an archaeology of European attitudes toward the foreigner that examines the Stoics, Saint Paul, Dante, Thomas More, Montesquieu, Fougeret de Monbron, and others, her book valiantly extols that thread of European thought standing "as a rampart against xenophobia."[54]

Much more artfully written than its predecessors, it positions itself disturbingly in a therapeutics of guilt, now scolding, now cajoling contemporary France (which it addresses quite openly as "we") for its abject prejudice toward its resident immigrants. Led inexorably to Meinecke's question "Might not universality be . . . our own foreignness?"—although she, of course, knows nothing of Meinecke—she also intimates his final point about the national pride lurking beneath these generous abdications of uniqueness that serve ultimately to reassert uniqueness:

> Nowhere is one *more* a foreigner than in France. Having neither the tolerance of Anglo-American Protestants, nor the absorbent ease of Latin Americans, nor the rejecting as well as assimilating curiosity of the Germans or Slavs, the French set a compact social texture and an unbeatable national pride against foreigners . . . And yet, one is nowhere *better* as a foreigner than in France. Since you remain incurably different and unacceptable, you are an object of fascination: one notices you, one talks about you, one hates you or admires you, or both at the same time. But you are not an ordinary, negligible presence, you are not a Mr. or Mrs. nobody. You are a problem, a desire—positive or negative, never neutral (38–9, Kristeva's emphasis).

If much of the literature of the 1950s sought a gritty realism by formulating projects for enforceable legal structures of global government, Kristeva's personalizing of the issue in the decidedly psychoanalytic register of the opening passages is fully developed in the body of the text—"The foreigner lives within us: he is the hidden face of our identity . . . by recognizing him within ourselves, we are spared detesting him in himself" (1).

Given the body of thought she surveys, the book in many ways invites speculation on the sort of state a proper cosmopolitanism might produce, treating as it does Dante on monarchy as well as the arcane legalistic categories of the *alibi natus* in the medieval seigniory. This scholarly review of civic life, especially strong and detailed in its passages on classical Greece, stands distinct from other sorts of examples, typified, for example, by the more polemical showmanship of the Prussian/Dutch member of the Jacobin Club, Baron de Cloots's "universal republic" (91, 108, 161), or the cosmopolitan as "cynic" (her term) or bon vivant—the part played memorably by Fougeret's "lumpen-intelligentsia . . . refusing to belong to phantom kingdoms and ravaged countries" (140). Nevertheless, it is much more the loose ethos of a cosmopolitan outlook as put forth in Montesquieu's *Persian Letters* that wins her heart, and the book culminates in a romantic anarchism typical of recent musings on globality: "From a legal standpoint, the problem of foreigners follows from a classical logic, that of the political group at its peak, the nation state. A logic that, amenable to improvement (democracies) or degeneration (totalitarianism), acknowledges its being based on certain exclusions and, consequently, surrounds itself with other structures, moral and religious, whose absolutist inclinations it nonetheless tempers" (98).

Kristeva's exposure of the self-defeating logic of legal or civic amelioration ushers the reader on to better alternatives to nationalism: namely, the literary heroism exemplified by some of her nascent modernist iconoclasts—the sixteenth-century "visionary missionary" Guillaume Postel, for instance—as well as to the heroism performed by the book itself. More visibly enthusiastic about Montaigne's "universal self" than Thomas Paine's "denationalized" passion for rights and protections, Kristeva has scant feeling for those moments when the force of her learning unearths the cosmopolitan temper in its colonialist mode. Noting with disapproval François Charpentier's 1664 report on French trade with the West Indies that had argued that France had a duty to spread its civilization to barbarian peoples, she can manage little more than worried explanations: "Undoubtedly colonialism was already beginning but the initial intent was a cultural expansion of which all men are worthy. The brutality of colonizers has been emphasized to such an extent that one should point out, on the other hand, this other design of universalistic explorers who, on the contrary, balanced their own culture with the thought of a 'concord of the terrestrial globe'" (124). It is so unthinkable to her that her ethical preference for cultural "concord" might actually *be* the form in which imperialism expresses itself, she refuses to entertain the possibility. What enables the oversight is her starting point. She is firmly and ingenuously, almost atmospherically, *in* France, looking with French eyes (suggested in part by the overwhelmingly French congregation of thinkers she considers), but also *against* nationalism, unbothered by her own investments in a fiercely ethical take on French culture. The dialectical necessity of her position is to reinvigorate France the more she extols not-France in the very mastery of her inclusiveness.

It is significant that Kristeva chooses to hang her investigation on the peg of "cosmopolitanism" rather than on terms like "worldly," "global," or "international." The distinctions among the historical senses of those terms arises again in the sparks created by the collision between two of the Enlightenment thinkers often considered in this genre of intellectual history but not considered by Kristeva: Kant and Marx. In his *Perpetual Peace: A Philosophical Essay* (1795) and his "Idea for a Universal History with Cosmopolitan Intent" (1784), even Kant had been more wary than she of the drift of a good cosmopolitanism into an imperial apologetics. Like Schiffer and Borgese after him and Grotius and Rousseau before him, he sought to promote relations among states so they "may at last come under the public control of law, and thus the human race may be brought nearer the realisation of a cosmopolitan constitution." All the same, he knew about rhetorical sheep's clothing:

> Let us look now, for the sake of comparison, at the inhospitable behaviour of the civilised nations, especially the commercial states of our continent. The injustice which they exhibit on visiting foreign lands and races—this being equivalent in their eyes to conquest—is such as to fill us with horror. America, the negro countries, the Spice Islands, the Cape etc. were, on being discovered, looked upon as countries which belonged to nobody . . . Oppression of the natives followed, famine, insurrection, perfidy and all the rest of the litany of evils which can afflict mankind.[55]

The Greek ideal of perpetual peace, after all, was the search for a constellation into which other nations would be absorbed. The term "cosmopolitan" itself, according to Stephen Toulmin, arrived to the Greek mind following Alexander's conquests, when the Stoic philosophers fused the natural and the social orders into a single unit: "Everything in the world (they argued) manifests in varied ways an 'order' which expresses the Reason that binds all things together. Social and natural regularities alike are aspects of the same overall *cosmos* + *polis—i.e. cosmopolis.* The practical idea that human affairs are influenced by, and proceed in step with heavenly affairs, changes into the philosophical idea, that the structure of Nature reinforces a rational social Order."[56]

As the idealism of cosmopolitanism marched on, Thomas More, Erasmus, and the Abbé de Saint-Pierre all provided schemes of international peace that, under scrutiny, amounted to plans for a European coalition against the Ottoman Empire. Open-eyed about such depressing realpolitik, Kant sought a much more modest analogy: if individuals submitted to law within states, nations could between themselves. Anticipating a popular argument against nationalism voiced today by, among others, Basil Davidson, who favors an "interterritorial federalism" rather than "nation-statism" as such (a view that lies equally at the core of the enormous false consciousness surrounding the likely outcome of the European Economic Union),[57] Kant logically supposed that the analogy would "give rise to a federation of nations which, however, would not have to be a State of nations."[58] Realizing that individual states seek to subject others, Kant set his readers and himself at rest by noting that nature, in the end, prevents them from intermixing given "the differences of language and religion" (156). Of course, Kant could not have foreseen the felicity of a cosmo-American global culture uniting people, like Christianity, at the spiritual level, making that intermixing possible, and for their own good.

Neither could Marx, whose scattered writings on the United States remain some of the least known and most interesting for suggesting that the U.S. role in a future world culture was not exactly unforeseen. Nor was it—for the German communists at least—especially ominous. In what must surely seem today a monstrous irony, the "Address of the International Workingmen's Association" to Abraham Lincoln in 1865 (written by Marx) proclaimed that "the workingmen of Europe felt instinctively that the star-spangled banner carried the destiny of their class."[59] Writing from London to his friend Joseph Weydemeyer in New York on March 25, 1852, Marx began excitedly with the greeting "Best wishes to the new citizen of the world," sensing great things from the country. In a euphoria of technological prophecy, he imagined a time in the future when the trip from London to Calcutta would take only "seven days," and then continued: "The workingmen of Europe feel sure that as the American War of Independence initiated a new era of ascendancy for the middle class, so the American anti-slavery War will do for the working classes. They consider it an earnest of the epoch to come, that it fell to the lot of Abraham Lincoln, the single-minded son of the working class, to lead his country through the matchless struggle for the rescue of an enchained race and the reconstruction of a social world."[60]

This excessive optimism about the forward drift of American history—so reminiscent of José Martí's equally ecstatic writing on personalities from the U.S. nineteenth century—did not lead to the outcome Marx hoped for, as the pathologies of race continued to undermine the labor movement.[61] But Marx's upbeat view does indicate the love affair of Europe—even left Europe—with America prior to the aftermath of World War II. This particular spin on the globalism debate (examined more fully in Chapter 5) lives on vestigially, although unaccompanied by Marxism's traditional distinctions between imperial and socialist internationalism.

Classical Marxism's theories of nationalism and globalism—which date from before the start of the century—are, as Michael Sprinker has vitally pointed out, almost completely ignored in the current literature.[62] In the period from the rise of German social democracy in the late nineteenth century to the outbreak of World War I, it was conventional wisdom that capitalism had become international. As a system of strategic foreign investment as well as a brute colonialist occupation, imperialism meant (according to Karl Radek and others) that capitalism had outgrown the boundaries of the nation-state. It was precisely the dismal scenario then unfolding in Eastern Europe (and now resurgent), as well as the unlooked-for German prowar patriotism of Lenin's comrade-in-arms Karl Kautsky, that pushed Rosa Luxemburg's social-democratic left wing to see nationalism as an ugly impediment—a position based both on an indignant outrage against her party's support for the war and a dispassionate, "scientific" observation about the larger financial dynamics of an emergent global capitalism. In writings of unacknowledged subtlety, Lenin disputed her claims, predicting that a viable nationalism would continue to emerge in "backward" regions (his term for the third world).

In Pyatakov and Trotsky this incipient, and still novel, solidarity with the colonies was even more pronounced. They theorized that independence there was impossible under capitalism, and that to be successful nationalist movements would have to be, paradoxically, socialist and international—the substance of Trotsky's infamous and misunderstood "Theory of Permanent Revolution." It is remarkable, although not surprising, that the relevance of those ideas to decolonization has not been emphasized of late—particularly as they might be applied to the 1950s and 1960s, when the modest reform programs of Julius Nyerere's "Arusha Declaration" in Tanzania and Cheddi Jagan's victorious 1953 election platform in Guyana brought about merciless destabilization schemes and a further realization that "bourgeois democracy" would elude the two countries short of some broader socialist and international solidarities.[63]

Recent projections of the borderless future, by contrast, find comfort in an often hysterical writing on nationalist evils—writing that has all the clumsiness and one-sidedness usually accorded Marxism. It is not hard to find examples in cultural theory: "Universalist nationalism [is] a dangerous and cruel ideology . . . From the position 'all men are my brothers' it comes to follow easily that 'only my brothers are men, all others are animals.'" Or this: "The golden age of a nation-state's memory proved to be neither pure nor just, nor even available, but a utopian dream often turned into a bloody nightmare." Or this: "It is not the twilight of nationalism but its bloody new dawn—[one of] sanguinary disintegration . . . imperial collapse has brought on a crisis in . . . national legitimation . . . nations are forgeries."[64] These quotations are familiar, very easy to find, and symptomatic in evident ways—above all in the choice of crises (that predictable and belabored horror show, the Balkans, for example), in the reference to "imperial collapse" (when empire has gotten stronger), and in the unsurprising inside news that "nations are forgeries" (as if their citizens did not know this and the interesting question were not why, in spite of this, they are believed in).

Once again from the perch of high cultural theory while sharing the outlook of a more generally philistine intellectual culture of the ponderous "poli-sci" commonplace, these angry dismissals echo, say, William Pfaff's *Wrath of Nations: Civilization and the Fury of Nationalism,* which ahistorically laments that after World War II progressive hopes were pinned on nationalism in the form of the independence struggles (in fact, antinationalist rhetoric was at least as intense then as it is now) and concludes—in the customary gesture of the genre—that "the misgovernment of the contemporary African nations is part of a larger tragedy of Africa in the twentieth century, which has nothing to do with the nationalism of modern Europe."[65] Even though it would be hard to find anyone in academic theory who shares Pfaff's endorsements of what he calls, frankly and innocently, "paternalist neocolonialism," the positions on nationalism above are suspiciously similar (158). It would be overstating slightly to say that the logic here is often not far from saying that national struggles are bad since people die in them; or that states are bad since people are thrown in jail; or that nations no longer exist since teenagers in Beijing listen to the rock group Nirvana and the U.S. military has no worthy rival on the horizon.

Because of its proximity both to pressing metropolitan concerns and the larger theories of postnationality, the European Union deserves a closer look here. It is, for one thing, the ideal site for soberly assessing the durability of the nation form in a way that avoids the complicating clichés and prejudices toward the third world. Given its timid and uncertain beginnings as a narrow trade-oriented venture following the Treaty of Rome in 1957 and its sweeping projections today, after Maastricht, for everything from a common currency, indirect European-wide taxation, the end to internal borders, and even a common foreign policy, being for or against the Union may not be the question so much as what to lobby for after joining. Late entries like England quibble with the terms of inclusion, while Finland, Norway, Sweden, and Austria stand in line (although, significantly, Sweden has in two recent referenda declined to enter the Union). That I am talking about a fait accompli does not get past the fact that the European Union in fact (rather than in the humane heart of Jacques Delors, the Union's major architect) is a catastrophe for trade unionists, peace activists, and that rarely mentioned constituency in debates over the Union—nonwhite European immigrants and their fully credentialed descendants. If the only game in town is, according to Perry Anderson, regaining the momentum of a left internationalism in the face of corporate internationalism (and in large part, that may well be so), one has to do so soberly—and the Union may be precisely *not* the way of achieving it.[66] The international contacts and momentum on the side of business are fantastically well advanced—from easy access to jet travel to the polylingualism of elite trainings and private access to fax machines. The structural openings for global labor or solidarity organizations barely exist. To move from national government to the European Parliament is to make accountability a vain hope.

How, anyway, do massively divided local constituencies from the Urals to the Aran Islands, without great technological resources or the habits of travel or cosmopolitan fellow-feeling, build an international anything? It is good to recall in some of these concerns that Denmark in 1991 voted down Maastricht (although that vote has since been reversed); as late as 1993, union continued to be opposed by sizable majorities in Norway and Sweden and smaller majorities in Austria and Finland; as of 1994, Russia similarly remained unconvinced, at times by overwhelming numbers (although the figures fluctuate wildly).[67] When one considers the disenchanted second-class citizen-capitalists of Eastern Europe and their shabby treatment at the hands of hard-nosed European Community negotiators, a weighty opposition to Brussels's dreams for the future reveals its potential—although in the near future only at the level of pressuring their own governments not to take them down the primrose path.

But these justified fears of the corporatization of Europe in the name of "internationalism" only lend support to the conclusion that nationalism is far from over in the minds of the Union's architects. As some have stressed, both the ongoing principles and the actual fine print of the current legislation of the Union allow for an immense array of strictly domestic national decision-making and initiatives. Once again, this important fact has often been obscured, as Perry Anderson notes in his essay "The Light of Europe," where he concludes that "national differences, however relative compared with conditions outside the metropolitan zone, continue to count for those who fall under them." If the left needs to be "global in its conclusions . . . , it has not yet ceased to be national in its conditions."[68] An indication of how often this point is lost is the view of one writer that "national-populist movements are the major mass enemy of progressive ideas in years to come."[69] It is not hard to think of evidence for this case: Zhirinovskii, Buthelezi, Thatcher. In part the comment betrays the weakness of the focus on Europe—still surprisingly resilient at this late date—and the conceptual models it cripplingly provides in a large range of theoretical takes on state formation and national culture. Along with enthusiasm for a left international posture or doubts about preserving current national development strategies in Europe must come a more detailed awareness of the full scale of what is being lost. These developments place labor and the immigrant communities in a desperate position without even mentioning the two- and three-tiered hierarchies inevitably to be created within the European Union with the so-called G-12 countries at the core, late-arriving Scandinavia and middle-Europe next, and the East at their margins.

One cannot approach the issue of union so exclusively within Europe. Proposals for a common foreign policy have in practice already included plans from the U.S. Army War College to coordinate military action in the Middle East, Northern Africa, and Yugoslavia—a sort of NATO model for the new European army. Mariano Aguirre has interestingly argued that a link exists between such "discriminate" military interventions and the emerging pattern of "discriminate" economic ties that establish special relationships between some countries and zones in Europe while leaving the rest to the margins of the global economy.[70] This vision of a meganation Europe as a close ally of the United States would seem to militate against the hopes of Régis Debray in *Les Empires contre l'Europe*. Here, shortly before perestroika, without the benefit of seeing a bastion Soviet Union laid to rest (thus the plural *"Empires"* of his title), he sardonically felt his way toward a spirit of union from a position of indignant vassalage rather distinct from corporate arguments of efficiency. For Debray the so-called East-West conflict was a "cynical metaphor which could not continue except by never being precisely named," since it actually referred to a Soviet-American relationship, with Europe caught in the middle.[71] Borrowing his language from the related North-South conflict—with France situated firmly in the South—he voiced a common European position with uncommon bluntness: "The vital question for Europe and France . . . is today to know if it ought to acquiesce to the imperceptible but progressive American satellitization of the globe and satisfy itself with the modest regional subservience assigned to it by the chief of the West who believes himself to be, not without reason, the President of the United States of America" (22).

In Debray as in other advocates of union, the conceptual apparatus itself cannot go unquestioned. It is now lodged in an unsatisfactory dualism between older state structures and a new federated system of higher efficiency and world economic viability. What now looks like sizable minority opinion agitating within the borders of present nations for "their" government to oppose union might tomorrow look like disparate minorities fighting for sectoral interests against a government in what we now call Belgium. The shift is not merely definitional, however. Admittedly, one could argue that this perspective opens up a way of freely accepting the inevitability of union on the grounds that it would prompt national minorities to perceive their own common interests—that it would facilitate alliances that at the present moment appear "international." But the shift from a federation of states to a "Europa" involves the important matter of a common European *culture*—and propaganda to that effect is now evident in essays stressing the commonality of Greek thought and Roman law:

> Building a European consciousness must, however, extend well beyond the education of our young. It needs to permeate everyday concerns and interests of Community citizens, including sport, cultural pursuits, and television . . . The most important role in promoting a European consciousness is that of the media, with television obviously playing a decisive part . . . Symbols can play an important part [too] . . . The adoption in 1986 of the old Council of Europe flag, consisting of a circle of twelve gold stars on a blue background, has helped. So could increasing use of the European anthem—the prelude to the "Ode to Joy" from Beethoven's Ninth Symphony.[72]

Black and immigrant Europe has a reason to fear the effects of such thinking on domestic civil rights, the policing of Europe's borders, and an emergent common European foreign policy.

Corrupt, homicidal, anachronistic, bourgeois—nationalism only rarely gets a more nuanced look. One of the rare times it does is in James M. Blaut's book *The National Question: Decolonizing the Theory of Nationalism.* Of immediate interest for literary theory is its recollection of a Marxist legacy that departs, finally, from the view that the problem with theory is its "cultural nationalism."[73] Sorting out nationalism's tangled threads—less creatively, perhaps, than recent work on the nation and sexual and racial identities—Blaut restricts himself to a set of homely distinctions. In a slightly impatient rehearsal of the obvious, he reminds the reader of the practical varieties of the national question and, consequently, the fatuousness of approaching "it" as an attitude, urge, or ideology, however much it might be (in Tom Nairn's famous term) "Janus-faced."

For Blaut, much current theory evaluates a primal entity that is in reality many distinct and even antagonistic projects. As opposed to its ideas, the projects of nationalism cover a bewildering range of contradictory efforts. They include efforts by one state to annex another or part of another to its own territory; efforts of a part of a state to secede (as well as efforts to prevent secession); efforts of a colony to win independence (as well as the colonizing power's counterefforts); efforts of nominally independent countries to win sovereignty; and efforts to form states by unifying previously distinct or partly distinct political entities—the version behind the European Union.

Blaut's great contribution in the book is to argue that the "nationalism" of independence movements (he happens to be personally involved with the *independistas* of Puerto Rico), cannot simply be subsumed under, say, Fichtean protofascism or ethnicity-based European secessionist movements. This crucial point—continually obscured in current theory—is supplemented by Blaut's equally minoritarian views on immigration in which he contests the idea that emigrant groups, once they have left the territory of their own nation, stop culturally meshing with it. It is capital that *depends* on ghettoization; "migrant" rather than immigrant workers are by definition foreign, and their illegal entries are encouraged. The "air-bridge" connecting New York with Puerto Rico does not for the most part imply the fluidity evoked in James Clifford's allusion to the Puerto Rican airbus in his "Traveling Cultures" essay—where "everyone is more or less permanently in transit," and the question is not "'where are you from?' but 'where are you between?'"[74] What it implies, rather, is the terribly common situation reflected in the song lyric of Los Tigres del Norte quoted earlier: being so much *of* a place, and so insistent upon clarifying "where I am from," that one tries impossibly to be there even while being—by the tyrannies of work—away.

Managerial Training Manuals: Transnational Nationalism

> To read Max Frisch, Paul Bowles, Gabriel García Márquez, Anton Chekhov, Jane Smiley, Malcolm Lowry, or Norman Mailer is to consume a rich diet of relationships, chance, interconnectedness, muons, songlines, things large within small, small within large, things within things that nonetheless encompass things that are beyond them. Perhaps there are Cartesian novels, hierarchical novels, Newtonian novels. If so, one presumes that they have been quickly—and mercifully—consigned to literature's dustbin . . . If fiction and poetry (drama, opera, etc.) capture

> life better than other cultural media, and who would disagree with that, then why not think of fiction as a model for organization?
>
> —Tom Peters

While making the crucial point that "the current academic preoccupation with 'postcoloniality' and multiculturalism" prevents critics from seeing that colonialism is "even more active now in the form of transnational corporatism," Masao Miyoshi succinctly expresses a view of the transnational corporation that in this sense alone echoes the argument of Robert Reich: "TNC's are not beholden to any nation-states but seek their own interests and profits globally. They represent neither their home countries nor their host nations but simply their own corporate selves."[75]

But to begin with, what sort of coherence can there be in a cultural identity that is a "corporate self"? It is true that TNCs have fewer and fewer restraints placed upon them by national legal structures, and the very nature of how transactions are performed and communications secured precludes their having a single national base. And it is true that stockholders and management are often from many nations, and that many corporations historically from one nation are now run by majority interests from another. Yet it is also true that TNCs continue to have a distinct national character, not only because they depend on the nation-state system for their functioning and the products they sell often rely on perhaps fictional national-cultural associations (kimonos, baseballs, cuckoo clocks), but also because they always approach their own multicultural inner workings and public faces from the perspective of a single—usually American, West European, or Japanese—base culture. In the words of David de Pury, cochairman of Asea Brown Boveri, a Swedish-Swiss electrical-engineering firm, "there are very few multicultural multinationals; the truly global multicultural company does not yet exist." Executives at big American and Japanese firms, according to the *Economist,* think that "globalisation means having occasional board meetings in London or Paris."[76]

It is important not to allegorize vastly reorganized and streamlined business practices or more flexible, more classically "liberal" legislation by ignoring the culture of the day-to-day decision-makers.

While the corporate "body" has its members flung widely over the globe, living corporations such as Viacom, Nestle, or Philips have traditions and lines of succession made up of men and women with a single native language and a fund of memories shared overwhelming with one, rather than another, nation. The Japanese managers who ruffled feathers at Toyota plants in the American South and Midwest—who in fact pushed workers into lawsuits with their haughty attempts to transplant a style of corporate family discipline—did not cease being Japanese upon their arrival. The profits of the TNC networks go to members of various nationalities. But the members acutely share the same interests with, are enjoyed and spent in accord with the aspirations and status seeking of each profiteer's country. That the Chicago executive might choose to send his daughter to the Sorbonne, or the Iranian to Harvard, is not the main point. Those sorts of preferences (like the Japanese's for baseball) are nationally defined. TNCs are not really unencumbered with nationalist baggage; the meaning of the present system is that they are able more readily to manipulate national meanings and constraints for their profit-making purposes. As Reich puts it, if much of the value that so-called American corporations sell comes from other parts of the world, "ever more of the value of what other nations' corporate champions sell around the world is coming from the United States."[77]

Thus, *The World Directory of Multinational Enterprises* lists TNCs with their national affiliations in parentheses at the head of each entry—and the vast majority are from the United States. In the very effort to sort out definitions, the compilers necessarily employ a framework in which national boundaries persist. They define a "multinational" as having "25% or more voting equity in companies in at least three foreign countries . . . , 5% of its consolidated sales attributable to foreign investments . . . , [and] at least $75 million in sales originating in other countries."[78] Even before reading about them, many of these companies contain a lifestyle imagery of distinct national resonance in their very names (Levi Strauss, Revlon, Guinness, Eastman Kodak) while others are names of famous robber barons with their own national historical rumblings (Du Pont, Eli Lilly, Rockwell) or impervious stone-reliefs of ponderous anonymity, whose real line of production is not generally known (Ciba-Geigy, Olin, Burroughs).

As Roy C. Smith and Ingo Walter point out, there is also the matter of business style, which continues to exert influence even in the supposedly diffuse TNC "mobile picket" form: "Differences between corporate restructuring in continental Europe and the Anglo-American experience reflect the fundamental differences that have existed in national financial systems. In much of continental Europe, corporate finance has been heavily bank-oriented."[79] At stake in these demonstrations of the national culture of the transnational, of course, are central problems of theory. While resurgent neoethnic warfare—as much a focus of academic literary studies as of the U.S. State Department—is generally interpreted as marking the decline of the nation-state, it may, in another paradox, alternately be seen as the great cause latched on to in the absence of communism to find a worthy world enemy—not, that is, the proof of such decline but the cynical opportunity for furthering it. Are the ethnic strongmen who personify such clashes—Milosevic in Serbia or Johnson in Liberia—reacting desperately to the TNC's incorporation of power and seizing a bit of real estate before it is too late, or are they, rather, facilitating that incorporation (an option that suggests that the ethnic component of the national struggle is not as decisive as its social character)? Managerially trained to be color-blind and multicultural, the TNCs increasingly operate in the lingua franca of English, implying that in spite of a title that connotes the unprovincial and the nonidiosyncratic, the TNCs may better be seen as spreading a kind of global parochialism.

Viewed up close, the flavor of that multicultural training reveals the cultural centeredness of this bid for freewheeling globality and the degree to which the admittedly gripping prophecies of one-world theorizing are premature. Actual managerial training manuals provide insights into how the corporate elite talks to itself on such matters. Stephen H. Rhinesmith's handbook *A Manager's Guide to Globalization: Six Keys to Success* is an exemplary case within a crowded genre whose best-selling contributions include the work of business gurus such as Peter F. Drucker and Tom Peters, author of the enticingly titled post-Freirian reflection *Liberation Management.*[80]

Aiming his book primarily at "middle and upper managers of large international, multinational, and globalizing companies," Rhinesmith has very little difficulty distinguishing, in a quiet pact with his readers, between "them" and "us." Thus, in setting up the need for his earnest and energetic advice to down-at-heart white-collar decision makers bewildered by a "complex and changing world," he cites data that not only firmly place him as an American talking to Americans about foreigners but indicate the tardiness of present realities in catching up to a nationless theory: "Pre-departure and in-country training has [*sic*] been uneven in cross-cultural issues, language and adjustment support. Recent surveys indicate that while up to 70% of expatriates transferred overseas receive some form of language training, fewer than 50% receive any pre-departure cross-cultural training, but some form of in-country orientation is usually provided by the local expatriate community."[81] Actually, Rhinesmith's aim is to be done with this sort of tail dragging. He strives to break the mold of the older "multinational" that seeks "mini-replicas" of itself abroad—the corporation that plays the game of merely trying to gain "domestic competitive advantage" (47)—in favor of the "very sophisticated" business strategies of truly global organizations like IBM, GE, McDonald's, Philips, Sony, and Unilever, strategies that emphasize process rather than structure, adaptability rather than fixed gain. But on every page, Rhinesmith makes it clear we are not yet there. Indeed, his multicultural primer is informed by the idea that "people never give up their own national backgrounds and differences" (4); one could say that is the rationale for carrying out such training among decision makers who, stepping on toes and failing to draw information from all of its possible sources, allow prejudice to hamstring their efficiency.[82]

Diversity is no less than "the engine that drives the creative energy of the corporation," as Drucker puts it, ". . . because management deals with the integration of people in a common venture, it is deeply embedded in culture . . . Thus one of the basic challenges managers in a developing country face is to find and identify those parts of their own tradition, history, and culture that can be used as management building blocks."[83] Drucker's extended discussion of what he calls the "new pluralisms" weirdly echoes Foucault in its suggestion that "both society and polity in developed countries are now full of power centers that are outside of, and separate from, government"—a development he applauds since each pluralist institution now "serves a specific, limited function [and] this narrow focus is its greatest strength" (78).

Peters's book is a literary masterpiece in its own right, written by someone who could easily make a living at *Rolling Stone* magazine.

With chapter subtitles like "Yo, Fashion!" "Toward Zany," "The 'Soft Stuff,'" and "Soul (Again)," Peters so dresses up Wall Street wisdom that, stylistically, *Liberation Management* is to funds analysis what *Gödel/Escher/Bach* is to the history of science; and for the laptop-carrying commuter by plane, it is a much more punchy read than a market report. But Peters's ambitions go well beyond color. He is a deadly serious philosopher, liberated by metaphor to describe a better, more indirect road to profit than the one obstructed by the unimaginative puritanism of discipline and coercion. Although the utilitarian cast of his supposedly open-ended musings could well be noticed by a skeptical outsider, the pop-psych power of his truths for managers has the sound of a mass movement. At every step of this extraordinarily long book (834 pages), the ethics of the author's message lurk at the philosophical level. Peters's watchwords are "anti-realism," the "permanently ephemeral," "productive anarchy," "slippery intangibles," "the image." And the literary is not simply a mode of expression for him. He writes that in Bruce Chatwin he finds the means of breaking out of "traditional, linear, Cartesian modes of thought."[84]

Similarly, with shades of Reich, Rhinesmith finds himself rising to true joy only in the presence of a philosophy of culture, when he edges over from routine shoptalk of sales figures and employment stats toward an inflated rhetoric of mystified "skills." In a work very much like other books of its type, Rhinesmith tries eagerly to make the mind of the accountant shimmer with the light of the Crocean traditional intellectual—a pronounced feature also of *The New Realities,* in which Drucker is addicted to illustrating his points about the new American business management with copious anecdotes culled from the novels of Henry James, Charles Dickens, Leo Tolstoy, Elias Canetti, and Anthony Trollope. But this, too, is not simply a quirk or a transparent coloring of a lusterless message. "Management," advises Drucker,

> is what tradition used to call a liberal art—"liberal" because it deals with the fundamentals of knowledge, self-knowledge, wisdom, and leadership; "art" because it is practice and application. Managers draw on all the knowledges and insights of the humanities and the social sciences—on psychology and philosophy, on economics and history, on the physical sciences and ethics. But

> they have to focus this knowledge on effectiveness and results—on healing a sick patient, teaching a student, building a bridge, designing and selling a "user-friendly" software program.[85]

It is in passages like these that readers begin to learn about one of the functions of the humanities under American capitalism.

For Rhinesmith, abstraction is positive in this no-nonsense, broadly urbane, corporate culture where "intuition," "adaptability," "complexity," "creativity" and "play" become gloriously reified substitutes for discipline, loyalty, and systematic thinking. Under chapter subheadings that give a scent of this yearning—"Chaos Theory," "Continuous Play," "The People"—Rhinesmith has George Soros ("one of the most successful investors in the history of Wall Street") enter as Hegel in the closing pages, quoting Werner Heisenberg and offering a "theory of reflexivity" in which he warns potential investors not to expect systematic thought to make them wealthy, since "events follow a path that is irreversible and unreplicable" and participants change the very world they observe.[86] With philosophy in the air, Rhinesmith moves on to stress that his emphasis on "culture" is not without credentials. "Remembering my days as a comparative European literature and philosophy major at Wesleyan University," he writes in a discussion of the book's antiphonic structure, "I decided to take a chapter from some of the original thinkers about life and its challenges: the Greek chorus" (xv). And with such heady substance, his study's functionalist attitude toward culture is clearly expressed: "Globalization is ultimately the business of mindset, behavior change. The human factor—as Gorbachev, Yeltsin, and other reform leaders have learned—appears to be the key to change and development . . . The test for managers from throughout the world today is what can be done to radically transform people's thinking and behavior within the context of democratic *ethics*" (xi, Rhinesmith's emphasis).

Indeed. But while showing that IBM-Japan's tax contributions to the Japanese government were three times greater than, say, Fujitsu's, or when noting in passing that for all the talk of identityless corporate frameworks, "ICIPP and Philips all have board-level involvement in all appointments of the top 100 managers," Rhinesmith unwittingly gives evidence for the national identity of the transnationals. While those inside bear witness to the fact that the

TNC does have a narrowly national character, globality-speak is largely about getting the public to a point where it ceases believing they do. Although Rhinesmith addresses himself to the business professional, Reich's more umbrella-like audience the "symbolic analyst," floats in the background, leaving those who make a living with ideas and images little choice but to become either irrelevant or (in Reich's coercive sense) global. Current cultural theory aids this myth of having no choice, of the economy being less about physical toil than about the enticing ephemera of "skills" and "images." But as the discussion above suggests, the cultural theorist does not simply aid corporate public relations in a passive sense. He or she often takes an active part in promoting what the TNCs want the public (inaccurately) to believe.

4

Cosmopolitanism and the Explorer's Eye

> . . . that poverty might find ways of expressing itself as never before.
>
> —Jim Philips

> A human garden a botanical class menagerie with its own avant-garde beatnik color guard.
>
> —Paul Beatty

The term "nostalgia" has been a powerful one in cultural criticism, and its effects have been powerfully mixed. On the one hand, it has clarified the dead-end romanticism that often marks symbolic protests against modernization made by first-generation migrants to the urban centers who are sequestered by race or ethnicity and forced to play the role of equally symbolic civic threat in an ongoing battle with the forces of public order. There are many examples to cite here, and they justify in one sense the term's widespread uses. Lee Tamahori's *Once Were Warriors,* for example—a 1995 film about the Maori in New Zealand, based on a novel by Alan Duff—deserves to be called "nostalgic" in this sense. For while depicting a minority pushed to the slums, beset by chronic alcoholism and domestic abuse in a humiliating life on the permanent dole, the film—without any irony whatsoever—suggests an impossible solution. Its protagonists recover their dignity by relearning Maori war chants before moving to the countryside under the care of richer relatives whose prosperity and calm are implicitly linked to their observance of ancestral traditions.

Fine for them, one might say, but what of the chronic urban pathologies portrayed throughout the rest of the film? A return of this sort hardly speaks to the problems besetting the populations left behind, or to the fact that cultural will is a rather ineffectual response to a brutal process of late-stage colonization with its systems of labor management, law enforcement, and social disarticulation. But while granting the term's appropriateness in such cases, I think it is just as important to say that the charge of nostalgia (for it is never a compliment) has been an effective way of foreclosing alternatives based on a past that is rarely as dead as the term implies—alternatives staked out by those aware of the impossibility of a simple return. Up to this point I have been looking at the way globalism functions in a variety of intellectual forums—how it complements an intellectual ideal and entails versions of a usable past as opposed to nostalgia. But as the genealogy of cosmopolitanism shows, the term itself conceals a continuity with a past its adherents would either prefer to forget or remember in significantly partial ways.

The important theoretical issue of the permeability of borders, for example, has found its proof as much in the personal outlooks and instincts as in the work of the cultural theorists formulating it. Receptions of the culturally strange abroad end up lending themselves to analyses of "underdevelopment" at home, where outlooks first formed in colonial settings arise again in theories of domestic pluralism. The sort of ethnocentrisms found by scholars when they look at the border crossings of earlier, more imperially unself-conscious eras are dutifully exposed and rejected while, at the level of taste and form, the scholars often find their way back to the politics they rejected. This process is lively at the point where postcoloniality and cultural studies meet in American settings. With reference, as above, to the idea that the local is (in Saskia Sassen's words) always global, I want to look at my own neighborhood, New York's Lower East Side, before moving on to cases that suggest alternatives to the kind of work that recent studies on the area have generated. I begin with this example because the Lower East Side is where I have lived since 1978, and my responses are an attempt to rethink characterizations that strike me in many personal ways as strange and inaccurate.[1]

The Sublimation of Poverty: New York's Lower East Side

"The Fine Art of Gentrification," by Rosalyn Deutsch and Cara Gendel Ryan, showed some of the intellectual fascination with New York's Lower East Side that existed throughout the 1980s.[2] In their essay about the displacement of a poor, largely Latino community by a wave of art gallery openings in the early Reagan years, these writers forecast something of the symbolism of New York's traditionally "Red" ghetto as it gave way to a more contemporary story of racial politics, urbanology, and cultural resistance when white professionals and students began moving to the neighborhood in large numbers.[3]

A former settlement of Dutch farmers and Black freedmen in the seventeenth century, and a fashionable district of upscale townhouses in the eighteenth, the Lower East Side began to acquire an air of unrespectability with the arrival of the Irish at the beginning of the nineteenth. Thereafter it played host to a succession of "undesirable" immigrants: Italians, Slavs, East European Jews, and, more recently, Puerto Ricans and Dominicans. Physically set apart from the North-South flow of Manhattan's central avenues in a region jutting sharply out into the East River, the area has traditionally represented an encampment of neglect, overcrowding, and minimal social services. These conditions conspired to make it a favored meeting place of communist intellectuals from Europe between the wars as well as (largely Jewish or immigrant) movements of social reform, exemplified best, perhaps, by the Jacob Riis houses along FDR Drive, now largely Latino in composition.[4]

With the charged imagery of the former Communist Party and trade union rally site of Union Square at its northernmost end, the Ukrainian National Home at its middle (where Leon Trotsky had raised funds for the Russian Social Democrats on a visit in 1916), and the memory of the famous workers novelist Mike Gold in the southern haunts of Chrystie and Rivington Streets, by the mid-1980s the area was giving way to a tale of more confused conflict between a local lumpen proletariat and New York University film students looking for inexpensive housing within walking distance of the school's studios. Meanwhile, in an act of historical memory, the neighborhood continued to be a site of white or middle-class leftist forms of protest art found in such established venues as La Mama, Theater for the New City, the socially conscious performance art of PS-122 and Judith Malina and Julian Beck's Living Theatre.

The studies of gentrification that followed, and in some cases preceded, Deutsch and Ryan's—most notably works by David Harvey and Neil Smith—did the most to carry on these leads, and they placed their emphases on the issue of most interest to community leaders themselves: the control of public land.[5] In its contemporary incarnation, the Lower East Side was a particularly telling example of the process of gentrification, not only because of the symbolic appeal of the area as immigrant warehouse and its attraction to developers by virtue of its proximity to the shopping districts of South Broadway, New York University, and the fashionable off-Broadway venues of the Orpheum and the Public Theater, but because historical neglect had created its own opportunities. It is the one place in southern Manhattan with sizable stretches of abandoned (and, by default, city-owned) buildings and vacant lots whose residents are, in the most "undeveloped" areas, politically vulnerable and often exclusively Spanish-speaking. The housing conflicts there had also received some public notoriety outside the community. The widely publicized riots over the city's physical removal of the homeless from Tompkins Square Park had only given added attention to an area already known from former President Jimmy Carter's Habitat for Humanity project on East Sixth Street—a project visited by Nicaraguan president Daniel Ortega on one of his rare visits to New York at the height of Sandinista rule.

As a former encampment of the homeless, and later as a site of battles between police and demonstrators over the use of public land, Tompkins Square Park is also a rough boundary between, on its east side, a Puerto Rican and Dominican neighborhood (known by the name—a bilingual homonym—"Loisaida"), and the gritty trendiness of Avenue A's cafés, jazz clubs, and bohemian outposts (popularly called "the East Village"). In *Ethnocriticism* Arnold Krupat evokes the Tompkins Square Park riots to criticize "comfortable, middle-class, male, white academics" out of touch with the desperation experienced by the neighborhood's poor.[6] The riots had occurred following a police action ordered by then mayor David Dinkins to clear the park of homeless people who in large numbers had set up permanent settlements. A fence was placed around the square and for over a year the park was officially closed for "renovation." Following its reopening, both the park and a block-deep perimeter surrounding it have been under a police occupation to enforce a midnight curfew in the park itself.

With so much symbolic capital, it is not surprising that the area has found itself represented also in postmodern cultural studies. It did so notably in Dick Hebdige's treatment of a Krzysztof Wodiczko art piece, "Redeeming Witness: In the Tracks of the Homeless Vehicle Project," and to an even greater extent in Celeste Olalquiaga's *Megalopolis: Contemporary Cultural Sensibilities.*[7] By looking at these two examples, I would like to suggest something of the inadequacies of the discourse of globalization in a concrete case, particularly by focusing on a crucial maneuver found in the act of appropriating non-Western, ethnic, or "third-world" art. Turning to this locality is also motivated by my desire to suggest the way nativism might be seen as situatedness in a place rather than location in a place of birth or belonging to a race or a class into which one was simply born—a contrast similar to the one I made in Chapter 2 between positionality and identity.

Implicit in Deutsch and Ryan's study, although not spelled out, is a description of the following process: The enticements of culture as a form of bohemian becoming motivate gentrification. With the decline of interest in a temporarily defunct SoHo art scene, the galleries entered a new and more dangerous space, supplying personnel to fill the cramped stages of such showcase venues for punk and new-wave music as the Pyramid Club and "8bc," whose pathways to the after-hours clubs crossed those of the Puerto Rican heroin dealers pushed farther east toward the river by a police initiative known as Operation Pressure Point. Complaints at the time that this East Village art gallery scene was a pseudo-avant-garde, that its audience was too small or transitory, largely missed the point.[8] It was rather (as Deutsch and Ryan skillfully pointed out) that the "avant-garde" was an ironically appropriate name for a virtual army of middle-class painters, poets, performers, and punks who entered as crusaders, spiritually and for a profit, with emotional and intellectual violence, and whose work might be described best by the phrase "the sublimation of poverty."

Pregentrified communities gave to the denizens of the Village and Midtown a jolt of energy, something to live for in the ennui of café small talk, a vocabulary to copy, a way of moving to mimic. The artist could enter this world of clashing inspirations to recover them, use them, and eventually make something beautiful of them, even as the act of sublimation pushed the "raw material" deeper into poverty and into exile from their tenements and the public parks. The galleries and clubs made the unsettling bad joke of living in underprivileged neighborhoods adventuresome by transforming the distasteful features of gunfights, abandoned lots, and heroin into the content of paintings and songs. What had been talked about generally by Deutsch and Ryan, moreover, was written large in the image of two artists who especially marked the 1980s as sublimated lowlifes: Jean-Michel Basquiat and Keith Haring, both originally part of a grumbling underground graffiti culture who were plucked by impresarios such as Bruno Bischofberger and Henry Geldzahler to enjoy stardom in a more well lit, gallery culture that for the two artists was not altogether propitious.

There is a sense, however, in which this process—supposedly finished after the collapse of the East Village galleries by the late 1980s—is not over. It continues in many ways in the forum of the left-intellectual exposé. Hebdige's "Redeeming Witness"—brilliant as a reading of Wodiczko's political aesthetics, and acutely sensitive to the obscenities of homelessness itself—is marred by the inability to fathom the home that his essay on homelessness discovers. In an extraordinarily layered essay that roves (or in his own, somewhat embarrassing double entendre, "tramps") from intensive documentary evidence and autobiographical witness to expert summaries of the New York art world, Hebdige explores the meaning of Wodiczko's "homeless vehicle"—a parodic art piece shaped like "a streamlined four-wheeled metal object, reminiscent of a high-tech version of a supermarket cart," with "a gleaming metal nose-cone" such that "the whole vehicle bore a strong resemblance to a missile primed and locked on to some invisible target."[9] Ostensibly a vehicle designed with great seriousness to provide mobile shelter for the homeless (the "bed" is located in the cone), the ironically titled *Poliscar* also contained a storage area for possessions, but it was never intended for actual use. Rather, commenting on absurdly technocratic short-term solutions to social problems, it was a "parody of professional design and display codes."

But it is actually the problem of codes in another sense that troubles the essay. Too careful to be found guilty of ignoring the realities of the shantytown dwellers themselves in some overheated exaltation of "art," Hebdige poses these doubts before others can and takes them as his own. In an essay so ingenuously devoted to an avant-garde construct, where the risk is that of converting a potent image into a merely imaginary poverty, he guards himself by making an emphatic point of fingering "art's complicity (as investment and decorative adjunct) in the logic of real estate development" (177) and by pausing to hammer away at the "enduring failure of the capitalist city" (175). The argument with the essay, then, would not be something like elitism, but rather exaggeration of the claims of a self-interrogating avant-garde art-activism carried bodily from Dada into the present, where the deliberate ambiguity of the real and the represented are once again found to be salvational—although this time operating under the crushing finality of the racially and ethnically laden term "nostalgia." As such, it is a lucid confirmation of the cosmopolitan ethos.

As with many of the pieces after Deutsch and Ryan's, the area around Tompkins Square Park features centrally in Hebdige's essay, not because it can in any way be construed as the Lower East Side's most representative sector (although he does not mention this), but because it is a region of intense cross-referencing: the site of the earlier experimental-art-gallery boom, as well as the physical dividing mark between bohemia and barrio, itself marked off by a wall of occupying police. Apart from being the area in which Hebdige lived while researching the essay, it yields a gritty environment into which a café culture has seeped, and therefore a space where Wodiczko's project would be at least theoretically imaginable—a feature that the tawdry workaday intersection of Norfolk and Delancey Streets (only half a dozen blocks south) would decidedly not have. For the sorts of ironies Wodiczko uses and that Hebdige even more emphatically repeats demand the imagined presence of the more recent, and more temporary, residents of the Lower East Side who are likely to be readers of *Art in America*—a population that only the Tompkins Square Park area has in abundance.

But again, the weighted case of focusing on Tompkins Square Park rather than Avenue C—the heart of the Latino neighborhood—is not acknowledged or, perhaps, even noticed. For in making his case for the ideas latent in Wodiczko's marvelous construct, Hebdige insinuates an audience of definite cast, and in the most inadvertent moments—that is, those not ostensibly about audience—he explains himself in terms that involuntarily mark his clientele. Beggars are found everywhere in the city, but of all the areas on the Lower East Side, Tompkins Square Park alone houses a permanent community of artists and intellectuals from white middle-class backgrounds chafing communities whose poverty is historically—even famously—tied to their status as immigrant refuse.

The pluralism of the area is not only overdetermined but consciously theatrical, ranging well beyond the white/Latino nexus to include elaborate divisions within the white communities themselves: relatively well-off Poles and Ukrainians contemptuous of the art scene, weekend cultures of disaffected punks and New Jersey tourists, army-helmeted Hell's Angels bikers, and a significant subculture of avocational anarchists who occasionally turn Tompkins Square Park's southwest corner into a New York version of Hyde Park. As much as the somewhat lower rents, it is the totality of precisely this combination that lured would-be scriptwriters, adjunct professors, and performance artists into the area in the early 1980s. Only against this background is it possible to hear the odd ring of Hebdige's comparison of his own street-trekking through the neighborhood with "wandering around a gallery in a daze" (182), or to bristle as he notes that Wodiczko's project forever alters one's perceptions of homelessness, which "will never seem quite the same again" given "the dreamlike incandescence of [its] after-image" (185)—a comment in which the very desirability of change (replacing the vulgar apprehension of inequality with incandescence) is surprisingly untheorized.

For the issue is not, as I said, one of elitism, but of an exaggerated claim for a kind of art in the very act of countering a complicit aestheticism. As one example of a much larger "cultural politics," this exaggerated claim is, perhaps, the mirror image of the actual cultural services provided by the cosmopolitan intellectual to corporations, as analyzed in the preceding chapter. For, if the machinations of government and landlord are ridiculed in passing blows, they are altogether too obvious for Hebdige to dwell on them; and by far the most important target of his piece is—in a revealing allocation of energies—an unnuanced, unimaginative, and ineffectual (older) style of politics that deals with inequality in too nostalgic a form. In its full light, Wodiczko's accomplishment can be expressed only by what it manages not to be: the "empty rhetoric of moral outrage," the "limited effectiveness of 'radical' polemic," "the archaic nineteenth-century discourses," or simply "another utopian deliverance-machine." The savagery of Hebdige's own language toward the traditional language of social protest is restless and defining. It is the thesis one is left with when the writing is done—beefed up with a panoply of anecdotes. In that way, Hebdige prefers Lautreamont's bricolage to Tatlin's tower, whose heralding of the streamlined city of the socialist future was "as luck would have it, eternally delayed" (175).

The morality play in such juxtapositions pits "abstract, technocratic regimes" against the vivid potentials of the "situationist device," and in so doing stands tough against an overly "ordered" city planning, but without reference to the order—in world-historical terms—that actually produces homelessness. Reasonably unsatisfied with the style of protest in, say, the chant of a demonstration, and opting instead for the semantically richer parodies of the gallery exhibit, Hebdige fails to guard his other flank.[10] His disenchantment with moral outrage is highly reminiscent, after all, of one brand of popular conservative realism. It is, rather, an outrage pushed beyond outrage into sublimation; and that, Hebdige suggests is a harder task, a lonelier one, but one that allows his audience to venture into a complex truth by way of an art whose wry indirections demonstrate an ability to outwit the old nostrums of patchwork reform. Such a creation, he believes, is cleverer even than ideology; one step ahead of the marketeers, it co-opts the co-opters. From the comment that Wodiczko's work makes "the darkness surrounding [gentrification] visible"—a comment that can only be describing its effect on those who do not already know gentrification's violence personally—he inexplicably moves to the essay's starkest exaggeration.

The vehicle is said, romantically, to "work under cover in the labyrinth," where it offers a position "from which nomadic evicts could begin to talk back—to resist or reverse police surveillance, exchange information, and co-ordinate tactics."[11] Community or party organizing is apparently too valuable to dismiss, so it is reinserted metaphorically. At the same time, in a blur, the gallery audience simply becomes the homeless with the latter acting as a symbolic model for the former.

The essay's compensatory pleasures in describing the aesthetic apprehension of the project move Hebdige to a series of brilliant wordplays in which the idea of homelessness is expanded to include the concept of worldliness itself. Excited by the vehicle's capacity to fill dead landscapes with new and unexpected meanings, to create a sense of "familiar unfamiliarity," he takes note of the practice of the poor to collect redeemable cans and calls the vehicle "uncanny." He similarly picks up on the idea of unfamiliarity to call it, after Freud, *unheimlich* (literally, "unhomely"), and this brings him to his intended destination. For elsewhere, Hebdige has spoken of the "sedentary metaphysics of roots," arguing that "we all live in border country."[12] And so that move in which the witness as "tramp"—the scholar-artist Hebdige wandering through Tompkins Square Park—*becomes* in spirit "homeless" is here repeated more forcefully, and a good deal more problematically.

The reader is then brought to the fundamental conflict of the essay, which expresses itself in a telling disjunction. For although Hebdige concedes that the "homing instinct" and *heimat,* or the "nurturing source," are "fundamental ontological forms of security," he poses them as little more than fantasy. By contrast, the trope of the tramp as "outsider-seer types" the "flaneur/nomadic intellectual," although romantic, has "eschatological nuances worthing hanging on to."[13]

Despite differences of mood and outlook, Celeste Olalquiaga's work repeats many of these gestures with a surprising consistency. In spite of her sustained attacks on authenticity in *Megalopolis,* it is significant that early comments on the book refer to hers as a "new situated voice" on the topic of U.S. Latinos, a point underscored by her own careful allusions to her Venezuelan upbringing in the text itself. Apart from being an informative set of case studies and a graceful and concise piece of writing, the book attracted readers because it promised a view of postmodernism from inside a specific ethnicity. As the jacket blurbs attested ("exotic sights," "hybrid forms"), the selling point of the study to the readers' market involved an implicit and powerful argument that Latinization of this topic demanded a Latino voice.

While depending in this way on authenticity in the form of ethnic belonging, Olalquiaga dismisses authenticity in the form of "first-degree kitsch." Wandering along the storefront stalls of New York's East Fourteenth Street (a "frontier-like bazaar . . . of rubber flowers, pelicans made with shells, [and] rubber shoes"), she finds it endowed with a naive belief in the hierarchies between reality and representation. Here cheap, artisanal products "exhibit a certain rawness" that makes them appear handmade, and therefore more honest and authentic.[14] She is struck by how the Fourteenth Street stalls juxtapose tawdry objects for use with works of ridiculous artistic ambition—forms of "gaudy" household decoration that almost attain the status of folklore (felt tapestries of the Last Supper, for example, or 3-D photos of a winking Jesus).

There is a close connection for her, then, between the iconography of Latino Catholicism as practiced in the blocks below Fourteenth Street and the kitsch (whether religious in theme or not) that fills the storefront stalls—an inconography with an authenticity based not on the rawness or simplicity of craftsmanship so much as the "straightforward iconic value" of the religious objects on display (iridescent scapulars, votive candles, Christ mugs, and the like). She laments that both impede the acculturation of first-generation immigrants by way of a defense network of images and artifacts beckoning a home culture that no longer exists—a view that, although wrapped in a story of late-breaking news, actually repeats a standard American view of immigrant arrival, a sort of description as coercion: thus Stephen Sondheim's well-known lyrics from *West Side Story*'s "America" (now three decades old) where Puerto Rican couples on a New York tenement rooftop play the dozens, the men declaring that when they return, "everyone there will give big cheer," and the women responding, "everyone there will have moved here."[15]

With misleading words like "suddenly" and "nowadays," Olalquiaga gives us the impression that Catholic iconography now provides people with a source of "amused fascination" in venues outside of its Latino provenance. But Catholicism has always served this function in Protestant America—either in the form of the antipapist quip or the anticlerical jibe, whose forms range from those of the 1960 Kennedy campaign, through Tom Lehrer's "Vatican Rag," to gags about population control on *Saturday Night Live*.[16] The Christian memorabilia that Olalquiaga finds in discos, head shops, and the punk jewelry outlets of St. Mark's Place is not exclusively Catholic but generically Christian—a comment on the popular consciousness of a country whose origins and present conduct are coercively so. The marketing of such tokens as forms of youth alienation dates from the 1960s (it is not, as she argues, new) and is given its current boost by the skeptical or satanic imagery of heavy-metal and grunge rock videos against a backdrop of a resurgent fundamentalism.

One, again, is reminded of the sheer familiarity in popular culture of the critique of Christian kitsch—say, in *Cool Hand Luke*'s protest against a Southern disciplinary order with a song about the comfort given by a "plastic Jesus" and a "bright Madonna" on a "pedestal of abalone shells." Her link between the kitsch in the street markets of the poor along Fourteenth Street and the Catholic iconography of Latino altars is partial, and for that reason inaccurate—not the least because her conflation of Latino culture with Catholic kitsch overlooks the contributions of Ukrainians and Poles, whose garish wooden Easter eggs and Byzantine icons line the shelves of the stores adjacent to Taras Shevchenko Place, a few blocks west of Tompkins Square Park. Mistaking the Christian for the Catholic, she also ignores the African. The herbs and oils of the botanicas and the bones and photos of the altars are objects that do not translate very well as "bad taste." They are too foreign for her audience. There is no overlap with a culture whose popularity could register the artificial or the sentimental.

For those who do not greet Fourteenth Street with "amused fascination," it is unsettling to hear her speak as confidently as she does. It is very odd that she does not make more of the fact that, Catholic or not, people who shop on Fourteenth Street do not experience the same transgression she feels when viewing "Rita Hayworth towels [and] two-dollar digital watches" alongside "velvet hangings picturing the Last Supper."[17] They are there, naturally, to buy what they can afford. The paradox in all of this, of course, is that she undermines the very claim to ethnic authenticity that permitted her original indulgence in this class conflict through taste. She comes off as someone very foreign to the place she describes, repeatedly making basic errors describing Latino New York—neglecting, for instance, to mention "El Barrio" (Spanish Harlem) as one of the city's "traditional Latino outlets" in an apparently comprehensive list in the introduction, or sizing up the Rivington sculpture garden as being "of—and in—hell" (60)—a revealing misreading of the codes at work in the sculpture itself as well as in the spirit of its local audience, who naturally would find it strange to learn that they lived in "hell." For the sculpture is actually an aggressive act of *desublimation* in the sense that it solders together the consumerist refuse littering abandoned lots, clearing and ordering public space even as it makes itself a monument to the uncaring arrogance of a material production at odds with the interests and ambitions of the people who live there. It displays the exact logic of the intentionally hideous sculptures found as well in the corner garden at Sixth Street and Avenue B and in the courtyard of the popular summer nightclub known as the Gas Station. It is, unlike Wodiczko's *Poliscar,* Lower East Side art par excellence.

What is the culture lived as a resident of the Latino Lower East Side? To answer this is to be brought up against Olalquiaga's powerful restatement of the central theses of the now familiar critique of salvage ethnography: namely, that market media culture cannot simply be reduced to an impoverishment of imagination, nor to an obliteration of native cultures. Rather, the media and the market have stimulated new forms of creativity, allowed culture to reach new publics, and led to a general reinvention of political symbolism that in many ways is salutary from the perspective of social change. What had formerly been called cultural imperialism would then be seen—as Jean Franco accurately summarizes—an "inventive cultural bricolage, whereby imported technologies and fashions are used to create new cultures."[18]

Thus, in a study that ranges across a series of individually perceptive insights into AT&T advertising campaigns, the 1964–1966 New York World's Fair, and the modern science fiction film, Olalquiaga holds her study together with the tightly wound thread of a single, emphatic position on the death of the native. In one characteristic aside, therefore, she concludes that "ethnicity and cultural difference have exchanged their intrinsic values for the more extrinsic ones of market interchangeability: gone are the times when people could make a persuasive claim to a culture of their own, a set of meaningful practices that might be considered the product of unique thought or lifestyle."[19] Or later, that "cultural specificity has given way to the internationalization of its signs" (42), or that the older duality between modernity and tradition has been shattered by "the contemporary globalization of ethnic attributes" (80). It is exactly here that her reflections on authenticity meet the topic of gentrification and the sublimation of poverty and as such the practical outcomes of a cosmopolitan ethnography in urban America.

Striking in these formulations—which are so appealing in their general form—is the disregard they show for Loisaida's ostentatiously "typical" cultural practices, as though Olalquiaga was either unaware of, or wanted desperately to forget or explain away, what anyone living in the area everywhere sees: the *perico ripiao* dances at the Ecuadoran café on Twelfth Street between First and A; the Sunday fiestas along the north end of the East River Parkway, with their gaming tables, portable stands selling *pasteles* and rum, and traveling *disqueros,* whose sound systems blare salsa and merengue for the couples leaving the stands of the nearby baseball lots and soccer fields; the shops selling Santerìa herbs, potions, and votive candles (the botánicas) on Twelfth Street and on Avenue C; the trios that perform on special occasions in the little garden cabanas at Sixth Street and Avenue B; the plentiful murals of protest and commemoration, particularly in La Plaza Cultural on East Tenth Street; the roving *piraguas* vendors; and the Avenue C street market each Sunday afternoon (much more representative than the border country of Fourteenth Street), where in all kinds of weather, all year round, one can buy everything from a used vacuum cleaner to pirate tapes of Tony Vega and Ismael Rivera.[20]

Congealed in public space, these activities only spill from an indoor-outdoor culture of a subtler kind—the street chatter on doorsteps, the gatherings of amateur car mechanics on weekends by the Riis houses, all with their protocols of speech and manner—those, say, of Santiago, in the Dominican Republic, or Bayamón, Puerto Rico. There is nothing picturesque in the area's restaurants or bodegas. This is not, like the French Quarter of New Orleans, merely the memory of a place. In the slow ease of the interactions, the staccato Spanish, a good deal of Santiago and Bayamón remain. To be in the neighborhood east of Avenue B, between Fourteenth and Houston, is to be struck by the surprising degree of its imperviousness to cultural importations—the enormous energy expended in protecting home against an avalanche of assimilationist appeals and threats. At least as interesting here as the story of hybridity (which exists, of course) is the *lack* of it. But that is not the story of the cosmopolitan moment.

On the far side of Tompkins Square Park—closer to the East River and farther from the subway system—sits a massive former high school over whose main entrance hangs a hand-painted sign reading "El Bohio"—a slightly ironic reference (because of the disparity in size and scale) to the small wooden structures, usually one room, typical of the Puerto Rican countryside. The home base of Charas, a community housing and cultural organization founded by Puerto Rican ex–gang members in 1967, El Bohio has for over two decades hosted a series of art exhibits, martial arts and *capoeira* classes, *bomba* and *plena* performances, and alternative film series. Along with the Henry Street Settlement—whose adult literacy classes attract hundreds of students each year—and Miguel Algarín's Nuyorican Poets Café on East Fourth Street, Charas is arguably *the* organized cultural center of the Lower East Side, although it receives no mention in Hebdige or Olalquiaga.[21]

It is in the spaces of El Bohio that troupes from Puerto Rico and, lately, Mexico perform political satire, or that working-class art outside the loop of the gallery system finds public exhibition—as in a very successful 1988 show on Puerto Rican *independentista* painting, echoed somewhat later by nearby Kenkeleba gallery's ironically titled "Puerto Rican Embassy Show." Slightly east and downtown from Charas on Avenue C can be found a one-story-high mural of Bimbo Rivas, one of Charas's most gifted leaders, and the man who coined the term "Loisaida" (a word created to approximate the way "Lower East Side" sounds to Spanish ears). When Rivas died suddenly of a heart attack in 1990, the mural appeared overnight, and for weeks afterward, dried flowers and lit candles covered the sidewalk at the painting's feet. A crowd had earlier gathered to watch Chico paint it in the spray can style on the evening of Bimbo's death.

Charas has not only been important culturally. It has served as a planning center for long-term strategies to secure low-income housing and to turn garbage-strewn lots into community gardens—one of the center's more conspicuous local successes in the 1970s, when it established more than fifty of the gardens. The key, and deliberately old-fashioned, obsession of Charas has been in its own words, "development," and it applies the term to three interrelated aspects of its work: housing, cultural education, and urban environmentalism. According to Daniel Chodorkoff, Charas had always been a kind of fortress of "traditional Puerto Rican culture" standing "against assimilation" while being fully cognizant of the tension existing between these traditional forms and a neo-urban "street sensibility."[22] No "simple-minded return to the *Jivaro* customs," says Chodorkoff, their projects amount rather to a "reemergence of selected aspects of the traditional culture, adapted to the needs of life in a New York City ghetto" (167).

Founded under the cumbersome but appropriately ironic name of "The Real Great Society" in 1967 during Lyndon Johnson's administration, what would later become Charas limped along on government grants and volunteer work while experimenting with community self-sufficiency. Inspired on the one hand by Buckminster Fuller's geodesic domes and on the other by the "Libertarian Education" theories of the British economist Robert Theobald, Charas used both while hammering out alternatives to the "War on Poverty" apparatus and its unsupple plans for urban renewal. With an eco-consciousness at its heart, the organization built voluntary recycling centers as early as the 1970s and launched community farming on tenement rooftops, sketching out plans (only partly realized) to use the portable, elegant, and low-cost geodesic domes for housing, planting, and play—if necessary (and it often was) while on the move. At its height, Charas's "University of the Streets" program attracted more than sixteen hundred students. Its activities now reach from the Environmental Action Coalition, in joint sponsorship with the Avenue C Merchants Association, to various "sweat equity" schemes ("Adopt-a-Building," among others) that promote urban homesteading, to the creation of La Plaza Cultural—a 5,000-square-foot playground and theater space surrounded by murals and executed by the Seven Loaves arts coalition and the City Arts Workshop.

Charas, in other words, is—as much as any organization can be—the organizational face of the Latino Lower East Side; its emphases are those of the active majority of the community. Its work has complemented that of other organizations, such as CUANDO (the Cultural Understanding and Neighborhood Development Organization) and Pueblo Nuevo—a former storefront housing organization that now restores, rehabs, and manages on a scale belying its modest origins. Along with New City Theater and Asian-Americans for Equality, Charas also commissions many of the neighborhood murals that have found their way into discussions of urban resistance and guerrilla art in *New York* magazine feature articles and academic slideshows, as though these phenomena were the fruit of anonymous, underground, or individual outbursts rather than forms of strategic civic counterplanning. And it is not simply a matter of "decentered creative assimilation," as cultural critics often describe youth countercultures. To talk, by way of contrast, with professional muralist María Dominguez is to learn how the earlier warfare among graffiti artists, who went around "tagging" one another's fleeting creations, has given way to a form of local business typified by her successful bid for funding from the Banco Popular to finance her ongoing mural projects, which employ neighborhood children as assistants.[23] The artist behind the murals *To Our Homestead* on Shakespeare Avenue in the Bronx and *Baile Bomba* on Clinton Street in the Lower East Side, Dominguez makes her living teaching at the Guggenheim Learning through the Arts program and at the Henry Street Settlement. There has been a massive gentrification of the area since World War II, she argues, and it will not cease until it reaches Avenue D. But "art can be used as countergentrification as well," she insists, equating her vocation with "wak[ing] up the Puerto Rican mind."

As one of the founders of Charas, Chino García holds similar views. Although unaware of Wodiczko's "Homeless Vehicle Project," he was not hostile to it when told what the artist was trying to do. "A lot of the people involved in the first gentrification were artists," he noted. "The question we had to face is what we were going to get as a culture. One thing we did was organize people to take buildings over and fix them for themselves. When we first moved in [to El Bohio], almost all of Tenth Street and most of Ninth Street was empty . . . If Charas could adopt a building, we could mobilize people not to use the buildings across the street . . . But first you had to have momentum. What was it? It was the cultural movement."[24] On the most basic level, this involved bringing in volunteers to help entertain those working on the renovations; in the longer term, it meant music, dance, and theater programs—among them, workshops on composition and on Puerto Rican traditional percussion at Union High School 22. All were crucial, he says, in "motivating the antigentrification movement."

From García's standpoint, as with Dominguez, the debate around culture has been misconstrued as a theater of images, as a struggle in and through representation. Blunt and obvious though his position might seem, he puts it frankly when he says, "I've already been through the sixties listening to Abbie Hoffman and his nonsense. No, I'm more interested in the mortar and brick." When confronted with Olalquiaga's thesis, García allows that "what she says has some truth, but that truth has a base. It comes from a bunch of different cultures, and they are not necessarily dead. I don't know where she comes from, but in spite of mixing in a place like New York, you got Polish, Puerto Rican, Indian, Jamaican, you know, and they keep the things that are their own. Now, there are those people who want to destroy, consciously or unconsciously, cultures," he adds, "but whatever little bit is left is trying to carry on through the years, you know, even if it is not one hundred percent traditional."

In a few of the local gardens of Charas's domain, actual replicas of the Puerto Rican *bohio* have been built. Dubbing them *casitas* ("little houses"), Olalquiaga brands them as "the most extreme representations of Latino nostalgia." Such nostalgia, she argues, has "kept the majority of Latino communities from developing the parodic distance characteristic of the third type of acculturation."[25] Dominguez and García would respond to this view by saying that this is exactly the point.

GATT Poetics and the Traveling Critic

What arises in contemporary cultural theory in examples like these has its roots in a language and sensibility developed in distinctly literary genres of an earlier period. A mollifying beauty in decay has its own historical momentum. Associated with Baudelaire and the Decadents, beauty in decay is the central trope of late travel narratives from the same period—the late nineteenth and early twentieth century. There is a type of late travel narrative, in other words, that is generically distinct from the early explorers' accounts or later scientific expeditions, and it relies in part for its tropes on writing with no explicit relation to the conquest. It belongs with journalistic reportage.

Written by those who could no longer claim to be encountering unknown regions, these were reports on territories already dismantled and reassembled by Europe in which the task was often to glean from successively more subtle signs and gestures little atavisms of difference. Inherent in the long-term pillage and repression of the subject matter, endurance in poverty was an important subtext. From an emphasis on the "never-before-seen" and the primitive wholeness of the strange, one moved in this later literature to an emphasis on the versatility and invention of the reporters themselves, working variations on now familiar themes. Like the cultures under observation, the forms were in decay, which demanded a greater writerliness to sustain interest, one that moved gradually to that mode of contemporary travel writing made to order by the literary magazines.[26]

One of those favored themes had been a specialized form of colonial sublimation expressed in eroticized tropes of the female body whose goal was typically (and paradoxically) to make a case, via a set of masculinist assumptions, for the attractions of cultural difference rather than for otherness as a mark of civilizational inferiority. This advance, such as it was, forecast in many ways the logic of advertising's contemporary tourist lure in which other lands "invite" the traveler by way of a doubly fortified *hetero*sexual masculinity, where men are offered not only a fund of women assumed to be available, but women of an other, more intriguing, type.[27] With the emphasis not on converting, transforming, or merely recording difference but instead merging with it, cultural attraction could itself under commercial incentives be more confidently cast as a specifically sexual one, although that sublimation of politics was often itself sublimated by a calculated language of aesthetic beauty.

Even if the works of the earliest conquistadors, mariner-pirates, naturalists, and proto-ethnographers had been packaged in popular commercial forms from the time of Marco Polo onward, there existed a later literary traveler's market with none of these scientific pretentions or claims to originality—one that sold its style and attitude in place of the pressing dispatch or the startling discovery.

A variety of sources might be summoned here to show this lineage, although no writer fits this type better than Lafcadio Hearn, born of an Irish father and a Greek mother, whose very name ("Hearn") meant to wander or stray. Coming to the United States in the late 1860s at the age of nineteen, he took his first job at the *Cincinnati Enquirer,* where he made his name as a reporter of murders and other harrowing events. Summarily fired for marrying his mixed-race maid—and thereby running afoul of Ohio law—he relocated in 1877 to New Orleans, where he made his living translating the oriental tales of Pierre Loti and the works of Theophile Gautier, Gustave Flaubert, and Guy de Maupassant. There he remained until 1887, finding a post eventually with the *Daily Item.* But among his many American stays, it is what he himself took to be the Caribbean city of New Orleans that had the greatest effect on his formation. After moving from there briefly to Martinique, where he composed the novel *Youma* and a series of memorable prose sketches, he departed for Japan on assignment with *Harper's* in 1890. He eventually lived out his life in Japan as a professor of English literature at Government College and as an editorialist and collector of Japanese folktales. After an earlier divorce, he there married his second wife, a Japanese woman, and assumed Japanese citizenship in 1895.

Hearn was in this sense a promoter in his time for the dignity and value of foreign cultures—propagandist on their behalf in popular media venues. Although he is best known for his Japanese writings, it is his work on Martinique and on those Caribbean outposts of North America (he considered New Orleans a "tropical" oddity, and wrote a book of "Floridian reveries") that say most about the techniques of the professional traveler. An extraordinarily prolific writer, Hearn leaped from one curiosity to another. Many of his early pieces for the *Daily Item* are extremely short works—he called them "supernatural and occult fiction"—in which colonial erotics are never far from view; a dead girl, the most beautiful he saw in Havana, smiles at him in the last paragraph; three conquistadors raiding a Lima tomb on Good Friday kill each other fighting over a gem that falls like a "carbuncle" from the mummy's wrappings.[28]

Stuffed with Spencerian notions of "hereditary memory" and Jack Londonesque sorties into metempsychosis, the fiction looks forward above all to the civilizational taxonomies of Spengler, although with a much less grandiose, less historical method that operates on hints or on trivial incidents with the object of creating, as Hearn put it, "vivid and mystical visions" more interesting than mere political contests.[29] Apart from the orientalist writing of his early twenties in Cincinnati, which did not really fit this model, his style was rather one of admiring fascination and, in the way of things, a certain envy. From confident sensationalist reports about how Tartars, Arabs, and Indians typically torture their enemies to death, he moves to a lyricism influenced by his training in the French and dependent throughout on vivid portrayals of women's bodies ("There are tropical lilies which are venomous, but they are more beautiful than the frail and icy-white lilies of the North"). In a sketch entitled "Arabian Women," before vigorously defending the "vast and variform" literature of the Arabs, he finds the theme that comes up repeatedly in his American writing: these women have, he argues, "a sensitiveness to beauty—the aesthetic sense . . . an indication of the possession of powers which under favoring circumstances would enable the people possessing it to occupy a high rank in the hierarchy of nations."[30]

In spite of the dated racial typologies, the voyeuristic eroticism of its aesthetics, the embarrassing naturalistic assumptions of social types, the project shares with the contemporary travel narrative of the Hebdige sort the idea of compensation in cultural mixing—one developed, moreover with the aid of a literary sensibility refined in France. Hearn adopts a posture unrecognizable today for its lack of self-consciousness, speaking at one point in *Youma* about the "soft and musical speech of slaves," while going on to note that the matronly housekeeper-counselor type "was a product of slavery largely created by selection: the one creation of slavery perhaps not unworthy of regret—one strange flowering amid all the rank dark growths of that bitter soil."[31]

It is in his writing on Martinique, however, that the boldest compensations can be found, and they are made lively by a sexual titillation whose sincerity could not have been questioned by the readers of *Harper's* magazine, where the book's passages first appeared. If he finds Black faces "uncomely," the "half-breeds" at the same time are a "population fantastic, astonishing . . . It is many-colored, but the general dominant tint is yellow . . . The interblending of all the hues characterizing mulatresse, capresse, griffe, quarteroon, métise, [and] chabine."[32] He is impressed by their "dignified carriage and easy elegance of movement"; the sounds of their naked feet on the pavement make a "whispering sound" (36).

It is not at all the case, of course, that contemporary writing (especially academic writing) on crosscultural negotiations necessarily employs such tropes, but the tropes in modified form continue to be found in high- and middlebrow journalism, now joined to a more explicit rhetoric of international politics. Hearn is not meant here, then, to stand for a limited or exclusive case, but only to serve as an example of a much wider genre of late journalistic reportage—that of Carleton Beals in Mexico, for instance, in his comments on the excessive sensuality of "life in tropical countries."[33] Both writers used the attitudes of earlier exploration narratives even while attempting to modify their excesses with a sophisticated, more knowing and modern sensibility. Then as now, literary cosmopolitanism, as I said earlier, is very much about *not* partaking in the clichés of exoticism; rather, above all, it portrays itself as standing for a literature of the public sphere in which politics, with a large, thematic "P," forms the core of its creative play. With a taste for commitment, it extends that democratization lauded by the market analysts into areas of previous invisibility—only one reason why cosmopolitanism *in* the market in the West has been all but synonymous with the work of resident aliens in an act of conspicuous inclusion. Hearn's erotic aestheticism, at any rate, is not a part of its repertoire, even while his political-aesthetic lure of inclusiveness is.

The sentiments of the travel narratives mastered (and made into a kind of code) by the likes of Hearn have actually repelled authors like Nadine Gordimer, Salman Rushdie, and Ariel Dorfman, whose work has always been situated precisely against Hearn's brand of literary transcendence. Their well-crafted public personae in many ways depend on rejecting aestheticism. Rushdie's own Nicaraguan travel narrative, *The Jaguar Smile,* for example, was more than anything an intervention in a public debate and an exposé of official U.S. mendacities surrounding the war against that country—quite different, in that sense, from Beals's sensationalism. And yet, once real politics became more officially acceptable to high fiction, once "imperialism" could be uttered without clearing one's throat—as one was forced to do, for instance, under the withering invectives of those like Arthur Schlesinger, Jr., who maintained in the early 1960s that "the word 'imperialism,' much like the word 'capitalism,' belonged only 'to the vocabulary of demagoguery, not to the vocabulary of analysis'"—once that happened, more traditional gestures, if more guardedly, found ways to express themselves.[34]

It is always easier to find imperialism in the past than in the present, and the refashioning of the exotic has not often been seen as an unacknowledged continuity with the past. If in late-nineteenth-century travel narrative the sublimation of poverty took the form of a colonial erotics, it changed form later, but without disappearing. Scholars are, of course, well aware of the earlier erotics by now.[35] Even a scholar like Gordon Lewis, who precedes the more recent theoretical focus on such patterns, observes that the seventeenth-century French memoirist, Jean-Baptiste Labat (one of Hearn's sources) looked at Black slaves as "handsome enough to inspire an artist." And Lewis also takes note of Du Tertre, with his sense of "generous pity which almost makes the unfortunate appear to the reader in an illusive . . . ideal aspect."[36]

But these examples of colonial erotics are, of course, no longer common in so crude a form, even as they have given way to a political aesthetic that does not fundamentally alter their function. The contemporary travel journalism of Pico Iyer's book *Falling Off the Map: Some Lonely Places of the World* illustrates this.[37] Here politics, in the proper mode of literary globality, assumes the role of erotics in the aestheticization of underdevelopment, without changing its sublimating function. The "lonely places" he refers to are not simply places. They are countries—states—that either by geographic extremity (Australia and Iceland, for example) or, more typically, a past or present refusenik posture in the world capitalist economy (North Korea, Cuba, Vietnam) are—to revise a phrase from Jane Tompkins—"East of everything."

For to Iyer, "Lonely Places are places that don't fit in; the places that have no seat at our international dinner tables . . . Each makes its own accommodation with wistfulness and eccentricity and simple, institutionalized standoffishness" (4–5). But anxious that his writing not stray from the travel narrative's traditional appeals to sensuality in this dour talk of international relations, he provides the reader with an image that splices the one onto the other: "Vietnam, at present, is a pretty girl with her face pressed up against the window of the dance hall, waiting to be invited in" (5). Thanking in a prefatory note the editors of *Condé Nast Traveler, The New Republic,* and *Time* for helping him (in his words) "dream up" these voyages, Iyer wrote a book that can be seen in part as a warm-up to his first novel, which is at once predictably and surprisingly set in contemporary Cuba.[38]

The many inaccuracies and superficialities of his accounts are not the main point—even if he imagines, for example, that one typically hears "steel bands" in Havana's Lenin Park (steel bands are a Trinidadian, not Cuban, musical form), and that Cuba's only ally is North Korea ("a xenophobic hermit state run by an octogenarian madman"), an assertion that is simply—and trivially—untrue. Rather, it is the way in which a certain discourse of international relations implied by his list of patrons offers, as he says in a typically loaded phrase, "bridges" in place of "[Berlin] walls." An abstract politics of association replaces globality's retort to identity politics. To contest the retort is to risk an intemperate assault reserved for all who fail to accept the association of the approved global citizenry: "Before long, they have come to resemble the woman with a hundred cats in a house she's never cleaned . . . They grow three-inch nails, and never wash, and talk with the artificial loudness of someone always talking to himself."[39]

The almost audible growl of these images suggests the value of the stakes in nonassociation, although an air of politeness is then called forth to avoid spoiling the mood of cooperation. In a talk delivered at the Institute of World Culture, Iyer therefore argues somewhat inconsistently that difference is good. It is there to "enrich our lives"; the "charms of foreignness" alone rehabilitate what is less charming in these places' political differences: "the featureless gray blocks of Marxism have simply been set down, incongruously, on a sunny, swelling, multicolored quilt, so that much of the sauce and sensuality of the louche Havana of old keeps peeping through" (59).[40] On Vietnam, while ignoring what many Vietnamese are only too willing to state as the signal achievement of their country's recent war with the United States—namely, national unification—he brings erotics even more forcefully to his politics in talking, anachronistically, about the differences between a North and a South Vietnam that no longer exist: "the two aspects of the country are as different as past and future, silence and frenzy, maiden aunt and bargirl—as different, ultimately, as Beijing and Hong Kong."[41]

A properly cosmopolitan literature *about* third-world reception merges here with late travel narrative as a sublimation of poverty. The merging is by no means implicit, either. Iyer openly invokes "Salman Rushdie, the apostle of a new internationalism" singing "the possibilities of a fresh, cross-pollinating world," while diminishing Rushdie's more nuanced treatment of global politics as well as his care in preserving the sense of a real and interventionary imperialism. The necessary precondition of Iyer's sort of writing is the assertion that the truth of the "global village" is simply unquestionable. It requires no argument by virtue of the untraceable—although compelling—evidence of American mass culture. Thus, the fears and fantasies of a villager in Mali are like those of Americans because that villager "is moved by Michael Jackson rhythms and transfixed by *Dallas* archetypes," even if that real heterogeneity is often veiled by surface similarities. Culturally speaking, he argues, people read differently. *Rambo III* for them is "a political piece and not an entertainment." For them, "McDonald's may be a status symbol, as surely as that quaint Central Asian restaurant is for us" (15).

But it is the mark of such a piece that even in a moment of concession, Iyer muscles forth a set of views designed to pass by virtue of an authoritative referencing of long-standing literary tropes and contemporary novelists (Rushdie) of greater stature, clearer thinking, and less philistine intentions. Even if one did not question whether a McDonald's in Mali could be so confidently grouped with one in Prague or Warsaw (is the South simply the East?), or whether it is accurate to speak of McDonald's as a "status symbol" in any sense remotely analogous to U.S. ethnic dining—what strikes one here is the ease with which Iyer gives back what he had earlier taken away. The questionable reasoning appears almost irrelevant in the presence of an imputed globalism, to which he gives the attractive name "family responsibilities." He consistently slides between different referents for the words "our" and "we." If the "global village" is uncontestable, then the cosmopolitan continuum logically makes self-definition and local autonomy artificial. Far from taking ethnic conflicts as a sign of resistance to the very enforced globalism he is busy constructing, Iyer sees them rather as a symptom of the fact that there are no decisive differences. Now all in the family, "*we* are obliged to create and consolidate our own new and artificial ones" (13). But from sentence to sentence, this global "we" gives way to a particularist North American and European one: immigration enriches "our" lives. The collectivity in both cases cannot be the same, although the piece thrives on our willingness, through style or allusion, to accept them as such.

The highly publicized literary writing from Eastern Europe in the wake of perestroika shares a great deal with this method and is already present in Iyer's references. In that mental space of the politico-exotic enjoyed by third-world writing in the metropolitan book markets, the literatures of Eastern Europe found a similar pride of place, spawning new publishers' series of high production quality and yielding predictions of literary renaissance. If never quite accorded full membership in the West, Eastern Europe provided examples of the creative energies, undeveloped economies, and escape from Soviet influence lingering behind portraits of the postcolonial world, although without the civilizational and racial alienation felt by many metropolitan critics toward the latter.[42]

Bridges between the two regions had already been forged by journals like *Granta* in Britain and its counterpart, *Grand Street,* in the United States, which juxtapose writing from India, Africa and Eastern Europe under the same marquee.[43] The energetic and acerbic raconteur of foreign places Ryszard Kapuscinski appears often in these pages as a physical embodiment of the ideological marriage, and his writerly type (like Iyer to Hearn) has its predecessors. In the diaries of the great Polish novelist Witold Gombrowicz, who left Poland for Argentina in 1939 and remained there for most of his life, there can be found a set of commentaries brilliantly suggestive of the present conjuncture.[44]

As so many before him, Gombrowicz found in America a naïveté: provincialism, a "new childish whine" as distinct from European "oldness, world-weariness, and ill-humor." And one is not very far here from the pleasures of the poor. Argentina, he discovers, is "full of miracles and magic"; it has no Notre Dame, but does have "graceful bodies" that are "low earthy."

And yet Gombrowicz is after much more austerely mental game. He consciously reverses the process of third-world authorial flight to the big cities, where a certain kind of training can occur, or a certain kind of sensibility be indulged, in a modernist gesture reminiscent of Conrad's Kurtz.[45] That is, he travels to Argentina (he says) to escape the sense of "we"—and it is this point about the extraterritoriality of the writer that obsessively recurs in the pages of the diaries. The division into continents and nationalities is a "lousy schema imposed on art." There is nothing, he insists, special about him. He is just one of the many "deprived of even a longing for the past" then coming to the pampa. Although he usually avoided it, he sometimes succumbed to presenting himself as an "escritor polaco." But as a Pole, if he wanted to enter high culture as someone who mattered, he could not "hide my immaturity, but [had] to admit it; and with this admission to break away from it . . . [O]ne has to demonstrate that *everyone is like us,* that is, one has to reveal the complete inadequacy of the civilized man in the face of the culture which is too much for him" (emphasis added).[46] Disdained by Western Europe, he sets out logically to position himself among others who have been as well.

As a contemporary continuation of this tradition, it was a case of some symbolic significance, then, when the Czech head of state and celebrated dramatist Vaclav Havel delivered a speech at Philadelphia's Independence Hall on "self-transcendence" and "our common global destiny" as recipient of that city's prestigious Liberty Medal.[47] Accompanying the reprinted speech in the *New York Times* was a large caricature of a man faintly resembling Havel himself. In the drawing, the man's head is in the shape of a pyramid whose apex is severed from the base and hovers above the whole—an image, in other words, evoking the Great Seal on the American dollar bill and its well-known slogan "E pluribus unum." The speech offered a particularly clear example of how the literary intellectual—as symbolically resonant for being political (in Eastern Europe) as for being "literary"—is enlisted on behalf of a cosmopolitanism whose themes are now familiar in a variety of discourses from anthropology to finance in an interchangeable, and furiously functional, rhetoric at the service of Western social and economic needs.

Havel finds the present to be a transitional period of history where "cultures distant in time and space are discovered or rediscovered. New meaning is gradually born from the encounter, or the intersection, of many different elements." With the solemnity of the poet's vision, he urges his readers to see that "we are not here alone, nor for ourselves alone." In a display of the catholicity of his own interests and erudition, he summons on his behalf such mind-broadening recent theories of science as the "anthropic cosmological principle" and the "Gaia hypothesis" to make the case that ecology too has found all humankind to be "part of a greater whole . . . We are an integral part of higher, mysterious entities against whom it is not advisable to blaspheme."

And yet all of this wonder at the "miracle" of the "mixing and blending of cultures" appears at once religious and strangely utilitarian. Seeking a map through the thicket of values created by the cultural mixing of this period of transition, Havel is able to locate two stable points for his compass: democracy and science; and he finds both in the United States—"the first civilization that . . . binds together all societies, submitting them to a common global destiny." While this dyad is hardly unexpected in a talk delivered at Liberty Hall, it is rather the rhetoric of insistent, even threatening double entendre that is of interest here. Rather than peoples or polities, science itself becomes a "civilization"; and because it has as such no flag or face, the word "submitting" can be used without fear of offending anyone's sense of jurisdiction. Even so, under the caring hand of the poet, science finds its way (through the Gaia hypothesis) to God, and by way of several passages extolling the "miracle of Being," Havel declares that human rights in the new world order depend on our submitting "to the authority of the universal order and of creation"—a view that sounds suspiciously like the authority that believes itself to have allowed science and democracy to span the globe—that is, the authority of his hosts in Philadelphia.

Despite the dragging influence of these tropes—or perhaps because of them—attempts have arisen to explode their conventions from within. Eyeing the social costs of a double-edged literary knowledge, efforts to dismantle the politico-erotic travel narrative have led to a genre designed to cancel its meanings: the travel parody. The two cases I examine below are self-consciously poised against the brand of cosmopolitan sensibility I have been analyzing. But in one of those cases, at least, the distaste for a threatening or self-congratulatory worldliness seemed to have grown out of an earlier personal familiarity with it. In *La Vuelta el día en ochenta mundos (Around the Day in Eighty Worlds)* (1967), the Argentinean novelist Julio Cortázar regarded travel as both explicitly and theatrically a metaphor of an extraordinary mental inventiveness.[48] Similarly, more than any in the long train of Latin American writers and painters who preceded him in Paris, Cortázar captured in the novel *Rayuela (Hopscotch)* the seductive national anonymity a "third-world" author could attain in European high culture.[49]

Remarkably, however, it is exactly when "third-world literature" becomes an issue in the reviewers' pages that Cortázar leaves those exquisite entertainments and moves on to what defines his final years: work of deliberate testimony, and undistilled attempts to set the political record straight. In *Nicaragua, tan violentamente dulce* (Nicaragua, so violently sweet), he flees from these meditations on the willful eclecticism of the artist comfortably abroad and by avocation (rather than nation) "foreign." As an account of his experiences in Nicaragua in the last years of his life, the book takes a most unmodernist stand on the real by way of an appeal for writers to "live with the people of a country . . . [to] enter into the rhythms of many different lives." His argument on behalf of national realities focuses on the matter of conversion, where he is struck by the "lack of any sense of flesh-and-blood reality, of a visceral day-to-day existence" in most Western reporting, which typically falls into "the old

European habit of reducing everything . . . to an almost geometrical analysis of positive and negative facts"—the other side, perhaps, of the politico-erotic travelogue.[50]

To imagine Nicaragua, Cortázar finds he must talk about Cuba, and on that matter he explicitly parts company with some of the "boom" novelists in passages that were excised from the English-language version of his book. While the English translation is careful to retain the very moments in which Cortázar reproduces the formulaic ironies of hybridity (as when he remarks, for example, on a sign he saw on a "humble store" in Havana's Oriental barrios: "'Dimitri's Barbershop, Unisex Technique'"), it deletes the entire first chapter, provocatively titled "Marginal Notes on a Rereading of 1984," where he addresses himself to the views of Octavio Paz and Mario Vargas Llosa. Here is an example of what was cut from the English-language version of his book:

> Personally, I share many of their misgivings [about Cuba and Nicaragua], with the difference that in my case I have them in order to defend an idea of the future that they appear to imagine only as a meliorating present, without accepting that things must be changed at the root . . . No ideological argument justifies plotting the whole over the parts—the global notion of the "people" over the individual (but only to the extent that the notion of the individual does not wipe out that of the people, as in the case of that type of critique, always egocentric, that speaks of Sakharov and Padilla) . . . In the face of the cult of sadism through which the enemy often persists in turning children into little murderers awaiting their hour, the ethical and political orientation of socialism is the best and most legitimate portrait of life.[51]

It was, I would argue, precisely as a result of his experiences in Nicaragua that Cortázar came to produce his send-up of the explorer and the rootless wanderer in his mock travel diary *Los Autonautas de la cosmopista: Un viaje atemporal París–Marsella* (The autonauts of the global highway: An atemporal journey from Paris to Marseilles), an account of a car journey from Paris to Marseille in which he and a companion trundled out a typewriter at the highway rest stops in order to keep a running record of their "adventure."[52]

Although the treatment of the travel genre as one of imperial knowledge-production has been very lively in criticism in the last decades, the accompanying—if somewhat later—genre of the travel parody as a form of anti-imperialist critique has not been as quickly appreciated. Right there from within the ranks of the travel narrative's intended audience has come a politics of prank, exposing some of the literary devices that have eased the task of domination no less than the novels of Jane Austen and Anthony Trollope did in theirs. Cortázar's book can be seen as part of an antigenre whose representatives in recent years have included Margaret Randall's *Albuquerque: Coming Back to the U.S.A.*, Richard Rodriguez's *Days of Obligation: An Argument with My Mexican Father*, and others, in which the travel narrative is seen not so much as a specific genre as the dominant mode of address in a setting of suspicious globalization.[53] In other words, what is complicit in Hebdige, Olalquiaga, and Iyer is, for Cortázar, the very object of critique.

Cortázar's book is "atemporal" because it is written (tongue-in-cheek) in 1982 in the toadying, florid manner of an eighteenth-century supplicant to his benefactor. It relates events of unremarkable modern experience—too common to be interesting, too contemporary to be exotic—but (as the work progresses) more and more appearing to need explanation by the very fact that the obvious is, after all, very strange. Composed over the course of a month, the book is a deliberate hybrid of the eighteenth-century novel and the explorer's missive, as though the artificiality of their own project in France demanded the outward shell of historical fiction.

It begins with the traditional letter of dedication to the patron (here, the Director of the Society of Highways), moves on to a weighty "prolegomenon," and then passes on to the journey itself in carefully dated entries at two rest stops per day, for thirty-two days, which form the body of the text. The parts are divided under headings that use the familiar phrasings of a Tobias Smollett or a Jonathan Swift in a language whose archaism is attempting to show that the pretensions of the past still continue in the present. Even as the work casts a winking eye at the pomposity of the explorer's "scientific" collection of foreign data, it throws an ironic glance at the here and now in which that past continues to live. Thus, one section opens under the italicized heading *"Where the patient reader will join in the presentation of the protagonists, and will come to know its characteristics and most notable traits"*; and later, *"On the origins of the expedition: its genesis, slow elaboration, and sinuous ripening, and about how the pale reader will see not only that scientific reflection tends to transform the vision of the world in which it is practiced, but will become aware of the obstacles that are found in the researcher's path."* This is a section, it should be remembered, about sitting at a picnic table on the edge of a parking lot, eating *pommes frites,* and watching Renaults idling as their passengers duck into a nearby brick building to relieve themselves: *"Where the reader will follow our heroes along a road that jointly shares day-journeys filled with sunshine, proofs of the existence of human generosity, and also latent threats."*

Not a mere trip, Cortázar's journey must always be referred to, with calculated pretentiousness, as an "expedition." Ranging freely across the related discourses of the naturalist (he pauses to remark on the "entomological fauna of rest stops and other ecological considerations"), ethnographer (he takes notes on one rest stop's "indigenous customs"), and the specialist in military science, historical romance, and utopian prophecy (as revealed in his inspired "vision of Parkinglandia"), Cortázar never loses sight of the underlying philosophy of them all—indeed, of every travel account: "Our valiant expeditionists will discover that at times it is advantageous not to be from anywhere." The humor depends in part on the persistence and elaboration of the joke—that he and his wife (Carol Dunlop) would put themselves through an actual car trip rather than just invent one; that they would compose a three-hundred-page narrative without once dropping the language of literary play, recording faithfully the details of an unmistakable tedium that is everywhere enlivened by voguing on the explorer's genre.

A similar voguing, at least as clever as Cortázar's, comes from a writer of very different stripe but with similar literary aim. Only now the strategy is not to place Europe in the role of ethnographic object, but to stage its pernicious exoticism by savaging its most contemporary and most practical literary form: the tourist manual. The writer is Subcomandante Marcos, one of the leaders of the Zapatistas insurrection in southern Mexico. Following interviews with him in *Vanity Fair,* the *New York Times,* and elsewhere, and after efforts by some sectors of the Mexican press to paint him as an outsider, readers who followed the exploits of Mexico's Zapatistas (if they knew nothing else) knew that Marcos had a flair for phrasing and was disarmingly witty. The charge of being an outsider was, in fact, closely related to the guarded praise—part of a broader effort by enemies of the Zapatistas to weaken the authority of Marcos as an authentic representative of the Tzotsil, Tzeltal, Chole, Zoque, and Tojolabal peoples—those who formed the rebel cadre that took San Cristóbal, Altamirano, Ocosingo, and other Chiapan cities on January 1, 1994, where they read a now famous declaration of war against the Mexican government for its endorsement of NAFTA.[54]

But while a variety of mainstream feature articles have succeeded in giving a portrait of Marcos the iconoclast and moralist, the actual writing of his dispatches from the Lacandon have not been widely read outside Mexico. It has not been appreciated, I think, how bitter and how funny that writing is: the most unapologetically passionate, self-mocking, and uncynical acts of counter-postmodernity available anywhere. Speaking directly to the assumptions of the cosmopolitan moment, whose theoretical distrust of "speaking for others" or of merely inverting power dynamics by replacing one set of rulers for another, Marcos systematically addresses himself to the problems of leadership of people's movements by intellectuals, of the category "nostalgia," and of the viability of the term "indigenous." All are bound up tightly in a literature that is also counterliterature.[55]

Marcos in this sense represents a strain of anticolonial literature most invisible in third-world reception, as much for the quality of its art as for the conditions of its composition. Many of his pieces were written in the cold of the Chiapas winter on a hard wooden desk as military search helicopters hovered overhead. Conjunctural and ad hoc, alternating between programmatic statements and autobiography, between official demands and personal vignettes, they cast their light on the act of writing itself, bringing literature into an expansive humanism rare in recent metropolitan literatures. The dispatches from the Lacandon are nevertheless wildly varied in texture, returning more than once to simple storytelling: parables about a beetle who steals tobacco from the "sup's" pipe and counsels him on the ways of neoliberalism (15); deliberate adaptations of the Popol Vuh about a *compa* named Old Antonio who passes on a tale about the "people of gold" and the "people of corn" (17).

By contrast, the initial dispatch to the local Mexican newspaper, *La Jornada,* at the outbreak of hostilities was entitled "Chiapas: The Southeast in Two Winds, a Storm and a Prophecy"—the first piece of direct communication between the rebels and the outside world. It seems significant that this first communication was an extended mock travel narrative, with much of the same dry humor as Cortázar's (whose name actually comes up in one of Marcos's letters to the press on May 28). In the crucial moment of lifting the veil for the first time on the mind of their movement, the EZLN chose to address itself to the shibboleth of globalism and the problem of cosmopolitanism—themes that (except for the word "cosmopolitan" itself) come up repeatedly in their communiqués of 1994. The inaugural outreach to Mexican civil society is therefore not a dry set of accusations or demands, but a sort of short-story-cum-pamphlet that parodies a tourist brochure. "Welcome! You Have Arrived in the Poorest State of the Country: Chiapas" reads one subheading, introducing statistical data on the region in a mock-jaunty tone. Told in the intentionally corny direct-address format of a brochure, the essay gives the reader driving directions with all the forced cheeriness of a tour group guide: "Continue driving," we are enjoined, or, "No, you better not go down this third-rate road;" as we pass a corrugated shack passing for a school, it cautions, "Don't get close, don't look inside, don't see the four groups of children brimming with worms and lice."

After meandering, we finally reach our destination: "Welcome to San Cristóbal de las Casas, a 'Colonial City' say the *mestizos,* though the majority of the people are indigenous . . . Did you add it up? Yes, that's right. While there are seven hotel rooms for every thousand tourists, there are .3 hospital beds for every thousand Chiapans. Fine, forget the figures and move on, take care to avoid the three lines of cops in camouflage berets trotting along the side of the road" (4).

Like Cortázar, Marcos establishes a continuity between the genre of the explorer's account and the related genre of historical romance. While implicating this literary machinery of Western knowledge, he repeatedly demonstrates his ability to carry it off, thus making the piece a self-conscious act of abnegation rather than a sullen or defensive act of resentment. In the form of italicized chapter precis, the reader gets a sense of Marcos's literary loves when he uses this culpable genre now purged by parody:

> The one from above tells how the almighty government was so touched by the misery of the indigenous people of Chiapas, that it gave them hotels, jails, a military barracks, and a military airport. And also tells how the beast feeds on the blood of the people, and

> other unhappy and unfortunate events. [And later, under Chapter 3] Tells how the viceroy had a brilliant idea and put it into practice, and also tells how the empire decreed the death of socialism, and enthusiastically took on the job of broadcasting that good news, bringing joy to the powerful, consolation to the fainthearted, and indifference from everybody else. It also tells how the people say that Zapata has not died. And other upsetting facts.

One gets a hint here, but only a hint, of Marcos's brand of humor—humor coming, after all, from a hunted guerrilla being tracked by a well-armed military force. As the work of an *anonymous* representative of a movement whose job throughout 1994 was to act as a public liaison under the discipline of the EZLN, this piece is a remarkable kind of public relations effort given that its effects would help determine whether or not the insurgents physically survived.

For here is a particularly tense and textured meeting of the postmodern and the old left in which the latter exhibits what is usually thought only to exist in the former: versatility, humor, self-criticism, novelty. Only the flavor of Marcos's writing as a whole drives this observation home, however, and it does so contextually as much as textually: an intellectual and satirist who smokes a pipe and who comes from the metropolis (Mexico City), but who lives in Chiapas and submits himself to the command of the people living there: "I have the honor to have as my superiors the best men and women of the various ethnic groups . . . I have lived with them for over ten years and I am proud to obey and serve them with my arms and soul . . . [For] he who commands, obeys if he is a true leader, and he who obeys, commands through the common heart of true men and women" (8, 12).

These sentiments would be much easier to expose as naive—or "literary" in the bad sense—if it were not for Marcos's constant admonitions to appreciate that he knows the score. Clearly believing in guerrilla warfare, he knows a good deal about the society of the spectacle as well. Almost a third of the communiqués are efforts to cajole the press or to salve its ego, and like any thinking intellectual of the information age, he knows that the media are where the war must be won.[56]

In an almost poststructuralist moment, he says that change will come "from neither an armed revolution nor an unarmed one: . . . It will be the result of struggles on several fronts, using a lot of methods, various social forms, with different levels of commitment and participation. And the result will be not the triumph of a party . . . but rather the creation of a democratic space."[57] The democratic space, he notes, will be defined by the revolt among the Zapatista women, who laid down a series of guidelines they called "the Laws of Women," which were then translated into the relevant Indian languages. The occupation of San Cristóbal was originally carried out under the leadership of a woman, Comandante Ana María.[58]

Surely one of the things that empowers Marcos's prose is precisely his anonymity. One reads and critiques him under his nom de guerre, knowing only his social type. What pours forth from his sharp retorts and deceptive pleasantries is not the mind of a single person but the minds of many filtered through his. This is part of the literary and media mastery of his rhetorical strategy as a whole rather than a simple military necessity to avoid capture. At the same time, for sustaining interest in the genre at all, the allures of anonymity require a definite, individualized personality, even if a typical one—"Marcos" the person. Often, at the end of the communiqués, in the form of elaborate postscripts, the personality comes out with a vengeance. He draws attention to them as such with just this distinction in mind, calling them "the *sup's* section: 'The repeating post-script,'" and asks ironically in a moment of rebuke to mainstream book reviews, "Did you notice the exquisite, cultured air of these post-scripts? Aren't they worthy of our entry into the first world?"[59]

A mind familiar with metropolitan obsessions leaps out here, as when, having fun with his audience by recalling his days as a student at the Ciudad Universitaria in Mexico City, he dubs his postscripts "nostalgic" before others can. At another moment, he thinks out loud about his quandary if the EZLN decides to send him personally to the dialogue in Tuxtla Guttiérez: "I am quite frantic, trying to decide what clothes to wear . . . I look critically through the giant wardrobe I carry in my pack and I wonder anxiously whether winter clothes are still in style or if I should wear something a little more flirty for spring" (12). Commenting on the wide public anxiety over his real identity, he jokes with the newspapers in yet another postscript: "How about a ski mask *'streap tease'*? (is that how it's spelled?) *How much for this show?* You know, how much dough for that? . . . how much for a minute of saying silly things? How much for half a minute saying truth?" (12).

And thus, in spite of his obvious urbanity, he intentionally departs from its modes of celebration or acquiescence, resolving that society must "wake up from the long and lazy dream which 'modernity' imposes on everything and everybody" (8). His comments are founded not on the political integrity of the gesture of negation (the restless moving beyond any fixed point of the dialectic) but on that of standing in a single place with wide-open arms, traveling broadly, and experimenting supplely in ideas and attitudes, gestures and concessions, while remaining fixed to the point of the essential conflict on a limited tract of land. When the Mexican government labeled the EZLN "professionals of violence," Marcos countered that they are "professionals of hope," dubbing the chief administrator of Mexico's ruling party in Chiapas a "chocolate viceroy with a peanut nose" who tries to pacify the region with radio programming of "marimba music and rap, proclaiming a brand new world." The flourish here wins the reader over even as its pointed talk of a popular cultural invasion from foreign territory (in both a class and an ethnic sense) sharply distinguishes Marcos from a ritualized embrace of hybridity. He portrays the government's bid to sell NAFTA as going hand in hand with the selling of an accompanying cultural style that equates modernity, capitalism, and worldliness: "lies and rap."

The Zapatista's veto of this equation in 1994 is a significant repudiation of the view of "subversive consumption." While national struggles are often said to be giving way to regional or ethnic ones, this movement of indigenous peoples instead emphasizes its unity with Mexico as a discrete political entity: "Our EZLN does not have a single foreigner in our ranks or in our leadership bodies, and never has received help or training from revolutionary movements of other countries or from foreign governments. We did not learn our military tactics from Central American insurgent movements, but rather from Mexican military history: from Hidalgo, Morelos, Guerrero, Mina" (6).

In arguing for the specific makeup of the mediation commission, Marcos stipulates further that "they must be Mexicans by birth. We think problems among Mexicans should be resolved by Mexicans without outside involvement, even if the foreigners might be honest, upright men and women" (7). The desperate goal is to preserve the integrity of the national state in order to have something meaningful to wrest away from the patriots posing in the current Mexican government. And in that struggle, literature is seen as national while mass culture is seen as *corporate.*

The Literary in the Light of the Nobel Prize

When recounting the features of literary value in the metropolis, one should distinguish between its inspired creators and its later, routine functionaries: the difference, say, between Arnold's *Culture and Anarchy* and the essays of professors in the 1990s complaining about the decline of standards for New York literary magazines. The sublimation of a liberal anti-imperialism so central to the imagination of the recent wave of non-Western films, novels, and song lyrics is part of a process of taming that comes with sudden success and recognition. But it is not so much about inspired African musicians or Chinese short-story writers as it is about an ex post facto *framing* of their work by an apparatus of organic literary intellectuals.

The cosmopolitan script is largely written afterward, and then superimposed on work whose tempos and tortured uncertainties are subsequently blurred. Everything painful and slow and suspicious in them is converted to a set of moral maxims. The glory days of third-world literature in its current phase are no more. Its three originary moments are gone: the period of Black liberation (circa 1964–1972), when an extraordinary amount of writing from and about the third world found its way into English (even into print) for the first time; the 1970s themselves—the period of the Latin "boom" with its (largely male) cast of epic satirists, originally pro-Castro in their sympathies, and deliberately New World in their rhetorical repertoire; and, finally and most recently, in the 1980s and 1990s, the era of a counter-counter-reformation, in which a culture of shrewd, good-hearted, and politically responsible writers (whose most brilliant spokesman was Salman Rushdie) copped the lessons of the "boom" and extended them to accounts of the British and French colonies and former colonies.

Striving to hold on to the moral sense of the rule of law, of nonconformist opinion, and of the inherent dignity of the world's many races and cultures, third-world literature in the Reagan era captured a much larger market than in the other two decades—in part because the cumulative impact of the other two had created an audience for it, but more because the perceived collapse of activist options drove a huge number of the disenchanted into the compensations of books at a time when Western governments were busy retaliating against decolonization and the progressive social legislation launched by the earlier two eras. At all events, a *politics* of names and faces was the calling card of this literature—from the poetics of Fanon's defense of the Algerian National Liberation Front (FLN) to Isabel Allende's unforgettable allegories of the Pinochet coup. Politics was in large part what its audience was hungry for, and what, in part, its by-products were in the public sphere of new university curricula and PBS specials: a greater discussion of politics from a mildly left, but critical, point of view.

Instead of confirming the victory of reform, the awarding of the Nobel Prize in literature to authors from Colombia, Egypt, South Africa, Nigeria, Mexico, Saint Lucia, and Afro-America in an almost unbroken succession in the 1980s and early 1990s gave ongoing lessons in the varieties of containment, and it is here that sublimation and cosmopolitanism have been largely identical.[60] Shortly after Derek Walcott's award of 1992, for example, James Atlas was rather franker than most in observing that the Swedish Academy had singled out his "historical vision, the outcome of a multicultural commitment," but one whose value lay in rejuvenating both the classical formal properties of pre-*vers libre* Western poetry (meter and rhyme) and the now threadbare devotion to a poetic lineage from which Walcott would at first seem to represent a departure: "In Derek Walcott, we can discern the history of what is most enduring in our tradition, invigorated, as it has always been, by the voice of our most recent immigrants." Atlas even continues, very ungraciously, to note that writing "in the cadence of Yeats" or borrowing "shamelessly from Robert Lowell . . . Mr. Walcott's apprenticeship to his English masters has a slavish feel to it," although that slavishness (remarkable word!) accounts for the confidence he feels in the Academy's decision to enlist Walcott to its ranks.[61]

Although by no means a political poet in the Caribbean tradition of former French Communist Party member Aimé Césaire, the Walcott found in such poems as "A Map of Europe" or "The Sea Is History"—with their divided sympathies and historical burdens—is simply ignored. And there is no hint of the dramatist who, often in a nation-language largely absent from his verse, explored native myth and Rastafarianism *(Ti-Jean and His Brothers; O, Babylon)* and parodied English tradition in *Pantomime,* a send-up of *Robinson Crusoe.*[62] Nor did Atlas's postmortem pay much attention to the content of Walcott's Nobel acceptance speech, which set out to highlight the misapprehensions people have of places like the Caribbean, thinking them "illegitimate, rootless, mongrelized."[63] Contesting that view with virulence, the speech sets its tone with an opening evocation of a festival in the small central village of Trinidad where *Ramleela* (the epic dramatization of the Ramayana) was being performed—not only buying in, in that sense, to the loaded connotations of "roots" in any mention of the "village" but doing so defiantly and (to Atlas, one assumes) anachronistically, strategically placing himself in the very position of his audience.

For in the very moment of acclaim, Walcott foregrounds his own cultural strangeness as an Afro-Caribbean from Saint Lucia in the face of an Indo-Trinidadian festival, having to convert himself painfully from assumptions of beleaguered loss to an understanding of what the villagers themselves do not see as loss. Whatever else he does, Walcott here makes a point of exposing his own role as a literary man and drives home a point about the sheer imaginative labor involved in entering and exiting the lives of the "people." Walcott in this speech is busy chiding his audience's unwillingness to travel knowledgeably. "For tourists," he laments in a contentious mood, "sunshine cannot be serious . . . In the unending summer of the tropics not even poverty or poetry (in the Antilles poverty is poetry with a V, *une vie,* a condition of life as well as of imagination) seems capable of being profound" (28).

A year later following Toni Morrison's award ceremony, John Darnton performed a feat similar to Atlas's by placing her in the memorable company of William Faulkner—who in his famous Nobel speech of 1950 spoke (as Morrison did) of "language as redemption"—without dwelling too long on the social pathologies of the American South that her language was supposed to have redeemed.[64] Remarking on the event's ambience—and with the excited air of one who has been part of a happening—Darnton related how appreciative the Stockholm audience was to this message: it burst forth in unsolicited applause as Morrison delivered her speech "with sequins that reflected light from 13 chandeliers in the Grand

Hall above the 18th-century Bourse." Relieved from the themes of genocide and Jim Crow that course through Morrison's novels, he applauds her talk as itself a "prose poem" that wisely chose to stress the ineffability of language—its inability to "pin down" issues such as war and segregation. With abundant leads provided by Morrison, he is able to steer the troubling political symbolism inherent in the award itself (she being the first Black woman ever to receive it) away from any awkward finger-pointing.

In a striking neglect of her actual work, the Swedish Academy had defended its choice by pointing out that Morrison has always "liberat[ed] language from the fetters of race." And with race thus dressed in sequins, and in the imagined company of Faulkner, matters of taste and realpolitik converged again in a moment (from its own point of view) of literary affirmative action. In a political event of some significance, Morrison felt moved to write, and Darnton urgently to stress, that value lies not with "official language or the censoring language of the state or the trick language of journalism, but language as words, with the magic they contain when they are learned by children." It seemed hardly to matter that most of anyone's canon would be excluded by this description—from the Baldwin of *The Fire Next Time* to Edmund Burke's *Reflections on the Revolution in France.* But pointing out this "obvious" fact seems strangely beside the point. A greater issue than the prima facie absurdity of the claim is the nimbus of the literary itself and, paradoxical for a "nimbus," its dead weight. Public affirmations of an abrupt insiderism push Morrison to deliver these conservatively liberal meditations, practicing a form of censorship against a writing of (or in) the state that is just without being "ineffable," that is beautiful without being "gnomic."[65]

With its burning eyes trained on a specific America in which it makes sense to speak of the "obscuring state language or the faux language of mindless media . . . the proud but calcified language of the academy or the commodity-driven language of science" (6), the speech drives with an unerring sense of self-preservation into a retreat disguised as an attack. With lively jabs against "fascist boots under crinolines," racist demagogy, and the "bottom line," the essay instinctively finds refuge in ambiguity. It knows that all is permitted so long as one makes *this* politics, "Politics"; makes *this* state, the "State."

The blurred language of Morrison's speech in this sense skillfully conceals where Natopolis begins and third-world dictatorships end;

and her wording is carefully crafted to allow readers to persuade themselves that one or the other is the real target of her railing against the "state." They can always comfortably assume that their enemy is hers. Thus, in order to buy space for her message that women, nonwhites, and youth are the great creators of tradition—only the vulnerable have truth, and only so long as they burrow from below—she aims to sell off the literary legacies of more organized sensibilities like those of Debsian socialism, abolition, and the suffragist movement while praising the graceful (although in this company, almost honorific) "state language" of Lincoln at Gettysburg. It is only one of the piece's contradictions.[66]

A Few Thoughts on What the Postcolonial Leaves Out

Recent work suggests that criticism of cosmopolitanism, at least as a type among literary celebrities, has already begun to appear with some regularity—that its recognition as such is in certain places now evident.[67] But the durability of an idea is clearest when it appears as common sense, not as the exemplary work of a few masters. The social significance of a fiction of hybridity does not lie with the "boom" novelists, or later with Rushdie, or even later with Bharati Mukherjee, but with the fiction they spawned in what might be called a fourth wave. Several younger writers have entered a genre of third-world metropolitan fiction whose conventions have given their novels the unfortunate feel of ready-mades. Less about an inauthenticity of vision than the context of reception, such novels—typically grouped together in the display cases of library foyers—unjustly come off as a kind of writing by numbers.[68]

The phenomenology of a "third-world literature" not only affects the reception, but in part dictates the outcome. As the work pours forth, authors ranging from Brazil to South Asia tend to exist not as individuals but as elements in an intertextual coterie that chooses them as much as they choose it. Placed in the company of other hybrid subjects, they take their part in a collective lesson for American readers of a global pluralism. They are unable to enter the scene of letters as innovators in the way, for example, that a talented North American novelist without ethnic baggage might be packaged as the rude boy or girl of a new generation. Their "movement" is based on being rather than doing, and so it is not a movement so much as a retrospective categorization. At the same time, the oppressive persistence of the role the public critic implicitly asks them to fill—and rewards them for filling—constructs a discourse that conditions the novels they set out to write.

The striking thing about Arabic fiction now available in the West, for example, is how completely it fails to live up to the charges typically made against the cultures of Arabic peoples. Since the work is generally not produced for cosmopolitan reception in Anglo-America (as I described in chapter 1), the point here is not so much routinization of theme in a Western marketing of the third-world "political" subject, but its opposite: the confounding of subject that becomes evident finally when a country's literature finds its way accidentally into translation and then is noticed. Although the mistreatment of women is a theme by which the West virtually defines the third world—and it forms one of the principal arguments for modernization—it has been especially the Arabic world for most Americans that has epitomized the horrors of "traditional" societies in this regard. But perhaps as a response by reform-minded intellectuals from within, Arabic novels in English have consistently been about sexuality, male hypocrisy, and women's consciousness. This has been true in some cases since before the *fatwa,* and even before the rise of modern feminism itself, as can be seen in the well-publicized women writers, not all of them recent: Nawal El-Saadawi and Hanan al-Shaykh, or in the work originally written in French by Etel Adnan, Andrée Chedid, and Assia Djebar. But even the two most well known Arabic novels in translation—Naguib Mahfouz's *Palace Walk* (1956) and Tayeb Salih's *Season of Migration to the North* (1969)—are extended studies of sexual politics whose point of entry is the troubling image and reality of male sexual privilege.[69]

The slogans of empire vary with time. At the simplistic but important level of pop knowledge found in journalism or trade history texts, empires past are projected usually in single, consolidated images. In these, Egypt gave the world the pyramids; the Romans, law and military organization; the Chinese, efficient bureaucracy and public works; the English, proper speech, good breeding, and the life of the mind. What, then, of the U.S. empire? Its contribution to the world seems to have been pluralism itself. Pluralism is the slogan of American empire. The immigrant has become a fetish, and the images of immigration as heroic survival have become the new mixed-race, intercultural products of the American crucible seen as a source of American strength. It is here that one finds a continuity between the travel narratives of high empire and the ethnographically inflected cultural studies of today's traveling critic.

Through its media interlocutors, cosmopolitanism's original impulse (ambiguous to begin with) has begun to decay, becoming in many cases a politico-exotic: a troping on democracy in a setting of poverty, disease, dictatorship, and revolution. Implicit in the acceptance of a third-world literature whose politics is unashamed and central to its aesthetics comes a potentially radical expansion of the degrees and types of aesthetic value appreciable in the metropolitan centers. But the very emphasis on "politics" paradoxically disables that appreciation. Now that "politics" is out in the open, one sees *less* clearly the narrow range that politics is allowed to have at the aesthetic level. A very unpredictable and asymmetrical set of conditions for literary reception has been the result.

For university administrators and commercial book reviewers, the final resting place of multicultural training has tended to be American pluralism, and, without it being said openly, the passport is the final arbiter of where the disciplinary boundaries begin and end. In a related way, the crucial move from literature into the extraliterary field of popular culture has led to an enormous interest in the export of American mass culture but much less to an interest in the vitality of indigenous popular cultures—especially as massively influential exports to Europe and the United States in a variety of forms, some of them apparently trivial, yet with significant effects at every level of American everyday life: among them, ethnic cooking, martial arts, urban carnivals, soccer, film, commercial dub poetry, and the varied offshoots of "salsa" (a problem I take up in more detail in Chapter 6).

The North-South divide is inflected by a peculiar kind of critical paralysis when it meets that of the East-West in its political and artistic senses. There is relatively little said about the latter's aesthetic beauty as an epic politics of class or imperial confrontation. Take, for example, the Guatemalan poet Otto René Castillo's "Apolitical Intellectuals."

One day,
the apolitical
intellectuals
of my country
will be interrogated
by the simplest
of our people.

They will be asked
what they did
when their nation died out
slowly,
like a sweet fire,
small and alone.

No one will ask them
about their dress,
their long siestas
after lunch,
no one will want to know
about their sterile combats
with "nothingness"
no one will care about
their ontological manner of obtaining pocket change
they won't be interrogated
over Greek mythology,
nor about the self-disgust
they feel
when someone within them
begins to die like a coward . . .[70]

It is next to impossible to read this sort of poetry in the United States today and be able to communicate the logic of its art. Insufferably "p.c." to most readers, the poem relies on a historical sensibility and an ethical integrity that have been systematically evacuated from American common sense. And yet etched into a history of torture, these lines are marked by a kind of classical restraint, and certainly part of the aesthetic marvel of the poem is what it avoids indulging in: the gratuitous gibe, the programmatic declaration, the envisioning of a revenge enacted by the wronged. Literary figures, of course, can be found here, although they are hitched to the assumption of a prior conversion. The word "interrogated" is well chosen, for example, and puns on the common knowledge of any guerrilla or peasant leader who has ever experienced the inside of a military barracks.

But satire rather than irony floods the poem's lines with an understatement calculated to make the reader scream, as philosophical inquiry is yoked to the vulgar ends of "pocket change." What appears so cloddish and overearnest is in fact jesting and subtle, although the subtleties would have no meaning without the *patria* and the *pueblo* underlying the whole—those very concepts that metropolitan criticism disarticulates and ridicules with the very same vigor as the popular press. The euphoria one can feel, similarly, while hearing the Namibian freedom song "Independence or Death" does not lend itself easily to analysis in a classroom because of the song's simplicity and the effects of its repetition, even though to grasp its meanings for Namibians would be a particularly potent way of illustrating the crosscultural values that are barely approximated in appreciations of the African novels chosen for most seminars.[71]

Be that as it may, even explicitly socialist writing is not always motivated by simplicity per se, or the desire at all costs to achieve a historical outward-turning—a view that may be implied by the examples just cited.[72] It is only one kind of confusion. For by contrast, and at the other pole, there is also a lack of interest in the explicitly modernist or experimental writing of those who are considered not to be political enough—those who do not fit the injunction that the third-world writer embody politics in a readily consumable form. This would be the process at work, I think, in the surprisingly weak reception of the Brazilian novelist Clarice Lispector, for instance, with her brilliant psychological portraits of love and loss; or of the Zimbabwean novelist Dambudzo Marechera, who often takes as his angry theme the bohemian nonconformism of the Black writer who is indignantly required to be—in the confrontational sense—more "Black."[73]

Tendencies such as these deserve more attention than I can give them here. As a matter of elaboration, I will look at only one problem of reception in more detail below. In the last two chapters I want to explore a protest within cosmopolitanism itself by looking at two writers whose worldliness is so pronounced that it seems virtually to define them. My interest is to examine why they distrusted what is now called global culture and, in one of the two cases, affirmed indigenous culture, redefining the "indigenous" while doing so.

5

Cosmopolitanism's American Base: C. L. R. James in New York, 1950

> For the European, even today, America represents something akin to . . . a phantasy of emigration . . . It is by an act of force or *coup de théatre*—the geographical exile of the Founding Fathers of the seventeenth century adding itself to the voluntary exile of man within his own consciousness—that what in Europe had remained a critical and religious esotericism became transformed on the New Continent into a pragmatic exotericism . . . To land in America is, even today, to land in that "religion" of the way of life which Tocqueville described. This material utopia of the way of life, where success and action are seen as profound illustrations of the moral law, was crystallized by exile and emigration and these have, in a sense, transformed it into a primal scene . . . The US is utopia achieved.
>
> —Jean Baudrillard

More than any other twentieth-century theorist and activist, C. L. R. James was obsessed with discovering a properly socialist desire. But what is socialist desire? Judith Williamson notes sardonically in her book *Consuming Passions* that desire is a radical topic, the one "most avidly consumed in academic work." It is the subject of popular cultural readings by coolheaded academics mixing business with pleasure while reveling in what they coldly analyze.[1]

From the unpromising vantage point of a journalist writing in the genre of the short-caption feature, her writing is an exemplum as well as a content. At the same time, she prophesies how difficult it would be after perestroika to see socialism, and desire as having anything to do with one another: "Consuming passions can mean many things: an all-embracing passion, a passion for consumerism; what I am concerned with is the way passions are themselves consumed, contained and channeled into the very social structures they might otherwise contain." In this way she returns to the Frankfurt critique of postwar American sociology, now reapplied to a cultural theory that imagines itself dispelling an empiricist cultural functionalism. And her complaint with the latter is like Leo Löwenthal's with the former in 1950: "Social research is, in the final analysis, nothing but market research, an instrument of expedient manipulation, a tool with which to prepare reluctant customers for enthusiastic spending."[2]

Without any of her ease of language, Ernst Bloch would have enjoyed Williamson's words (and certainly would have agreed with Löwenthal's as well), but he would have pushed them into a different, austerer mode. As the exilic counterpart of C. L. R. James in America (the subject of this chapter), Bloch deserves a brief discussion here, for he more than anyone articulated a socialist desire that is limited neither to the euphoria of Frankfurt's negative critique of existing society nor to today's uncritical populism. The overripe product of another generation, country, and intellectual repertoire, and holed up virtually as a hermit in the United States from 1938–1947, Bloch chose these bitter years to write *The Principle of Hope* as an act almost of spite. Its three long volumes are, on the one hand, a highly idiosyncratic anatomy of the daydream and, on the other, a compendious history of the world's utopias—environmental, social, medical, technological, athletic, religious. The book maps, in other words, what that urging and striving he had given the name "daydream" had created in history, what complicated mutant forms flourished in its soil. It is at the same time an agenda for those who seek something else, something better than the real.

As an early friend of Georg Lukacs and a student of Georg Simmel in Berlin, Bloch frequented the circles around Max Weber, who distrusted his mysticism. As a messianic socialist and comrade of Walter Benjamin in Zurich, and as a scholar whose knowledge spanned the whole of Continental philosophy, Bloch found himself in 1938 suddenly in an unspectacular bungalow in New Jersey surrounded by the rhythms and sheens of a civilization he despised. Reports of German emigré intellectuals and artists profiting from their imported talents in Los Angeles and on Broadway poured in along with a public appeal on his behalf by Theodor Adorno (another close, but former, friend), although it was only Bertolt Brecht with whom he could share the full extent of his abhorrence for a land, as he saw it, of hucksters, militarists, and fundamentalists. He never mastered English.

Although later revised in 1953 and 1959 after his return to the German Democratic Republic (it was first published in its entirety only in 1959), *The Principle of Hope* had been slogged out with a grim thoroughness as though by a man in prison conspiring against his jailers. With the original title "Dream of a Better Life," the book is one of a kind. A generic hybrid with a stamp of odd singularity and memorably strange coinages, it evokes at once the frivolousness of romance and the tightly reined discipline of the German Universität. In the words of its English-language editors, "he blends archaisms, Latin and Greek terms, obsolescent usages, '*Volksweisheiten*' (popular sayings and proverbs) . . . New and unexpired ideas appear as premonitory glimmerings and extended after-glowings, shining ahead or continuing to bathe history in their unextinguished light."[3]

Lacking the colloquial light touch of Marx or Heine, and missing the straight-ahead logical sharpness of Lukacs or Weber, Bloch produces a motley with exposed seams, but with patches of unforgettable imagery and humor. If in the first volume there is no illusion that these imageries of the "not-yet-conscious" and the "forward dawning" have a scientific referent in consciousness, they are given such stunning piles of evidence of all kinds—anecdotal, archival, imaginative—and are attacked from so many conceivable angles over the space of the 447 pages of volume 1 alone, that belief in the "world-improving" power of the daydream becomes the reader's idiosyncrasy as well. A very demanding book in that every item or tool of analysis is itself rethought and rephrased as Bloch's own, the book nevertheless is often and unexpectedly informal, confessional, offhanded, and contemporary, driving on from prolonged psychoanalytic discourses on sexual repression to extended close readings (in Greek) of a passage from the *Odyssey*.[4] Later still the reader finds a punning and impish excoriation of petit bourgeois murder as seen in the Ku Klux Klan and as concealed by the glossy magazines.

The text's moods are the moods of Bloch over the extended period of its composition. Everything from the local Glee Club, Kierkegaard, Saint Anselm of Canterbury, and Philadelphia to mirrors, Nero, and Karl May is packed into his enormous brain, where it is then processed and annealed to a monumental human structure of urging, expressed "first as striving, craving to go anywhere. When the striving is *felt,* it becomes 'longing,' the only honest state in all men" (45, Bloch's emphasis).

What is it about key Marxist intellectuals in the postwar period, who, faced by theorists of moral exhaustion on the one hand and by a syrupy technicism on the other, turned their attentions to the philosophical intricacies of the plainest and most basic emotions—for Bloch, "Hope"; for Henri Lefebvre, "Trust"; and for C. L. R. James (as I discuss below), "Happiness"? From the god that failed in the 1950s to "after the Fall" today, the project of utopia is mercilessly under siege, as though one were grabbing the moment when the feared alternatives were weakest in order to erase the very possibilities of thinking them. This is only one of the calls that the archaic and eclectic misfit Bloch makes on the imagination, and why he blends so well with Williamson's searchings. His Wagnerian tome survived the cold war, but is it enough to make us reconsider utopia when it is widely argued that the problem of tomorrow's tyrants is the insistent lie of utopia itself? This question is never directly posed in academic cultural practice. And yet, both immediately before and after the fall of the Berlin Wall, criticism had been asking, and answering, it.

"The ghost has now vanished," reported Jean-François Lyotard. "The regimes that have pretended to be representative of the hero have fallen into appalling buffoonery. The collapse, one after the other, allowed the stage to be opened up for rebuilding in accordance with Western models . . . By invading the shops in West Berlin, the East Berlin crowds gave evidence that the ideal of freedom, at least of the market, had already invaded Eastern European minds."[5] On a very different side of theory, and from a very different politics, Stuart Hall struck a similar note when he once claimed that "the war of position is the only game in town"—a view that underscores his turn in the 1980s to a politics suspicious of progress, a politics of microlevels that explicitly rejects the utopian "high church" socialism of the former communist parties.[6]

Does utopia belong in the world of *Dr. Strangelove* or *The Battle of Algiers*? For an aspect of literary reception "across cultures"—the euphemism for writing that is not only "ethnic" but extranational—is the part it plays in shoring up the utopian ideal of what formerly was known as socialism, an ideal described well by Williamson in her attempt to give light and color to a passion that for generations had, as Norman Mailer once put it, "given us psychic ammunition for the desperate silent struggle we have been fighting with sick dead hearts against the cold insidious cancer of the power that governs us." The labor of so much contemporary cultural commentary, meanwhile, has been intended precisely to clear from our mouths the taste of that ideal known personally to many from decades on the line. That history of socialist heroes, that soft-focus dream of the Other Way, was said to be a demon, not because the project was evil but because the well-formulated desire had settled into a permanent past. Inebriated by visions, the reform-minded could no longer see history rushing past them.

At the very moment of a strategic return by Western governments in the 1980s and 1990s to a new conformism, publishing and the media embraced writing from zones of neocolonial horror. More than simply an accompanying and (given the conservative mood) appropriate voyeurism, the literature attracted many readers precisely because a certain kind of no could be uttered through it. It presented itself not only as a weak and waning escape for bookish specialists in the archives, but blasted onto the screens and lit up the minds of the middlebrow editors eager for the new. Yet simmering beneath its lines, present even when it was absent, were hints of that older socialist hope. A flight from nostalgia in metropolitan circles, in other words, met the arrival of a kind of writing that suggested that socialism—or a certain kind of socialism—was still "on." Uneven development? Perhaps it was that the theory (which attacks utopia) had not yet fully taken hold in the provinces.

The very sensibility that would make one wonder about such matters, or be paralyzed by such ethical worry, is rare today in criticism, which skips over the intricacies of Williamson's generation with a few turns of phrase. Immediately after World War II, Henri Lefebvre was already wondering aloud about the viability of utopia in a context that the Fall has made to seem recent: "Today, the Revolution has lost its mythical meaning and the now-outmoded aspects of its former romanticism . . . Should we attempt to escape from platitude through the past, the tragic and the mythical, the surreal or the transcendental? Or through the marvelous, in other words through the trumpery of lost illusions and miracles?" Here is where he turns to "the new marvels which are being born at the very heart of mediocrity. They are simple, human marvels. Let us name one of them without further ado: *trust* . . . very close to naïvety, to foolishness; always abused from childhood on . . . always changed into a distrust which is almost as unexpressed as the initial naïvety—today trust in life is taking root in life and become a need."[7]

In much this same spirit of insisting on the homely and the plain, Bloch answers Lefebvre's initial queries with a resounding no. Where Bloch departs from Freud lies here in this turning away from a search for origins—a search in which Freud explains our profoundest desires, for example, in an implicitly antique drapery of Moses, tribalism, or childhood, by invoking the paradigms of the primitive, the archetypal, the illusive, and the repressed. Only too aware of the paradox of his own words in the neon glare of the fast sell outside his American windows, Bloch turns his audience instead toward the "Novum" whose motor and motive are built into them in a tactile feeling for the "Not-Yet-Conscious, Not-Yet-Become." And thus it becomes his project throughout the book to distinguish between resemblances—between the desire that utopia *is* not, but that utopia tries inadequately to capture, on the one hand, and capitalist addiction, on the other; the Novum as a "real possibility" versus the "new" of bourgeois philosophy: the "different rigidity of a surprise that is always the same."[8]

> The Novum as a whole in [Henri] Bergson is not elucidated by its path, its explosions . . . The eternal metaphysical vitality theory ultimately achieves a mere frenzy instead of the Novum, precisely because of the constantly required change of direction, required for its own sake . . . Consequently, the abstractly understood Futurum also ends in a l'art pour l'art of vitality . . . [and Bergson] has in fact only developed his concept from sheer excess into capitalistic fashion-novelty and thus stabilized it. (201)

The point is always how to venture beyond without "skating over" what already exists. Bloch spends all of his prodigious endurance and neologistic flair on bringing to life a philosophy of the future that has never been given a name, never been provided with its concept, even though it is "the horizon of all being." Whatever belies this extraordinary claim comes in for repeated acts of rhetorical bombardment: "Venturing beyond never goes into the mere vacuum of an In-Front-of-Us" (the American one-world) nor does it call the colossal banality of social pessimism the future, since the business of hegemony is to "make its own agony apparently fundamental, apparently ontological," relying always on "the illusory existence of its own bad immediacy" (4).

It is the day- rather than the night dream that therefore captivates Bloch, although not in any simplistic substitution of light for darkness. He wanted, rather, to add to the concept of desire. Associated biblically with vanity, psychoanalytically with the id, and functionally with the frivolous (and Bloch covers them all, from the desire of "being slim" to the "after-image of love"), the "waking dream of world improvement" requires for itself "the seriousness of a pre-appearance of the possibly Real" (95–7). The night dream moves in the forgotten and repressed, the daydream in what has never been experienced as present (115). That Bloch, like Brecht, suffered financial disappointments after his forced arrival in the United States does not explain very well the virulence with which Bloch loathed what he found on American shores. *The Principle of Hope* (or as Fredric Jameson more accurately translates it, "Hope the Principle") develops work begun much earlier, in *The Spirit of Utopia* (1918).[9] But the earlier work, dedicated to the practical matter of explaining how a future Real is created through the mechanism of utopia, now reads as a kind of revenge on the myths with which Bloch and his generation were weaned. James K. Lyon recalls how deeply those myths involved the United States:

> No sociologist can accurately measure what the idea called "America" did to the consciousness of a certain youth counter-culture in Germany. For many this exotic word carried a thousand overtones: gangsters and flappers; boxing and the latest dance steps . . . All of these and anything practical, useful, experimental, or new were considered "American." "America" was in the air. In Germany, books about its life and culture proliferated. Publishers rushed to translate any title that sounded as though it came from the mythical continent.[10]

From his travels in Tunisia in 1926, Bloch was positioned to critique that fairy-tale orientalism nowhere stronger than in the German's relationship to America. He is unable to resist associating cosmopolitanism with a "pax capitalistica," singling out particularly that process whereby the utopian function had become a "religion of dead slogans" in North America:

> The American Declaration of Independence and then the American Constitution contained their rights of life, liberty and the pursuit of happiness, their principles of liberty, justice, morality and law, still seen from the standpoint of the citoyen . . . But now all this is trapped in inert air, and the only real basic principle, the economic one, because of the abstract-statics of the other principles, permits any opportunism of content, above all in the case of liberty.[11]

Bloch, in fact, in his personal opinions went considerably beyond this critique. He finally could not bring himself to believe that fascism had lost in World War II. The very thing he had fled in Europe was being re-created in his American refuge.

Socialist Desire: Ernst Bloch in America

If Bloch represents one distinct tradition animated by the need to articulate a socialist desire, there is at least one other—secular, popular, and emotive, often depending for its viability on a third-world positioning where anachronisms are tolerated, or a frank disinterest in academic respectability foregrounded. The spatial and temporal lag between the two is disheartening given the harmony that exists between an often very specialized cultural theory and the attitudes and moods of the broad left press. As one might expect, the fall of communism plays centrally in this process.[12]

To say that sectors of the Soviet and East European bureaucracies were deeply reactionary or that they proved their appetites for personal profiteering by transforming themselves overnight into leaders of various ethnic chauvinisms is desperately true. But the fact of Soviet power in all its contradictions and conservatism was—as Iraq and Panama alone demonstrated—progressive in a global sense. It is from these intellectuals—not the media ones, now, or the advertising copywriters, but the intellectuals of the academy itself—that a certain image of the "good life" is still projected onto the reality of the global leftovers for whom the West cannot bring such a life, and for whom the Soviet military "threat," regardless of whether Marxism meant anything to them as an idea, was a line of defense. Many intellectuals are motivated by different desires—not the accretious ones of having ready access to fashion, beer, autos, and appliances, but the longing for an infinitely deferred utopia—longed for precisely because it *is* deferred. What needs to be analyzed is the way this logic steps to the rhythms of a larger structure in a specifically capitalist fulfillment of desire that is based on addiction, since addiction is the type of artificial longing whose virtue is regular and predictable but always an only temporary, and therefore an infinitely repeatable, fulfillment: a fulfillment without satisfaction.

One seemed much closer to this badly needed critique in the Benjamin of *One-Way Street,* with its familiar Frankfurt paradoxes, than in the dazed and angry—but deliberately "Leninist"—aestheticism of Guy Debord's *Society of the Spectacle,* much less in Baudrillard's *America,* with its baleful encomium to Disneyland. Taken together, these three works—roughly analogous as political reflections on the libido in practical encounters with capitalism—chart a sort of regress. None of them, however, asks what pleasure in socialism might be. There is no vocabulary for discussing the freedoms one feels, for example, listening to community-sponsored radio, where women and minorities are no longer token voices but in the majority, or even managers of the station—the sheer freedom one feels from commercial cant and the singsongy voices of the salesman's lie. What specific forms of humor, what lines of communication, what lore surround the mining communities of West Virginia in the heat of a strike like those of the late Carter years? What brand of literary transport takes place in the novels of Meridel Le Sueur or F. Gladkov? What aesthetic frenzy accompanies the smiling peasant faces of Dziga Vertov's *Three Songs of Lenin*? What samizdat-like enclaves of practical democracy are carved out of the public sphere by college students occupying a university hall to protest tuition increases? Fredric Jameson has been one of the few to recall the parallel universe of these values, as well as the obstacles to expressing them crossculturally in a satisfactory way: "The principal difficulty . . . lies in the utter disparity or incommensurability of the explanatory terms in which each side seeks to stage its discourse. To put it briefly, the East wishes to talk in terms of power and oppression; the

West in terms of culture and commodification . . . What we end up with is the inevitable comedy of each side muttering irrelevant replies in its own favorite language."[13] Hence the attempt to talk here about a socialist desire, a term that supposedly belongs only to the discourse of "culture and commodification." It is, in fact, the move from the one into the other that is of interest to me.

The emotional dynamics of the United States itself need to be studied more closely—its repertoire of ready icons for wiping the historical slate clean by destroying the vitality of an alternate utopia—a vitality that continues, weakened and more tentative, in spite of prognoses to the contrary. What needs to be explained is how all this relates to the ebb in third-world insurgency or (put much better and more accurately, I think) to an intellectual brutalization by the information classes that forces those insurgencies into a vacuum of nonsupport. The conversion of culture to a category of struggle makes a good deal more sense in the third world (or in those metropolitan regions where the third world has been imported) than it does among the communities so widely written about in studies of cultural resistance—computer hackers, New Age diet reformers, Madonna fans, and so on—simply because hegemony is less stable there. And one is struck by the anxious mirroring of an earlier anticolonial discourse in the current language of post-Marxism, a mirroring that it is not entirely conscious of and unintentionally inverts—most graphically, for example, in the work of Ernesto Laclau and Chantal Mouffe, whose championing of "radical democracy" and the "democratic revolution" has been plucked from the much more meaningful contexts of decolonization struggles against semifeudal, militarized, and absentee regimes.[14]

To apply this terminology to the modern neoliberal state, however, is to participate in a reversal in which (to take the English case) the entrepreneurship of Toryism provides answers to the very crisis it created. Debates over the new directions required by the success of capitalist desire, one might say, are attempts to account for the apparent passivity of subalterns in the West; and the borrowing of anticolonial terminology (that is, from a context in which subalterns have been anything but passive) is a way of infusing that passivity with the look of resistance.

The United States as a temptation does not exist merely as an exported idea. If it has begun to resemble the center of a centerless world government in the making, then it is that "capital" to which the ex-colonial intellectual makes a pilgrimage. As London was to the immigrant from the British colonies, as Paris to that of the French colonies, the United States is to the new cosmopolitan. When C. L. R. James arrived in the United States in 1938, little of this future was clear. But in the course of roughly fourteen years here, he found himself drawn to what he held to be the country's unique significance as an idea in the world. An internationalist by conviction, and an author of vast global sympathies and experience, he saw in the United States a way of reaching the world without ever leaving American shores. How that view affected his thinking on Africa and the Caribbean is an untold story, and his proleptic culturalism as well as his temporary retreat from anticolonial planning and strategy while resident here were directly related to the want of formulating a properly socialist desire. What follows, then, is critical of James's American detour while defending its continuities with an earlier and later period of his work. It also seeks to show the misconceptions that a concept like cosmopolitanism has when applied to a figure like James, who objectively seems so well to represent it.

Cosmopolitanism, America, and the Cold War

In 1950, soon after a divorce, James wrote a lengthy outline for a study of U.S. popular culture. Since 1947 he had been aware of government plans to deport him as a political undesirable, and partly as a result, the study had a tone of urgency. But in spite of some initial interest from friends (he circulated the work in typescript), it was not published until 1993, well after his death.[15] By 1953 he was forced to flee the country. In its form, the proposed book could not have been more unlike *Notes on Dialectics,* which was completed in a hotel room in Reno, Nevada, two years earlier in a decidedly different frame of mind. Instead of his ponderous and ultimately sectarian performance there, *American Civilization* unfolded at leisure, crammed with long quotations from *Life* magazine and the *New York Times,* struggling its way toward notoriety in a sustained dialogue with popular critics like Elton Mayo, Cyril Conolly, and Geoffrey Gorer.

The writing of *Beyond a Boundary* was still more than a decade away, but even more than that largely autobiographical work, *American Civ-*

ilization tells its readers hidden things about James's life.[16] Composed in a concentrated burst of activity over several weeks, the brilliant and bulky draft was a philosophical meditation on a national desire. It capped the brittle, far-left theorizing of the American years (1938–1953) and colored them beyond recognition even as it continued many of their obsessions. Although his concerns had been wide ranging, his major focus in the American years had been on the assimilationist role of the "Negro" and on the state capitalist character of the Soviet Union. Like the stage of his career that it embodied, then, the study was marked by extremes. At a time when James was giving lectures at Columbia University on such topics as "The Idea of Personality in Great Literature" and was organizing sharecroppers in Missouri, he was also elaborating views that anticipated both the highs and the lows of later U.S. cultural criticism. His comments on the "Negro" as a historical stimulant to American freedom expressed fully, and at a very early date, the centrality of race to the study of popular culture. But they did so, paradoxically, not by looking at Black popular cultures per se (about which James had surprisingly little to say apart from his well-known comments on cricket), but by focusing on political initiatives. Less important in itself, perhaps, his position on the Soviet Union was paradigmatic of U.S. cultural criticism in a more negative sense. It made his overestimation of American promise inevitable. And it is this American seduction, as it were, that says the most about his career as a cosmopolitan intellectual.

Despite the brilliant recovery work of scholars like Paul Buhle and Cedric Robinson, James's left milieu of the immediate postwar period often appears with a lopsided rendering of the spirit that compelled it. Cultural criticism has not sufficiently recovered the outlooks and assumptions of this era, as several critics have been strenuously pointing out—most notably, James's only de jure literary executor, Robert A. Hill. James's habit of arriving at momentous cultural abstractions based on the minutiae of textual and biographical anecdotes is weird to the critic today—and so much a part of his Hegelian training that his real positions barely register. The prolific recent scholarship on James records his impressive contributions to the contemporary study of political cultures, but it is often silent about ideas revealed by the project itself: for example, his unexpected identification with the United States as an adopted home and his bid to become a popular author in the market sense of that term.[17]

Although the American project until recently was not largely known even by James specialists, threads of its argument available elsewhere have given some critics the warrant to misstate his political intentions—misstatements that are aided by his own theoretical wanderings in the early 1950s as he struggled to adapt traditional Leninist positions to the era of McCarthyism (a task, it must be said, in which he was in great measure successful).[18] The study reasserts the classically Marxist side of James at the same time that it adds new reasons to question his coherence as an anticolonial theorist. Both the one and the other were related to the pressures of living in the United States as an adopted "American."

James's study is therefore a paradigm of sorts for a strangely understudied moment in his personal career, a period (as Buhle put it) "not as hotly debated" as others: the post-1950 "cultural James." More important, it came *before* the publication of *Beyond a Boundary*, which represents a cultural James that has been lately studied to the exclusion of almost everything else.[19] Instead, it captures a tendency within current U.S. cultural theory to creatively misrepresent earlier left structures of feeling that, far from suppressing the current cultural turn, fully enabled it, although in much more doctrinally consistent forms than most are led to believe.

Such structures of feeling helped empower the anticolonial project, creating the principles and even much of the vocabulary of what is now called multiculturalism. So much has been written lately about the migrant sensibility of the third-world intellectual abroad that one tends to blanket that sort of experience with Salman Rushdie's famous phrase about being a "translated man." But the most pertinent kind of "translation" is not so much an ontological state of mixing and matching identities as it is a critical selectivity after the fact, one that tends to excise uncomfortable continuities with the past found in the writing of key cultural innovators, who are then presented as exemplars of a radical break. This has occurred most strikingly with Antonio Gramsci, but in a New World context James is perhaps the clearest case. The matter, however, is more complicated than mere misreading. James's own experience in the early 1950s looks forward to a pattern of self-censorship and terminological maneuvering exhibited by the U.S.-based critics once they attempt to enter an anticommunist public sphere.

James's motives in this key text are, at the same time, deeply conflicted. One of the most salient features of the project is its eagerness to establish James as a commercially viable author of "philosophical" volumes on popular themes accessible to a mainstream reading public. At the moment of composing it, he was emulating H. G. Wells and Arnold Bennett more than Victor Serge, his Russian-French counterpart—like James, a celebrated anti-Stalinist and novelist. It seems not unfair to remark on the personal background in this way. At least one of James's intentions was to have the book demonstrate to the immigration authorities that, loving America so, he could not be an alien and therefore could not be undesirable. The other, personal, reasons for fighting deportation were in this case inseparable from the genesis of the project itself. James's whole style of living had become bound up with the crazy media saturations of American postwar life. After a day of solitary reading, his greatest pleasure was to slip away at midnight to see a film in Times Square.

The United States could not be left behind so easily. For it was also the home of Constance Webb, James's lover and confidante, with whom he discussed the proposed book's contents in a long and intimate correspondence. In these letters, the project's new turn and new emphases were starkly apparent. He wrote the following words, for example, after more than a decade of unrelenting work in various Trotskyist parties: "Some pseudo-Marxist has been getting at you, telling you that what you should do is join a party and work in a factory? Just tell them to go to hell, that's all. I worked at literature for years and made my own way to where I am. Nobody taught me; and, thank Heaven, I find that I am still making my own way while so many others are floundering around."[20]

American Civilization is crucial to a contemporary accounting of the cultural left in other respects as well. It makes nonsense of the view that Marxism arrived only recently at an understanding of the politics of culture. It launched the first of James's pioneering efforts of the 1960s, developing ideas that became widely accepted only much later: sport as the popular art of a national character, the distance of intellectuals from the correctives of "everyday life," the cultural interdependence of Europe and its colonies. He does precisely what Marxist intellectuals are repeatedly described as not doing. For James it was the humanist center, not Marxism, that reduced cultural inquiry into matters of brute economics and material rewards. Quite apart from its own prescience, the manuscript forces one to remember that the American debates on popular culture in the 1930s and 1940s were already rich, varied, and (by the 1950s) quite general—as Leo Löwenthal pointed out when he chided some for leaping into the fray like pioneer inventors in 1950. The popular culture of the newspapers, Löwenthal observed, had been a topic of discussion for a hundred and fifty years, a "voluminous writing produced on both the left and right wings" already existed "in the nineteenth century."[21]

Despite the limitations placed on the debate by the immediate postwar era (because it was begun before cable, MTV, or the personal computer), its contours were very familiar. At this point of tension James already can be seen talking in detail about what is called today (with unintentional irony) the "new social movements." Large sections of the manuscript are dedicated to the special demands and histories of women, youth, and Blacks—a fascinating passage that culminates in an analysis of the political importance of "homosexuality" in American life, in which James lays out a protoprogram of gay rights.

Most important of all, however, is precisely what is *not* new in James's typescript. European and Latin American intellectuals had long seen the United States as a place of utopian refuge from imaginative staleness and class fixities. But even more than that, apart from a populist Trotskyist gloss, the imagery, attitudes, and general rhetorical feel of the work fits in a rather banal way the contemporaneous debate on mass culture in the 1950s academy and the popular New York literary magazines. James's fight to stay in New York in that sense reminds one of the postwar German film directors'—or recent poststructuralist professors'—attachment to California. To be in the United States was not only a matter of taste, but to live where the future was unfolding: to live now what others would soon be forced to live.

The early 1950s, then, were a transitional moment in James's career. He was experimenting with his authorial voice after a long preparation of pamphleteering and exhausting theoretical debates within tiny, isolated far-left groups. At a personal level, it seems likely that he sought a return to the prolific *anni mirabili* of the 1932–1938 period in Britain, where his best work had been written.[22] He never disowned the concerns of the American years and persisted in viewing his intellectual performance there as conditioning his later thought. But the arcana of Trotskyist critique did not translate very well in this new mode of public address. If his writing on the "Negro" was ahead of its time, his attitudes toward the Soviet Union developed under American pressures into a suspicious dependence on a salvational image of American "democracy."

Never after the 1930s was the grace and brilliance of his writing equaled—particularly that of his fiction and his early studies on Arthur Cipriani and the San Domingo revolution. He needed social movement to write, and this he did not have in the United States. The memorable outburst of *Beyond a Boundary* in 1963 was itself the product of reflections on his recent reinvolvement in Trinidadian independence, muffled by the bitterness of defeat in his fight with Eric Williams over the Chaguaramas affair, and then sublimated in "culture." James's genius as a recorder, grand strategist, gadfly, and consolidator of ideas did not accompany a genius for organization, as anyone who has studied his years in the Johnson-Forest tendency will appreciate.

Nevertheless, one does not have to take the position, as Buhle and Stanley Weir have, that James was primarily an "artist." James participated in the pre–World War II Pan African conferences, the early work in England for the independence of Ghana, the Independent Labour Party (ILP), the movements to defend Abyssinia (Ethiopia) following the Italian invasion, the People's National Movement of Trinidad, unionization drives in the United States on the eve of the war, and the "Black power" and "Black identity" movements in Britain from the 1930s to the present. These are the principal material and practical encounters of James as a revolutionary.[23] Although he certainly was an artist, especially in the 1920s and 1930s, his political work was not any less bona fide for being "literary"—and I am arguing here that it primarily was, not only in the more derivative political writing (that is, in his translation of Boris Souvarine's mammoth biography of Stalin, or in the rehashings of Trotskyism found in his *World Revolution,* or in the vastly overrated study on dialectics), but in his cultural-political theory after World War II. This work is most impressive today as a model of method. Its content was largely, although not entirely, derivative.

James nevertheless remained a prophetic voice whose colloquial Hegelianism provided historical readings more accurate than others' and in advance of most. But to read his life as a reading of his prodigious work is to get a false impression of both. He took his era in completely, and made sense of it to himself and others in a plain and penetrating language. Yet the man himself, in spite of close friendships with people like Richard Wright, was much more isolated than one would suppose. He certainly had met Kwame Nkrumah, Theodor Adorno, Leon Trotsky, Edith Sitwell, Martin Luther King, Lionel Trilling, and others. Still, although a key catalyst in many ways—as in his introduction of George Padmore to Nkrumah, then a college student in New York—he did not really collaborate with them. Although critical of the academic intellectuals' political seclusion, James was very much a loner himself, despite seeking out the laborers of Lancashire, the sharecroppers of Missouri, and the everyday contributors to the journal *Correspondence.* Apart from rare moments like these, his populism was imaginary. His manner of working was to spend his days for the most part in disheveled bedrooms, under sheets, reading T. S. Eliot with the TV on.[24]

It is not that James was in the least naive about the merely nominal democracy of America; but with little faith in the progressive character of the United States' cold-war enemy, the only logical option was to exaggerate the power of the nominal. *American Civilization,* at any rate, looked forward to *Mariners, Renegades, and Castaways* by linking American exceptionalism to the country's immunities to the "Red threat." Although with a twist entirely his own, James was in 1950 anticipating his exposé of the Communist Party in *Mariners'* final chapter ("A Natural but Necessary Conclusion")—a very embittered tirade of which James criticism needs to take greater notice. It was so fiercely drawn, in fact, that it was suppressed in later editions by his own friends and associates.[25] In the end, both books fit in well with the general effort of the time to rally a slumbering America to more vigilance against the enemy within—that is, they were works of anti-Communism with a capital *C.*

Biographical sources from this period—including the manuscript itself—implicitly contest some of the recent attempts to revive interest in James's contributions. New canons and new assertions of race and identity have all looked to James for support, but have not given enough attention to the disparate logic of three key periods of his life: the euphoric James of the ILP years in Britain, the injured sectarian on the mend in New York, and the practical politician with Eric Williams in Trinidad. The latter period especially—wonderfully investigated recently by Paget Henry and Walton Look Lai—would create considerable doubts about the usefulness of James to an identity politics as such, where the cosmopolitanism of the world-roving Trinidadian found expression above all in a sober (and ultimately failed) attempt to extend his participation in Trinidadian nationalism to a federation of West Indian states in a single polity.

Later still, in England, conflicts with Williams over his nagging Marxism and his tendency to speak in his journalism "under" the prime minister's head directly to the people ended his political viability at home. He then made his impatience with "identity" known in the context of the British diaspora: "People are here as part of a movement that is worldwide in which people from the underdeveloped countries are being brought into developed countries to do a certain type of labour; they are coming because they are invited, they are coming because they can't help it . . . But don't tell me about utterly mythical values in the Caribbean."[26]

A related critical approach to James can be found among those who are devoted to his political rather than his cultural work. But the paradox is that "Jamesians" of this type stress precisely the views he elaborated in the American years: his emphasis on spontaneity instead of leadership, his apparent advocacy of a cultural politics, and, of course, his denunciation of the Soviet Union as history's greatest barbarism.[27] Both approaches have helped to create a contemporary cultural politics that takes a transitory (and, I think, misguided) moment in James's career for inspiration—cosmopolitan in the sense of setting up an American universal.

What, then, is so different about this period in James's work? Why could he not rekindle the fire of his brilliantly productive life in Britain? People are brought to James in part out of the sheer matter of *location*. He seems to have somehow involved himself in most of the events that mattered to his time; he knew who it was important to know. As a middle-class dreamer, dropout, athlete, and writer from the outback of Tunapuna, Trinidad, he would have led an extraordinary life even had he accomplished less, since he was so unlikely to have accomplished anything literary at all. But his influence had much to do with the intangibles of personality, a concept that plays a surprisingly small part in accounts of his career, although as a reality, James's own personality certainly attracts many to study that career. What needs to be highlighted much more is that startling feature of his oeuvre that consciously militates against his immense and obvious worldliness: his extemporaneous style, the resonance of his voice, his passion: "Why am I a revolutionary? . . . I dislike intellectual restraint. I like to let everything I have go. Against bourgeois society I can think and write freely—develop my ideas. That is why to go out of it now would be so hard for me."[28]

One has to appreciate not only that he wrote *The Black Jacobins,* but that he did so working in a foreign language that he had mastered in his spare time. Conrad Lynn in the 1940s remarked that in one public speech James addressed a New York crowd for seventy-five minutes "equally at home in English, Yiddish, and French." Add the voice of the playful specialist in his cricket columns, leap to the German phraseologies of his book on dialectics, and the cosmopolitanism of intellectual range and sympathies is thrown in stark relief against a deliberate method to which he gave the name "simplicity."

For political as well as aesthetic reasons, most of the recent criticism on James has as a matter of custom stuck to the conversational, personal, and, above all, cultural performance of *Beyond a Boundary* at the expense of *The Black Jacobins,* for political as well as aesthetic reasons. The thematic balancing act of the latter book is perplexing to those who have no feel for the élan of the anti-Stalinist communism that saturated James in that period and made the writing of that masterpiece possible. Certain of its lessons find willing echoes today in a combative multiculturalism.

The Black Jacobins, of course, dramatizes Africans outwitting (not merely desperately fleeing, or struggling in some impotent jacquerie) European demigods like Bonaparte, Robespierre, and Hedouville. Its thrilling reversals stand out: the colonies *created* Europe, and slavery *created* Western civilization. It is significant, though, that veneration for the book is typically paid in knowing nods of the head, rather than in extended textual appreciations. For to grapple with specific content would bring one to a James that, in style as much as in argument, is the very figure marked out for culturalist reschooling, despite the fact, of course, that straight out of *Capital,* volume 1, comes his insistent third-worldist reversal that the colony is only a "crazy caricature" of the domestic regimes in Europe. Modeled on Trotsky's *History of the Russian Revolution*—whose phrasemaking and temperament it closely mirrors—the book is devised as a direct response to the Italian invasion of Ethiopia and amounts, in a subsidiary sense, both to a prolonged defense for West Indian political unification (in the 1930s!) and a prediction of World War II and fascism.

It is impossible to mistake the descriptions of the San Domingan creole elite, whose barbarities are painted in words of intentional double entendre, pointing the reader securely to their contemporary counterparts—Mussolini, Hitler, Coughlin ("the mulattoes, unlike the German Jews . . ."); the denouement of Dessaline's rise to power, similarly, is the Stalinist Thermidor.[29] If these deliberate layerings are lost on many readers today (and they are, out of simple ignorance), other points are all too clear, explaining the respectful critical silence toward what is, by all accounts, James's major work. James believed, for example—and explicitly wrote—that class was a more fundamental conflict than that of race (38, 127–8, 283)—which is one of the reasons he relishes analogies like the one he employs when observing that in San Domingo white women were imported with the same calculations used in importing slaves and machinery (30).

But the book's more telling nonconformity lies in the very grandness of its scheme, including its gnomic utterances about the "science" of history and its literary interpolations coupled with ecstatic (and strangely timeless) truths, of which these are typical: "When history is written as it ought to be written, it is the moderation and long patience of the masses at which men will wonder, not their ferocity" (138); or better, commenting on the disparity between the nationalism of poor and rich, "Property-owners are the most energetic flag-waggers and patriots in every country, but only so long as they enjoy their possessions: to safeguard those they desert God, King and Country in a twinkling" (135). The entire narrative is constructed out of these memorable phrases interlarded with data as the narrative ticks off one by one all of the theoretical issues bedeviling the Trotskyist left: the individual in history, leadership and the mass movement, the peasantry *as* proletariat, the way revolutions occur whenever a split occurs in the ruling class, and so on.

As uncomfortable with the slogan "masses" as with the oracular flourish of the epigrammatic asides, many contemporary critics see the book only as a history of geniuses. And there is a close connection between James's focus on leaders and his literary reading of history as a mockery and, finally, transcendence, of tragedy (292). It is only in the early brief wanderings into the pre-Toussaint guerrilla operations of Mackandal and Boukman that James brings the actual culture of the people to light, and he shares Dessaline's scorn for voodoo as well as his scorn for their low intellectual level. He does not hesitate to call them "brutish." The awe James registers at Toussaint's ability to compose letters like a trained diplomat even though he'd been a slave until the age of forty-five places the reader in a position to admire James himself, who wrote his masterpiece like a born scholar, despite a lack of formal schooling at the advanced levels.

What he misses in failing to excavate the role of *African* cultures in the war with France, he gains in his elaborate demonstration of "African" scholarship as brilliant and wily as Toussaint's military campaigns—a point that relies on concepts of Toussaint as a "world actor" in his squabbles with Rigaud, Roume, and Hedouville, and one whose activities were a pattern of considered *thought.* African liberation and Caribbean unity would depend, in short, on the demonstration of leaders who could play Europe in their very parlors, in white ruffled blouses, quoting Abbé Raynal.

It is quite wrong, in other words, to make of James an anticolonial intellectual of new departures alone—a point Buhle makes convincingly while showing James's usefulness to the New Left. He was, much as Gramsci, a basically orthodox Marxist-Leninist, and that may be precisely *why* he was innovative, although such a view conflicts with the current doctrines of "progressive" cultural theory. Even Buhle's excellent biography treats James's life in a series of documentary readings with little reference to the Jamesian category of personality, which would have demanded a more operatic score of conversations, reminiscences, the minutes of meetings, and encounters. *The Black Jacobins* had been written, according to James, against "the booming of Franco's heavy artillery, the rattle of Stalin's firing squads and the fierce shrill turmoil of the revolutionary movement striving for clarity and influence" (xi). The startling conceptual leaps, the elegance and assurance of phrasing, the immense theoretical originality of the book belong to personal as well as intellectual inspirations that coalesced at the point of his American debut as a professional writer.

James had said often that, weaned on Thackeray, he packed himself off to England with little politics and with only the keen intention of becoming a novelist. In his nonfiction of the time, a novelist's care seeped out of the prose to a degree that was never quite repeated after the war. But apart from the sparkly-eyed ambitions of the (not-so-young) writer disembarking in England—an England that for him, like many colonials, meant the home of Cricket as well as Literature—other personal events conspired to give magic to the decade of his arrival, and they were filled with discoveries.

Reading Marx seriously for the first time seemed especially vital given James's involvements in the Independent Labour Party, which seemed to bear out those bookish prophecies. He spent time with Karl Korsch and Daniel Guerin; met George Padmore and Jomo Kenyatta. The new ideas seemed to gather force in his extensive pub talk with the workers of Nelson, Lancashire, where he was then living with the cricketer Learie Constantine, who was James's first important benefactor—a friend from the Trinidad days recruited by the English leagues.

Indeed, his setting off to do research in the Parisian libraries—as the text of *The Black Jacobins* shows through numerous contemporaneous allusions—had been motivated by a desire to bring Marxism and African independence together, to make them part of the same constellation of thought. The linkage of Marx and Africa itself was enabled by another event of these years, one that more than any other had been a catalyst for his intellectual awareness of the stakes of African liberation: the Italian invasion of Abyssinia in 1935. Turning to 1950, one is struck by how few of these impressive communities and conjunctures remained.

American Civilization was, of course, equally a creature of its age, but raw enthusiasm and high-talking hopes now substituted for movement. There is a certain sadness in James's uncircumstanced optimism, and there is certainly much of dubious warrant. James saw the American workers poised for victory on the crest of a vast media wave; popular culture was not the neo-Blakean "mind-forged manacles" of an ascendant corporatism but final proof that the common people had in a sense already won: that *their* image and *their* values were now regnant. In this James presaged a libertarian politics of style that today marks the outlooks (and liabilities) of American-left criticism—a criticism whose authority has been enhanced by the prominent work of foreign intellectuals resident in the United States, who share many of the study's drawbacks.

Despite the well-known reach of American popular culture abroad, the foreign commentator has typically not been saturated by

American advertising while growing up, nor trained as a consumer with quite the same unrelieved intensity, or as part of a total national ethos. This aspect of many of our most well-known cultural theorists—so evident in a negative sense in the Frankfurt school—has not been widely appreciated in those critics for whom the United States is an ecstatic object of morbid fascination. The non-U.S. commentator on "America"—an intellectual type from before Tocqueville—is very much with us, as is the tendency to exaggerate, if not idealize, American popular culture's vaunted futurisms and potentials.[30] For many critics who are also "natives"—if such a term can be used—mass culture is often already a bad joke.

But here as elsewhere James has become a model-for-use. To what extent did he deserve to be? Contemporary criticism often translates James as an "artist," an "independent" radical, even a "deconstructionist."[31] At the level of epistemology and of method, James's antagonisms to poststructuralism are too obvious to make a refutation interesting, although he certainly did in some ways predate a poststructuralist politics, especially in his distrust of centralization and his belief in an active consumer. More interesting is Cedric Robinson's claim that James tried to "level Marxist theory to the requirements of black radical historiography."[32] This makes the case too strongly, however. The principle deviations in James from a standard interwar Marxist historiography were the result of his attempts to demonstrate the compatibility of Leninism to a libertarian populism; they were not the result, as Robinson argues, of James's interest in forging a distinct "Black radical tradition." James's emphasis on the necessity of Black leadership in African independence, for example, or his novel formulations on slavery's centrality to capitalist development were, for James, organically related to the outlooks and sensibilities of bolshevism. To insist on this point is not to preserve the sacred, but simply to remark how his very prescience and originality were bound up with a stubbornly classical position.

Indeed, the traditionalism of James's study reveals itself in his literary models. Seeing his book as a contribution to an established genre on the American social character, he explicitly cites Tocqueville's *Democracy in America* and Viscount James Bryce's *American Commonwealth,* while bringing them into a postwar recognition of the new stakes of "individuality" in a media society. Less about than *in* that social character, the typescript is almost quaint in its motives. It was to be the first of a series of books designed for the public to read "on a Sunday or on two evenings," a profound and embattled philosophical reflection in the form of a fireside novel. Versions of the books in this planned series appeared as *Mariners, Renegades, and Castaways* and *Every Cook Can Govern,* but the spirit of the project was there already in 1943 in James's plan to write a historical play on Harriet Tubman starring Ethel Waters, whom James said he loved "beyond idolatry."[33] It was, then, precisely that attempt to reach the public he had missed in the difficult years writing tiny-circulation documents for a minuscule sect of American Trotskyism. In spite of spirited arguments by compilers of his journalism that the book was a simple continuation of his concerns of the 1940s, his correspondence suggests otherwise.

The Struggle for Happiness

The America project is in many ways a more thorough and sustained example of James's applied cultural theory than *Beyond a Boundary* (1963), which is usually seen as the place to learn about this side of his thinking. Both works talk about the artistic tastes of ordinary people in a language of rhetorical enthusiasm, giving them a status usually reserved for the museum and the concert hall. James had a name for this process of linkage, which he defined elsewhere as "the coalescence of the cultural tradition with the popular audience," or simply "integration," a concept he derived from lecture series he had given at Columbia University on personality in Greek tragedy. The Athenian festivals placed judgment in the hands of "sausage vendors" rather than professional critics—an operation that James warmly approved of, of course. Similarly, in a letter of 1953 he returned to the decisive issue of the popular audience. There he comments on Malcolm Cowley's "truly philistine introduction" to a journal containing an article by Kenneth Burke: "I see that we have to do something with Kenneth Burke and his idea which I have met before that literary form depends on the psychology not of the author but of the audience." And then, with his peculiar brand of defensive self-confidence when it came to the academics, he adds: "He does not understand it really, but he is close to something."[34]

Unlike his first book, on the Trinidadian labor leader Arthur Cipriani, or the future book on cricket, *American Civilization* speaks to a global English-speaking audience. The grand narratives to which James was typically drawn, and that he had enlivened with the oddly obscure case studies of a Trinidadian unionist and a sport unknown outside the commonwealth, were now linked to a popular cultural language of American images and characters that was known virtually everywhere. His aspirations to be more like the great popular artists of history—Shakespeare, Aeschylus, Chaplin—had shifted from the idiosyncratic to the symptomatic. He finally had a topic that could reach millions: the "cultural tradition" as an unbroken line running from Greek tragedy through Dick Tracy and as a precise record of the very outlooks and designs of history's great revolutions. The spirit exalted there was the spirit of Dessalines, John Brown, and Patrice Lumumba.

And yet if the contemporary site of productive upheaval was the United States, James was unavoidably—like Tocqueville and Bryce—a foreigner. Fortunately, he did not have to rely entirely on the old adage that foreignness itself was a prerequisite for insight into the American social character. For he, unlike his famous predecessors, was a New World foreigner, and both qualifications were necessary for the task he set himself: "I have seen and have heard over and over again American intellectuals apologizing for their 'coca-cola civilization.' Though their ancestry may go back two or three hundred years, they are greater enemies of the American people than I am."[35]

In words like these, one hears very clearly the actual defense strategy James would use in the face of deportation. The energy behind the project—and the particular charge infusing the word "American" throughout—lay in the way James contrasted the United States with Europe. He was also saying that Americans, in a way that a world-traveling Caribbean man would not, still abased themselves before Europe; they did not know what they had. James's essays of the time therefore set out to show that Europe's postwar literature was all "incessant soul-searching and wailing and misery" that "express[ed] no future. It is the end of something."[36] The primary ideological conflict for him was New World versus Old, not first world versus third, and the United States was the only fully realized New World society. His preferences are very easy to misinterpret, however. Refusing to be sentimental, and faithful to what he saw as the "science" of politics, James saw the United States as a standard in spite of its imperial involvements: the place where any fight worthy of the stakes would occur. That calculation empowered his optimism in spite of such contrary details as the Platt Amendment, the occupations of Haiti, the railroading of Marcus Garvey, and the creation of the Panama Canal.

Far from oblivious of these precedents, he nevertheless chose to direct his anger at that brand of American cultural groveling before Europe that was then evident in one strain of the mass culture debate. Not unaware of the contradictions of doing so, he wanted to disrupt the pattern of American radicalism as an immigrant affair, by developing a way of thinking about political change that relied entirely on indigenous American traditions. These had not been theorized adequately, he argued, because America's intellectuals (both right and left), cowed by Europe, had not given them sufficient attention.

The point was not simply to battle over what was aesthetically pleasing in popular culture by exposing the prejudices of the opponents of "kitsch." The argument mattered only as a means of demonstrating that popular culture provided documentary evidence for an American "happiness"—an uncompromised hunger for what socialism alone could provide. The revisionary impertinence of the thesis is appreciable when one grasps the return here to the classical notion of the revolutionary leadership of the most "advanced" countries—a highly strange thesis, in fact, for a man who had been involved in African decolonization in the 1930s. Predicting in so many other ways the obsessions of the 1960s—the rise of "youth," of non-Party forms of organizing—the study directly contests the writing of Fanon, the ideology of peasant war and third-world encirclement—a rarely noticed corollary of James's message.

The intended sting of his message cannot be felt without recovering the prominence at this time of the thesis of "American exceptionalism"—a very widely and publicly debated issue that James takes up in order to stand it on its head. The question to ask, however, goes to the heart of the migrant intellectual abroad: How well did James understand the United States? Proposing to enter mainstream publishing on the eve of his incarceration at Ellis Island (which immediately preceded his departure from the country), James seemed almost self-flagellating. The typescript comes off with a numbing desperation. The selflessness and moral vigor of the move alone seemed to justify it; to become "popular" rather than merely commenting on the popular was to realize practically the critical emphasis he had placed on "audience" in his earlier readings of the European literary classics. The polemical point was in this sense embodied in the project rather than explicitly argued in its pages. The key political questions are always posed "from below"; they are the ones so obvious that the cultivated flee from them, thinking them banal. Thus the intentionally naive framing of the study itself: "What is it that people want?" (*AC*, 166). What makes them happy?

His answers to these questions in the opening movements of the outline, however, suggest some of the difficulties of adopting "America" for his purposes, and these too are problems of cultural translation: of the foreign intellectual faced by U.S. centrality of power and resources seeking to be professionally acceptable and honorably dissident at the same time. He sets out to acknowledge that power, but then, in an act of subversive interpretation, to convert it. What people want, he writes, is "to manage and arrange the work they are doing without any interference or supervision by anybody . . . to work and love handling the intricate scientific masses of machinery" (167). The vision might be called "industrial-pastoral," as though overlaying the sentiment and heroism of a socialist realist novel upon a wish fulfillment in McCarthyite America. It attempts to splice a typically American frontier scorn for government interference with a very different tradition of workers' control from the socialist movement.

Several theorists at the center of an international postwar Marxist stock-taking were involved in similar queries, not always so sanguinely. Thus Lefebvre, with an eye on America, finds himself asking: "Will there ever be anything great which is not dehumanized—or a form of happiness which is not tinged with mediocrity?"[37] Almost as a proleptic riposte to *Beyond a Boundary*'s basically Brechtian argument that sport is the high art of ordinary people, Lefebvre muses ambivalently over the metropolis's Athletics, Inc.: "Thus leisure and work and 'private life' make up a dialectical system, a global structure . . . Sport has developed by presenting itself as the culture of the body, of individual energy and team spirit: as a school for health. What have these lofty ambitions achieved? A vast social organization (commercialized or not) and a great and often magnificently spectacular *mise en scène* devoted to competitiveness" (40).[38]

Leaving aside the historical issue of whether the movements James revered (among them, the early Bolsheviks and Cipriani's labor movement) ever believed in a workplace without "supervision by anybody," James's answer to the question about what people want elides progressive and reactionary desire. In the United States, "government interference" had already in Reconstruction a resonance James unexplainably forgets in his eagerness to locate a univocally progressive American populism. Moreover, this resonance would not change in coming years, during the school desegregation battles of Little Rock or in today's standoffs at the abortion clinics or in the militia movements. By tapping into an instinctively anarchist response to an overbearing state, James was making the same gesture familiar in today's culturalism—a gesture in which the "state" is doubly damned as an object of desire: it is, for one thing, the code word for what failed in the Soviet experiment; it is, for another, the nemesis of the methodology at work here—that is, a viewing "from below." And yet what James is doing is punning on the notion of workers' control to draw on the vocabulary of Marxism by applying it to a specifically national conception of freedom that was, in many ways he chose not to discuss, hostile to Marxism.[39] A similar slippage occurs in his focus on individual happiness, the book's central concept.

The typescript begins with the thesis that individual happiness had found in the United States a fuller expression than anywhere else in the world and that, as a social expectation unlike that of Europe, individualism had the force of rallying mass movements: "Freedom of the individual . . . cannot be abstracted from the nation. It is the peculiar, the special contribution of the United States to international civilization" (*AC*, 106). This beguiling observation is put so energetically that one almost forgets to add the obvious provisos. It is not only a looking backward from the 1980s that allows one to complain about this unguarded way of putting the matter. To say that individualism in its American form has also meant cars rather than cheap mass transportation, picket fences rather than public housing, the lottery rather than guaranteed health care is to say only what Lewis Mumford and Thorstein Veblen had been saying before the war.

It is not that James does not remark on the potential contradictions of his thesis. He just neglects to explore them fully. For example, the book sets out to distinguish between two eras. One of them is characterized by the enviable individualism of the pre–Civil War days of Jacksonian democracy, Tocqueville's yeoman farmer, and the abolitionists, all of whom he sees collectively embodied in Melville in much the same way that medieval Europe had been embodied in Dante. To this he opposes the cant of the rising Northern magnates after the Civil War who, in a sense, colonized the idea of freedom. Their unwitting mouthpiece, for James, was Whitman, who becomes in the book Melville's alter ego. Diverging sharply from José Martí before him (another Caribbean intellectual resident in New York, but in the closing decades of the nineteenth century), James compared Whitman's poetry to Voice of America broadcasts.[40] The last one hundred pages of the four-hundred-page manuscript are dedicated to an ambivalent reading of John L. Lewis and the Congress of Industrial Organizations, an assessment in which James criticizes the union for being limited to narrow material demands rather than concerned with the larger and more insubstantial issues of the quality of life.

In the early sections, he explores the paradox of American society that had been recognized already in the 1830s by Tocqueville: its authoritarianism alongside its outbursts of mass democratic protest; its cultural expressions of an undying hunger for individual happiness that had been reduced to general prognoses on the "boredom of freedom" and prosperity by existentialist intellectuals and *Partisan Review* contributors, whom he loathed. Tocqueville thought that America was unique because of the individual—that "puny" thing of the self—as against the social stratification of Europe. To him, the American individual had a "capacity for free association," as James puts it. "Individuality and universality achieve a fusion unknown elsewhere" (*AC,* 48).

And yet, by contrast, the rule of the majority was dominant, leading to an apparently untroubled conformity: "I know of no country in which there is so little independence of mind and freedom of discussion as in America" (48). Taking these observations of Tocqueville and reapplying them to the 1950s, James predictably blames this conformity on the routines of life brought about by the social regimentations of the captains of industry, but also, and less predictably, on the Communist and trade union bureaucracies, whose unimaginative choices emphasizing social "security" rather than "freedom" failed to challenge the vicious system of industrial peonage and its attendant welfare "statism."

At this point, James steps into novel territory, for he concludes that this factor of "individual freedom," although apparently evanescent, had been precisely what powered Jacksonian democracy, as well as the uprising of Denmark Vesey, the first National Negro Convention of 1830, and finally (and following their inspirations) abolitionism itself, in the form of William Lloyd Garrison's *Liberator* (1831) and the great speeches of the New England radical Wendell Phillips—the clear hero of James's early chapters, and one he refers to often in his correspondence.[41] James had always angrily denied that the moral imperative of freeing slaves had only been a cover story for the investment designs of Northern federalists in the Civil War.

Linking the high drama of abolitionism with the jeremiads of Melville, James subsumes both in a striking association under the subheading of "Nineteenth-Century Intellectuals." He establishes an indigenous American radicalism that had proven itself the equal of revolutions everywhere, thereby venturing into a dimension of the doctrine of "American exceptionalism" that was not a customary part of it: "Out of America, with no assistance from any alien tradition but from the very genius of the country emerged this clearly recognizable replica of the early Christians, the Puritans, and later the early Bolsheviks, types which have appeared only when fundamental changes are shaking a society to its depths" (*AC*, 91). A homegrown idealism grounded in a stubborn resistance to threats against the sanctity of the person had given abolitionism a resilience and a clarity that Europe no longer had.

The novelty of James's thesis arises when he theorizes the need to recover the diluted passions of this era by excavating mid-twentieth-century mass culture. Capitalist social rationality (and for James this would have included, of course, life in the "capitalist" Soviet Union as well) was not simply "the daily grind of the assembly-line workers. It is that the whole of productive life is tuned to this pattern" (115). If opposition to this broad web of disciplinary culture marching to the rhythms of the factory had become increasingly narrow and defensive in the hands of union leaders, there were abundant signs that the workers themselves had not lost their memory of "freedom." Workers were continually striking, not for wages, but for the dignity of free association.

What James develops, then, is the proposition that American popular culture, particularly the pre-1929 cinema, the detective novel, and the "serious" comic strips of Al Capp and Chester Gould, did not reflect an impoverishment of the human spirit; it was, by contrast, the direct descendant of the pre–Civil War classics of American literature. Popular culture expressed a desire for individuality that could be found in present American society in a twisted rhetoric of enterprise hiding a new authoritarianism: "Melville has left no serious descendents . . . [one must turn to] radio and the comic strip, to Charles Chaplin, Rita Hayworth, Sam Spade, Louis Armstrong, Dick Tracy and Gasoline Alley . . . after the writers of the middle of the 19th century, [these] are the first genuine contributions of the U.S. to the art of the future and an international art of the modern world" (35).

What is unique about James's take on the matter is (1) his linking of the classics of nineteenth-century American literature with mass art, where the latter is actually portrayed as the fulfillment of the former; (2) his finding the motor of development of mass art not in "technology" or the demands of advertising or wartime lessons about the uses of propaganda (the then familiar lines), but in the fundamental character of American society—"individualism"; and (3) his clear formulation, at this very early date, that culture, like politics, was "concentrated economics" and could give direction to political activity.

> Where formerly we had to look at the economic relations of society, the political and social movements and the great artistic expressions to get a whole, complete and dynamic view of the society, while as far as the great mass was concerned, we had to guess; today it is not so. The modern popular film, the modern newspaper (the *Daily News,* not the *Times*), the comic strip, the evolution of jazz, a popular periodical like *Life,* these mirror from year to year the deep social responses and evolution of the American people in relation to the fate which has overtaken the original concepts of freedom, free individuality, free association. (118–19)

Mass culture was not something for the left simply to exploit; nor was the issue to give mass culture its due as entertainment. For James, it was an unsullied archive of popular desire. It provided a space for intellectuals to readjust their sights, wake up from their reveries. With an enormous confidence in the wisdom of the people and their trudging power, James felt that the future glimmered back at him from the dancing images of the commercial cinema. What interested him, and what he found historically new, was the "day-to-day correspondence between the ordinary experiences of many millions of human beings and their transmutation into aesthetic form" (139). Consuming mass culture, the people watched themselves, and liked what they saw.

James's Art

Apart from being the fruit of a decade of hotly debated thought on "American exceptionalism," *American Civilization* was not only, like *Beyond a Boundary,* a diagnosis of a national popular culture, but a work intended specifically to orient radicals in their postwar wanderings. It may have been a contradictory piece given James's personal life, since a part of the book wanted to be fireside reading for a general audience, as well as an outsider's last word on the fashionable media debates of the 1950s academic intellectuals. But its aspect as "movement" tract had little to do with its better known successor, *Beyond a Boundary.*

Although packed with commentary on race, on cricket as a site of colonial enmity, and on the Victorian uses of the sport as social discipline, *Beyond a Boundary* was James in a eulogizing mode, not the beckoning one of his organizational Trotskyist days. The cricket book established the importance of popular culture in defining national character but did not ask how that knowledge bore on the Peoples National Movement of Trinidad or the Caribbean Federation—perhaps the major political bases for James immediately prior to 1963, when the book was published. Eric Williams and Michael Manley belonged less with *Beyond a Boundary*'s famous question "What is Art?" than John L. Lewis and Harry Truman did with the America book's question "What makes people happy?" Nodding in the direction of pre-1923 Bolshevism, the forms of struggle James liked to talk about were workers' councils, which would place him in a classically syndicalist position.

In fact, this is misleading. James's emphasis in *Mariners, Renegades and Castaways* on the formula "centralization equals capitalism" and his chiliastic descriptions of spontaneity fell soon enough into moralizing abstractions. In the book on dialectics, immediately before writing *American Civilization,* he declares: "If the free activity of the proletariat is to emerge, it can emerge only by destroying the communist parties . . . Only free activity, a disciplined spontaneity, can prevent bureaucracy . . . The proletariat has reflected itself in organization after organization until it now will see organization for what it is. The impulse, spontaneity, with which it created new organizations, the means by which it created them, must now become the end."[42] The focus on "personality" was, as here, deep enough to seek foundation in a Hegelian recovery of the actualization of "Essence"; but in his own manner of constructing words, James reflected this focus on personality in the sense that his historical work is always a biographical case study, clear from his early book on Cipriani, through the Toussaint focus of *The Black Jacobins,* and the later book on Melville, as well as the long sections of *Beyond a Boundary* dedicated to Garfield Sobers, Matthew Bondsman, and others. In a protracted theoretical way (as I have said), personality is the principal theme of *American Civilization.*

James had written of "the modern aesthetic" in his laudatory comments on Griffith's films, which he adored (like those of Chaplin) since they repeated the accomplishment of Aeschylus and Shakespeare in pleasing a mass popular audience. His intention here, of course, was not merely to match wits with the university pundits, but to refurbish the instincts of Marxism toward mass-cultural popularity, however creative and self-critical he knew Marxism to be in other ways. And yet, turning again to contemporaneous intellectuals like Lefebvre and Bloch who shared many of James's political coordinates but not his pact with America, one can see that, whatever the validity of comments like James's for individual rarities, the dead weight of the institution of mass culture as a whole cannot be left for "popular opinion" to clear away. For both, doing so was simply entering the Panglossian realm of the market analyst. In what must appear as a direct response to James's argument, Lefebvre wrote:

> Chaplin gave us a *genuine reverse image* of modern times: its image seen through a living man, through his sufferings, his tribulations, his victories. We are now entering the vast domain of the *illusory reverse image.* What we find is a false world: firstly because it is not a world, and because it presents itself as true, and because it mimics

> real life closely in order to replace the real by its opposite; by replacing real unhappiness by fictions of happiness . . . This is the "world" of most films, most of the press, the theatre, the music hall: of a large sector of leisure activities.[43]

James, on the other hand, does not dispute that masscult gives one only "fictions of happiness"; his point is only that these fictions engender a Blochian striving. A more radical departure from Lefebvre can be seen in James's willingness to accord individual artifacts of masscult the finesse of sophistication. At first glance focused on formal techniques (the flashback, crosscutting, the mobile camera, the close-up), James is not interested finally in the joys, so familiar in film criticism, of technological options and film language. He quickly moves on to the key figure of his art theory, the *audience,* bridging his observations with a graceful metaphor: "The twentieth century is *panoramic,*" suggesting both the Griffithian long take and the crowds of Atlanta and Saint Petersburg that inspired it.[44]

The audience, for James, did nothing less than create the artist. There was no more extreme view than James's on the movement of influence in the "culture industry" from bottom to top, and his final opinion that every program or film idea would simply die if the people did not want it had emerged from a lifetime of nearly fanatical confidence in the common people's collective good sense—an outlook that dovetailed strangely with the behaviorist sociology discussed in Chapter 2. The credo of that wing of social science (and the inevitable counter to any charge of upscale manipulation of product) was and is that masscult gives people only what they want. As for James, he attributed the power of his own study on Trinidadian labor leader Arthur Cipriani, for example, to pub talk with ordinary workers in Lancashire. The point, he told his nephew Darcus Howe on another occasion, was not to find what was good for the workers, but rather to take their lead. It was not "what the working class *ought* to be doing, but what it *is* doing."[45]

Such inflexible optimism left its footprints everywhere. As George Lamming observed, his own first novel was based on James's early play version of *The Black Jacobins,* in which the crowd was the major character—an ideological style that the "yard" fiction of James's early short stories as well as his novel *Minty Alley* plays out in great detail.[46] Even the origins of cricket in the "artistic instinct" of

Victorian artisans and rural laborers had everything to do with James's dedication to the sport. The key, he argued, to the great art of our time is the art that "takes the people seriously"—something literature, for the most part, had failed to do. For one who stated very plainly that content called forth form—or, to put it another way, that Griffith's camera did what his subject matter told him to—James was little occupied with the mechanics of beauty as such. The conflicting combinations that he embodied—Victorian theorist of cultural studies, third-world European, anarcho-Leninist—rose up fully in his plans for "The Struggle for Happiness." It would be not only fireside reading for the petit bourgeois listeners of Walter Winchell, but a sort of handbook for a new politics. While the going debate in mass art criticism was, predictably, over "taste" and the decline of art, James was busy redefining what a discussion of aesthetics ought to be about.

Apart from an open hostility to the literary modernists he called "magists, textualists, and metaphoricals," and apart from his primary emphasis on audience, there are two aesthetic categories that recur in James's work with impassioned emphasis: "rhythm" and "simplicity."[47] The former has an obvious bearing on audience. As for "simplicity," James applies that concept to the genres standing midway between highbrow reflection and public contact—another way of stating, perhaps, his earlier category of "integration." Thus, it is the art of Lincoln's political speech that surpasses even Burke, Demosthenes, and Pericles in its "simplicity."[48] In James's own prose, it is primarily the grace and balance of his early fiction, the dramatic monologues of the first English period, and the guileless, conversational tone of his later criticism that he stands by. One might say that James's particular strength as an author was the majestic explanation—the putting into words of what had been either unforeseen or (more likely) thought already known.

In a letter to Constance Webb in 1946, James laid out what he believed to be rhythm's "positive universal." Prompted by the viewing of a film starring Jennifer Jones whose lines James believed to be "our modern poetry," his observations detail the great directive of art to repeat the accomplishments of Shakespeare using "the prosaic sharp disjointed urban speech of our time."[49] It is a fascinating passage, not only for its technical detail (which James's criticism often lacks), but for its privileging of "America" over the Caribbean, an odd focus when the subject is "rhythm." With puzzling evasion, James speaks of "the great rhythms of history" as "the Greek hexameter, the Elizabethan blank verse, the heroic couplet." But the point here is not James's quirky Eurocentrism. These rhythms were "expressions of the human soul" and, as such, social; and they came each in their own way through a process of distilling the "'normal' speech at the time."

Yet James's preferences for European art cannot be explained away by pointing to his admiration for the postwar West Indian novel, or by saying that the postcolonial mixture of cultures renders all claims to a purely "European" or "indigenous" art spurious. In fact, only in his semiofficial capacity as nationalist commentator for the *Nation* in Trinidad did he, rather colorlessly, express his admiration for carnival, and even here one feels that he wants to like it much more than he actually does. Concern has marked the vexed topic of James's Europhilia in the present climate of cultural nationalism, but James caught the balance of his actual posture in a side comment in *The Black Jacobins* by applying to Toussaint what he would have applied to himself:

> It is Toussaint's supreme merit that while he saw European civilisation as a valuable and necessary thing, and strove to lay its foundations among his people, he never had the illusion that it conferred any moral superiority. He knew French, British and Spanish imperialists for the insatiable gangsters that they were, that there is no oath too sacred for them to break, no crime, deception, treachery, cruelty, destruction of human life and property which they would not commit against those who could not defend themselves.[50]

What excites James about the United States is that "the people's speech . . . distilled into poetic rhythm . . . becomes not only echoes but positive expressions towards the freedoms, powers, sentiments, etc., of previous generations enjoyed by only a few."[51] In other words, the authenticity given popular speech by the ritualized fame of the cinema confers power on the ones represented.

This audience, though, is different from those of the past, argues James, in that its knowledge of the past and present can only be learned "in art, and above all, literature." By stressing the saturated nature of representation in a period of media control, James significantly departs from his emphasis on art as cultural infrastructure. A major postwar statement of his more typical position is in "Lenin and the Problem," where he admiringly remarks how Lenin, when speaking about culture, ignored Pushkin and Chekhov, who "even outside of Russia were acknowledged as the greatest artists of the nineteenth century."[52] Instead he speaks of education. Following Lenin's lead, James finds the major tasks of cultural study to be universal literacy and the curbing of the power of governmental bureaucracy. These to him are the major issues in studies of culture. They refer not only to the classical problem of the Soviet state but, step for step, to the postcolonial African elite, whose "culture" did *not* mean literature, or even mass culture, but the ideological means of access to thought.[53]

Exceptional Americanism

By the time he wrote the America book, James had already collaborated in the early 1940s with Dwight MacDonald—the founder of *Partisan Review*—on Irving Howe's journal *Labor Action*. He had in that way been introduced to the mass-culture debate with a vengeance. James had also mingled with the New York intellectuals, but he never felt a part of them, given their fascination with psychoanalysis, which he deemed to be of little use. Although Theodor Adorno was too alien in temperament and outlook to be considered a friend of James, the two had coffee together more than once in the lunchroom of the New School for Social Research.

What James would highlight in *American Civilization* he had already explored among his small circles of like-minded thinkers—for instance, in his arguments with Communist Party member Herbert Aptheker over the latter's book *The Negro in the Abolitionist Movement,* a work that prompted James to complain that Aptheker had minimized the role of John Brown and deleted the fierce debates between the radical and moderate wings within abolitionism.[54] In an ongoing way, James's participation in the journal *Correspondence* (whose first issue appeared in 1953) also grew directly out of his work for the America book. The rationale of the journal was to "encourage the workers to speak for themselves" by petitioning their comments, printing them, and then simply sharing them with others. Divided into four sections dedicated to "factory workers, women, Blacks, and young people," the journal, again, anticipates in great detail the "'new' social movements"—an anticipation that was common in Marxism elsewhere. The idea of cultural sites of political work was fully developed here in the early 1950s with specific attention going to "sexuality, male chauvinism, [and] high school alienation." The themes of abolitionism as intellectual legacy and the "masses" as variable identities reachable through sites of culture—both central to the America book—were thoroughly worked through by James and others in a political milieu for over a decade.

James's study was, in this sense, deliberately contemptuous of academic production, and the tenor of the typescript evolves from a deep and jealous resentment of those intellectuals whose academic connections gave them a visibility he lacked. In 1950 he was writing defensively and out of worry that he would not be heard, but from a position he believed to be a superior one since he (unlike the academics) understood "ordinary people."

Although he had won Trinidad's prestigious scholarships as a younger man, and although his impressive archival performances in *The Black Jacobins* and *The Life of Captain Cipriani* had suggested something of the acclaim he might have won in the university, James had thrown all of that away because it would isolate him from "ordinary people." His pain and his anger are apparent in his correspondence with the Melville scholar Jay Leyda, and, later, Lionel Trilling, and still later, Frank Kermode. It is hard to avoid the conclusion that they saw his missives as the work of an interesting crank. As if in response to that sort of treatment, he writes in the America project that "the whole thesis of this book" is to show that "the American intellectuals have nothing to say that is new. They will make no special contribution to the future of American society . . . Not only are they powerless before the process [of bureaucratization]. The intellectuals contribute to it, and then either drown themselves and their doubts and hesitations in it or desperately seek a retreat in their own individual psyches" (*AC,* 225).

Not only was his outline written in the middle of an enormous outpouring of work by U.S. intellectuals on mass culture, but his eventual spin on the content of that debate reflected many of the ritual enticements of leftist European emigrés during the war. Like

Brecht, for example, James endorsed the common 1920s view that America represented "an exciting alternative to a Europe which . . . [the intellectuals] thought to be depleted of its imaginative resources"; unlike him, by the 1950s James would not have recognized the disillusionment reflected in Brecht's comment that in the United States "everyone tries to turn themselves and everyone else into thoroughbred Americans in record time. It makes me seasick."[55]

As for the popular cultural reading itself, the European predecessors had been, for example, José Ortega y Gasset, much of the Frankfurt school, and (through the *Partisan Review*) George Orwell. In the United States, the chief predecessor had been Veblen (*Theory of the Leisure Class,* 1899). Characteristic American work of the period included MacDonald's "Theory of Popular Culture" (1944), Clement Greenberg's "Avant Garde and Kitsch" (1946), and Edmund Wilson's "Who Cares Who Killed Roger Ackroyd," from *Classics and Commercials,* a book that is exactly contemporaneous with James's manuscript in 1950.[56] Inasmuch as the mass-culture debate was about aesthetics, the familiar complaint was with mass culture's insincere imitations of high art. More relevant to James, predictably, were the arguments about social effects—arguments not at all unique to him in kind. The mass-culture debate was littered with them. How can the people be protected from the blandishments of big business? Such a view often blended imperceptibly into the perspective of liberal critics like Paul Lazersfeld and Frank Luther Mott to the effect that masscult could not be "bad" when so many chose it democratically. At the other extreme, Wilson perhaps best summarized the minority conservative position: "With so many fine books to be read . . . there is no need to bore ourselves with this rubbish."[57]

James's innovation was to pinpoint the reversal at work within the troubled notion of a U.S.-centered "popularity." Without denying its apologetic covering for the principle of freedom as market "choice," he saw no reason to recoil from the principle of individuality itself. It was too precious for that. But in the face of the truism that the United States was "exceptional"—that is, immune to revolution because of its racially divided working class, its high standard of living, and its replenishing frontier—James countered by turning the thesis on its head, not unlike Bloch in this respect, who, although anything but committed to resurrecting "individuality" in James's sense, still believed ardently that the "chicken in the pot and two cars in the garage . . . is also a revolutionary dream, not just a French or American or 'general human' dream."[58]

Taking Warren Susman's position, James believed that the United States was the best, not the worst, site for building the socialist future, and the reason had precisely to do with its racial divisions. In America, the African diaspora had reached its fullest sense of self; African Americans would either lead the revolution or the revolution would not be. James here was simply echoing Garvey before him: "The American Negro is the peer of all Negroes, the most progressive and the foremost unit in the expansive chain of scattered Ethiopia."[59] What poorer countries were struggling for, what decolonization was (and would be) mainly about, was achieving what already existed in the United States.[60]

Intellectually, though, the all-important tone of James's arguments came from his personal life, and they are perhaps responsible for an overstatement of potential within mass culture that diminishes the validity of the claims. James's letters to Constance Webb between 1939 and 1948 were both a courtship and a literary preparation. A married woman twenty years his junior, a highly successful model and actress, a Trotskyist militant, and an eventual biographer of their close friend Richard Wright, Webb ultimately married James after a protracted courtship represented in part by the correspondence itself. It is true that through this correspondence James worked his way out of his sectarian milieu, but the study's almost millenarian optimism offers to all but the most careful reader the temptation to mistake James as an advocate of a purely culturalist politics. From 1944 onward, the themes of *American Civilization* were hinted at and even loosely outlined in the Webb letters, which ranged in subject from unguarded comments on political discipline, to Wilhelm Reich's theories of the orgasm, the verse of Pope, and the male psyche. In a sense the letters were the culmination of his relationship with Webb, a relationship that was not by any means only intellectual (they had a son) but nevertheless clearly depended on the free association of intellectual desire James felt uniquely able to employ in her imagined presence.[61]

The Webb letters suggest that there were other, hardly personal motives; but they do put an appropriate emphasis on personality (as a key historical category) and at times reveal a touching vulnerability that betrays the extent to which James dramatized his own: "Curious the affinity I find myself always making now with you and the proletariat . . . If I write to you I will in time write better for the proletariat. And if the proletariat does act and a voice is needed to give its actions their fullest implications, I not only know that I will do it, but that I'll write to you as never before. No one will ever write as I shall write then. No one. The revolution is a release of power—and release for me too, in every direction."[62] *American Civilization* is a record of this type of sublimation: Constance becomes the working class just as the libertarian dream of the United States is translated into being the true goal of socialism—a standard culturalist position today that James foreshadowed. As a militant and a model, Webb brought the manuscript to James as a photo of the "real mind" of the working class in the thoroughly American, thoroughly marketable form of the "good read."

If he was not the first to claim that, as a connoisseur of the "high," he actually *loved* Hollywood films and comics, his argument in 1950 was still sufficiently iconoclastic to raise eyebrows. Still, as Jackson Lears has shown, "personality" as such was a patented part of the intellectual production in the 1950s and manifested itself at the convergence of two myths, one of which saw the social conflict of the American past "concealed by a renewed stress on individual heroism."[63] Here as elsewhere, the familiar scope of James's concerns is more or less blatant when one returns to Warren Susman, whose genealogy of twentieth-century appeals to "personality" places James in very crowded company.[64] In this period, similarly, Tocqueville was, according to Lears, "ritually invoked"; literature took on the aspects of a "surrogate religion"; "national character" sorts of studies swamped the bookstalls; and Philip Rieff, among others, found the "mature and still dynamic industrial civilization" constitutive of a "happy psychic condition."[65]

What James seemed clearly to be trying to do was absorb and deflect a very overdetermined thematics, making all the familiar gestures, citing the same gods, pouring on the required patriotic praises, but subtly changing their valences. It is not, after all, that this managerial/media society created happiness, only that it uniquely created the *image* of happiness; it was James's novel move to find hope in this. Here too, however, in the very moment of his bid to seize and invert the clamor by claiming contact with "ordinary people" (his American myth, unlike many of his contemporaries', was anything but classless), and to emphasize the utopic prodding of representation rather than—in the words of David Potter's *People of Plenty*, "the already arrived utopia of material abundance"—in this very moment his argument still overlaps with the prominent acclaim for the virtuous American folk, a U.S. variant of the originally left *volkische* ideologies on the Continent.[66] All the same, in some ways his study is completely original.

First of all, *American Civilization* combines two familiar genres of the time and so is unique in combination. It fits in not only with the popular-culture media work being done (very differently) by people like MacDonald, Louise Bogan, Clement Greenberg, and the Frankfurt school, but with the other, Brycean and Tocquevillian explorations of the American "character" that virtually flooded scholarship and media in these years, including Carl J. Friedrich's *New Image of the Common Man* (1950), Geoffrey Gorer's *American People: A Study in National Character* (1948), and Henry Steele Commager's slightly more academic *American Mind* (1950).[67]

Instead of going exhaustively through each of these, we might look only at Friedrich's book to get a sense of its common tenor with James. A battling liberal, Friedrich declares himself against the condescension with which the image of the "common man" is widely treated. His Jamesian point is that the common man is not someone else—it is you and I. According to Friedrich, only the critics of democracy itself, like Ortega y Gasset or, before him, Nietzsche, speak of the "incompetence of the masses," and these are food for the witch hunts "now sweeping the country."[68] In one section entitled "Independence of Thought and Propaganda," Friedrich attacks elitism and pleads, much like James, for a Veblenian "sense of workmanship" (9).

The similarity of his approach does not end here, either. Friedrich isolates in the United States a distinctive "appreciation for the diversity of national cultural backgrounds" (273). With his more acute, and more personal, awareness of race relations, James would pause before such an idea. But in the same passage, Friedrich looks back to the nineteenth century to discover, much like James discovered in Melville's use of Anacharsis Cloots, a general movement among the intellectuals from "nationalism to cosmopolitanism"—an idea that is central both to the priority James gave America over Europe (its classlessness in *culture*) and to his understanding of the distinctive mixing of the West Indian character (its unity despite a linguistic and racial heterogeneity).[69] Building on these traditions, Friedrich wanted to see what he called a "pan-humanism" and a "new world order": the creation of a "world citizen" with the United States supplying the moral lead.[70]

In 1950 the only really new twist possible to give to the genre of Bryce and Tocqueville would have been the discovery of the "masses." Both of these forerunners, of course, had written as if in a private conversation with Europe about a famous oddity. Tocqueville, in his famously ambivalent phrase "the tyranny of the majority," officially expressed sadness at the "universal uniformity" of social status in America—its lack of extremes that might produce "great poverty" but also "great learning" and men of "great importance." The necessary features of the genre are encoded here: a mixture of awe (never before had the like been seen), of daring to enter the future, and of regretting the loss of distinctions. A challenge to monarchy in its time, Tocqueville's work has always been used educationally in the United States as proof that America was (and is) a paradise for the small entrepreneur, a perennial golden mean: "Extraordinary prosperity and irremediable penury are alike unknown. The sentiment of ambition is universal, but the scope of ambition is seldom vast . . ."[71]—all untrue, of course, if one considers the slaves and the captive nations of the western territories (both Latino and Indian).

The Viscount Bryce, on the other hand, is much shriller and even less ambiguous. "Levelling down" is his phrase, and the good and the bad of it are not balanced. He despises the United States' "commonness of mind and tone, its want of dignity; the apathy among luxurious classes and fastidious minds," while he favors its "stability, the obedience of the law, . . . [and the fact that there are] no struggles between privileged and underprivileged orders." Intrigued by the unofficial or semiofficial respect for law—its marvelous avoidance of bureaucracy—Bryce even has some good words for lynch law justice![72]

However much one toys with the liberalizing intent of these two books, a cold reminder of their contents places James in a hard position. One could say he was merely taking the genre over, but these precursors mark the milieu with inherent hostility toward social leveling and with paeans to entrepreneurship. They were basically the work of admiring snobs. So then why say, as James did in the age of Henry Luce and Douglas MacArthur, that "America is the greatest country in the world"? *American Civilization* is much more of a continuity than a departure. Such a book had to be written, James seems to say, not by a European, who dissects the country from the vantage point of imperial experience and a settled culture, but by an "American" who is to the United States what the United States was to Europe then: raw, mixed, energetic, new.

Between this and the more applied sociological approaches of postwar media studies, there lay another sort of model for James in the work of Thorstein Veblen and, more close to home, Lewis Mumford, whose *Condition of Man* (1944) speaks with James's very enthusiasm for the "renewal of the personality" pitted against the shadowy forces of "war" and "machinery." "Technics" had been Mumford's term since 1934 for the enslavement of modernity to the machine—the point James reintroduces when he speaks of the "rhythms" of conformity. Significantly, both Mumford, in 1929, and Van Wyck Brooks, in exactly the same year as James, had also written revisionary studies of Melville. There were also telling differences. Mumford's doctrine of "organic humanism" may sound pretentious today. All is conducted at a moral level, and his reference points are unrelievedly "high"—Le Corbusier, Brancusi, Emerson.

To rehearse in detail the criticism of mass culture in the first decade of the postwar period would obviously be impossible here. But both the issues of James's novelty and his political intentions demand a general accounting. The preface to Bernard Rosenberg and David Manning White's *Mass Culture: The Popular Arts in America* (1957) suggests both the limits and the maturity of such writing, since it speaks already of the "postmodern world" and yet explains the rise of mass culture in terms of Madame Bovary. While discussion of the popular culture of newspapers had been around for 150 years, examination of the effects of mass media on audiences was much younger than that. The anthology claims it is the first of its kind and that "no traditional sourcebooks [are] available." For the editors, at least, the possible positions seesaw between only two: the critics repelled by vulgarity (a position shared by both radicals and conservatives for different reasons) and those who believe the situation is mixed.

With some of Friedrich's euphoria for America's postwar power to create "world citizens," the editors speak proudly about new labor-saving technologies, yet they doubt their merits when brought to the realm of "culture" in the sense of spiritual cultivation. That is, the irrepressible progress of American civilization in the field of politics and economic organization is not only unquestioned here but in fact provides the operative irony of the whole inquiry: "we" solved problems on one side, only to discover that we created a dulling monster on the other. "Before man can transcend himself he is being dehumanized. Before he can elevate his mind, it is being deadened. Freedom is placed before him and snatched away" (5).

Throughout the considerable range of the anthology—with essays by such unlikely companions as Edmund Wilson, Siegfried Kracauer, Hortense Powdermaker, and Theodor Adorno—the "quality" of mass culture is not the only or even the major issue. As in James, there is a deliberate attempt to fathom the political character of capitalism and the policies that the weapon of the media demand. If one finds predictable comments about the horrors of standardization like Greenberg's "sameness develops everywhere" (right out of Tocqueville and Bryce, incidentally), or Rosenberg's claim that mass art will "cretinize our taste" and "brutalize our senses while paving the way to totalitarianism," there are also the stands of Frank Luther Mott and Leslie Fiedler, who boasts about reading comic books "with pleasure." In a letter to Clive Bell, James similarly had protested: "You hoped, when I spoke about my admiration for comic strips, I was speaking with my tongue-in-cheek . . . I would never speak tongue-in-cheek to the general public."[73] Both Marshall McLuhan and Fiedler join James in saying that mass culture is dismissed only because intellectuals are hypnotized by books, and that self-righteous attitudes toward mass art come from a simple middlebrow fear of difference.

But both the specific attitude toward the "people" and, even more, the methodology of this writing as a whole place James apart. The pattern that emerges in the anthology is one of a contest, supposedly exhaustive, between those who worry about the effects of "rubbish" on impressionable viewers (feeling, like Orwell, that its political content is often right-wing and probusiness), and those who see it as proof of the mass's inherent bad judgment, its ease of satisfaction. Formally, the work exhibits psychosocial studies of wish fulfillment and fantasy, pseudoempirical surveys on the need for escapism, plain market research, winking insider talk by those who have done a little slumming, liberal "understanding" of people's entertainment desires, and so on. At the same time, declarations sounding very much like James are everywhere: rhetoric on the future of American "democracy," comparisons between popular culture and the art of ancient Greece, links to the "forgotten literature of tradesmen," and arguments about the special force of mass culture in permitting people to "have the satisfaction of knowing that they are identified with a vast and forward movement, which is giving to everyday folks their right to laugh and flourish under the sun."[74]

As I suggest above, the contribution of James's America project is not found so much in its insights but in its *location*. The typescript's resilience derives in part from its tone. The ecstatic drive of the narrative, its rigorous but plainspoken enthusiasms are based on a conception of an American social and artistic conscience in evolution. Both derive from James's assumption of place within the ranks of everyday people, whom he conceived, unlike Friedrich's panhumanist "you and I," as a class that stood in opposition to the "industrialists." This aspect of being in a class, and in solidarity with it, is completely absent in the other books. James's location ensured "integration" in the simultaneously aesthetic and political sense of the term: "I have sat for hours in America, listening to people, all sorts of poor working people, telling me all about themselves. It is indispensable for any understanding of anything. It must go side by side with the books" (*AC*, 225).

If the separate sections of the larger study found echoes in the work of others, they are altogether different in James because he fits America into an apocalyptic narrative of global liberation from an explicitly Marxist point of view. Moreover, they fit together altogether differently in James because of his own clarity of purpose. The part of the manuscript that is a revisionary account of Melville, for example (and in this way like Mumford, Jay Leyda, and Van Wyck Brooks) makes enormous claims about the essence of New World originality. Melville, says James, did not just record as a novelist an American "individuality" or predict the social type that would threaten it (Ahab); he showed, in addition, "an absolutely unique objectivity about ordinary labor without sentimentality which cannot be found in any other novelist." He was the best of all time because he created "realistic description[s] of process and personnel" in ordinary business life. Similarly, James's examination of the abolitionists (unlike Aptheker's) was not just the uncovering of a domestic radicalism. All of these themes, right up to the examination of the CIO, are part of a seamless fabric, expressed in a single outburst of energy that gave the study a rare sincerity.

The unmistakable feel of mass-culture criticism in the 1950s, like the postmodernism debate today that repeats it in a barely modified language, is that of helpless witness: recording by inches the approach of something too powerful to resist.[75] The evils conjured—the leveling of value, standardization—are horrible precisely because they are popular; that is, a vestigial memory of Marx's focus on the working class produces in the researcher a terrifying loneliness since "they" have willingly joined the anonymous culture of the "machine," making its victory certain. In these accounts, apart from the "masses," there are no human agents. How different all this looks in James, where he talks instead of a colonization of American ideology by businessmen: "It is perhaps the most astonishing thing about the way modern America thinks about itself—the need to believe that the individual industrialists and financiers who organized the vast industries of the West were merely new forms of the individualism of 1776–1861."

A true "individualism"—as distinct from this bogus one of the financiers—becomes for James very much like a collectivism. He begins to see individualism as a collectivism without centralized leadership. Mass art portrays with complete fidelity what people are and what they want. But mass art also reveals to the people the commonality of their desires, and thereby gives them the self-consciousness of class: "It is the writer's belief that in modern popular art, film, radio, television, comic strip, we are headed for some such artistic comprehensive integration of modern life, that the spiritual, intellectual, ideological life of modern peoples will express itself in the closest and most rapid, most complex, absolutely free relation to the actual life of the citizens of tomorrow" (*AC,* 150).

In a way similar to Rosenberg and Manning White, but with an inverted sense of value, artistic taste and political consequence are here yoked. One felt with the former that the ugliness of "standardization" was the real complaint—that is, an aesthetic complaint—but that the animus toward it could only be defended by arguing that it led to "totalitarianism." For James the case is just the opposite. The artistic thrill of mass culture lies in its documentary testimony of a people grasping at a fleeting individuality. The key concept here—

the point at which the artistic integrity and political benefits of mass culture intersect—is what James calls "integration." Media art was integrating "all aspects of the life of modern man" by projecting into a new public forum both "ordinary" life and "the great social and political events of the day," allowing the one to belong to the other.

Leo Löwenthal, writing at exactly the same time, reminds his contemporaries that mass culture was inextricably bound up with advertising; while it gave expression to vivid desires, the desires had the effect of pacifying the audience: "Wherever revolutionary tendencies show a timid head, they are mitigated and cut short by a false fulfilment of wish dreams, like wealth, adventure, passionate love, power, and sensationalism."[76] As a counterpoint to James, Löwenthal is invaluable in part because he shares with him a common platform as a foreigner schooled in a wider, more impressive literary and philosophical tradition who wants those dreams to bear the present crisis against the resistances of a parochial intellectual audience. Like him, he is unsatisfied with the missing middle of masscult criticism's peremptory polarity between, on the one hand, "a positive attitude toward all instrumentalities for the socialization of the individual" and, on the other, a patronizing "concern about the inner fate of the individual under the impact of the leveling powers of . . . leisure activity" (47)—precisely the dualism James sought to revise by denying instrumentality out of hand and polemically asserting that individuality was enabled by the official celebration of a leisure activity that was basically working class.

Löwenthal's departures from James cannot simply be dismissed as the top-heavy work of a Frankfurt mandarin. Yet it is difficult to rephrase the former's worries in a more appealing contemporary form; in the end, one is talking about agreeing or disagreeing with the unarguable stakes of the cultural juncture James extols. Is American masscult's undermining of high art an appreciable problem or not—the undermining, that is, of precisely the creators of those artifacts James delightfully portrays as masscult's ancestors: Aeschylus, Melville, Lincoln, Phillips? James may well argue that these classics in their day were like the comics of our own, but the system of masscult's dissemination ensures that the audience for comics will not have read the earlier classics. Similarly, why is there no room in James, as in Löwenthal, for a distinction between masscult and "folk" culture, which the former was busy extinguishing from the

American earth? Löwenthal's analysis was simply more demanding. Despite what is often said about the Frankfurt approach, Löwenthal did not suppose the masscult audience to be sheep, or to be brainless; merely that it appeared they lived a split personality, which made him want to know more about "the mechanisms of interdependence between the pressures of professional life and the freedom from intellectual and aesthetic tension in which popular culture seems to indulge." This extremely promising and, to me, more convincing way to account for the popularity of mass culture is at the same time a built-in safeguard against that Jamesian doctrine Löwenthal especially singles out: "Better popular culture presupposes a better society."

On a different matter, it needs to be said that James glorified the traditional values of the American working class while attributing ideas to it that ring very false to natives and seem a part of that exended myth of America believed by the foreign left. U.S. workers, argued James in 1945, believed in a nonsectoral, unified world community; he thought their religion was a merely formal affair ("[the worker] may call himself a Catholic, but he is a confirmed humanist . . . [who] would not dream of persecuting his fellow-worker for his religion"); he felt they believed that everyone had "the right to the best possible education."

In context, James's comments are not as wildly wrong as they first appear. In contrast to the European tradesman of the Reformation—the kind of comparison he would typically have had in mind—there is some truth to what he says. At the same time, it is a fundamental misreading of the American heritage, the origins of the United States as refuge for religious zealots, and its character (especially after World War II) as meeting ground for right-wing exiles. Then as now there were mobilizations by the religious right—attacks on "secular humanism" nurtured by a long-standing anti-intellectualism and focus on "technical" education. Fierce ethnic chauvinisms appeared frequently at the community level and expressed themselves in national politics as well. James had even brought himself to the point of believing that the United States would aid anticolonial liberation movements following the war![77]

His optimism about a progressive America came at a price. It is astounding that by the time he wrote *Mariners, Renegades, and Castaways* James had practically nothing to say about one of the most prominent aspects of Melville's premature modernity—his treatment of ethnocentrism, the corruption of the West at the cusp of imperial trade, the concept of differential values among cultures, the connection between slavery and genocide *within* the United States, and the nation's barbaric attitudes toward nonwhites abroad—all of it connected, in turn, with the exploitation of labor. The avoidance is so absurd, in fact, that James actually quotes a passage where Melville, tongue in cheek, praises the great "naked Nantucketers" who would "overrun and conquer the watery world like so many Alexanders; parceling out among them the Atlantic, Pacific, and Indian oceans, as the three pirate powers did Poland." His response to this passage, uttered without a trace of irony, is precisely this: "Melville understands what America has given to the world—none better. He has chosen whaling for his unit of demonstration. And in a brilliant page he sums up the grandeur of the American past." By considering the contrast between these lines and those he would proclaim only a few years later in Trinidad, one gets a sense of the damage done by James's failed bid to nudge American worldliness into the scope of his own antithetical designs, and also of the sharp corrective to his thinking given by the unpredictable force-fields of (an albeit small-time) liberation struggle. Not long after in Britain, aware of the final reckoning, James would again speak of the "seeds of the new society" planted by imperialism in the form of London's diaspora communities.

The implications of this transformation are, I am implying, this: "American exceptionalism" as a mechanism for explaining the lack of U.S. revolutionary prospects is in the end valid, although not because of U.S. affluence, the customary explanation. It is valid for the reasons that James had the perspicacity to see, but not to interpret correctly—that is, America's mass-cultural mirage. What is obvious and "crude" is not necessarily wrong. Mass culture has indeed been the appropriately American means of stifling protest in a society of consumer pleasures.

It would be wrong to suggest that James's theses on "American exceptionalism" were confined to this moment of transition. He retained them throughout his life. In a letter to Maxwell Geismar in 1961, for example, he is again planning an essay on "American character as I have known it and as I have seen it reflected in American literature." The difference, he says, between Americans and Europeans (always his major point of contrast) can be "crudely" put as follows: "Americans expect to be happy. They want to be happy. They see no reason why they should not be happy. And when it turns out that, despite material promises which they know are for many of them reasonably satisfactory, happiness seems to elude them, their fury and frustration is the fury and frustration that permeates Styron's book [*Lie Down in Darkness*]. All this of course for me has enormous social and political implications."[78]

He punned on that image of happiness (and of "America"). But the rediscovery of James by the New Left, and the largely unconscious repetition of many of his findings in current cultural theory misses the joke. For James, the mass-cultural image potently captured a life that could not be lived in the America of 1950; it was historical backwash from the future—an enticement, a lure, rather than a record. Behind his love for what could be salvaged here lay an elaborate set of reversals—Lenin as an anticolonial writer, Al Capp as the child of Melville, happiness as an urge that is intensified by a milieu of evident and growing unhappiness.

Taken whole, James's career is remarkably consistent. There is the emphasis on labor, dialectics, personality, and happiness, all underwritten by a specifically populist bolshevism. The America years—particularly these recently resurrected ones—are in that sense a detour, which is why they are so instructive. His reading was brilliant, but too subtle. Its transformation today—or better, its unwitting echoes—in various theories about the politics of style, of subversive consumption, and of the opportunities for resistance opened up by the new technologies leave all of his ironies behind. In part, of course, the reasons for this are not hard to find: they are partly generational. They have to do with lacking James's cross-generational experiences and intersectoral training in the wake of combined colonial and second-world defeats. Living again at the gateway of another "American century," we perhaps know better than to mistake the comforting familiarities and controlled excitements of mass art for a socialist rallying point, despite the multiple confusions on this score in the recent cultural criticism of Britain and the United States. For mass art is not only an American affair, as I try to show in the next chapter.

6

The World Cuban: Alejo Carpentier and Cuban Popular Music

In Cuba, we watched American films constantly; the Soviet Union did not. The difference is why we are still here.

—Mayra Vilasis

The *bongó* antidote to Wall Street! . . . No hotdogs with the *santos de mayeya!*

—Alejo Carpentier

In debates over comparative social systems, much has written about the viability of economies, about the relative merits of human rights and social services, about the success or failure of forms of art, but rarely about the categories of joy and relaxation. And yet, no issue is more decisive for a mass-cultural product than desire, nor for socialism than an image of voluntary attraction to its distinctive kinds of entertainment—particularly now in a period of dismal prospects and anxious self-interrogations. Does socialism have anything unique to offer pleasure?

As U.S. mass culture continues to appear to many a normative center, it is forgotten that history is full of alternative cosmopolitan models in societies long seen as the nemesis of U.S. mass culture. In the case of Cuba this is certainly true in what Fernando Ortiz once called "the cosmopolitan triumph of the Cuban drum."[1] It may at first appear willful to state what is nonetheless true: that in the 1920s and 1930s this *international* success of Cuban music was instrumental in shoring up the project of Cuban independence, many of whose intellectual leaders (among them, Ortiz himself) greeted the revolution of 1959 as that project's completion.

The fact of that international triumph cannot be seriously doubted. It has become a commonplace in Latin American musical criticism. What Emilio Grenet wrote in the introduction to *Música popular Cubana* in 1939 has been repeated dutifully by a variety of later commentators, although Alejo Carpentier has put it best: "The island of Cuba had an ability to create music with its own distinctive form that from the earliest times found an extraordinary success abroad . . . our little island produces one of the great popular musics of the twentieth century."[2]

The case of Carpentier is especially interesting in this history. He was a singular chronicler of the Americas' impact on Europe who told a story that departs from (or rather, extends) the better-known stories of jazz and "primitive art," and who did so in a way that redefines customary views of the European avant-gardes (of which he was harshly critical). But Carpentier, although rightly identified with high literary novels and essays, was arguably as important a theorist of music as Theodor Adorno. Consequently, there is an inherent interest in the way in which he promoted forms of popular and symphonic music while analyzing the Adornian problems of radio and recording technologies but arriving at vastly different conclusions.

Furthermore, as a supporter of the Cuban Revolution after 1959, Carpentier suggests a great deal about the importance of Afro-Cuban culture to the ideology of the revolution and about the specific role that popular music has played within it. He embodies a history that contests the many accounts of the Sovietization of Cuban culture and the numerous assessments of that culture's failures in regard to the image of "Blackness" that have appeared in recent decades—issues that in important ways are related, as I argue below. When analyzed at all, Carpentier's writing on music has been used to chart its effects on his novels. By contrast, I want to look at the way his extensive music criticism over half a century led him to attempt a union of high and low culture in a distinctively Cuban *mass* culture for export.[3] To do so, he took on the very European avant-garde themes he had once been deeply involved in—themes that provide the basis for the contemporary critiques of salvage ethnography that lie at the heart of recent dismissals of indigenous culture.

To explore the case of Cuba today might appear impertinent or simply nostalgic given the island's rapid transformation under the diktats of U.S. policy. But doing so allows one to examine how the intemperate, generalized attacks on the nation-state have been, at one step removed, the contemporary form that an attack on socialism takes. Images of a stillborn or prescriptive cultural life under socialism have always been powerful means of dispensing with the attractiveness of socialist alternatives. The debate over mass culture, after all, is a debate over the articulation of a type of experience—a type of relationship to fantasy associated in advance with the libidinal free play and spectacle of image capitalism. One does not have to deny the liberatory feelings that U.S. mass culture unleashes in various third-world communities to urge that critics treat more carefully, and unearth or explain more fully, the forms of alternative desire that socialist movements and societies have actually created, and are still creating. There is almost no vocabulary for doing so right now.

From Paris to Havana

Alejo Carpentier could not have been invented less nationally authentic. "I can say without irony," he remarked in 1963, "that the fact that I was born in Cuba and am a Cuban writer in the Spanish tongue is the fault of Dreyfus."[4] Descended from an old French family, his father had relocated to Cuba to escape his homeland's anti-Dreyfus ways, but also, according to Carpentier, because Cuba had seemed attractive to him as a new republic (its independence had been formally declared in 1902). Passing his adolescence in the Cuban countryside, Carpentier traveled to the capital on horseback periodically to purchase books, living a life, as he would later put it, *"totalmente campesina"* and listening to "old Cuban blacks who used to tell me stories that their grandparents had told them" (73).

If not literature and storytelling, it was classical music that marked his childhood. One grandmother had been a superb pianist under Cesar Franck, his father an excellent cellist and student of Pablo Casals. By profession his father had become an architect and designed some of the most important buildings of Havana in the early part of the century. His mother was a Cuban of Russian origin.

When Carpentier arrived in Paris in 1928 at the age of twenty-three, he did so fleeing the police of Gerardo Machado, in whose prisons he had begun his first novel, *¡Écue-Yamba-Ó!* the year before. Jailed for his activities in the Grupo Minorista and its vanguardist journal *Revista de Avance*—a group whose platform of political reform featured ill-tempered protests against U.S. interventions in Cuba, Mexico, and Nicaragua—he had written the novel (published at Machado's fall in 1933) in the atmosphere of Cuban *negrismo*.[5] As a movement, *negrismo* was roughly analagous to the Harlem Renaissance in the United States: the first serious attempt to give Black Cuba a position of deserved importance in the national patrimony. Most famously associated today with the ethnographies of Fernando Ortiz in his pioneering work on Afro-Cuban religious and musical cultures, and, after World War II, with Lydia Cabrera in her work on *ñáñigo* rituals and *palo monte, negrismo* had been a significant factor of resistance to the Machado dictatorship and, in Carpentier's hands, an expression of literary vanguardism itself.[6]

In a wildly impressionistic experimental prose modeled, contrapuntally, on a work of music, *¡Ècue-Yamba-Ó!* casts its Black protagonist, Menegildo Cué, in settings that record with an ethnographic delirium the rhythms of the *zafra* (cane harvest), the ecstatic spirituality of *batá* drumming, and the sort of innocence of the humble then widely accorded the "primitive." He later considered the novel an artistic and political failure, although the Cuban conjuncture had forced on it an interesting, and paradoxical, twist: an avant-garde writing that sought at the same time to be "nationalist."[7]

Although Carpentier was described in later life as speaking Spanish with a French accent, his arrival in Paris invited a variety of misunderstandings.[8] In spite of his impeccable avant-garde training and ambiguous personal history, the interwar European intellectuals' use of the "primitive" on behalf of ventures into the erotic and the unconscious was bound to play differently for him, coming from a culture of emergent racial syncretism and political dictatorship—the two forces behind the word "nationalist" as he used it. And so the act of negotiating a view of vanguardism in the *Revista de Avance* as a kind of activist study group, and of vanguardism in general as an explosion of creative and epistemological possibilities, did not remain altogether submerged during his preparatory intellectual formation in Paris between 1928 and 1939.

It was, nevertheless, significantly complicated by the auspices under which he found himself there—as a correspondent for Havana newspapers. The topics of his essays were relentlessly Continental and belonged above all to that type of art criticism suggestive of the leisured amateur: the gossipy and idiosyncratic reviews of recent European symphonies and operas. With the possible exception of the painters Francis Picabia and, especially, Wifredo Lam (a close friend of André Breton, and the subject of an entire chapter in Breton's *Surrealism and Painting*), no Cuban intellectual had such intimate contact with the interwar avant-gardes as Carpentier.[9]

Left penniless on his arrival—and unable for that reason to live, as he put it, the "sweet cosmopolitan life"—he took over the editorship of the South American journal *Imán* for a short time, befriending contributors such as Michel Leiris, Georges Bataille, and Raymond Queneau (he had met Robert Desnos already, in Havana, in 1928). Like the English Caribbean writers of the 1950s in London, however, Carpentier made his early living in radio. After the collapse of *Imán,* he collaborated with Desnos on a series of text-and-music programs broadcast by Poste Parisien and Radio Luxembourg—programs on which the young Antonin Artaud worked as an artistic interpreter. In this company he developed a type of ambitious, experimental radio featuring poetry readings by Paul Eluard, Langston Hughes, Miguel Hernández, and Nicolás Guillén, and one improvisational wordplay piece with text by Jacques Prévert and Desnos. He was later to collaborate with Bataille on the famous surrealist journal *Documents,* in 1930.

Carpentier's return to Cuba, by contrast, had none of the compulsions of his arrival. Well established and financially independent after a decade in Paris, he left behind "an enchanting apartment on the plaza Daupine overlooking the Seine," and did so out of an inner need: "The necessity of returning to find contact again with Latin America had become absolutely overwhelming."[10] Traveling to Havana via New York, he continued his extraordinary output of music criticism for the Cuban journal *Carteles,* to which he had been contributing while still in Paris, with particular attention to trends in European classical performance, and with a special interest in Edgar Varèse.

It was his trip to Haiti with Louis Jouvet in 1943, however, that marked the clearest break in Carpentier's career—the inspiration for that series of novels he would call his "American cycle," whose first volume (*El Reino de este mundo* [*The Kingdom of This World*]) saw the appropriate union of his French and Caribbean interests in a fictional history of the San Domingo revolution. *El Reino* was remarkably, and perhaps expectedly, an inspiration with sources both ethnographic and musical. For his Haitian trip was quickly followed by one to Mexico, where he was commissioned by the Center for Economic Culture to prepare a history of Cuban music as part of an encyclopedia the center was organizing on South American history, philosophy, literature, and the arts. Although crucial in helping him realize two of his most important pieces of writing—*La Música en Cuba* and the novel *Los Pasos perdidos (The Lost Steps)*—the assignment did not so much force him to see for the first time the global significance of Cuban music as it allowed him to refine and complement arguments he had been making about that music throughout his Parisian sojourn. When he wrote, spectacularly, in the early 1960s that "Cuban music . . . has conquered the world, is listened to virtually everywhere" (85), he was only repeating points he had made in the 1930s and 1940s while watching the influence of *"cubanismos"* on the Parisian café crowds in the form of touring Cuban combos in the age of European jazz.[11]

For all of Carpentier's early devotion to the culture of locality, Cuba in these years could not hold him. In 1945 he moved to Caracas to work for a publicity agency while continuing his reviews of music for the Venezuelan paper *El Nacional,* and there he remained until 1959, writing the novels for which he is now mostly known. Beginning in poetic ethnography and moving to ethnomusicology proper, he found himself after the Cuban Revolution involved in cultural policy. In the Castro years, he became subdirector general of culture, a member of the National Council of Culture, and (within that) the chief commissioning agent for the National Publishing House. It took the victory of the 26th of July Movement to bring him back to Cuba, and upon his return, he later recalled, "I placed myself at the disposal of the Revolutionary Government."[12]

Why someone with this background and these inclinations chose this option seems a significant and unasked question. For one has to appreciate Carpentier's reputation in Cuban letters as the impeccable novelists' novelist whose Spanish flamboyance has typically been given the name "baroque," a concept whose centrality to Latin American letters was clarified above all by his countryman, the novelist and Proustian recluse José Lezama Lima.[13] The critical account of Carpentier's oeuvre has had relatively little to say about his work on music or the way in which that work moved his understanding of literature away from Lezama's sense of the baroque as an "erudite polyphony." His seminal essay "The Problematic of the Contemporary Latin American Novel," for example, while extending this familiar rhetoric of cultural mixtures in images of the "untiring transience" of Cuban cities in which "every imaginable style meshes with another" is actually about how writers too easily pretend to assimilate cultural differences superficially, without really knowing a place.[14] They imagine that after spending "fifteen days in a mining village" they know it (10). The essay is a strongly worded defense of the "indigenous" understood politically and ideologically, rather than through folkloristic color. Its recurrent references to Sartre and (more indirectly) Brecht summon the categories of race and class to make a case for the novel as being a form of knowledge and information as well as aesthetic pleasure.

A gifted connoisseur with salon credentials, Carpentier was also, after Ortiz himself, the best known and most quoted musicologist Cuba ever produced. The languorous architect of a fiction—to use his own words in a different context—of "indefinable charm, a fabric of vague, remote memories and partly remembered longings," he was also the author of a 470-page political-historical trilogy about Cuba extending from the Spanish Civil War to the Bay of Pigs: *La Consagración de la primavera* (characteristically titled after Igor Stravinsky's *Rite of Spring).*[15]

The question one might ask is "Why?"—particularly now, when the very viability of the concept "indigenous" is questioned, and when a general rehabilitation of surrealism as a model for ethnographic work is so common. Why, that is, would someone who knew surrealism so intimately—a collaborator and close friend of many of the same figures who are retrospectively invoked in contemporary ethnographic surrealism, someone enlisted in the Latin American baroque as precursor of today's cultural hybridity—why would someone such as Carpentier be so useless, finally, to literary cosmopolitanism in its present form?

A number of issues are striking here. Even after 1989, in spite of its rapid and coerced transformation, Cuba remains as a sore point for cultural theories of globalization: the last New World refuge of the wrong subversive politics and an atavistic paradigm of third-world independence.[16] And this is the state, after all, that Carpentier not only supported but joined. With a few notable exceptions, it is remarkable that the culture of revolutionary Cuba has played almost no role in Euro-American cultural theory, even among the U.S. academy's many prominent and prolific Cuban-American critics.[17] Carpentier's example is similarly key for understanding the contributions of contemporary ethnography to an understanding of cultural studies. By ignoring his sustained and often violent criticisms of surrealism, for example, it is easy to lose a sense of the Marxist milieu in which the continental avant-gardes were largely articulated, and to miss the force of his complaint in the 1970s that the avant-gardes had been "hopelessly separated from [their] political contexts."[18] Although Carpentier is, one would think, a significant precursor to cultural studies in that he promoted, and even embodied, the turn to popular culture, he continued comfortably to live (and in Cuba, largely to stand for) the life of letters in a traditional sense.

Apart from his links to the avant-garde, Carpentier importantly revises the discourse on traditional literary modernism's view of diasporic Black cultures and the novel of empire. As I have been arguing, one of the problems in the reception of third-world literature in the age of globalization is, paradoxically, the provinciality of its references. It is only too easy to cite Theodor Adorno's essays on jazz, for example, when looking at the cultured European Marxist's limitations in the face of expressive Black cultures. The great modernist novel of the classical composer is, similarly, Thomas Mann's *Dr. Faustus;* and it is to Conrad's *Heart of Darkness* that critics inevitably turn when exploring modernism's dramatization of the river journey as archetype of the imperial quest for the source.

It is not only that Carpentier in *La Música en Cuba* and *The Lost Steps* covered the same territory as these divergent works, but that he did so with an intimate, localized attachment to the geographic locale he was fictionally exploring. I am talking, in other words, about two kinds of absence: political, in the clipped treatment of Carpentier's contexts, and referential, in traditional English studies, whose creation of a postcolonial subjectivity relies on a cramped list of representative works. Writing from within the field of current English studies—even inflected as it is by postcoloniality and multiculturalism—one is simply unable to discuss Conrad with any degree of adequate comparative knowledge. *Heart of Darkness* would look very different alongside logical counterparts like Walter Raleigh's *The Discoverie of the Large, Rich, and Beutiful Empire of Guiana,* Wilson Harris's more polyphonic or cubist novel *Palace of the Peacock,* and Carpentier's *The Lost Steps*—all about river journeys that allegorize the conquistador logic at work in the search for a primitive source.[19] To avoid an undifferentiated third-world literature demands, paradoxically, a greater investment in a vastly expanded comparatism, and that is one of the interests of this chapter.

These are only some of the ways in which Carpentier, the literary cosmopolitan, refuses to act like one. Thus, in spite of his obvious links with the Latin "boom" novelists who provided the model for that cosmopolitanism in American book markets—above all in his famous coinage *"lo real maravilloso"* ("marvelous reality") in the preface to *The Kingdom of This World*—he is not typically placed in their company. What I argue below is that Carpentier's apparently naive insistence on autochthony has a political rather than a cultural-nationalist meaning, and that this view is deeply linked to his mixed views of the interwar avant-garde as well as to his later involvements with revolutionary Cuba—a stand inseparable from his involvements with Afro-Cuban musics. I examine this record—which has been largely overlooked in accounts of his work—by way of reviewing the recent interest in what James Clifford and others have called "surrealist ethnography," while I also question related assumptions about the universality of U.S. mass culture, since both of these concepts have been instrumental in attacking the intelligibility of the indigenous.

Both of these theoretical views rely on invoking the new, the fresh, and the vibrant that themselves depend on New World tropes that Carpentier helped define and extend, but also amended in particularly situated ways. In that sense, the quaintness of returning to this baroque novelist is calculated, and I intend it as a trope of return that is also a going forward. For the version of the "new" in surrealist ethnography approximates in its own theory (often at the level of style) the very imaginative rupture with tradition found in the artistic avant-gardes. Its approach is fundamentally aesthetic and literary in that sense, however much it is true that vanguardism (as Peter Bürger notes) is about "the liquidation of art as an activity that is split off from the praxis of life."[20] Many of the moves in mass-culture theory, though, have been antagonistic to literature and are motivated by the populist desire to read social meanings allegorically in public entertainments of a nonliterary sort. Carpentier unites and subflates these two positions, and does so inflected by a personal relationship to Cuban socialism.

Ethnographic Surrealism: The Red and the Black

What, first of all, did Carpentier mean by the avant-garde? The answer is clearer after Vicky Unruh's brilliant recent study of the Latin American vanguardist movements of the 1920s and 1930s, including its brief account of Carpentier's part in it.[21] Her work is crucial for showing not only the sheer range of these movements, but their parallels to and independence from the European avant-gardes that are typically assumed simply to have spawned those in Latin America and elsewhere. In the work of writers like Roberto Arlt, Oswald de Andrade, Martín Adán, and Vicente Huidobro, Latin American vanguardism had been Continental in its development. It found expression in every genre, produced a wealth of manifestos, and was "simultaneously international and autochthonous in its orientation" (10).

Along with Andrade, Huidobro, and Miguel Angel Asturias, Carpentier had been one of the important "transcontinental links" stimulating *vanguardismo* with leads from the European avant-gardes at the same time that he and others denied the debt. Andrade's "Manifesto antropófago" (1928), for instance, had "stressed Europe's debt to the New World for its conception of natural man" in Rousseau and Montaigne, and had proposed the creation of the "bad savage"—a "New World model of cultural critique and capacity for creative assimilation" (130). The claim was common in Latin American circles of this type that "vanguardism itself was a fundamentally New World event" that Europe had been copping for generations (132). Carpentier himself had suggested that "Latin American writers needed to pay attention to European clamorings for a New World vernacular art" (134).

Carpentier's autochthony, then, has to be seen against this larger background of a protracted and widely articulated "Americanism" in its hemispheric sense. Autochthony was in some ways nothing more than the great rhetorical club of vanguardist motifs of originality and discovery in the New World context, and they perpetuated earlier "romantic, organicist myths of America through images of an integrated, telluric body-continent, rooted to ancestral origins"—a modernist spin on what could be found already in Martí: America as the "radically disparate" (27). To Unruh, then, *The Lost Steps* (1953) is primarily an "encounter between modernity and the autochthonous" that had its roots in Mário de Andrade's *Macunaíma* (1928) and Asturias's *Leyendas de Guatemala* (1930). Both she and Roberto González Echevarría see Carpentier's novel to be an ironic rewriting of what both call "organicist myths of America" that rely on the idea of nature or the landscape as a field in which a new and original being expressed itself in the Americas. As in *Macunaíma,* the Latin American vanguards had "simultaneously epitomized and parodied" this position.

Yes and no. Much had happened to Carpentier between 1928 and 1953—immersion in Afro-Caribbean musics primarily, as well as a decade and a half of skeptical looking back on the pros and cons of the avant-gardes themselves. Unruh superbly sets the political stage for these movements by describing how they coincided with the first "interlocking of Latin American economies with world markets" and the "gradual shift in hegemony from Europe to the United States." Along with the growth of major Latin American city-centers came the growth of a "more politically aware and active middle class," the "development of significant workers' movements," and the "formation of Latin America's first socialist and communist parties" (4–5).

But although Unruh observes that a few struck discordant notes in their attitudes toward artistic vanguardism as such—most notably César Vallejo—she leaves Carpentier completely out of that picture, saying only that he defended surrealism against the charge of being aloof and affirmed that his was an era of "passionate faith in the value of intellectual and artistic pursuits" (24). She is quite right about Vallejo, who wrote from Paris for the Lima-based paper *Mundial* between 1925 and 1930, and whose broadsides against surrealism were eventually published as a separate pamphlet. But she misstates Carpentier's second thoughts on the European avant-gardes. What is more, she suggests that Vallejo's complaint was that the avant-garde "ap[ed] Europe," when what bothered him was at least as much the intellectualist pretense of a purely cultural resistance. The interesting tension for Unruh is the one between the avant-garde's sense of Latin America as the "homelessness of a cultural void," on the one hand, and a "ground zero of artistic creation to be forged from autochthonous sources," on the other (143). *The Lost Steps* is about a great deal more than this, as I argue below.

Unruh's argument, at any rate, speaks to the assault on the concept of the "indigenous" today. The term can be understood here in the sense of Hal Foster's related term the "primitive," which he argues has two suspicious and mutually hostile strains: "a spectacle of savagery or a state of grace, a socius without writing or the Word, or a site of originary unity, symbolic plentitude, natural vitality."[22] The assault against the second of these meanings—a salvational primitivism—has come from within ethnography, whose late borrowings from literary criticism have provided compensatory capital for a discipline endangered by the extermination of its very object of study. What ethnography lost by giving up the primitive, it gained in theory.

The critique of ethnography offered by James Clifford, which I refer to in an earlier chapter, charted its new course by returning to France of the 1920s and 1930s, the very years Carpentier spent there as a Cuban surrealist, critic, and musical director of Radio Luxembourg. A similar ethnographic critique, with the same attention to France, later arrived with Michael Taussig's book *The Nervous System.*[23] Rather than a tight artistic circle, surrealism for Clifford is a broad, and broadly social, reinvention of the primitive in a manner that transcends what Foster saw as its unacceptable dichotomy between the inarticulate and the naturally pure. It subsides finally in the aesthetic of the fragment, a reshuffling of order, "delight in cultural impurity and disturbing syncretisms"; a "cultural reality composed of artifical codes, ideological identities, and objects susceptible to inventive recombination."[24]

For Taussig, the same period in France has become an immediate and obsessive point of interest. For him, the focus is more explicitly on magic, a concept he uses to explore the power of the state in grotesquely arbitrary and militarized zones like those of today's Colombia. Yet Taussig discovers in the Cuna shamans rather infinite malleability, accommodation, and evasion in the act of interpreting terror. In a long essay, "Homesickness and Dada," he draws very strict homologies between shamanistic magic and the outlooks of the European avant-gardes. Homesickness for him becomes the now outdated plight of the anthropologist fleeing to the womb of the Great Mother to find cultural roots. But Dada is what the researcher who is really looking ought to find: the "arbitrariness of the sign"—that is, the "mimetic vertigo" that the shaman uses to copy without copying, to assimilate an encroaching Western culture only by reenchanting it. Magic is the renarrativization of an alien artifact: subversive consumption.

As I have been saying, this image of a cultural resistance in the form of an appropriation and mixing—Clifford's "delight in cultural impurity and disturbing syncretisms"—blankets the study of non-Western cultures in the United States and Britain. It presents itself as an answer to Lévi-Strauss's ethnographic romanticism and his moving accounts of the decimation of the last remnants of a prelapsarian world.[25] The indigenous today is therefore seen to be naive, and its ready substitute is, of course, hybrid culture.

These fascinations with juxtaposition, the fragment, "fortuituous or ironic collage" are a deliberate effort to give value to an interwar aesthetic for contemporary intellectual work: to stamp the present with the seductions of an era in French intellectual life.[26] Yet anyone who has returned to the documents of Bataille, Jacques Rivière, and Marcel Mauss—not to mention Louis Aragon or Breton—recaptures a network of feelings absent from Clifford's work but present in the sympathies of writers both in France and in Latin America until the mid-1950s. Continental socialism had close ties to an emergent third-world modernism in much the way the Continental vanguards have to an emergent American postmodernism. In retrospect, it is surprising how little is known of the story of these links at the level of individual careers or aesthetic projects. What are these connections between Popular Front socialism of the 1920s and 1930s and the Caribbean arts?

In Europe on the eve of the French Popular Front's emergence following the 1936 elections, much of the avant-garde had seen in "America" not so much a preindustrial idyll as a domestic communism before Marx. It was not simply exoticism, but a social utopianism that can be traced back through Rochefort's history of the Antilles in the late seventeenth century (on "primitive communalism" among the Caribs) and, in a sense, all the way back to Las Casas. The specific mood, which should not be mistaken for Rousseau's, was expressed again recently by Eduardo Galeano: "Community—the communal mode of production and life—is the oldest of American traditions, the most American of all. It belongs to the earliest days and the first people, but it also belongs to the times ahead and anticipates a new New World. For there is nothing less alien to these lands of ours than socialism. Capitalism, on the other hand, is foreign: like smallpox, like the flu, it came from abroad."[27]

In its stark contrasts, the emphasis in surrealist ethnography on the extreme case—the "last-chance rescue" of primitive peoples—frequently obscures something more brutal than the inventive, mutually beneficial transculturations that tend to be these critiques' conclusions. For even when looking at those regions where hybridity is most pronounced, one often finds mestizo, mixed-economy zones in which a kind of terror capital has staked an outpost but not yet pacified the natives. The degree to which metropolitan images and values have actually penetrated village life abroad or been internalized there is never comprehensively established or argued in any sustained way. It remains a largely unjustified originary truth from which sweeping reassessments can be made in an atmosphere of visible relief from earlier "dogmas."

The new anthropological critics of "salvage ethnography" vastly overstate penetration of U.S. commodity culture and its array of social pathologies into the underdeveloping world, and by doing so, they weaken the outcry against the very practice. In this discourse, words such as "indigenous" and "source" are safely made to slide over into, and eventually become, images of "cultural nationalism" and "ethnic purity" where they can be disposed of more confidently. Again, in a pattern of argument I have tried to identify repeatedly in these pages, the trope of racial or national identity (here in the form of the well-intentioned ethnocentrism of the romantic ethnographers) is brought in to silence a *political positioning:* in this case, that of a left intellectual (like Carpentier).

Is there not some value in focusing on the vastly different political stakes confronting metropolitan writers from imperialized countries and weaker nations for whom that hopelessly romantic concept, the people, continues to matter—the kind of position that in metropolitan theory has been relegated to the single figure of Fanon, although its is widely present elsewhere?[28] Unlike the work of the largely European cast of characters whom Clifford targets, Carpentier's own ethnography offers an interesting middle space between Clifford and Lévi-Strauss.

In his retrospective prologue to *¡Écue-Yamba-Ó,* Carpentier in the 1970s had written that of all the isms of the era, he considered surrealism "the last and most important artistic and poetic ism of the century," although not without pointing out that for the Latin American writers, at any rate, it was not surrealism so much as "the two novels that arrived to shatter, in less than two years, our vision of the Latin American novel: [José Eustasio Rivera's] *La Vorágine* (1924) and [Ricardo Guiraldes'] *Don Segundo Sombra* (1926)." These, he argued, prompted "a nationalist, vernacular novel endowed with a new sound and look (prefigured already in 1916 by [Mario] de Azuela's *Los de abajo*)."

This reference to Azuela's famous novel of the Mexican Revolution, a typical Carpentieran gesture, brings us quickly back to the domestic class issues simmering behind his understanding of Latin American surrealism. Roberto González Echevarría in his well-known study of Carpentier argues emphatically (and with some justification) that the novelist "had been a champion of the avant-garde in the twenties." But the *Carteles* columns do not exactly confirm this view. Well before Carpentier's return in 1939, when he set out to write a full-fledged "manifesto of American autonomy" announcing the dusk and decay of Europe,[29] his articles from France brimmed with jaunty satires on "the cosmopolitan enchantment with the Latin Quarter," its students with their "oversized pipes and little beards carved to a point," where Nordics locked elbows with Russians, and the "inductees from 'Our America' [made] sure to be seen with the blondest women around."[30]

By 1945, after his return to Cuba, Carpentier's comments were even more strident. "It is much more interesting," he observed, "to talk about the ceremonies, traditions, and legends of certain Black mutual-aid societies in Cuba than to search, as Lautreamont used to love to do, 'for the beauty of a chance encounter of an umbrella and a sewing machine on an operating table.'"[31]

> Surrealism has remained despoiled of all its polemical potential and for that reason has died as a movement. Its founders, who labeled their contemporaries cadavers, today interrogate in turn their stomach rumblings, with white heads, on the streets of New York or Mexico . . . But its school had profound justification. Surrealism has raised today's language, as any inherited tradition would.

> Almost all poets writing today owe it something . . . Nevertheless, those who underline its influence breathe a strangely pure and self-assured air. They puff up their lungs as Ulysses must have when meeting the Sirens while tied to the mast. (20)

He reserves his most brutal portrait for *The Lost Steps,* where his fatuous lover Mouche, with her "astrological pretensions" is said to have acquired her intellectual formation in the "great surrealist bargain basement."[33] Not simply weary, Carpentier lashes out here by suggesting a Dionysus-Nietzsche-Nazi link in which surrealism itself is held to be complicit:

> The White musician, Indian poet, and Negro painter . . . would soon land in . . . the great manger of Saint-Germain-des-Près . . . The topic of conversation would be the longing for evasion, the advantages of suicide, the need to slap the face of corpses . . . Some high priest of delirium would initiate them in the cult of Dionysus . . . though without telling them that the one who invoked this Dionysus, the officer Nietzsche, had had himself photographed on one occasion in Reichswehr uniform, sword in hand, and helmet on a console table of Munich style, like a prophetic prefiguration of the god of horror whom reality would unleash in the Europe of that Ninth Symphony. (72)

It is true that González Echevarría concedes Carpentier's firm native footing and contentious anti-European broadsides, as well as his profound skepticism toward surrealism itself. But while trying to make Carpentier an ambivalent disciple of Spengler and Vico, he portrays *negrismo* as an exact homologue of surrealism in an act of Cuban mimicry—a simple "frivolous élan of the avant-garde"—a tweaking of the bourgeois nose. This is so, argues González Echevarría, because the indigenous properly belongs only to the Indian—to peoples whose "richness of culture," unlike the Africans', has been known for centuries. While revealing the not altogether noble motives of Ortiz's rather patronizing efforts to recover Black culture, for example, and in capsule form identifying the conflicting pressures on Carpentier with immense historical precision, he also views the turn toward the Afro-Cuban as a basically bad-faith gesture prompted by the already existing taste for Africa in the artistic avant-gardes. In other words, it is not a matter of social consciousness generated by the national struggle but of a modernist erasure of European influences.

Thus, González Echevarría concludes that the Indian could not provide the fuel the avant-garde needed in Cuba's case, not only because indigenous peoples were so little in evidence on the island, but because Indians have "rarely played a prominent role in avant-garde narrative"—an unsustainable thesis for many of the reasons outlined by Unruh. He therefore drives a wedge between the "primitive" (African) and "indigenous" (Indian) strains of creole gesturing in a manner that particularly marks the distance between later intellectual supporters and denouncers of the Cuban Revolution itself, whose promise or threat resides precisely in one's attitude toward the triumph of Afro-Cuban culture launched in *negrismo* and consolidated by the revolution after 1959.

In the *Carteles* articles, Carpentier announces the invasion of Europe and North America by *cubanismos*. He writes of the "hundred sumptuous cabarets decorated with Asiatic luxury frequented by the cosmopolitan 'gems' that habitually walk the banks of the Seine," and then adds, "but of all the fashionable tastes for such foreignness, only one exotic value has remained firm in the Parisian market: Cuban music, whose irresistible impulse has not been slowed up at all."[33] The observation is all the more telling in that he later finds surrealism lacking in its inability to say anything interesting about music: "The doors surrealism opened for us by showing us the magic of everyday life as reflected in commercials, street posters, and shop windows" made it a "marvelous movement in the plastic arts and in painting. But that movement never touched music." Breton was one for whom "music did not exist," and who considered music a "dissolute art."[34]

Finding this gap in sensibility fatal, Carpentier greets it with a scandalized national-cultural pride. With persistence and anecdotal vividness, he details throughout the 1930s the huge importance of Latin music on the European intelligentsia. Citing the rumba record collections of Paul Derain and Tristan Tzara, he relates how he is constantly being hounded to "translate things from Latin America," explain their value, dig up "new popular Indian, peasant, and Negro poetry."[35] He notes with some exasperation how even the minor articles he writes on the subject are picked up and exerpted on the front page of *Le Soir* the next day. But with apparent delight, he also notes how the appeal is for

> the pallid daughters of Albion to forget for a moment their Pre-Raphaelite poses by burying themselves in the sonorous sortilege of the Antilles . . . To give you an idea of the communicative power of his interpretations, I will tell you that, on one evening, I saw Fernando Collazo pull enthusiastic applause from a French public recounting a certain story about "maja enroscao" that no one who was not Cuban could possibly understand . . . And from a corner, Buster Keaton—who assiduously frequents La Cabaña Cubana—presents himself full of the odds and ends of our rhythms, contemplating the magic painting with the sleepy eyes of an old alligator. (323–4)

In "Sóngoro cosongo . . . en París," written for *Carteles* in 1934, Carpentier charts out more specifically this impact of the *negrismo* movement on contemporary Europe via rumba and the new dance known as conga "whose canons have been officially approved by the Association of Parisian Professors of Dance." In such clubs as La Cabaña Cubana, Melody's Bar, and La Coupole came performers like Moisés Simons and Eliseo Grenet, the trumpet player Julio Cuevas, the brothers Barreto, the brilliant saxaphonist Castellanos, the "excellent pianist" Rogelio Barba, and Frontela, the "virtuoso of percussion," who together constituted what the foreign correspondent called a virtual military "offensive of our rhythms" placed "at the service of our most authentic creole traditions" (322–3).

While Unruh and others have mentioned that Latin Americans abroad took note of the European avant-garde hunger for New World authenticity, she has never mentioned its specifically African inflection in music. Nor do they appreciate the kind of critique the Afro-Cuban element suggests of the avant-gardes themselves. For example, Unruh cites Carpentier's "America before the Literary Youth of Europe"—where he comments on Philippe Soupault's confession of European decadence and disgust at the European tendency to "suavely agonize, stuttering, slavering, bragging," a passage in which Soupault compares European civilization to a "microbe" that Latin America would be better to avoid (298). But even here Carpentier's revelation of the political context of this rejection has been suspiciously edited. The explicitly Marxist references have been left out.

Nino Frank's comments in the article, for example, suggest a New World attraction not exactly covered by the "romantic" and "organicist" motifs of authochthony found in Latin American primitivism: "If one day the Soviet experiment is destroyed by the forces of reaction, only one thing will stand in the way of old bourgeois civilization: Latin America" (299). For his part, Robert Desnos is even more explicit: "What interests us is the destiny of the Cuban cane cutter, the Brazilian coffee worker, the Argentine cattle worker, the Peruvian miner, and the Chilean wine grower . . . In the present epoch in which all the power of capitalism is due to a long social experience, a received technology, inflexibly realized plans, it is important that the Latin American proletariat not let itself be vanquished by that science, by the capital in whose service they labor . . . Fewer phrases, less lyricism" (300).

Carpentier's development of these ideas in the popular culture of music is remarkable not only as a methodology but as a deliberate highlighting of the centrality of Black culture in Cuban national politics—one that was being realized internationally already in the 1930s. It was not operating from a position of defensive New World European mimicry. While granting that there was a kind of popular "folkloric" music played at exhibitions and festivals at the behest of official institutes, Carpentier was interested rather in "that other class of popular music . . . arising from the people of the cities." Of its "strongest and most legitimate exponents in the twentieth century," there were only two: "jazz and Cuban music. It is not a matter of talking about their 'possibilities' in the world. Cuban music IS. It covers the planet. It is listened to in Moscow as in Mexico; in Paris, as in Egypt. And its perpetual evolution (through mambo, cha-cha-cha, the style of Beny Moré, of the 'feeling' song, or whatever you like) serves as a guide to the instrumental and vocal combos that are now performing everywhere."[36] Like Vallejo, Carpentier belonged to a tradition of skeptical critiques of surrealism from within. It was a tradition that embraced many European writers as well, and along political as well as national-cultural lines.

The Marxist milieu in which the interwar avant-gardes flourished was far more important to their articulation, as well as what they perceived as "new," than current cultural theory acknowledges. Clifford, for example, has so expanded the definition of surrealism, so fully qualified it for his purposes as a "utopian construct," an "attitude" that constitutes no actual movement or "stable tradition," that his treatment of individuals becomes "foreshortened . . . in an attempt to disengage its ethnographic dimension."[37] Marcel Mauss, whom he does in fact glancingly describe as a "Dreyfusard and socialist" is nevertheless presented without any of the links that existed between his political and ethnographic imaginations. For Clifford, the organizational identities of Mauss and others form no more than a minor biographical detail. He has nothing to say about the important enlistment of Jacques Rivière and Rivet—two of his principal actors—in the Popular Front organization known as the Maison de la Culture, and Georges Bataille's antagonisms to the avant-garde are never mentioned.

Although Bataille plays a key supporting role in Clifford's account, he had at first actually ridiculed surrealism for many of the same reasons that Clifford embraces it, although one would not know this from reading the essay. Coming to most modern readers through the well-known appreciations of Foucault, the philosopher of transgression would be unrecognizable to contemporary readers on the basis of his essay "The 'Old Mole' and the Prefix *Sur* in the Words *Surhomme* and *Surrealist,*" where he urges surrealism to live up to its undermining of bourgeois values by coming "back to the subterranean action of economic facts." The Old Mole (Marx's nom de plume) is, for Bataille, "revolution"—a word "repugnant to the noses of utopians."[38] He analyzes the bourgeois guilt that produces the empty verbiage of surrealism, that places everything above rather than below in the proletariat. None of this can be found in the language of Clifford's portrait of the "idiosyncratic scholar . . . and pornographer," who, for a time at least, was also a Popular Front believer whose sharpest weapon against Breton was the charge of political "inauthenticity."[39]

Surrealism has often served as a positive model for appreciations of non-Western cultures, just as it has served, particularly lately, as a way of misappropriating interwar Marxism. Walter Benjamin, for example, is presented by Michael Taussig as above all a hermeneut with insights into the "miraculous."[40] But this portrait hardly fits the author of "Surrealism," where the movement is presented (with some reservations) as a pathological manifestation of European aestheticist pretense and fellow traveling. Even more, with some defensiveness, one can observe that Benjamin casts the essay as a German view of French intellectual fashion, portraying Germany's own backwardness as an unforeseen safeguard against contagion. The complaints he outlines there are prophetic. They forecast a contemporary disenchantment with many of the turns that literary theory has taken and that ethnographic surrealism has embraced, for he sees surrealism as a movement in which, lamentably, "language takes precedence." The surrealist, he avers, did in fact accomplish what he himself had been after in his own version of a materialist theology: the "profane illumination, materialistic, anthropological." But the more salient judgment would have to be, he goes on to say, that the surrealist remains in "the humid backwaters of spiritualism" among "down-at-heel dowagers, retired majors, and emigré profiteers."[41] In one final charge in the same essay, Benjamin declaims surrealism for "organiz[ing] pessimism and giv[ing] politics over to images." In spite of what several Benjamin critics have recently argued, his position was not fundamentally different from that of Carpentier, Vallejo, the early Bataille, and Desnos after 1928.

This particular set of misreadings has been crucial for marshaling a set of tropes and attitudes that dispenses with an adequate understanding of interwar European Marxism. Moreover, that misunderstanding empowers the currently cramped view of the scope and direction of non-Western cultures. In his recent work, for instance, Taussig's in many ways sensitive and nuanced revision of surrealism's effect on Latin American modernity is linked directly, through Benjamin, to an account of Carpentier, who is said in the end to be only "carrying out a western European avant-garde project . . . [and] perceiving the popular culture of the poverty-stricken third world with exactly the same primitivistic optic that Surrealism itself stimulated."[42] While the discussion above demonstrates the untenability of that approach, the violence done to Benjamin has been, at all events, the critical mechanism for revision, as evidenced by a barrage of studies transforming Benjamin into a poetic illuminatus.[43]

Peter Osborne's *Politics of Time,* for example, goes so far as to say that "Marxism and surrealism converge in Benjamin's approach to the everyday" since surrealism transforms "everyday objects into the site of what Benjamin called 'revolutionary' experience."[44] There is a striking hermeneutic denial in passages like these, I would argue, that corresponds closely to what I described in Chapter 2 as "conversion" in the meeting of the socialist legacy with postwar American sensibilities. One is compelled to posit an ideological impasse that is larger than a simple idiosyncracy to explain how so many readers could miss the attitudes evident even in Benjamin's very subtitle, with its barely concealed distaste and its whittling down to size: "The Last Snapshot of the European Intelligentsia."

Among the things lacking in the accounts by Osborne, Taussig, and Margaret Cohen is the appreciation by Carpentier, and no less by Benjamin, of the avant-garde represented by the new Russian cinema and the theater of Vsevolod Meyerhold. In his interwar journalism Carpentier describes himself as being "absolutely awed by the technical assurance" of both. The rapid evolution of technique is due, he says, to the "centralization of forces that allow for a focus on higher ends"; and he marvels at the films' "economy of gestures" and strongly approves that "Russian films concede more importance to the idea of a film than to the art of the actors."[45]

These are some of the sensibilities that have to be taken into account when interpreting Carpentier's "ironic" commentary on origins in *The Lost Steps,* a commentary that serves in the ethnographic surrealism of Taussig, for instance, as an example of somewhat clumsy masculinist and indigenous nostalgia. On the contrary, I would argue that the novel places its readers in the process of looking, rather than at the inexpressible end where autochthony supposedly lives. *The Lost Steps,* then, is finally not, as it is often said to be, about the Latin American intellectual who discovers his "real" identity in the jungle backwaters of the southern continent—or in González Echevarría's words, about how the "fugitive seeks redemption through art."[46]

It is about the class exasperations of crossing over. It is about the hopelessly vain act of "literature" in working-class surroundings, and of the vanity of civilizational niceties in surroundings outside those of polite society. The steps back in time that the journey into the jungle recounts do not reveal an ineluctable core of primitive reality, either bestial or divine. They reveal instead a moment of invention where Carpentier sees clearly for the first time the necessity of creating a culture that can unite the high-art sensibilities of the classical repertoire with the "crude" chants of ordinary people, at once ritualistic and simply entertaining in an unreflective sense. It is about the creation of a total art drawn from the various threads of Carpentier's own training in an urbane classicism and his later research into the national-cultural power of Afro-Cuban rhythms. In short, it is an allegory of the role of music in the Cuban nationalist movement.

The novel tells the story of a partial conversion. In spite of the work's relative fame, it seems a good idea to summarize its major features briefly before continuing my argument. The hero of *The Lost Steps* is a Latin American composer and aesthete who, based for many years in Paris, finds himself languishing in New York. Married to an actress who is involved in an interminable production of a Civil War melodrama set in the Old South, he spends his days idly peering into the windows of Brentano's, feeling guilty about not finishing the score of a sonata based on Shelley's *Prometheus Unbound:* "Between the I that I was and the I that I might have been, the dark abyss of the years gaped."[47] The hero's musical vocation particularly weighs on him via the metronome, the ultimate "Measurer of time's passing."

Meeting one day with his former teacher, a museum curator, he is presented with a proposal. His teacher has found an obscure recording of music played on crude wooden instruments that appear to mimic the whinings of birds, and he presents this to his former pupil with great satisfaction as proof of the latter's theory on the origins of primitive music. The hero had published a thesis positing that those origins derived from attempts by native peoples to copy the movement of animals and the songs of birds. Collecting funds, the curator then sends the hero on a mission to collect rare instruments in a South American jungle and thus provide the definitive evidence. This he heads off to do, reluctantly and out of boredom, taking along his mistress, Mouche, whose circle of friends sets up a stark aesthetic contrast with the curator. The former teacher belongs to the generation of Wagner's Bayreuth and the "sublime"; Mouche and company, by contrast, are bohemians given to practicing a form of asceticism. They are, the hero says, "wild about primitive painting."

Cynically, while en route, the hero dawdles in the capital, supposing he might simply find old instruments in a bric-a-brac shop on the outskirts of Caracas, and then dress them up as native artifacts in order to please his sponsor. Here at a storefront window, there at the shelves of a friend's private library, the hero is cast as a browser. But placed in the position of performing a duty, the hero is tormented by the dream of the still-unfinished sonata, which he believes his research trip is annoyingly impeding.

Delayed still further when street fighting confines him to a decaying luxury hotel during a revolution in the capital, he and Mouche eventually are able to set out for the interior. More and more estranged from his lover, who seems to be a "hangover from the days when women proclaimed themselves revolutionaries to meet intellectuals for sexual encounters they enjoyed in literary coteries," he begins to fall in love with a woman he meets on a bus during the journey to the jungle's depths. Once the switch from the bus to small boats for the journey upriver begins, the hero is consumed with meditations on a series of what he calls primordial "trials." The narrator speaks of "the inexhaustible mimetism of virgin nature"—a "world of deceit, subterfuge, duplicity, stratagem, artifice, metamorphosis." Of the people he sees, he finds only "complete masters of their culture. Nothing could have been more remote from their reality than the absurd concept of savage." All of this he experiences as he falls more deeply in love with the peasant woman, Rosario.

When he witnesses, finally, in the remotest region, the dirge of a shaman, and hears his spells against death become a gasped and rhythmic chant, he understands that music is not mimetic, but ritual. His original thesis had been wrong. Music could be seen to be in its origins the desperate soul-call of a people without power over nature, and therefore—once translated to its modern surroundings—a soul-call of deliberately utopian social connotations. Suddenly inspired, he buries himself in his tent to write his sonata in an unbroken burst of energy lasting several days: a "threnody with a cell-word, its verbal exorcism turning into music—a form which, in this case, was demanded by its magic function."

Technology intervenes, however, in the form of the lack of something so trivial as paper. He cannot write his sonata without it, and he has run out. Without the sympathies of his companions who consider such writing worthless, he leaves the village to return to the capital "for a few days" to assemble the goods he needs for a permanent stay. But delayed month after month by one misfortune or miscalculation after another—or (it is implied) by the waning sense of the importance of returning—he never does so. Later he learns from a distance that Rosario has married someone else.

One notices that the more the hero penetrates the jungle, the less writing matters, and that writing gives over to music as the origin of language in ritual. But these are not the decisive themes for this discussion since, as many others have argued, they securely place the work in the traditions of the modernist primitive. What has mostly passed without comment in the novel, though, is the relentless self-criticism entailed in its parody of the unreliable narrator—a rewriting, in a sense, of the musican protagonist of Thomas Mann's *Death in Venice,* whose aesthetic perambulations dull the hero to his surroundings.

Carpentier's novel is rather, an allegory of unrealized conversion. First of all, the narrator is placed not within surrealism but outside of it—and to the right of it, as it were—in order better to send up both the avant garde and the flaneur, a type familiar to Latin American letters from the time of Domingo Faustino Sarmiento.[48] Second, both the hero and his sponsor occupy a dubiously ethnographic position that is portrayed not simply as ethnocentric but fraudulent. Carpentier in that way dispels the two logical roles for a visitor of his type: reporter and anthropologist. Thus, the Rosario subplot. For he suggests that the narrator wishes not only to witness or to understand but to become the culture that he sees—to cross over and to stay, to make it his life. Once that decision is made, his symphonic writing begins to flourish at precisely the point he is freed from mimesis—a term not only ontological, of course, but intercultural in its related form of "mimicry"—a central trope of Taussig's argument of the welcome transformations, through imitation, that U.S. mass culture undergoes in non-Western settings.[49]

Quite a bit more than wholesale rejection is implied by the allegory, moreover. What one appreciates here from the outset is that the indigenous as Indian stands in for the indigenous as African—the actual role the latter played in Cuba of the nineteenth and twentieth centuries in the absence of Indian communities. The indigenous as African is found, above all, in a history of musical origins in Cuba's African communities—such as that Carpentier had just completed in *La Música en Cuba.* The writing of his study on music six years earlier had been important for taking Carpentier into archives of obscure church circulars, unpublished memoirs from the colonial period, forgotten eyewitness accounts of early musical performance, and arcane early histories. The process indelibly marked his fiction with historical novelties and archaisms that helped transform his style from the daring metaphors and oxymoronic neologisms of the avant-garde into the archaic, layered prose of the baroque.

But, again, while that tells us about Carpentier the novelist, it says nothing about his role as musicological agent of the national struggle. Two decisive sources for *The Lost Steps* have not been noticed.

The first relates to Carpentier's most immediate predecessor in exploring Afro-Cuban music, Fernando Ortiz, whose investigations into rumba were significantly limited to an earlier version of the form—the so-called *rumbas del tiempo de España.* Unlike the later virtuosic dance of the urban ghettos, these had been based on naive mimesis—"pantomimic rumbas"—about "taking a shower or hunting blackbirds," and were folkloric in the bad sense. Reviewing Ortiz's writing, Carpentier must have seen how useless such examples were to establish the influence of popular music on Cuba's cultural elite.[50] *La Música en Cuba* had in a way been dedicated to charting that influence of the working classes on elite cultural life at all levels from the earliest colonial times. What *The Lost Steps* offers, in other words, is an allegory of Cuban musical evolution and an argument about the role music played in establishing a Cuban source required for the national movement.

What Carpentier had uncovered in the earlier study of music directly matches the exploits of the hero in *The Lost Steps.* And therefore the second unnoticed source has to do with the argument of *La Música en Cuba* itself. Through much of the nineteenth-century, a more or less rigid distinction remained between so-called traditional orchestras playing at popular village gatherings (brass, violins, kettle drums, and guiro) and official ones influenced by the French (where piano and flute reigned). As Carpentier perceptively notes, however, the breakdown of such distinctions occurred as a result of pressures from below in the popular street musics whose appeal was great enough to influence the compositions of the elite. The breakdown was also the result of recruiting lower-class and Black performers for high European chamber ensembles. Quite apart from their profound influence as performers of popular dances (still strictly on the margins of musical propriety, but present as atmosphere), Black musicians between 1800 and 1840 were a substantial minority among the professional musicians of official European music in Cuba.

Far from merely learning their trade as apprentices, artists such as Juan Peña, Bartolo Avilés, and Claudio José Domingo Brindis de Salas—who took on the role, according to Carpentier, of "political men"—put a characteristic stamp on the development of classical and orchestral music in Cuba. Thus, by 1879, Miguel Faílde was writing the first *danzón*—a slightly syncopated, still elegant, but sensual dance music that took polite Cuban society by storm, although not without the fearful reservations of guardians of public taste like the accomplished habanera musician Eduardo Sánchez de Fuentes, who angrily denied "the presence of black rhythms in Cuban music."[51] This melding of the high and the low is precisely the sort of move embodied by the symphonic musician protagonist of the novel.

As for the related Afro-Cuban form known as the *son,* although Carpentier marks its origins only a few decades after the arrival of the Spaniards in the era of the first slave uprising of 1522 (citing the songs of Teodora Ginez, a Black woman of Barracoa), this attribution is dubious, and its distinctive sound became widely known only in the mid- to late nineteenth century when a virtual legion of *soneros* began playing at popular and religious celebrations. Nevertheless, as both a song and a dance, the *son* had been banned in Cuba until as late as the early twentieth century, and it had to wait for *negrismo* itself to become accepted in an atmosphere of restless national self-definition.

Alluding, then, in his novel's very title to André Breton's influential book of essays *Les Pas perdus* (meaning, significantly, both "The Lost Steps" and "The Not Lost"), Carpentier explicitly rejects that book's evasion of the "ridiculous conditions of existence here below" and departs from the book's determination to remain unattached to anything "in a state of perfect *disponibilité*"[52] Carpentier's book is for that reason about attachments, in fact. It is saying that although the space on which to stand is always shifting, it is still a space; that in the passage of time a transcultured Cuban becomes—just as working-class Blacks became after the elimination of the Indians—an autochthonous one, mixed with the upper classes in a "soul-call of the powerless," to recall the words the novel's hero uses to describe the chant of the shaman. The contribution Carpentier makes to what was, after all, a very familiar Latin American genre of the novel dedicated to finding the elemental core of Latin American cultural origins was in effect to jest. The indigenous is necessary, he suggests, but has to be constantly reinvented.

Salsa and the Cuban Image

The global reach of Cuban music found its contemporary expression in the rise of salsa—arguably one of the most popular mass-cultural forms that is not at the same time a U.S. creation. As a style of music and as a public sound, salsa has often seemed easy to ignore—at least for readers of popular-music theory in the United States. Covering the terrains of reggae, jazz, hip-hop, and rock, a barrage of brilliant studies of wide-ranging form have appeared to explain popular music's political and philosophical codes.[53] Not so with the Latin sound, which has also had its day, although usually in smaller or more out-of-the-way venues.[54] In spite of the well-publicized explosion of so-called world music in record stores, U.S. publishers' catalogs seem to say that salsa does not have the same resonance as rock or jazz for the English-speaking world, nor the proved international appeal of the great Jamaican-British breakthrough sounds of Bob Marley and Peter Tosh. The French inflections of Haitian and West African rock, as well as the South African sound, have similarly had a larger following than salsa among very mixed communities of concertgoers and buyers of CDs.

It is not obvious why this is so. To the students of the Broadway musical—from the 1897 hit "Cuban Song" on through the work of Sammy Kahn and Cole Porter—a vital history has been lost. As Carpentier repeatedly observed, U.S. popular culture has been more or less inundated by Spanish Caribbean rhythms and composers for at least a century and a half. To take only one item from the written record, Nicolas Slonimsky in his heralded history of Latin American music averred that the work of the Cuban composer Ernesto Lecuona, made up something like a "North American hit parade."

Salsa nevertheless, has played a small role among critics of popular music in U.S. cultural formation. Greil Marcus, Gene Santoro, and Nelson George are only some of the first-rate pop music critics who have nothing to say about this massively influential genre that, among other things, left its marks all over jazz. The neglect may have to do with salsa being a notoriously difficult art on the dance floor, one that violates the freestyle ethic of the flop-dance and slam of British punk and American grunge. Its polyrhythms are, unlike Jamaican rub-a-dub, impossible to fake. It remains, much more than reggae or commercial concoctions like lambada, the most intractably "ethnic" of the popular forms—in part because it is so implausible once wrenched from the Spanish language, as it sometimes has been in order to increase sales.

Or perhaps salsa registers to the novice ear as simply old-fashioned. To many American audiences, the salsa performers' uniforms are corny, the big-band orchestration anachronistic, and the vocals croony or infantilizing. It is true that there is a devoted following of non-Latino initiates in every major American city taking salsa lessons at nightclubs and community gyms or learning steps to enjoy themselves in mixed company. But the numbers are not large and the interest is in being adventurously unpopular and (in short) foreign. Despite the Latino flavor of a Cuban-American artist like Jon Secada or Gloria Estéfan, salsa remains immune to anything like a genuine crossover sound.

As a term, "salsa" may have been coined first in 1928 by Ignacio Piñeiro, one of the pioneers of the modern *son,* in his song "Echale salsita" (Put a little sauce in it). Except to devoted listeners, though, Piñeiro's song, with its broad trumpet section and rough, crackly vocals, would simply not sound like the driving, brassy studio-dance music known widely as "salsa," and so its coinage is less interesting than its inaugural appearance as a significant and meaningful term. As most are familiar with it, the term refers simply to the commercialization of the Cuban sound in New York in the late 1960s and 1970s. That commercialization was first made possible by the rise of a pan-Latino group, the Fania Allstars, who modeled themselves on the Cuban-style band Sonora Matancera and in 1964 made it big with hits like "Para ser rumbero" (To be a rumba player) by Roberto Roena and "El día de mi suerte" (The day my luck changes) by Willy Colón and Héctor Lavoe. When Johnny Pacheco and the New York lawyer Jerry Masucci founded Fania Records in the mid-1960s, a distinctively New York type of Latin dance music became viable after two decades of meager survival in lowlife bars and all-male Caribbean social clubs in the long drought following the mambo fever of the 1940s and 1950s. With the film *Nuestra Cosa Latina* (Our Latin thing) based on a Fania Allstars concert at the Cheetah Club in the Bronx in 1971, salsa had stormed out of El Barrio (East Harlem) into a much broader public awareness, if not exactly the mainstream.

"Salsa," then, is a generic term. Its calculated fuzziness and sweep made those who had been performing it for decades resentful. By the time earlier generic tags like *bembé, amor, sabor,* and *fuego* had given way to "salsa," Mario Bauzá was calling it simply "a publicity stunt" and Ray Barreto a "marketing ploy." But there was no serious dispute about its origins in Cuba, or the exclusive role that Cuban musicians played in the early days in bringing it to the United States. In a basic sense, there had been three musical forms that launched the process leading to El Barrio: the rural song-dance complex known as the *son,* from Cuba's Oriente province; the Cuban working-class urban dance music of rumba (never absent from its African religious base, and for the most part an *individual* display of virtuosity); and the *danzón,* a popular couples dance performed in the high society of nineteenth-century salons but also scandalously marked by the improvisation and rhythmic motifs of Black musicians.

The pioneers of the transition in U.S. metropolitan centers—particularly New York—had not only come from Cuba, of course, but from Puerto Rico and the Dominican Republic, Venezuela, Colombia, even Peru and Mexico. In New York the existing musical repertoires were vastly expanded, fine-tuned, even redeveloped in the hands of "Nuyoricans" of divided sympathies and jostled national memories over a period of almost four decades. Yet it is important to grasp that salsa today is nothing more than the *son* (as a rhythmic structure) and rumba and danzón (as secular dance rituals) with some important late additions of coloration, orchestration, and stylistics. None of its commentators has disputed that salsa *is* Cuban music in its New York life.

Like many popular musics, its lyrics record its own history, stars, and conditions of formation. Much of the subject matter of salsa is precisely salsa. So, even in its late, atavistic, New York setting, "Cuba" is omnipresent as a source and site of generation and fertility, musically speaking—a reminder of what Cuba means to the world of Latin popular culture as a whole. Developed in the *barracones de patio* of slave times and the *cabildos,* or mutual-aid societies, established along ethnic lines after slavery for religious observance and recreation, ur-salsa had been the breeding grounds of new genres even after the revolution, in the so-called *solares*— "large houses that were divided into crowded living quarters . . . where poor Cubans were forced to live," and that served also "as meeting places to relax, play, and dream in song, dance, and poetry."[55]

The question becomes the degree to which the specific history of Cuban revolt and achievement retained the aural allusions to and thefts of the Cuban sound in generic salsa. That is, Cuba can be said in a sense to have become through the mass-cultural export of music a significant source, perhaps even the principal source, of indigenous Latino Americana, with important contributions from Colombia, Puerto Rico, the Dominican Republic, and, more recently, Mexico.[56] To claim this is to confront what is precisely at issue between theories of diaspora, on the one hand, and the rather distinct phenomenon of an exported national-popular culture, on the other.

One can begin to negotiate this difference by looking at the structure of salsa itself. Compositionally speaking, the *son* announces what is distinctive to salsa: a three-part polyrhythm with a central 2-3 or 3-2 beat known as the *clave;* an antiphonal (call-and-response) lyric structure; and an overall two-part structure to the song itself, consisting of a solo singer's story (the *motivo*), usually in slower tempo, set against the collective affirmation of the chorus in the song's second movement (the *coro-pregón*), in which the tempo typically explodes in a flurry of vocal improvisation and frenzied instrumental solos (the *montuno*). In other words, formally as well as substantively, the *son* was a living homage paid to the plurality and diversity of its origins: a vital enactment of imperfectly merged hybridities.

And yet, for the ones who made Cuban music into salsa in the United States, Cuba, although ritually invoked and loved, came less to stand for a place than a style in its basically New York settings. This is not, however, how it played in Cuba itself, where from an early date music defined the culture, the culture was significantly Black, and Blackness was explicitly the crux of the national movement. Hence one of the principal questions to raise is the sense in which "Cuba" became, through music, a home base through which a generic Latino identity arose under U.S. conditions. The well-known and well-researched story of the effect of Cuban-exile attitudes and postures on U.S domestic politics is, in that sense, a very partial one.[57] A different influence was being exerted in the underground, lower-class regions of musical pleasure that (for reasons I explore below) tended to signify in part—just as Cuban sport continues to signify—a specifically revolutionary achievement, even though the provenance of the music predates 1959.

For one thing, the magnetic pull of the Cuban sound did not abate after the revolution. As some have noted, "the music of salsa musicians often came from contemporary recordings made in Cuba as well as old collector's items. Current recordings were at first difficult to get, but many musicians went out of their way [after the revolution] to get them via Martinique."[58] Streaming into New York after

1959 were a torrent of new Cuban rhythms that continued to define innovation in an increasingly canned commercial setting: *chaonda, paca, mozambique, pilón, songo,* and *pachanga.* The Cubans were bitter that "many musicians and record companies took advantage of the U.S. blockade against their country to plagiarise their music in a scandalous way."[59] In spite of well-known stars who fled to the United States and made celebrated careers—among them, Celia Cruz and Willie Chirino—the majority of the most prominent remained: Irakere, Los Van Van, NG La Banda, Grupo Sierra Maestra, Orquesta Revé, Anacaona, and others. And the motivating sentiments were not merely defensive or altruistic: "Daniel Ponce [felt] that current popular Cuban music is 'absolutely superior' to salsa . . . This attitude to salsa on the part of the younger generation of Cubans seems to be widespread."[60]

Cuba's very pariah status has paradoxically preserved its Africanicity (as it has its Spanish-colonial culture) to a degree that strikes foreign visitors deeply, and surprises them. The indigenous becomes under such sudden apprehensions palpable and intoxicating. And because isolation and perceiving the indigenous as Black are in this way related, they are related to Cuba as a socialist country—which is the feature accounting for both, and an object also of that intoxication the foreign visitor feels.

What has to be described, and what is all but impossible to describe without color docu-footage or a saturation background training in salsiology, is the sheer euphoria of the *son*-complex in the hands of the at-home musician. This can be seen clearly in the contemporary Cuban-based group NG La Banda's "La expresiva," for example.[61] The song's feelings are so intensely permeated by an aesthetic joy based on the subtleties of rhythmic innovation and on the jockeying of traditional song fragments into new constellations that its humble lyrics are not noticed at first for what they are: the site of a different and related utopia based on *being poor* and *being Cuban.* For the lyrics are a systematically boastful rendition of all of Havana's neighborhoods, listed reverentially by name one after the other and sparked by observations about the abilities of each to be represented in that company where the poor and the Cuban create sounds and movements unmatched anywhere, and envied everywhere.

Cultural theory's recent emphasis on mixed cultural formations as "hybridity"—although certainly well founded and in its own way significant—masks the indigenous tropes within which hybridity has actually operated in Cuba's case. Even the best Cuban-American criticism and memoir of recent decades hammers away with images borrowed from a more general cosmopolitanization of theory: Gustavo Pérez Firmat's "life on the hyphen," Coco Fusco's "border culture," and perpetual recyclings of Ortiz's much abused (but still central) concept of transculturation. (Now a somewhat tired gesture, transculturation has been a familiar one since Bronislaw Malinowski's introduction to Ortiz's *Cuban Counterpoint* as early as 1940, although most cultural historians are unaware that the "discovery" of Ortiz's concept has existed that long, or that Ortiz himself justified the term by appealing to the endorsements of Malinowski himself, who applauded his coinage.)[62]

Pérez Firmat's *Life on the Hyphen* would appear at first to be an exception to this generally cosmopolitan approach, since it addresses mambo in one extended chapter on Dámaso Pérez Prado, the (significantly Mexican-based) Cuban musician of the 1940s and 1950s, and even uses the term as an organizing scheme for the book as a whole. But Pérez Firmat conflates salsa with a variety of musical genres exemplified best by Estéfan and Desi Arnaz in a symbolically laden narrative of American arrival. Even images in studies of *batá* drumming now lend themselves effortlessly to what María Teresa Vélez calls the "diasporic musics . . . of transnationalism and globalism"—the story of moment centered on the United States and on the concept of mass culture as a largely U.S. affair.[63]

The point is not so much whether Cuban music was forced to enter the U.S.-owned distribution networks in order to become influential but, rather, what it still manages to convey once there about its national-popular cultures of origin. For those who know salsa well, the Cuba of Oriente and Matanzas, of Beny Moré and Vicentico Valdés, and (more pertinently) of the contemporary, postrevolutionary Cuban groups is omnipresent. It is a matter of ritual, in other words, to dwell on these nativist memories in the act of consuming the music, and it forms one of the music's principal pleasures.

Misconceptions have extended also to the political function of such music—in Cuban domestic settings, first of all, and later, in its exported, transcultured forms. The customary attitude is that "it was only in 1979 . . . that the left totally accepted the new music [of salsa]."[64] On the contrary, as the Cuban musicologist Leonardo

Acosta has pointed out, salsa grew out of a long history of political wrangling in which even at the level of form its disturbing African and lower-class styles and attitudes had about them the tones of a frightening populist and egalitarian demand. From the time of the war against Spain, the *guaguancó* and *batarumba* signified "left" even when their lyrics were apolitical.

For Cuban popular music was dangerous not only for being simultaneously Black and emergent during the turn-of-the-century's relatively confident creole rule: it also included more than a few examples that in a variety of periods and in different ways were explicit political protests at the level of content. In speaking of Gonzalo Asencio, "the best and most prolific author produced by our country in that popular variant of the rumba known as the *guaguancó*," Acosta puts his finger on a familiar misunderstanding about the politics of the popular:

> Obviously, the *social record* of the meek and humble has frequently been a *Red record*, which refers us to the supposed Marxist conception on the bourgeois media, which posits that while the dominant classes occupy the privileged spaces of communication, the space given to the proletarians is the *Red record*. In neocolonial Cuba, it is a situation doubly alienating by virtue of the dependence on the imperialist metropolis and the submission to its values by the creole bourgeoisie. It is undeniable that the mechanisms of the bourgeois press created a favorable atmosphere for the injection of these images into the dispossessed and marginalized population. But the flesh-and-blood fact is that the media version constituted a vision *directed to* the poor, while the very same event narrated in *guaguancó* reflected *the vision of the dispossessed themselves.*[65]

Created in the era following World War II, Asencio's composition "Cubanos! ¿Donde estan los Cubanos?" ("Cubans! Where are the Cubans?") passed by word of mouth and won him a six-month jail sentence. From the last century to the end of the neocolonial republic there were abundant "protest *sones* and protest *guarachas*" (95). After the revolutionary triumph, Asencio continued composing rumbas with revolutionary and anti-imperialist themes, and Acosta calls them "a species of popular chronicle, singable and danceable, of the accomplishments of our country during these last twenty-odd years" (96).

Acosta's point need not be limited to Asencio either. Although it is difficult to determine with any specificity who or how big the actual listening audiences were for the popular musical forms that predated the revolution and that, after the upheaval, were filled with a revolutionary content, it is equally difficult to mistake the latters' massive popularity in the realms of simple leisure. These nightclub mambos and rougher, more traditional rumbas in the immediate posttriumph years sang with enthusiasm and an obvious joy of the social goals and achievements of the 26th of July Movement in power. Original recordings of these songs from the opening years of the 1960s were distributed widely in European anthologies such as *Les Chants de la revolution cubaine,* which includes this typical example:

> We are now in the year of education
> And the people are getting reading to teach the lesson.
> Cuban women and men, it's now up to you
> Teach us how to write, teach us how to read
>
> It's all over for the privileged
> Because the poor are going to college
> It's all over for the privileged
> Because the poor are going to college
>
> This is the rumba of the nation
> Send the message that we're going to study
> Forward, Cubans, now's the time:
> you can learn if you don't know, and if you know you can teach.

It is likely that such lyrics, in spite of their "p.c." flavor in MTV America (all the more so rendered in English), were as widely indulged in by the public as more contemporary examples of such political translation—say, the indigenous musical forms in Nicaragua, adapted by the Sandinistas, about which more recent documentation of actual reception exists.[66]

There is, moreover, in Cuba's case a wealth of such examples in a variety of forms, from the early trio compositions of Carlos Puebla y Sus Tradicionales, with his *sones* "El Comité de defensa" and "El Son de la alfabetización," to the traditional rural *guateques* "Mi tierra es así" and "Mi bandera nacional" as sung by such popular performers as Celina González, Carmelina Barberís, and Ramon Huerta. There is nothing somber or official about the drive and beat of the rumba above, nor about the abandon of its performance, which rocks with the same assurance and sincerity as the teaching-pieces of U.S. rock and rap—a place where an incipient political ethics at odds with acceptability is itself a critical part of the song's appeal. In spite of their mass attractions, these adapted musical traditions were able to retain an underground flavor in an *international* context.

As Van Gosse has suggested, early revolutionary Cuba's beleaguered position vis-à-vis the combined forces of capitalist conformity in the 1950s and early 1960s allowed it to be both in power and subversive at the same time. This continues to be the case. Avid listeners of popular music can discern the impossibility of faking the emotions that motivate this message-rumba, and can immediately distinguish it from the glorified anthems and marching songs that, with all their good intentions, played a role in the lore of the socialist internationals similar to that of the church hymns of Protestant Christianity. By contrast, the forms here speak in the popular idiom of entertainment and play, rather than devotion, and for a brief time became indistinguishable from them.

It would be rash to argue that all of Cuban music could confidently be reduced to a subterranean force inseparably tied to an explicit anticolonial politics, and that is not what I am suggesting. Such a view would, in fact, be absurd. Nor is it the case—as might appear from my emphases here—that the African influences on Cuban music were the best, exclusively important, or invariably political ones in Asencio's limited sense. What I am arguing is that Afro-Cuban music—at the same time that it achieved an astounding success abroad as an exported mass culture in the arenas of nightclub leisure and Broadway novelty—was the proudest cultural brag of the national movement in Cuba. As such it signified very differently within Cuba than outside of it, retaining (as a hybrid form) its primary meaning as an indigenous artifact: a display of national self-definition.

As it found its way into the markedly different cultural life of the U.S. metropolis, Afro-Cuban music nevertheless retained the hints and gestures of these original domestic meanings and helped forge a Latino identity with significant Cuban roots. And one has to remind oneself here of the privileged place that music as a cultural form enjoyed throughout the Caribbean, and the national-cultural role it tended to play in a way analogous to literature in the Anglo

North.[67] I am further arguing that post-revolutionary Cuba not only continued this well-developed sense of sacred secularity and cultural politics in Afro-Cuban music, but did more to document it, to promote it, and to solidify its prestige than any other source in Latin America or in the diaspora, before or since.[68]

The early *negrismo* movement had been led prominently although not exclusively by white intellectuals, and in the hands of Ortiz, for example—as González Echevarría carefully points out—had not avoided a paternalist idealism: "Black music, especially when it is most genuine, offers the delight of immersion in a torrent of virginal waters springing from dark forests to anyone who has known only baths in a routine commode or fashionable beaches. The sophisticated find there all their pleasures bared."[69] The same primitivistic indulgences, I would argue, were not a part of the writing of Carpentier or Cabrera, however, in spite of what has been widely written about *The Lost Steps*. More important, *negrismo* made the political implications of Blackness cultural for the first time, and it was precisely here in Ortiz's creation with Guillén of the Society for Afro-Cuban Studies in 1926, in Carpentier's *La Música en Cuba* in 1945, and in Cabrera's folkloric recovery work that the national movement through Blackness became self-conscious.

Again, it is to Carpentier that one can turn to find the history that music had had in the national movement from the time of the French Revolution in the work of Manuel Saumell, who rejected the bourgeois suspicion for anything but sentimental romances and Italian opera by expanding the repertoire of rhythms available to orchestral music and by writing the first opera scores in macaronic. Expanding the rhythmic innovations was Luis Espadero, a personal friend of Louis Gottschalk—the American pianist who, in visiting Cuba as a concert performer toward the end of the nineteenth century, helped popularize Afro-Cuban musical forms in North America. In this same line could be found Ignacio Cervantes, the master of the *zarzuela,* the *sinfonía,* and the *danza,* who after studying in Paris, lived for four years in the United States giving concerts while in exile from the independence struggles against Spain.[70]

Cuba's ability to figure as a significant actor in mass-cultural desire had a great deal to do with race. This feature of its development is what Carpentier understood and helped explain. Castro's Cuba has often been accused of having a "problem with race"—of still feeling shame for the Afro-Cuban elements upon which it has been forced to rely after the flight of the educated, wealthy, and mostly white Cubans to Miami and New Jersey in the early years of the revolution. In fact, as Wyatt MacGaffey points out, to the revolution's tories Castro "invented the issue of race."[71] The virulence of anti-Castro politics in Miami is marked not only by the hatred of dispossession or lost privilege, but by a sense of outrage that Blacks have assumed roles of authority and power. Pedro Pérez Sarduy and Jean Stubbs, for example, have pointed out that white Cubans living in exile are currently obsessed with the slogan "the Haitianization of Cuba" and that the slogan "Neither Black nor Red" formed part of a white backlash against major redistributive measures in the early revolutionary years.[72]

Underlying a larger distrust of socialism has been the refusal to accept the new rights given Cuba's Black population as well as the government's explicit and official cultural valorization of *cubanismos.* Hatred of socialist Cuba is a hatred rooted in race, and the issue of race politics itself—curiously elided today as an implicit reprimand to an older class-centered politics—has one of its more venerable expressions precisely in the current home of an older socialism. The immense relevance, therefore, of Cuba to New World theory and history is often missed.

The role played by revolutionary Cuba in transforming official attitudes toward Black culture in Cuba has been as extensively documented as it has been ritually denied. Santiago Colás, for example, has written of what he calls the "creole symptom," which in Cuba's case, he argues, expresses itself as a "condescending moral and political arrogance" associated with Guevarist *foquismo* (an insurrectionary strategy based on the *Foco,* or guerrilla "cell") and its vision of the artistic intellectuals as "guiding angels" of helpless peasants.[73] Revealed in his argument is a popular set of assumptions surrounding the political conduct of Cuba in the realm of culture. It is no exaggeration to say that such belief systems are among the most symptomatic reasons that non-Western cultures remain marginalized, inaccessible, or poorly understood in metropolitan discourse in the United States. For, far from looking at the people as peasants to be led in matters of culture, the Cuban government has consistently taken its leads from them. In that sense, the weakest of the critique's formulations has to do with "authenticity" and the "native," which are grotesquely caricatured in just the sense I have been explaining here in reference to salvage ethnography.

Researchers who have actually explored Cuban popular culture (and Colás very obviously has not) attest, for example, that the government's promotion of rumba and other Afro-Cuban forms has been part of an "embracing cultural education program" conducted precisely in the name of combating "internal colonization."[74] Not at all limited to packaging a friendly egalitarian image for foreign consumption, these moves made rumba the national dance of Cuba, demanding it be given a prestige that had earlier eluded it and that the culture as a whole might then be identified with in international circles. In a simultaneously racial and class sense, such promotions were about "interconnectedness, diverse world views, uniting liminal worlds" (146). Since 1959 there has been an explosion of research into Afro-Cuban music unknown in any other time, with the government dedicating articles to the forms in its official journals and publicly showcasing African culture in annual independence celebrations.[75]

To understand the historical importance of such measures, one has to appreciate (again) the relationship between "race" and the "people" in this domestic context. While the 1953 census had 26.9 percent of the Cuban people listed as Black or "mixed race," the true proportion was much higher. "Mulattos consistently underreport their Blackness because of extensive economic and social discrimination . . . Even today, however, at least 50 percent of the population is Black or mulatto while the census reports 33 percent." All the same, "demographically and socio-culturally, Cuba is far less white after three decades of revolution than it was in 1959."[76] That is to say that for the Cuban government, racial discrimination was considered antination, and by declaring it so, officials were drawing on a rich tradition from the nineteenth century. Many of the best-known soldiers and insurrectionists against Spain had been Black: Antonio and José Maceo, Quintín Banderas, Guillermón Moncada, and Mariano Torres. In order to create confusion among their Mambí army, the Spanish press created fear of the coming Black republic, while the wealthy landowners echoed the watchword: "Cuba, better Spanish than African."[77]

To guard against this sort of thing, the revolution of 1959 targeted racial discrimination, and did so (according to Pedro Serviat) by promoting "mass study of all the popular arts."[78] The gestures were not lost on the people of the streets and villages. The *Regla de ocha* and Santería believers announced that their *babalaos* were standing with Fidel. As Pedro Pérez Sarduy and Jean Stubbs have observed, "whatever the shifts in official ideology, blacks are arguably one of the groupings in Cuban society with the fewest illusions about any switch to Western-style market democracy or Eastern-style perestroika. The contemporary resurgence of racism in both of those camps has not gone unnoticed in Cuba."[79]

Rogelio Martínez Furé, moreover, has explicitly linked earlier Black traditions of protest with modern-day Cuban socialism: "We share from food dishes to proverbs, stories, riddles, prejudices, historic ill-fate and above all a tradition of struggle against exploitation, symbolized in the settlements founded by Indians, continued by runaway slaves, nationalized by the *mambises* and now taken up by modern-day revolutionaries."[80] John La Rose, one of the founders of the Caribbean Artists Movement and an English-speaking delegate to the 1968 Havana Congress, seconds this view. The Black consciousness of this half-white Caribbean island was only strengthened after 1959, which saw the launching of a "neo-negritude movement" in which the artists and ethnographers were usually themselves of Afro-Cuban origin.[81] It was in this sense that Jamaican novelist Andrew Salkey affirmed that as much as Jamaica, Cuba was part of the West Indies he called his own. It had the effect of making him, as he put it, "acquainted with myself." If the "Red" and the "Black" in postcolonial theory are treated as incompatible, they are presented this way in the context of a "creole symptom" displayed by the theorists themselves, and one that is vastly enabled by the mass media.

Reading Mass Culture through Youth

Carpentier's position on sovereignty is an uncharacteristic one in that the popular culture he acclaimed was not only national but had been exported globally by a country (unlike the United States) that had no imperial claims. The importance of this view today is inseparable from the almost universal assumptions that exist about the supremacy of U.S. mass culture as a political foundation for a new globalism. Jacques Derrida joins many others in making the claim:

> The movements for democratization [in Eastern Europe], in all their diversity, in the too often neglected difference of their style or rhythm, would not have been possible without a profound and, I think, determinate transformation of causality said to be cultural . . . It is well known that without the ultimately irrepressible circulation of techniques of reproduction, of televisual images, of music, and film, discourse that could be conceived as new modalities [these movements would not have occurred].[82]

In Derrida, then, "mass culture" is not a matter of genre, one suspects, or a reference to the numbers of people who consume this culture, but a type of experience—a type of relationship to fantasy associated in advance with the libidinal free play and spectacle of image-capitalism. A crucial aspect of any account of mass-cultural allure is therefore youth itself, not only as that quality everyone would like a bit more of, but as a social sector acting as arbiter for what a society is likely to become in the next generation. Youth arises as a category in cultural studies not (or not mainly) as a sector restless with declining metropolitan options, but as a reprimand to an older, now outmoded "vanguardism"—which unlike "avant-garde" is here a pejorative term.

The predominant focus today on "subcultural style" or "rocking against Reaganism" produces images of cultural politics as performed by youth in what are arguably novel forms: the techno-nerd, the neo-1950s disgruntled wanderer or waif, the b-boy and fly-girl, the New Age environmentalist. Each is placed implicitly "in an age that rejects intellectual vanguardism and vanguardist intellectuals alike."[83] Youth becomes a potent image of the need to revise older political outlooks at the same time that it picks up the trace elements of those qualities—innovation, novelty, experimentation—associated with capitalist mass-cultural allure. At the same time (if, as suggested above, somewhat contradictorily), it gestures toward the anti-authoritarian "breaks" of the historical avant-gardes whose members were overwhelmingly young.

Behind much of this cultural theorizing about youth lies a verdict that has been expressed most bluntly by John Beverley: "The socialist countries were not (and are not) able to compete effectively with capitalism in the creation of mass culture (wonderful theatre and film, mediocre television)."[84] The political importance of this failure is crucial for Beverley in light of the massive social changes that U.S. mass culture has created in postwar Latin America, in which a new subject has arisen, one unresponsive to those examples of high culture that socialism has in fact succeeded at times in developing. He wants, then, to promote the sort of subject he finds represented in testimonial narrative—a "new, deterritorialized, organic intellectual of the subaltern, capable of acting effectively in global circuits of power and representation," a fitting match for Latin America's new "Lacanian desiring subject . . . whose sense of inner lack can never be compensated," a Caliban "interpellated culturally . . . by the mass media."[85]

The necessity of such a project is amply demonstrated in the pages of Beverley's text. Yet he seems oblivious of the way in which, unintentionally and from very different outlooks and ends, reflections on "youth" have figured centrally in the cold war. Marc Cooper's "Roll Over Che Guevara," with its portraits of seething, blue-jeaned Cuban layabouts hungry for a bit of rock and a quiet place to play guitar, captures this familiar genre.[86] So does Jay Murphy's essay "The Young and the Restless in Habana," which substantiates more convincingly than Cooper does the real fissure between the older élans and the pressing desires of Cuba's young.[87]

I am talking here, however, not only about a specific charge leveled against the socialist countries and against Cuba per se, but about a more pervasive instrumentality of youth in assessments of U.S. mass culture. "Youth," "women," and "gays"—as cultural tropes rather than as actual people in specific contexts of complexity and contradiction—have often been used in assessing third-world cultures for the purpose of holding on to a belief in Western superiority. This is doubly true when the third-world culture is also, like Cuba, socialist. In this sort of atmosphere—where art and the imagination play key political roles—the obvious comparisons between the plight of youth in Cuba and, say, Colombia do not typically get made, and there is no attempt to judge the comparative outcomes of the two system: on the one hand, frustrated rockers and weekend prostitutes, and on the other, a sociopathic, suicidal nihilism helped along by death squads delegated to "clean" the city streets.

The virulent opposition to Cuba in both official U.S. discourse and cultural studies is therefore double, and speaks to the dual burdens of its apparent anachronisms: its being a socialism and its being an independent state. Again, attacks on the viability of the nation-state have been the contemporary form that an attack on socialism takes. For, apart from ethnic purists and right-wing nationalists, socialists are the only ones who still defend national sovereignty in the age of the global subaltern, and do so for many of the domestic political reasons suggested by the material above. In vivid ways that material shows popular culture within Cuba as well as outside of it empowered by a desire for what Ortiz gave as the motive for his entire oeuvre: "national integration." Each bears directly on the assumptions in current theory that (returning to Beverley) "the socialist countries were not (and are not) able to compete effectively with capitalism in the creation of mass culture (wonderful theatre and film, mediocre television)."[88]

This comment is decisive when set against the playing out of "race," "youth," and "women" in the Cuban context. For it questions the ability of socialism to be culturally popular at a deep libidinal level of leisure, entertainment, and unguarded mental and emotional play. It is not just a technical distinction between the capacities of first- and third-world countries to create the studio finish and computer opulence of the Super Bowl commercial or the rap CD. In other words, one has to assume that Beverley's point about effectively competing is not just a point about brute resources, since countries without satellites, global press agencies, or global computer links cannot in obvious ways compete with countries that have them. He is talking, rather, about the kind of message that one system as opposed to another is inherently capable of sending. Socialism, he is arguing, is characterized by the "normative and pedagogic,"[89] which disqualifies it from the kind of appeal that U.S. mass culture has succeeded in generalizing globally.

Beverley also implicitly distinguishes between popular and mass culture, allowing the former to be seen in two ways: as the authentic art forms and practices that emerged anonymously in the past when something like village life still existed, or (by contrast) as the culture of an explicitly popular-democratic content that the revolution's intellectuals have devised to express their support for new social programs (the 1960s-type political folk song or the *nueva trova* tradition of Pablo Milanés and Silvio Rodriguez, for example). Mass culture (as opposed to popular), a form whose distribution relies on the media, has subsumed the former and outmaneuvred the latter. What the argument implies, in other words, is that authentic popular culture exists only in smaller and more insignificant pockets, while the post-1959 culture of popular-democratic content was never really "mass" in the sense that normal people ever embraced it as their own.

Again, neither of these views is really borne out by the record, and the pervasiveness of this opinion is itself a sign of the cosmopolitan moment. Almost never studied (or even mentioned) in this context would be the golden age of Cuban poster art from the 1970s, the international influence of Julio García Espinosa's "imperfect cinema," the revival of the so-called *filin* songs of the 1940s in the socialist 1960s, or, even after 1959, the continued export of salsa's raw material to the nightclubs of New York. Apart from the international success of individual Cuban film directors like Tomás Guttiérez Alea, Humberto Solas, and Pastor Vega, the annual film festival held in Havana has served as a regional spur to domestic Latin American film production and moved it into areas not modeled (at least un-ironically) on either Hollywood or European art-school cinema.[90] And even if it is not necessary to rely on such examples (as I have been arguing), in order to establish that a socialist mass culture exists, it is crucial to appreciate their actual appeal. Leonardo Acosta, for example, specifically confronts the question of whether *nueva trova* was mass culture or not: "If the Nueva Trova movement was not a mass movement, it would still have to be conceded that it constituted a fit means of channeling, on a mass basis, the artistic potentials of the people."[91]

It is initially curious, then, that to make his comment work, Beverley disqualifies film from mass culture since there are too many obvious counterexamples, not only in Cuba but in the former Soviet bloc. That, however, is not the point on which to focus. If it is true, for example, that the testimonial is *the* form at present of a kind of subaltern antiliterature, it has succeeded in expanding the Western reading public's sense of the subaltern itself by linking it to gender and colonial identities.[92] Unlike the vision of the lower orders as laborers, lower functionaries, urban riffraff, peons, and domestics in, say, French or American naturalism, the subaltern in testimonial is defined by struggles of nationality, gender, race, and cultural difference. Again, unlike naturalism, not only is the testifying done by the subaltern subject, who is marginal, repressed, endangered, or exploited, it is inseparable from testimonial meaning, thereby speaking to the uncompleted project of subaltern emergence and looking forward to an era in which the testimonial itself can no longer exist.

All of this has a special relationship to Cuba, and in two senses. First, the specific valorization of subaltern subjectivity as historical actor was implicit in the revolution itself and the resistance movements it inspired throughout the hemisphere. But second, in a more direct way, the consolidation of testimonial as a form is difficult to separate from the reception accorded Miguel Barnet's *Biografia de un cimarron (Diary of a Runaway Slave),* along with his later theorizations of what he had done in that genre-breaking book as well as the pioneering work of Margaret Randall who began her prolific string of testimonials of women in Vietnam, Cuba, and Nicaragua only after moving to Cuba (and she remains one of the few interlocutors to have written a how-to pamphlet on the writing of the genre). What is more, Cuba has been extraordinarily important in the institutionalization of the form, beginning in 1970 when Casa de las Americas began awarding prizes in the category in an annual literary contest—an action that undoubtedly encouraged some who might not have composed them to do so.

All of this is enormously resonant for the ongoing question of popular culture in Cuba and, more generally, for the possibility of a viable mass culture in noncapitalist countries—countries, in other words, where the subaltern is nominally in power. It raises the question, for example, of whether a corporate, technological mass culture has displaced the authentic, collective forms gestured to in the testimonial, and it makes one wonder whether a type of exportable mass culture—that is, one capable of global dissemination—exists differently from the varieties now made in the United States and (to a lesser extent) Western Europe.

If Beverley and others are right in locating the rise of the testimonial in the emergence of a social grouping we call, collectively, the subaltern, the question is not only whether it has found adequate expression in writing, but whether it has done so in other forms of cultural expression more appropriate to the technological disseminations of a properly "mass" culture. One doesn't have to rely on intellectual products like *nueva trova* or film to make such a case in Cuba. As suggested by Carpentier's *Carteles* articles from the 1930s, there were currents even before the revolution that were bringing Cuban subaltern musical forms into a "serious" representation, with its own heroes and heroines, its own exalted history, its own chroniclers. And like Cuban sport (another alternative mass-cultural form), these currents were disseminated globally. Even in the commercialized form of New York salsa, they continue to rely on injections of Cuban authenticity.

The politico-cultural troping of "youth" in the Cuban instance might also be revised after looking at Van Gosse's study on the historical connections between the Cuban Revolution and North American youth, especially its avant-garde.[93] The images of post-1959 Cuba as a country with origins at the head of a bearded, youthful army, and with early successful teen revolutionary journals like *El caimán barbudo* (The Bearded Alligator) have been legendary. Started in 1966, the journal launched a new wave of Cuban writers among its youthful target audience. According to Rio Vásquez, it especially attracted poets "committed to establishing a solid link between poetry and song . . . In the second edition, a manifesto affirming the poetic character of the song was published."[94] These efforts paralleled the early support given the Cuban Revolution by Beat poets like Lawrence Ferlinghetti and Allen Ginsberg (who had written "A Prose Contribution to the Cuban Revolution" in 1961), support that culminated in the founding of the League of Militant Poets by leading New York Beats and the publishing of the journal *Pa'lante: Poetry Polity Prose of a New World* (189).

These were the days of the revolution's "mass romantic glow," in which Fidel was seen as "merely one aspect of this generalized youthful nihilism" (126). For Norman Mailer, the ideologist of hipsterism, Castro had emerged as a hero who could combine, in Vasquez's words, "the existentialist's emphasis on the spontaneous act with the revolutionary impulse to purposeful action" (192). But, of course, none of this lasted, and as Gosse points out, its beginnings were shaky:

> The evidence suggests that Cuba's influence was felt primarily among those most insulated from political discontent: middle-class youth, especially males, in their teens and twenties, for whom World War II was mostly a faint memory and the Affluent Society was the overwhelming tangible reality . . . Nor had they inherited any vibrant traditions of cultural opposition, as both the 'people's culture' of the Popular Front left and the various avant-garde bohemias had been subsumed into the new high culture championed by repentant leftists from Sidney Hook to Clement Greenberg.[95]

The observation shows that relief *from* consumerism (rather than escape from its lack) is what early Cuba represented, and so reminds us of the range of desires possible in this cultural debate over comparative systems. It would be hard to imagine the U.S. solidarity movements without this desire to have a place to go to that was not-market, not advertising, not masscult.

The Indigenous and the In-Between

In the epigraph at the beginning of this chapter, Mayra Vilasis hints that the creation of consumerist mentalities and the shackling of those mentalities to a specifically U.S. form of capitalism are facilitated by mass culture but only in the environment of the market itself. To see American mass culture in Cuba, she suggests, is to be innoculated against the market. From a recognition of U.S. mass culture's popularity among audiences abroad, contemporary cultural critics quickly jump to the view that its pleasures involve an irrespressible choice of the system that produced it. Vilasis implies that this does not necessarily follow in the context of an alternative, internally coherent "popularity." Although highlighting mass culture, her comment about still being here suggests the ties between the mass-culture debate as a whole and political independence.

In 1991 twenty-one-year-old Yociel Marrero Baez began a project to determine what the novelist Alejo Carpentier meant to Cuban youth. In the course of his research, one schoolmate's candid answer raised a familiar problem with the popular: "I cannot read [Carpentier] . . . without hearing a voice scream 'you are ignorant' in my ear." For his own part, not without feeling a similar sensation at times, Marrero was impelled to read all of Carpentier "in search of something that until recently I had been unaware of wanting to find in him: knowledge."[96] He goes on to define his project's telos in terms of "Carpentier—the inexhaustible source in our journey towards becoming people of knowledge."

This view could never be mistaken for a North American statement on literary value. The pairings that come to mind are not so much the useful and the superfluous need, or social security and frill (as above), but two ideas of aesthetic reception. Carpentier and Vilasis both occupy a place where the literary, high, elite, and ennobled gloss the popular because they form a continuum with it: the aesthetic cannot be pried away from information, or poetics from policy. Carpentier's training within institutions like UNESCO allowed him to appreciate the principle of dissemination as distinct, say, from ideology as such—the belabored focus of social theories derived from studies of popular culture. This is to say that distinctions between the content of mass culture and its forms of articulation fatally bypass a point more decisive than either: the physical means of dispersion—one of those cultural questions that, again, rudely forces theorists to look squarely at the state, and thereby occupy a site of the very totality and collectivity whose passing theory laments.

For most people are not, after all, consistently ideological. They do not interpret their day-to-day lives in terms of abstractions like communism or capitalism. Working-class Cubans see the revolution above all as independence. Cuba is their country, and from all quarters the mantra one hears while touring contemporary Cuba is simply "We are Cubans." They are proud not to be owned—not yet, at least, and not lock, stock, and barrel. They associate this freedom with the changes Castro introduced; what journalists in the United States call "communism," the Cubans simply call national independence. At the time of this writing at any rate, that feeling is still undiminished among most sectors of the population, and it is why Castro has so far been able to maintain support in the face of significant obstacles. All of this, naturally, may change in the years ahead.

The indigenous, I have been arguing, continues to matter because it can be, and often is, a rejection rather than a nostalgia. The reality of Afro-Cuban culture in the Cuban national context moved Carpentier to see the indigenous as a constantly reinvigorated trope, intensely contemporary and mutable, rather than a strategy of enclosure or a static, arresting disclaimer. He sought a way to bring the sort of novels he wrote and the sort of classical music he adored into communion with popular nonliterary traditions from which both had borrowed and on which both relied. It is a view of the indigenous as a process of avoidance, of re-creation, on the terms of a different dignity and a stable polity. The essential political act was always to keep one step ahead of mimicry. Despite his cosmopolitan credentials, Carpentier's goal was not to occupy a convenient no-place but to be always on the move.

Conclusion

Cosmopolitanism? As opposed to what? In November 1995 the International Forum on Globalization met with some alarm in New York, setting out to describe a world economic system crippled by corporate centralizations, unwieldy bureaucracies, impersonal planning, and arrogant monopolies. Taking David Korten's book *When Corporations Rule the World* as its point of departure, the group castigated the evils of big business even as it promoted the virtues of local initiative, eco-responsibility, and a more sensible, small-scale competition.

In proposals like these, one can see the scope of contradiction in familiar terms and (more pressing for me) the possible misunderstandings in the way I have been using them. In my view at least, the charge of nostalgia would actually have some force here, and cosmopolitanism would be welcome if only to challenge a view that confuses the big with the bad while mystifying the past as a time when capitalism was more responsive, more rational, and more truly "competitive." The same could be said of the world's lingering precapitalist forms as well. Most of the subproletarians of the growing city centers, after all, do not want to return to their villages, however much they may have been forceably uprooted from them. But they do reasonably demand good wages, stable employment, and respect for their customs and ways. The point in that sense—or at least my point—is not to flee from the global, but to socialize it.

No doubt global economic restructuring has forced on everyone the need to build new international forms of communication and mutual support. An exact duplication of the national liberation movements as they existed in the immediate postwar period is impossible, as are the dependency theories that were their cultural corollaries. As I argued earlier, the laptop insurrectionist Subcomandante Marcos has grasped very well the importance of establishing new forms of international solidarity via the media in a contemporary language that manages to refashion postmodernism and its celebratory deracinations. And the observations could be pushed much further, and in a different direction.

To conceive of one's political goals or cultural objectives on a uniquely national basis has never been the position of a left culturalism, and it is not mine. It is a position that belongs more properly with the classical isolationism of the Republic Party or, in more recent ways, the literary patriotism of Lynn Cheney, former director of the National Endowment for the Arts. At the same time—as the 1996 presidential campaign showed—a populist and right-wing nationalism of a very different sort than Cheney's has arisen from below, attacking the partnership of big business and government for being indifferent to the interests of the American people, and demanding that the United States be separate and apart and superior by privileging the concerns of the white "mainstream" in what is seen as a return to an inward-directed patriotism poised against foreigners.

The major point in this shifting amalgam of positions for and against corporatism, for and against nationalism, is the reversibility of terms. The kind of cosmopolitanism I have been looking at here has paradoxically stood not against, but with, an Americanism distinct from patriotism yet also jealously supportive of an American imperial myth about the portable ethos of the United States as an idea and (with some modifications) an honorable longing. To build new international lines of contact in order to oppose, while mirroring, corporate consolidations, one has reasonably to stress what is *not* (or not yet) America.

In that sense, it is important to focus on how much of the undeveloping world still exists in large pockets oblivious of the rationalizing rhythms and obtuse ethical emptiness of capitalism. One of the signal problems with current criticism is its tendency to deny or downplay this important fact. It is striking to anyone who actually visits India, Africa, or Latin America how little the paeans to the Internet finally matter to a world populace whose familiarity with Western images is much greater than their belief that the images will ever be theirs. Yes, TV; yes, Coke; yes, Chicago Bulls T-shirts—but much of that is unintelligible elsewhere, and exists in the context of a metropolitan life whose architecture, language, and pace are inimical to the designs of Korten's corporate megaliths. This is simply how it is: large swaths of the world touched but also untouched by the great conformist family of European and North American man.

There is nothing particularly romantic in this fact, nor should the desire be necessarily to exalt these pockets of a happily undeveloped, pre–shopping mall third world in some Conradian escape from the funk of "civilization." But their existence is important to any strategy of how to build a cosmopolitanism worthy of the name. For the question is not so much the desirability of building a cosmopolitanism in the sense of a global cultural outlook that respects autonomy and contestatory values, as it is *how* to do it. Crucial in that sense is preserving the sense of a system of competing nation-states, both as a desired objective and as a more sober, less celebratory description of actual global arrangements. The struggle among the individual countries of the European Union; the conflicts over control of domestic resources and economic treaties in Mexico, Nigeria, and Brazil; the coming showdown between the countries of China and the United States—all of these characterize international development more accurately than a portrait of nongovernmental organizations or Web-users battling a new world order under the amorphous stewardship of the TNCs. The struggle may be primarily about the control of land, resources, and capital, but the symbolic mediations of intellectuals writing on mass culture, cultural studies, and literary cosmopolitanism help set the conceptual frameworks and ethical outlooks of the struggles themselves.

The territory covered in this study has been large, perhaps too large from the view of professional specialization. That has been part of the point. It is hopeless to try to embrace the world, either because of the necessary limits on knowledge or the technical impossibility of mastering the languages or cultural references to do so adequately. But too much is conceded by avoiding generalizations about an elusive whole whose parts appear often to be unaware of one another. I have been drawing examples primarily from the French, Spanish, and English Americas, because these are the areas I have studied most, and because here is where I live. Here also is where a specific New World rhetoric flourished—a rhetoric that the present globalist moment studiously mines.

I have placed many of the lessons of that work against the outlooks of a white, middle-class intellectual milieu in the United States. The rationale for doing so derived from my argument that cosmopolitanism is the product of precisely this sector in an era of unexpectedly subtle continuities with the big-power America that, more often than not, is the object of critique. Added to this has been an argument about the importance of a white, middle-class minority in the political sense of that term—a view that I believe dovetails in important ways with much of the underanalyzed colonial and postcolonial writing of authors who are neither white nor middle class. Thus, the meeting place of position with identity is what needs to be explored much more fully in the future. My own position as a critic in that sense is within a group speaking for the world in a language that often conceals its attempt to do so: a language of local identities, of revisionary ethnography, of authentic minority insider knowledge, of the infinitely liberatory and fungible uses of U.S. mass-cultural images and values.

In the space between the reading of novels, poems, and essays from Latin America, Africa, and Asia and the reading of postcolonial theory, much is missing. A massive network of emotions and sympathies found in the primary work does not always find itself expressed in the criticism. As a slightly dated term, "cosmopolitanism" may seem an unlikely entryway into such a problem, and yet its powerful provenance merges so effortlessly with a set of positive contemporary associations that it cannot be ignored. Those associations have to do with the supposedly inherent catholicity of outlook among intellectuals as a caste, and with a more local and more current interest in non-Western societies. In spite of their ranging concerns, the pages above have been about how an elusive and malleable construct like cosmopolitanism has served to limit a necessary confrontation with alternative values implicit in the reception of the "third world." While making it more difficult to talk about the concept convincingly, the term's very malleability and elusiveness were central to the success of its role as an arbiter of bad faith.

Lost in much of the writing on colonialism and postcolonialism is the mood of languorous attachments to native cultures, still in many ways premarket or anticapitalist, that were (in displacement) sites of nativity. If hybridity can be said to characterize them, then it is a hybridity reclaimed and reinvented as indigenous, defiantly posed against an increasingly insistent metropolitan norm. It was for me both a question of making this point and of trying to make it colloquially without giving ground to the charge of nostalgia or idealization. I think this is a very hard thing to do. Nothing is so widely accepted in U.S. cultural life as a commonsense cynicism. It has no political boundaries; almost everyone equates it with sophistication.

Postcolonial theory or minority criticism has in many ways been a powerful counterweight to a rising chauvinism and a stubborn, anti-intellectual insistence on the normative principles of European superiority in Europe, the United States, and the white-settler societies of the former British Commonwealth. Proof of the field's effectiveness and largely salutary impact can be found, I think, in the virulence of the "p.c." campaign itself, which forever dispels the argument that debates in the academic humanities are unimportant or powerless. In specific ways, discourse in the humanities has conditioned and even helped direct public debate, although it has often done so negatively.

A key part of the long-term romance with Americanism as a U.S. product—absorbed by and influencing European and colonial intellectuals for over a century and a half—has been the proposition that it stands for the *antiliterary:* that its attractions, in the words of Rudolf Kayser in 1925, were bound up less with literary models than with poorly understood and necessarily distant images of "trusts, highrises, traffic officers, film, technical wonders, jazz bands, boxing, magazines, and management."[1] As one of the stress points where cultural studies and postcoloniality meet, the observation suggests the need for examining literature itself more closely—or, more important, the ideology of the literary. This sort of move is different from being methodologically committed to a close reading of texts. Such a focus does not amount to an inconsistency, I think.

The scope of the themes of globalism (as an imputed sociological reality) and of cosmopolitanism (as an ethic of proper intellectual work) brings us by their very natures to the media through which literature is disseminated and consumed. In writing about literature proper, then, one is drawn to a phenomenological understanding of literature as it is received via trends in book markets, key educational anthologies, and literary tropes adapted for use in journalism, political essay-writing, and public policy. What is valued as literature? What is understood to be literature? How does the literary, even in a media age, continue to matter?

None of this is meant to suggest that the actual practice of teaching texts, of admiring their complexities and subtleties, or of relaying that admiration to others is no longer interesting. It continues to occupy the bulk of most teachers' time in the classroom, even if it seems much less compelling to offer in a published form. In doing so, there is no need to argue for the primacy of a certain kind of art—certainly not a socialist realist art, or an art of anticolonial struggle. All the same, it is true that a narrow concept of artistic value does dictate what is taught, and finds itself surprisingly replicated whenever one chooses which nontraditional art forms make the A-list of the new curricula. To that extent, works of art representing aesthetic strategies currently out of favor should find a place they have not so far.

It may be true that what matters most is how a work is read rather than what canon it represents. And there is no necessary directive for doing away with arguments over "better" and "worse" literature—for keeping a sense of aesthetic standards, in short—which in spite of unassailable arguments about the arbitrariness of all value is too strongly intuitive to give up, and too strong a weapon in the effort to extend the range of works that are read and discussed seriously by broad publics. The implicit message of world-historical variety in expanded lists and the type of discussion they tend to generate is decisively different from simply reading the canon critically. In that way, I think it is false to argue that the latter is alone sufficient. The ethnocentrism of an imperial culture has to be seen both from the vantage point of its victims as well as from the vantage point of the metropolitan critic unveiling ethnocentrism in the surroundings of a canonical text.

What also has to be grasped is that in order to transform English departments on the basis of a true comparatism one cannot be looking only at literature. This comment—almost banal after a decade of cultural studies—means more (and other) than what "cultural studies" usually implies. Cultural studies in practice has actually stunted an internationalism of value by glorifying a specifically U.S. mass culture, by superimposing literary critical readings onto nonliterary texts and thereby giving a cramped literary criticism a second life and by conceiving nonwriting (mass-cultural practices and the media) as the extraliterary without confronting the force of the literary itself.

The point should not be simply to expand what is studied but to give to the art forms of other peoples and nations the same authority and seriousness that the literary now enjoys. The international influence of other cultures has occurred primarily in music and in dance or in certain of the plastic arts. The challenge is to find a way of speaking that extends to such forms the same veneration that literature finds in the English department—and with the same felt need to master their complexities.

Educationally, a new comparatism would mean organizing knowledge in terms of theme, period, and topic rather than in terms of subspecialization within national literatures. Specialization could still occur (precisely *in* theme, period, or topic), but without the strictures against, say, literature professor being too sociological, or modern British experts impertinently wandering into Latin American themes. The sort of organization I am alluding to here already has a home at some universities, but trends point to a move backward to a past that has hung on with unexpected strength.

The resiliency of national-literature forms of organizing knowledge in terms of their own subspecialties (again, in the daily press as much as in academia) has been much stronger than is usually thought—not only in the well-known neotraditionalism of the National Association of Scholars, the public attacks on the Stanford core, and other efforts to put brakes on curricular reform in order to discredit postcolonial studies or minority literatures, but in the imperceptible move to transform a proper world literature into a study of American pluralism. Thus the paradox at the heart of those moves to reassert U.S. national identity at precisely the moment that the breakdown of national borders is vigorously and messianically announced: a paradox mirrored in many ways in U.S. domestic politics, where many political leaders claim they are against government while favoring an intensification of state coercion in the form of stronger penal codes, increased military spending, and rearmed police departments.

Cultural studies—although it challenges these forms of university organization in obvious ways—has maintained a hold in the universities in part because, with some exceptions, it leaves the U.S. national sense of preeminence untouched. What has to be done is to make basic high school and undergraduate training truly global in its scope, without making it cosmopolitan in the sense I have been outlining here: that is, to study U.S. culture as one of many historical cultures in a system of competing nation-states. We are very far from that, and many of the most progressive innovators in the academy are not proposing it.

Since, from a literary as well as a cultural point of view, the most pressing technical issue raised by cosmopolitanism is "translation," a few words should be dedicated to it here. The complexities of translation theory are deeply related to issues of interpretation proper—the cognitive abilities of people to understand any form of verbal communication, even those written in one's own language in the colloquial sense of a national language. By varying degrees, one is driven in such studies to issues of communicability, in the strict linguistic sense or in the sense elaborated in the common-language theories of analytic philosophy. Or, in a related way, one is led to a discussion of poetic-expressive means and the faithfulness of art to the original. These are vital questions about which much has been written, but I have intended here once again to bracket them.[2]

What I have been concentrating on, by contrast, is the immense financial resources of publishers to offer a mind-boggling repertoire of work written in languages other than English for monoglot English-speaking audiences—a condition that finesses such issues of faithfulness and poetic expression by presenting to an avid reading public a body of work that is known and discussed entirely within English and that is often referred to in the translated language of English even by literary professionals versed in a smattering of foreign tongues.

In other words, very much *un*like the multilingual philological settings of high European scholarship where many of the great theorists of translation operated, contemporary Americans are witness to a commercially defined writing where it is possible for literature to be read and reviewed entirely in English while registering as "foreign." The Leibnizian quest for a universal language begins to take on the coloring of the more pedestrian and programmatic world-English schemes discussed in Chapter 3.

Even if there are legitimate reasons to question whether the older technical issues of translation have an impact on the ability of a metropolitan readership to understand the original adequately, those who actually write about such works or who attempt to present them to the public (and who, at the same time, *have* read them in the original) know that an additional "translation" affects understanding—and in a practical sense, prohibits it. This translation has to do with specific national histories, social settings, consequent social values, and what can only be called a political aesthetic.

That, I am arguing, is at least as intractable a problem as the one outlined so well by more traditional theorists of translation such as George Steiner, whose own effortless polylinguilism (which forms the theme of one of his central chapters in *After Babel*) shadows the experience of the colonies in a radical translation of the stakes of reading and speaking. Nicolás Guillén, for example, gets at one aspect of the colonial translation problem in his poem "Tú no sabe inglé" (you don't know English):

> La mericana te buca
> y tú la tiene que huí:
> tu inglé era de etrái guan,
> de etrái guan y guan tu tri.
>
> Bito Manué, tú no sabe inglé,
> tú no sabe inglé,
> tú no sabe inglé.
>
> No te enamore má nunca,
> Bito Manué,
> si no sabe inglé,
> si no sabe inglé.
>
> The American woman is looking for you
> and you have to run away:
> your English is at the level of try one,
> try one, two, three.
>
> Bito Manué, you don't know English,
> you don't know English,
> you don't know English.
>
> She'll never love you again,
> Bito Manué,
> if you don't know English,
> if you don't know English.[3]

At the same time that a poem like this suggests the U.S. centrality of the language problem in an emergent globalism, it illustrates the very difficulty of translating plebeian experience that I have been referring to in these pages. It seems insufficient somehow to state simply that coloniality and postcoloniality are also about class; and yet, to understand why third-world art is so neglected, condescended to, or homogenized before it appears in cosmopolitan packaging, one would have to grasp the reality of censorship, evasion, and bad faith when it comes to addressing class in American surroundings.

While questioning certain critical roads taken, I have tried throughout to give counterexamples that seemed to me more fruitful, more honest, and more complete. I do not think, then, that here is the place to sketch out still more solutions to the problems I have already raised. References to what I think of as exemplary work are explicit throughout; I have tried not only to criticize but to invoke the sort of work I think has done what should have been done. Yet the question does have to be asked in closing: If not cosmopolitanism, then what? If the importance of the fate of nationalism to literary and cultural study has been too often theorized to repeat here, what exactly does a resistance to cosmopolitanism imply for the future of small nations in an age that carries globalization and transnational corporatism to new levels, particularly given the fact that I myself am writing from an overdeveloped global site?

There is only one way to express internationalism: by defending the popular sovereignty of existing and emergent third-world polities. And part of that defense is to preserve an ideological space where they can exist in the face of futurist prognoses that they have ceased existing. Crippled, vexed by the dangers of excess and exclusion, smothered by the weight of ethereal images from afar, the nation is a precious site for negotiating rights and for salvaging communal traditions. Nationalism of this type took centuries to forge, and its resilience in the face of the universalizing myths of U.S. benevolence is hopeful.

At the same time, even cosmopolitanism's critics are varied, and some (like those considered at the beginning of this section) are unwelcome. It is not enough to posit against cosmopolitanism, as several cultural critics recently have, the evasive category of "local resistance," whose theoretical grounding is often anarchist in the technical sense of the word—fearful or distrustful of states.[4] Critics of this type do not want to accept the responsibility for living, actual governments, which in the nature of things throw people in jail, train armies, collect taxes, and make enemies. As I have been arguing above, local resistance tends to develop an inflated cultural politics where change is effected at the level of response and attitude, but not at the level of civic power where so many responses and attitudes are directed. Even at this late date—as an emergent wing of the Republican Party fully understands—any meaningful politics is still about the control of states. The less cultural theory reflects that understanding, the less it can be called political, in my opinion.

American cosmopolitanism has been refining itself for the better part of a century. The process now heralded did not begin yesterday, and yet the forces it describes were not able to prevent nationalist insurgencies of very recent vintage—in Guatemala, Nicaragua, Grenada, East Timor, the Philippines, South Africa, Namibia, southern Mexico, and elsewhere. In exactly the sense that civil libertarians today struggle to keep alive terms like "freedom," "justice," and "equality," writers in the third world seek to give a content and a dignity to terms that are typically ridiculed by metropolitan theory. "Liberation" is one of those terms; the "indigenous" and the "people" are others. Tied as they are to the project of nationalism, these ideas and these words remain vital today because there is simply nowhere else to go. Anthony Appiah is right when he says that "there are many reasons to think that living in political communities narrower than the species is better for us than would be our engulfment in a single world-state: a cosmopolis of which we cosmopolitans would be not figurative but literal citizens."[5]

I cannot prove that the national liberation movements of weak and impoverished peoples are possible to sustain. Maybe Fukuyama is right. But there are reasons to doubt the inevitability of Fukuyama's thesis, and they can be seen by looking at the left nationalisms that have sprung up recently with the goal of breaking out of the world system and putting the great nightmare of capitalism behind them.

No one can be completely confident that such movements have a realistic chance, but what I do know is that ideas and opinions desperately matter, and that intellectuals help make them. The ideological climate created by the cultural work I have been analyzing saps the countermovements of their energies and robs them of support. If critics continue that sort of work uncritically, they are only helping to destroy what, at a later and more convenient date, they sign off on as obsolete. They doom what they later reject for being "doomed." Nationalism is not dead. And it is good that it is not.

Notes

The book's epigraph is from Henri Lefebvre, *Introduction to Modernity* (London: Verso, 1994).

Introduction

1. Tim Brennan, "Cosmopolitans and Celebrities," *Race & Class* 31, no. 1 (July–September 1989), 1–20.

2. Mary Louise Pratt, *Imperial Eyes: Travel Writing and Transculturation* (New York: Routledge, 1992), 143.

3. Tönnies' distinction had been between the "real and organic life" of community versus the "imaginary and mechanical structure" of society. Ferdinand Tönnies, *Community and Society,* Charles B. Loomis, trans. (East Lansing: Michigan UP, 1957; orig. pub. 1887).

4. Paul Rabinow, "Representations Are Social Facts: Modernity and Post-Modernity in Anthropology," in *Writing Culture: The Poetics and Politics of Ethnography,* James Clifford and George Marcus, eds. (Berkeley: U of California P, 1986), 258.

5. Anthony Kronman, "Duties of Descent," *Boston Review* 19, no. 5 (October–November 1994), 30.

6. See George Lipsitz, *Dangerous Crossroads: Popular Music, Postmodernism, and the Poetics of Place* (New York: Verso, 1994).

7. Ibid., 25.

1. Claims to Global Culture

The Dambudzo Marechera quote is from *The Black Insider,* Flora Veit-Wild, ed. (Harare, Zimbabwe: Baobab Books, 1990), 49.

1. Christopher Lasch, *The World of Nations: Reflections on American History, Politics, and Culture* (New York: Alfred A. Knopf, 1973).

2. Paul Rabinow, "Representations Are Social Facts: Modernity and Post-Modernity in Anthropology," in *Writing Culture: The Poetics and Politics of Ethnography,* James Clifford and George Marcus, eds. (Berkeley: U of California P, 1986), 258.

3. Marjorie Levinson, "News from Nowhere: The Discontents of Aijaz Ahmad," *Public Culture* 6, no. 1 (Fall 1993), 128.

4. Antonio Gramsci, *Selections from the Prison Notebooks,* Quintin Hoare and Geoffrey Nowell Smith, ed. and trans. (New York: International Publishers, 1971), 237, 108.

5. David Hollinger, "Ethnic Diversity, Cosmopolitanism, and the Emergence of the American Liberal Intelligentsia," in *In the American Province: Studies in the History and Historiography of Ideas* (Baltimore: Johns Hopkins UP, 1985), 59, 72.

6. Arnold Krupat, *Ethnocriticism: Ethnography, History, Literature* (Berkeley: U of California P, 1992), 4.

7. Julie Newman, "Buchi Emecheta's *The Rape of Shavi,*" manuscript submission to *College Literature,* December 1993.

8. Michael Eric Dyson, "On *Black Athena:* Interview with Martin Bernal," *Z Magazine,* January 1992, 57.

9. Edward Friedman, "World Culture, 'Global for Millennia': Scholar Supports Eclectic Curriculum," *L&S Magazine* (Winter 1992), 28.

10. Bruce Robbins, *Secular Vocations: Intellectuals, Professionalism, Culture* (New York: Verso, 1993), 196, 197.

11. James Clifford, "Traveling Cultures," in *Cultural Studies,* Lawrence Grossberg, Cary Nelson, Paula Treichler, eds. (New York: Routledge, 1992), 107.

12. Ibid.

13. Raymond Williams, *The Politics of Modernism: Against the New Conformists* (New York: Verso, 1989), 34.

14. Rabinow, "Representations Are Social Facts," 258.

15. Robbins, *Secular Vocations,* 196, 184–5 (his emphasis).

16. Oswald Spengler, *Decline of the West,* Charles Francis Atkinson, trans. (Oxford: Oxford UP, 1991; orig. pub., 1918, 1922), 25 (his emphasis).

17. Quoted in Dick Hebdige, "Guilt Trips: Coming Up Against the Wall," *Border/Lines* 20/21 (Winter 1990/91), 44.

18. See Galit Hasan-Rokem and Alan Dundes, eds., *The Wandering Jew: Essays in the Interpretation of a Christian Legend* (Bloomington: Indiana UP, 1986), 1–10, 107.

19. Eugène Sue, *The Wandering Jew* (New York: Random House, 1940; orig. pub. 1844–5).

20. M. Ageyev, *Novel with Cocaine,* Michael Henry Heim, trans. (Evanston, Ill.: Northwestern UP, 1991; orig. publ. c. 1930).

21. Hollinger, "Ethnic Diversity," 66.

22. Barbara Herrnstein Smith, *Contingencies of Value: Alternative Perspectives for Critical Theory* (Cambridge: Harvard UP, 1988), 54.

23. Robbins, *Secular Vocations,* 195.

24. James M. Blaut, *The National Question: Decolonizing the Theory of Nationalism* (London: Zed, 1987), 15.

25. Martha Nussbaum et al., "Patriotism or Cosmopolitanism," *Boston Review* 19, no. 5 (October–November 1994), 3, 34. Subsequent Nussbaum quotes are from this source.

26. Edward Said, *Representations of the Intellectual: The Reith Lectures* (New York: Pantheon, 1994), 113.

27. An exception can be found in William E. Cain, "From Liberalism to Communism: The Political Thought of W. E. B. Du Bois," *Cultures of United States Imperialism,* Amy Kaplan and Donald E. Pease, eds. (Durham, N.C.: Duke UP, 1993), 456–73. Cain sees this trajectory in Du Bois as "tragic."

28. W. E. B. Du Bois, *Color and Democracy: Colonies and Peace* (New York: Harcourt, Brace and Company, 1945).

29. For a reformed socialist like Régis Debray—an advocate of a fundamental political reordering on behalf of a Europe caught between the superpowers—it is thus a central tenet to deny such a polarity: "The East-West problem [seen as] a worldwide religious war between two ideas of mankind" is an "epic hallucination, a collective romance" (Régis Debray, *Les Empires contre l'Europe* [Paris: Gallimard, 1985], 11–12).

30. *Guelwaar*'s climax occurs when the main character delivers a lengthy speech against the importation of commodities from abroad, and against the complicities of the comprador elite of Senegal in enriching themselves by creating a detestable consumerism. Throughout the speech, the word *"diom"* ("self-esteem") is repeated forcefully, and the title (meaning "warrior") has intentionally archaic connotations, as though staking out a future in the past. *Time, Forward!,* a classic of socialist realism, is a remarkably personal drama of economic construction in a steel mill under conditions of external hostility and internal pressures—a drama, like Sembène's, both in and of a state in formation.

31. Joel Kovel's *Red Hunting in the Promised Land: Anticommunism and the Making of America* (New York: Basic Books, 1994) catalogs the global body count, numbering in the millions, of "communists" eliminated by the United States in various third-world campaigns during the cold war.

32. Frederick L. Schodt, *Manga! Manga!: The World of Japanese Comics* (Tokyo: Kodansha International, 1983).

33. See Henri Lefebvre, *Critique of Everyday Life,* vol. 1, John Moore, trans. (London: Verso, 1991; orig. pub. 1947), and *The Production of Space,* Donald Nicholson-Smith, trans. (London: 1974; rev. ed., 1991).

34. Pierre Bourdieu, *Distinction: A Social Critique of the Judgement of Taste,* Richard Nice, trans. (Cambridge: Harvard UP, 1984), 1: 227.

35. I am thinking here of writers I have explored elsewhere as a specific constellation—among them, the authors of the Latin "boom" and their

immediate descendents (Salman Rushdie, Bharati Mukherjee, Isabel Allende, Jamaica Kincaid, Ben Okri, and others)—as well as a second generation modeled on the successes of the former: Sashi Tharoor, Gish Jen, Cristina García, and many others for whom the descriptions above, I think, generally hold.

36. Thus, in a scene from Sarah Maldoror's film *Sambizanga,* set in prerevolutionary Angola, a tailor says to his apprentices as they labor in a small workshop: "There is no Black, no mulatto, no white—only the rich and the poor, [and] the rich give in a way that keeps the poor poor."

37. See Breyten Breytenbach, "Why Are Writers Always the Last to Know?" *New York Times Book Review,* March 28, 1993, 15–16.

38. Carolyn Steedman, *Landscape for a Good Woman: A Story of Two Lives* (New Brunswick, N.J.: Rutgers UP, 1991), 137.

39. Among the reviewers I contacted, Michiku Kakutani *(New York Times),* M. Mark *(Voice Literary Supplement),* and Robert Silvers *(New York Review of Books),* declined to be interviewed. Barbara Epstein of the *New York Review of Books* found the subject fascinating, but "too politically sensitive."

40. Sheena Gillespie, Terezinha Fonseca, and Carol Spica Sanger, eds., *Literature across Cultures* (Needham Heights, Mass.: Allyn and Bacon, 1994).

41. James Hurt, ed., *Literature: A Contemporary Introduction* (New York: Macmillan, 1994); James H. Pickering and Jeffrey D. Hoeper, eds., *Literature, Fourth Edition* (New York: Macmillan, 1994); and Sven Birkerts, ed., *Literature: The Evolving Canon* (Needham Heights, Mass.: Allyn and Bacon, 1994). The quotations concerning the Birkerts anthology are taken from a promotional pamphlet issued by the publisher.

42. Jerome Beaty and J. Paul Hunter, eds., *New Worlds of Literature,* 2d ed., (New York: Norton, 1993).

43. Shirley Geok-Lin Lim and Norman Spencer, eds., *One World of Literature* (New York: Houghton Mifflin, 1993); Elisabeth Young-Bruehl, ed., *Global Cultures: A Transnational Short Fiction Reader* (Middletown: Wesleyan UP, 1994).

44. Mike Featherstone, ed., *Global Culture,* special issue of *Theory, Culture, and Society,* 7, nos. 2–3, June 1990.

45. John Boorman's 1985 film *The Emerald Forest* demonstrates my point.

46. Laura Kipnis, *Ecstasy Unlimited: On Sex, Capital, Gender, and Aesthetics* (Minneapolis: U of Minnesota P, 1993), 27.

47. Achille Mbembe, "Prosaics of Servitude and Authoritarian Civilities," *Public Culture* 5, no. 1 (Fall 1992), 135.

48. Robert Young, *White Mythologies: Writing History and the West* (London: Routledge, 1990), 4.

49. Christopher L. Miller, *Theories of Africans, Francophone Literature, and*

Anthropology in Africa (Chicago: U of Chicago P, 1990), 42. For a pointed critique of Miller along similar lines, as well as for a brilliant and sustained treatment of blanket assaults on nationalism, see Neil Lazarus, "Disavowing Decolonization: Fanon, Nationalism, and the Problematic of Representation in Current Theories of Colonial Discourse," *Research in African Literatures* 24, no. 4 (Winter 1993), 69–98.

50. Achille Mbembe, "The Banality of Power and the Aesthetics of Vulgarity in the Postcolony," *Public Culture* 4, no. 2 (Spring 1992), 3.

51. Michael Taussig, *The Nervous System* (New York: Routledge, 1992), 207.

52. James C. Scott, *Domination and the Arts of Resistance: Hidden Transcripts* (New Haven: Yale UP, 1990).

53. Achille Mbembe, "Prosaics of Servitude and Authoritarian Civilities," 127.

54. Sara Suleri, *The Rhetoric of English India* (Chicago: U of Chicago, 1992), 4.

55. Tim Brennan, "Aijaz Ahmad, *In Theory*," *Textual Practice* 8, no. 2 (Summer 1994), 327–35.

56. The most reliable reviews, in my opinion, are Michael Sprinker, "The National Question: Said, Ahmad, Jameson," *Public Culture* 6, no. 1 (Fall (1993), 3–29, and Neil Lazarus, "Postcolonialism and the Dilemma of Nationalism: Aijaz Ahmad's Critique of Third-Worldism," *Diaspora* 9, no. 3 (Winter 1993), 373–400; useful additional points can be found in Benita Parry's somewhat less giving appraisal, "A Critique Mishandled," *Social Text* 35 (Summer 1993), 121–33.

57. Aijaz Ahmad, *In Theory: Classes, Nations, Literatures* (New York, 1992), 11.

58. Ben J. Wattenberg, *The First Universal Nation: Leading Indicators and Ideas about the Surge of America in the 1990s* (New York: Free Press, 1991).

59. Teresa Hayter, *The Creation of World Poverty* (London: Pluto Press, 1992), 53.

60. Ahmad, *In Theory*, 16.

61. Octavio Paz, *One Earth, Four or Five Worlds: Reflections on Contemporary History* (San Diego: Harcourt Brace Jovanovich, 1985), 86.

62. Ahmad, *In Theory*, 19.

63. See, for example, Theotonio dos Santos, *El nuevo carácter de la dependencia* (Santiago, Chile: Centro de Estudios Socio-Economicos, Universidad de Chile, 1968).

2. Cosmopolitanism and Method

The Fredric Jameson quote is from "Towards Dialectical Criticism," *Marxism and Form: Twentieth-Century Dialectical Theories of Literature* (Princeton,

N.J.: Princeton UP, 1971), 306. The Otto René Castillo quote is from "El antepasado más antiguo," *Let's Go! Vamonos Patria a Caminar,* Margaret Randall, trans. (New York: Cape Goliard, 1971), n.p.

1. Theodor Adorno, "How to Look at Television," *Quarterly of Film, Radio, and Television* 8, no. 3 (Spring 1954): 213–35.

2. Theodor Adorno, "Memento," in *Minima Moralia: Reflections on a Damaged Life,* 86.

3. Pierre Bourdieu, *Homo Academicus,* Peter Collier, trans. (Cambridge: Polity Press, 1991); *Outline of a Theory of Practice,* Richard Nice, trans. (Cambridge: Cambridge UP, 1977).

4. Gayatri Chakravorty Spivak, *Outside in the Teaching Machine* (New York: Routledge, 1993); *The Post-Colonial Critic* (New York: Routledge, 1992).

5. Renato Rosaldo, *Culture and Truth: The Remaking of Social Analysis* (Boston: Beacon, 1989), 197.

6. Jameson, "Towards Dialectical Criticism," 306–416.

7. Lauren Berlant, "Live Sex Acts," talk delivered at Rutgers University, December 1993. The idea is found also in Jameson's account of what he calls the "geopolitical aesthetic," the attempt of conspiracy theory films "to think the world system as such" (Fredric Jameson, *The Geopolitical Aesthetic: Cinema and Space in the World System* [London: British Film Institute; Bloomington: Indiana UP, 1992], 4).

8. Rosaldo, *Culture and Truth,* 170.

9. See Thomas Bender, *Intellect and Public Life* (Baltimore: Johns Hopkins UP, 1993), 117, 124.

10. Russell Jacoby, *The Last Intellectuals: American Culture in the Age of Academe* (New York: Basic Books, 1987).

11. Margaret Randall, *Gathering Rage: The Failure of Twentieth-Century Revolutions to Develop a Feminist Agenda* (New York: Monthly Review, 1992), 21.

12. Edward Said, "Introduction: Secular Criticism," in *The World, the Text, and the Critic* (Cambridge: Harvard UP, 1983), 1.

13. Paul Nizan, *Aden, Arabie,* Joan Pinkham, trans. (New York: Monthly Review, 1968; orig. pub., 1931), 158.

14. Paul Nizan, *The Watchdogs: Philosophers of the Established Order,* Paul Fittingoff, trans. (New York: Monthly Review Press, 1971; orig. pub., 1932), 6.

15. Tricia Rose, *Black Noise: Rap Music and Black Culture in Contemporary America* (Hanover,: Wesleyan UP, 1994), 5–6.

16. Barbara Herrnstein Smith, *Contingencies of Value: Alternative Perspectives for Critical Theory* (Cambridge: Harvard UP, 1988).

17. "The Man Who Knows Everything, Murray Gell-Man," *New York Times Magazine,* May 8, 1994, 24–7); Stephen W. Hawking, *A Brief History of Time: From the Big Bang to Black Holes* (New York: Bantam, 1988). For an even

clearer example of scientism as style—where a rather average writer and thinker (but first-rate biologist) counsels laypeople on the nature of things in an outrageously unsubstantiated argument based on cultural metaphors purchased with scientific authority—see Stuart A. Kauffman, *At Home in the Universe: The Search for Laws of Self-Organization and Complexity* (New York: Oxford UP, 1995).

18. Oswald Spengler, *The Decline of the West,* Charles Francis Atkinson, trans. (Oxford: Oxford UP, 1991; orig. pub., 1918), 35–6.

19. Walter Benn Michaels, "Race into Culture: A Critical Genealogy of Cultural Identity," *Critical Inquiry* 18, no. 4 (Summer 1992), 655–85.

20. Spengler, *Decline of the West,* 253.

21. As in Lisa Kennedy Montgomery, the star of MTV's *Alternative Nation,* "heroine of the new counterculture" (Lloyd Grove, "Young Glory," *Vanity Fair,* June 1994, 124–5).

22. In this vein one finds, for example, John Carpenter's film *They Live,* where the members of a Los Angeles subculture put on magic sunglasses that allow them to see the aliens in their midst who, posing as friends, have infiltrated the group for the purpose of enslaving them with television.

23. Edward Said, *Culture and Imperialism* (New York: Alfred A. Knopf, 1993), 65.

24. George Lamming, "C. L. R. James: West Indian, George Lamming Interviewed by Paul Buhle," *C. L. R. James's Caribbean,* Paget Henry and Paul Buhle, eds. (Durham, N.C.: Duke UP, 1992), 29; Walter Rodney, *A History of the Guyanese Working People, 1881–1905* (Baltimore: Johns Hopkins UP, 1981), xxi, xxiv.

25. See also Harry Wu, "China's Gulag," *New York Times,* February 4, 1994, A-23.

26. Marjorie Levinson, "News from Nowhere: The Discontents of Aijaz Ahmad," *Public Culture* 6, no. 1 (Fall 1993, 97–132).

27. Andrew Ross, "Cultural Preservation in the Polynesia of the Latter-Day Saints," in *The Chicago Gangster Theory of Life* (London: Verso, 1994).

28. Cary Nelson, "Always Already Cultural Studies: Two Conferences and a Manifesto," *M/MLA: The Journal of the Midwest Modern Language Association* 24, no. 1 (Spring 1991), 24–38. See also two other remarkable essays in this respect: Corey Dolgon, "Marxism and Cultural Studies: Politics and Theory in the Postmodern University" (unpublished essay submitted to *Critical Sociology,* 1994) and Jerry Leonard, "Is the Multi- in Multicultural Studies the Multi- in Multinational Capitalism?" (unpublished essay submitted to *Minnesota Review,* 1992).

29. See, for example, Paul Lazarsfeld and Patricia L. Kendall, *Radio Listening in America* (New York: Arno, 1979; orig. pub. 1948); Harold Lasswell,

Democracy through Public Opinion (Menasha, Wis.: George Banta, 1941); and Carl Hovland, Irving Janis, and Harold Kelley, *Communication and Persuasion: Psychological Studies of Opinion* (New Haven: Yale UP, 1953).

30. Alexis Tan, *Mass Communicaton Theories and Research,* 2nd ed. (New York: Macmillan, 1986), 6. Hall's important observations on American behaviorism and structural functionalism can be found, among other places, in "The Hinterland of Science: Ideology and the 'Sociology of Knowledge,'" in *On Ideology,* Bill Schwarz et al., eds. (London: Hutchinson, 1978), 9–31.

31. This was the motivation, for example, of Pierre Bourdieu, who, upset by this linkage, in 1972 declared simply that "public opinion does not exist."

32. Daniel Lerner, *The Passing of Traditional Society: Modernizing the Middle East* (Glencoe, Ill.: Free Press, 1958), 1–2.

33. Hall, "Hinterland of Science"; Armand Mattelart and Jean-Marie Piemme, "New Means of Communication: New Questions for the Left," *Media, Culture, and Society* 2, no. 4 (October 1980), 329; Armand Mattelart, *Mass Media, Ideologies, and the Revolutionary Movement* (Atlantic Highlands, N.J.: Humanities Press, and Brighton, Sussex: Harvester, 1980), 26–7.

34. See James W. Carey, *Communication as Culture: Essays on Media and Society* (London: Unwin Hyman, 1988); James Curran, Michael Gurevitch, and Janet Woollacott, eds., *Mass Communication and Society* (London: E. Arnold, 1977); Kaarle Nordenstreng and Herbert Schiller, eds., *National Sovereignty and International Communication* (Norwood, N.J.: Ablex, 1979); Tapio Varis and Thomas Guback with José G. Cantor, *Transnational Communication and Cultural Industries* (New York: UNESCO, 1982).

35. Stuart Hall, "Introduction to Media Studies at the Centre," in *Culture, Media, Language: Working Papers in Cultural Studies, 1972–79,* Stuart Hall, Dorothy Hobson, Andrew Lowe, and Paul Willis, eds. (London: Unwin Hyman, 1980), 22.

36. Richard Hoggart, "Literature and Society," in Peter Davison, Rolf Meyersohn, and Edward Shils, eds., *Literary Taste, Culture, and Mass Communication,* vol. 9 (Cambridge: Chadwyck-Healey; Teaneck, N.J.: Somerset House, 1978).

37. See Stuart Hall, "The Rediscovery of Ideology: Return of the Repressed in Media Studies," in *Culture, Society, and the Media,* Michael Gurevitch, Tony Bennett, James Curran, and Janet Woollacott, eds. (London: Routledge, 1982), 56–90, and "Culture, the Media, and the Ideological 'Effect.'"

38. See, for example, Jacques Lacan, *Television,* Denis Hollier, Rosalind Krauss, and Annette Michelson, trans. (New York: Norton, 1990; orig. pub. 1974); Jean Baudrillard, *The Ecstasy of Communication,* Bernard and Caroline Schutze, trans. (Brooklyn, N.Y.: Autonomedia, 1988); Paul Virilio, *The Vision Machine* (Bloomington: Indiana UP, 1994); and Mark Poster, *The Mode of Information: Poststructuralism and Social Context* (Chicago: U of Chicago P, 1990).

39. For example, Armand Mattelart and Michele Mattelart, *De l'usage des medias en temps de crise: les nouveaux profils des industries de la culture* (Paris: Alan Moreau, 1979) and *Penser les medias* (Paris: La Decouverte, 1986). For a fuller treatment of their work and a bibliography up to 1990, see Timothy Brennan and Ewart Skinner, "Communication and Cultural Theory: Armand Mattelart in Chile," *Alif: Journal of Comparative Poetics* 10 (1990), 73–92.

40. Simon Frith and Jon Savage, "Pearls and Swine: The Intellectuals and the Mass Media" (review of Jim McGuigan's *Cultural Populism*), *New Left Review* 198 (March/April 1993), 107–16 (107 quoted).

41. Armand Mattelart and Michele Mattelart, *Juventud chilena: rebeldía y conformismo* (San Francisco: Editorial Universitaria, 1970). This book predated the CCCS's later famous studies of youth subcultures and deviancy—one of the Mattelarts' many anticipations of later metropolitan theory.

42. Richard Johnson, "What Is Cultural Studies Anyway?" *Social Text* 16 (Winter 1986/87; corresponds to vol. 6, no. 1, 1987): 38–80 (p. 55 quoted); examples of Raymond Williams's notion of "cultural revolution" can be found throughout his writing, most recently in *The Politics of Modernism: Against the New Conformists* (London: Verso, 1989), 161, 170.

43. Henri Lefebvre, *Critique of Everyday Life,* vol. 1, John Moore, trans. (New York: Verso, 1991; orig. pub. 1947), 52.

44. In this respect, see William G. Rosenberg's anthology *Bolshevik Visions: First Phase of the Cultural Revolution of Soviet Russia* (Ann Arbor: U of Michigan P, 1990).

45. Laura Kipnis, *Ecstasy Unlimited: On Sex, Capital, Gender, and Aesthetics,* (Minneapolis: U of Minnesota P, 1993), 113.

46. Wendy Goldman, "Early Soviet Woman's Organizations" (talk delivered at the Institute for Culture and Society, Pittsburgh, June 1995); Katerina Clark, *Petersburg: Crucible of Cultural Revolution* (Cambridge: Harvard UP, 1995).

47. Alexandra Kollontai, "Make Way for Winged Eros," William Rosenberg, ed., *Bolshevik Visions,* volume 1 (Ann Arbor: U of Michigan P, 1991); Karl Korsch, "Basis and Superstructure," *Karl Marx* (New York: Russel and Russel, 1963; orig. pub. 1938), 215, 220.

48. Examples include bell hooks, Catherine Stimpson, Cornel West, Stanley Fish, Michael Eric Dyson, Andrew Ross, and others.

49. See, for example, Michael Berubé, *Public Access* (London: Verso, 1994), or the media strategies plotted by Gerald Graff and Stanley Aronowitz through the newsletters of Teachers for a Democratic Culture and the Union of Democratic Intellectuals.

50. John Leonard, "The Search for Signs of Intelligent Life in Brooklyn," *New York,* May 3, 1993, 68.

51. Bernard Weinraub, "Condensing a Riot's Cacophony into the Voice of One Woman," *New York Times,* June 16, 1993, C-15.

52. *Playbill* 92, no. 7 (Joseph Papp Public Theater, July 1992), 16.

53. John Malkovich, for example, from Chicago's Steppenwolf Theater Company, rose to stardom in a New York production of Sam Shepard's *True West* that was also produced for television on *American Playhouse.*

54. For a less successful effort in the same genre, see Dan Settani's play *Made in the U.S.A: Snapshots of the American Dream.*

55. *New York Times,* June 16, 1993, C-16.

56. David Roediger, *The Wages of Whiteness: Race and the Making of the American Working Class* (New York: Verso, 1991), 68, 145.

57. For an excellent treatment of this problem, see Hazel Carby, "The Multicultural Wars," *Radical History Review* 54 (1992), 7–18.

58. The excellent work, for example, of Ketu Katrak on Wole Soyinka, of Abdul JanMohamed on Richard Wright, of Hazel Carby on African-American women, of Paul Gilroy on rap.

3. The Culture of the Transnational Corporation

The Stephen H. Rhinesmith quote is from *A Manager's Guide to Globalization: Six Keys to Success in a Changing World* (Alexandria, Va.: American Society for Training and Development, 1993). The Peter F. Drucker quote is from *The New Realities: In Government and Politics, in Economics and Business, in Society and World View* (New York: Harper and Row, 1989). The Ted Turner quote is from an interview with David Frost, PBS, New York Channel 13, October 26, 1991.

1. Sigmund Freud, *Jokes and Their Relation to the Unconscious,* James Strachey, trans. and ed. (New York: Penguin, 1976; orig. pub., 1905), 100. Freud concludes about the joke that "A. has put an 'and' where only an 'either-or' is possible."

2. Michael J. Shapiro, "Moral Geographies and the Ethics of Post-Sovereignty," *Public Culture* 6, no. 3 (1994), 479–502 (479 and 482 quoted).

3. *Miami Herald,* December 27, 1992, 18A.

4. David Binder with Barbara Crosette, *New York Times,* February 7, 1993, A1, A14.

5. Robert B. Reich, *The Work of Nations: Preparing Ourselves for Twenty-first Century Capitalism* (New York: Alfred A. Knopf, 1991).

6. Pico Iyer, "The Global Village Finally Arrives," in *The New Face of America,* special year-end issue of *Time,* Fall 1993, 86–7.

7. Quoted in Andrew Ross, *Universal Abandon? The Politics of Postmodernism* (Minneapolis: U of Minnesota P, 1988), xii.

8. Ted Turner, interview with David Frost, PBS, New York Channel 13, October 26, 1991.

9. Masao Miyoshi, "A Borderless World? From Colonialism to Transnationalism and the Decline of the Nation-State," *Critical Inquiry* 19, no. 4 (Summer 1993), 726–751. Miyoshi goes on to state a rationale for his essay that I share: "How to situate oneself in this neo–Daniel Bell configuration of transnational power and culture without being trapped by a deadend nativism seems to be the most important question that faces every critic and theorist the world over at this moment" (742).

10. For a fuller discussion, see Tim Brennan, "Places of Mind, Occupied Lands: Edward Said and Philology," Michael Sprinker, ed., *Edward Said: A Critical Reader* (Oxford: Blackwell, 1992), 74–95.

11. Edward Said, *Culture and Imperialism* (New York: Alfred A. Knopf, 1993), xii–xiii.

12. Los Tigres del Norte, "Jaula de Oro," *16 Super Exitos* (PRC 90559, Profono Internacional, 1988; Discos CBS International, Miami). My translation.

13. See, for example, Benedict Anderson, Ernest Gellner, Eric Hobsbawm, Homi Bhabha, Etienne Balibar, Kum Kum Sangari, and others.

14. Robert Kaplan, "The Coming Anarchy: How Scarcity, Crime, Overpopulation, Tribalism, and Disease Are Rapidly Destroying the Social Fabric of Our Planet," *Atlantic Monthly,* February 1994, 44–76 (60 quoted).

15. Theodore H. Von Laue, *The World Revolution of Westernization* (New York: Oxford UP, 1987); Ben J. Wattenberg, *The First Universal Nation: Leading Indicators and Ideas about the Surge of America in the 1990s* (New York: Free Press, 1991).

16. Homi Bhabha, ed., *Nation and Narration* (New York: Routledge, 1990); Andrew Parker, Mary Russo, Doris Sommer, and Patricia Yaeger, eds., *Nationalism and Sexualities* (New York: Routledge, 1992); Etienne Balibar and Immanuel Wallerstein, *Race, Nation, Class: Ambiguous Identities,* Chris Turner, trans. (London: Verso, 1991; orig. pub. 1988).

17. Kaplan, "The Coming Anarchy," 60.

18. Perry Anderson, *A Zone of Engagement* (London: Verso, 1992), 323.

19. Eduardo Galeano, "A Child Lost in the Storm," in *After the Fall: The Failure of Communism and the Future of Socialism* (New York: Verso, 1991), 250.

20. Henry Kissinger, *Diplomacy* (New York: Simon and Schuster, 1994), 23–4.

21. Reich, *Work of Nations,* 309.

22. John Seabrook, "Building a Better Human," *New Yorker,* March 28, 1994, 109–14.

23. Ellen K. Coughlin, "The Emergence of the 'Global City,'" *Chronicle of Higher Education,* January 5, 1994, A8.

24. United States Department of State, "Application for Passport by Mail," Form DSP-82 (2-93), OMB No. 1405-0020.

25. Peter F. Drucker, *Post-Capitalist Society* (New York: Harper Business, 1993), 171.

26. See Michael Berubé's comment in "Egghead Salad, or, I Was a Tenured Intellectual," *Voice Literary Supplement,* December 1993, 28: "In the United States, whose civil society tradition is strong and whose central state is relatively weak . . ." One would have thought this relationship exactly inverted. Television and the automobile either substitute for or obviate the former, while the latter—voluntarily "weak" toward business—has a capacity for controlling dissent that is the envy of other Western governments. Because of the way individual citizens are tracked by information grids, spied upon by overfunded (and overlapping) federal agencies, or kept from meaningful forums of public speech, one could argue that the U.S. state is the most centralized the world has ever seen.

27. Joshua Meyrowitz, *No Sense of Place: The Impact of Electronic Media on Social Behavior* (New York: Oxford UP, 1985), viii. Meyrowitz draws many of the same unwarranted political conclusions about the democratizing effects of media now current in cultural and communications studies.

28. D. Steven Blum, *Walter Lippmann: Cosmopolitanism in the Century of Total War* (Ithaca: Cornell UP, 1984), 13.

29. See, for example, Ines L. Claude, Jr., "American Values and Multilateral Institutions," in *States and the Global System: Politics, Law and Organization* (New York: St. Martin's, 1988), 102–3.

30. *New York Times,* June 22, 1993, A-11.

31. *New York Times,* April 4, 1992, A-6. Perhaps predictably, the principle is not reciprocal. In the wake of the invasion of Panama, several civil cases were brought against individual American soldiers by Panamanian courts. Three of the soldiers—Mark McMonagle, Mark Gusser, and Paul Finsell—were court-martialed and sentenced to eight years in prison for shooting Edith Díaz de Panay in her home, while they were drunk and far from the combat areas. Although it has financially compensated Díaz's family, the United States government has refused to extradite the three to stand trial in Panama.

32. *New York Times,* November 22, 1991, A-30. In fact, the editorial was mistaken about the allowances of U.S. law in this matter. The United Nations charter specifically prohibits such activity, as does a key clause in the Organization of American States charter—"the territory of a state is inviolable"—a sentiment underscored by the relevant U.S. treaties.

33. *New York Times,* December 21, 1991, A-6. See essays in *Harvard Law Review,* November 1992, 318–28; *ABA Journal,* November 1992, 50–2; and *World Policy Journal,* Fall 1992, 687–703.

34. *New York Times,* July 6, 1993, A-16.

35. Amy Goodman and Laura Flanders, *The Morning Show,* WBAI-FM (New York), December 21, 1992.

36. Richard Falk, *A Study of Future Worlds* (New York: The Free Press, 1975), 59.

37. Saul H. Mendlovitz, ed., *On the Creation of a Just World Order: Preferred Worlds for the 1990s* (New York: the Free Press, 1975), 5.

38. Blum, *Walter Lippmann,* 12–13.

39. Edward Meade Earle, "H. G. Wells," in Edward Meade Earle, ed., *Nationalism and Internationalism* (New York: Columbia UP, 1950), 113.

40. G. A. Borgese, *Foundations of the World Republic* (Chicago: U of Chicago P, 1953), 1.

41. "Myth Information: Writers' Board Show Hits Belief that Sovereignty Can Keep Peace," *World Government News,* January 1950, 10–11.

42. Walter Schiffer, *The Legal Community of Mankind: A Critical Analysis of the Modern Concept of World Organization* (New York: Columbia UP, 1954), 5–6.

43. Jackson Lears, "A Matter of Taste: Corporate Cultural Hegemony in a Mass-Consumption Society," in Lary May, ed., *Recasting America: Culture and Politics in the Age of the Cold War* (Chicago: U of Chicago P, 1989), 38–57 (40–1 quoted).

44. Bernard Crick, *George Orwell, A Life* (London: Secker and Warburg, 1980), 81; George Orwell, *Collected Essays, Journalism, Letters,* Sonia Orwell and Ian Angus, eds. (London: Secker and Warburg, 1968), 2: 219.

45. Crick, *George Orwell,* xviii.

46. Ibid., 39.

47. Ibid., xviii.

48. Raymond Williams, *George Orwell* (New York: Viking, 1971), 14–5.

49. Orwell, *Collected Essays,* 2: 216, 24.

50. Ibid., 416.

51. Ibid., 219.

52. I. A. Richards, *Basic English and Its Uses* (New York: W. W. Norton, 1943) and *Design for Escape: World Education through Modern Media* (New York: Harcourt, Brace and World, 1968); C. K. Ogden, *The System of Basic English* (New York: Harcourt, Brace and Company, 1934).

53. Friedrich Meinecke, *Cosmopolitanism and the National State,* Robert B. Kimber, trans. (Princeton, N.J.: Princeton UP, 1970; orig. pub., 1963), 21.

54. Julia Kristeva, *Strangers to Ourselves* (New York: Columbia UP, 1991), 2.

55. Immanuel Kant, *Perpetual Peace: A Philosophical Essay,* M. Campbell Smith, trans. (New York: Garland, 1972; orig. pub. 1795), 139–40; "Idea for a Universal History with Cosmopolitan Intent," in *The Philosophy of Kant: Immanuel Kant's Moral and Political Writings,* Carl J. Friedrich, ed. (New York: Modern Library, 1949).

56. Stephen Toulmin, *Cosmopolis: The Hidden Agenda of Modernity* (Chicago: U of Chicago P, 1990), 68.

57. Basil Davidson, *The Black Man's Burden: Africa and the Curse of the Nation-State* (New York: Times Books, 1992), 106.

58. Kant, *Perpetual Peace,* 128–9.

59. Karl Marx "Address of the International Workingmen's Association," in Karl Marx and Frederick Engels, *Letters to Americans 1848–1895* (New York: International Publishers, 1953), 65.

60. Karl Marx to Joseph Weydemeyer, March 25, 1852, ibid., 46, 66.

61. See José Martí, *The America of José Martí,* Juan de Onís, trans. (New York: Noonday, 1953), especially the portrait essays "General Grant" (4–56), "Peter Cooper" (71–81), "Jesse James" (91–5), "Buffalo Bill" (96–101), and "Whitman" (239–258). For a brilliantly evocative study of post–Civil War race relations and the labor movement, see David Roediger, *The Wages of Whiteness: Race and the Making of the American Working Class* (London: Verso, 1991).

62. Michael Sprinker, "The National Question: Said, Ahmad, Jameson," *Public Culture* 6, no. 1 (Fall 1993), 3–29.

63. Julius Nyerere, "Arusha Declaration," *Ujamaa—Essays on Socialism by Julius K. Nyerere* (Dar es Salaam, Tanzania: Oxford UP, 1968), 13–38; Cheddi Jagan, *The West on Trial: My Fight for Guyana's Freedom* (New York: International Publishers, 1966), 139–40.

64. Marc Shell, *Children of the Earth: Literature, Politics, and Nationhood* (New York: Oxford UP, 1993), 22; Masao Miyoshi, "A Borderless World? From Colonialism to Transnationalism and the Decline of the Nation-State," *Critical Inquiry* 19 (Summer 1993), 727–51 (730 quoted). Rob Nixon, "Of Balkans and Bantustans," *Transition* 60 (1993), 5–6, 20.

65. William Pfaff, *The Wrath of Nations: Civilization and the Fury of Nationalism* (New York: Simon and Schuster, 1993), 157–8.

66. See Perry Anderson, "The Figures of Descent," *New Left Review,* and "The Ends of History," in Anderson, *Zone of Engagement,* 367.

67. "A Strange New Pattern of Stars," *Economist,* February 6, 1993, 56.

68. Perry Anderson, "The Light of Europe," in *English Questions* (New York: Verso, 1992).

69. George Ross, "Confronting the New Europe," *New Left Review* 191 (January/February 1992), 49–68 (67 quoted).

70. Mariano Aguirre, "Discriminate Intervention: Defining NATO for the '90s," *Middle East Report* no. 177, vol. 22, no. 4 (July-August 1992), 28–32.

71. Régis Debray, *Les Empires contre l'Europe* (Paris: Gallimard, 1985), 12 (my translation).

72. Ernest Wistrich, *After 1992: The United States of Europe* (London: Routledge, 1989), 86–7.

73. James M. Blaut, *The National Question: Decolonizing the Theory of Nationalism* (London: Zed, 1987).

74. James Clifford, "Traveling Cultures," in *Cultural Studies,* Lawrence Grossberg, Cary Nelson, and Paula A. Treichler, eds. (New York: Routledge, 1992), 109.

75. Miyoshi, "A Borderless World?" 728, 739. Miyoshi does point out, and quite rightly, that "the precise extent of the denationalization of a corporation is not readily determinable," although he develops the point only in regard to taxation and the military rather than culturally as here (736–7). The Tom Peters quote at the beginning of this section is from *Liberation Management: Necessary Disorganization for the Nanosecond Nineties* (New York: Alfred A. Knopf, 1992), 375.

76. "The Discreet Charm of the Multicultural Multinational," *Economist,* July 30–August 5, 1994, 57.

77. Reich, *Work of Nations,* 119.

78. John M. Stopford, John H. Dunning, and Klaus O. Haberich, *The World Directory of Multinational Enterprises* (New York: Facts on File, 1980).

79. Roy C. Smith and Ingo Walter, "Reconfigurations of Global Financial Markets in the 1990s," in Peter J. Buckley, ed., *New Directions in International Business: Research Priorities for the 1990s* (Aldershot, Eng.: Edward Elgar, 1992), 53.

80. Stephen H. Rhinesmith, *A Manager's Guide to Globalization: Six Keys to Success* (Alexandria, Va.: American Society for Training and Development, 1993). For a discussion of the eternal search for the business guru, see "Take Me to Your Leader," *Economist,* December 25, 1993–January 7, 1994, 21–5, which in its overview of the literature, interestingly, includes entries on Vaclav Havel, Octavio Paz, Noam Chomsky, and Jacques Derrida as well as the more usual business and governmental sources. Among the many works that compete more directly with Rhinesmith are Robert Allen and Charlotte Kraft, *The Organizational Unconscious: How to Create the Corporate Culture You Want and Need* (1982); Terence E. Deal and Allan A. Kennedy, *Corporate Cultures: The Rites and Rituals of Corporate Life* (1982); Glen Fischer, *Mindsets: The Role of Culture and Perception in International Relations* (1988); Paul Pederson, *A Handbook for Developing Multicultural Awareness* (1988); and Gert Hofstede, *Culture and Organizations: Software of the Mind* (1991).

81. Rhinesmith, *Manager's Guide,* 16.

82. In an excellent essay, Bruce Spear has made some of these same points; see Bruce Spear, "Multiculturalism, Inc.," *Transition* 61 (1994), 72–86.

83. Drucker, *New Realities,* 229.

84. Peters, *Liberation Management,* 370.

85. Drucker, *New Realities,* 231.

86. Rhinesmith, *Manager's Guide,* 142.

4. Cosmopolitanism and the Explorer's Eye

The Jim Philips quote is from "Reading Travel Writing," in Jonathan White, ed., *Recasting the World: Writing after Colonialism* (Baltimore: Johns Hopkins UP, 1993). The Paul Beatty quote is from "At Ease," in Miguel Algarín and Bob Holman, eds., *Aloud: Voices from the Nuyorican Poets Cafe* (New York: Holt, 1994).

1. Although I moved to the area before the gentrification wave of the early 1980s, I am aware that I was also implicated in the gentrification I describe in the sense that my physically being there, my willingness as a white professional to live there, was a motivation for investors to gentrify.

2. Rosalyn Deutsch and Cara Gendel Ryan, "The Fine Art of Gentrification," *October* 31 (Winter 1984), 91–111.

3. An interesting contrast between these historical moments can be traced locally in novels about the area. A treasure land of immigrant proletarian fiction from the turn of the century up to World War II—as seen in such works as Abraham Cahan's novel *The Rise of David Levinski* (New York: Grosset and Dunlop, 1917), Arthur Bullard's *Comrade Yetta* (New York: Macmillan, 1913), and Michael Gold's *Jews without Money* (New York: H. Liveright, 1930)—it has lately seen the light of bohemian angst: reflections on dissolution and drugs, as represented best, perhaps, by *Kill the Poor* (New York: Atlantic Monthly P, 1988), Joel Rose's novel about gentrification in "alphabet city."

4. As a police reporter based on Mulberry Street in what is currently Chinatown, Jacob Riis—a Christian Danish immigrant who arrived in 1870—particularly singled out the docklands areas of the Lower East Side for his project of exposing urban ills through narrative appeals and photographs. In *How the Other Half Lives: Studies among the Tenements of New York* (New York: Hill and Wang, 1957; orig. pub. 1890), he speaks of the graphic filth and degradation of "the Bend"—precisely the area where the Riis houses and the East River Parkway now stand.

5. Neil Smith, "Contours of a Spacialized Politics: Homeless Vehicles and the Production of Socialized Space," *Social Text* 33 (1992), 55–81; David Harvey, *The Condition of Postmodernity: An Enquiry into the Origins of Cultural Change* (Cambridge, Mass.: Blackwell, 1989). Although not specifically focused on the Lower East Side, Smith's early essays on gentrification predate Deutsch and Ryan's; see, for example, "Toward a Theory of Gentrification: A Back to the City Movement by Capital Not People," *Journal of the American Planning Association* 45, no. 4 (October 1979), 538–48.

6. Arnold Krupat, *Ethnocriticism: Ethnography, History, Literature* (Berkeley: U of California P, 1992), 4.

7. Dick Hebdige, "Redeeming Witness: In the Tracks of the Homeless Ve-

hicle Project," *Cultural Studies* (1992), 173–223; Celeste Olalquiaga, *Megalopolis: Contemporary Cultural Sensibilities* (Minneapolis: U of Minnesota P, 1992).

8. See, for example, C. Carr, *Village Voice* 29, April 3, 1984, 1; Kim Levin, *Village Voice* 28, October 18, 1984, 78–9; and Robert Smith, *Village Voice* 30, January 1, 1985, 67.

9. Hebdige, "Redeeming Witness," 176.

10. In spite of being built and distributed in four areas of Manhattan, *Poliscar* had its original reality only as staged photos, complex diagrams, and playfully overzealous explanations of the vehicle's "utility," all mounted on a gallery wall. In other words, it did not attempt to be a solution to a social problem, and Hebdige does not pretend it is.

11. Hebdige, "Redeeming Witness," 203.

12. Dick Hebdige, address to the Workshop on Localities, New Brunswick, N.J., March, 1994.

13. Hebdige, "Redeeming Witness," 198, 206.

14. Olaquiaga, *Megalopolis,* 81.

15. Leonard Bernstein, composer, *West Side Story: Vocal Score,* Jerome Robbins, conception; Arthur Laurents, book; Stephen Sondheim, lyrics (New York: G. Schirmer, and Chappel and Co., 1957).

16. Tom Lehrer, *Tom Lehrer's Second Song Book* (New York: Crown, 1968).

17. Olalquiaga, *Megalopolis,* 36.

18. Jean Franco, "What's Left of the Intelligentsia: The Uncertain Future of the Printed Word," *NACLA: Report on the Americas,* 28, no. 2 (September/October 1994), 18.

19. Olalquiaga, *Megalopolis,* 39.

20. It is only fair to point out that one of the Lower East Side's best known graffiti artists, "Chico," has in recent years been hired by local businesses to create advertisements—Coke cans and Tropicana orange juice cartons—on the stores' adjacent brick walls.

21. It does, however, receive passing mention in an excellent recent anthology: Janet Abu-Lughod, ed., *From Urban Village to East Village* (Oxford: Blackwell, 1994), 141–7. Still, in her introductory schematic map of the Lower East Side (which she restrictively calls "East Village"), Abu-Lughod inexplicably cuts the neighborhood off at Avenue C, thereby elminating the entire complex of the Riis houses, the vibrant Latino communities of Avenue D, and the highly important mixed cultural life of the East River Parkway across FDR Drive. As this lopping off of the Latino center indicates, the volume is, like Hebdige, inordinately centered on Tompkins Square Park as a liminal space.

22. Daniel Chodorkoff, "Un Milagro de Loisaida: Alternative Technology and Grassroots Efforts for Neighborhood Reconstruction of New York's

Lower East Side," unpublished dissertation, New School for Social Research, March 1980, 130, 149, 167, 169.

23. Personal interview with María Dominguez, New York, June 10, 1994.

24. Personal Interview with Chino García, May 10, 1994.

25. Olalquiaga, *Megalopolis,* 80.

26. See, in this respect, Charles Sugnet's superb anatomy of *Granta* travel writing, "Vile Bodies, Vile Places: Traveling with *Granta,*" *Transition* 51 (1991), 70–85.

27. This theme has been explored much more thoroughly elsewhere. See for example, Cynthia Enloe, *Banana, Beaches, and Bases Making Feminist Sense of International Politics;* (Berkeley: U of California P, 1990) and Mary Louise Pratt, *Imperial Eyes: Travel Writing and Transculturation* (London: Routledge, 1992), especially 90–107.

28. Lafcadio Hearn, *Fantastics and Other Fancies* (Boston: Houghton and Mifflin, 1914), 12.

29. Ibid., 13.

30. Lafcadio Hearn, *Writings,* vol. 1 (Boston: Houghton and Mifflin, 1922), 75.

31. Lafcadio Hearn, *Youma: The Story of a West-Indian Slave* (New York: Harper and Brothers, 1890), 5.

32. Lafcadio Hearn, *Two Years in the French West Indies: A Midsummer Trip to the Tropics* (Boston: Houghton Mifflin Co., 1922; orig. pub. 1890), 20, 36.

33. See Carleton Beals, *Banana Gold* (Philadelphia: J. B. Lippincott, 1932). Beals is perhaps best known for his admiring portraits of Augusto César Sandino while in hiding in Nicaragua during the U.S. occupation of that country. His solidarity with an anti-imperialist guerrilla is, therefore, juxtaposed with observations on tropical sensuality, a coupling of the political and the erotic that I am arguing characterizes the cosmopolitan "explorer."

34. Quoted in Van Gosse, *Where the Boys Are: Cuba, Cold War America, and the Making of a New Left* (London: Verso, 1993), 7.

35. As, for example, in Malek Alloula, *The Colonial Harem* (Minneapolis: U of Minnesota P, 1986); Kumkum Sangari and Sudesh Vaid, eds., *Recasting Women: Essays in Colonial Indian History* (New Brunswick, N.J.: Rutgers UP, 1990); Jenny Sharpe, *Allegories of Empire* (Minneapolis: U of Minnesota P, 1993); and Saree Makdisi, "The Empire Renarrated: *Season of Migration to the North* and the Reinvention of the Present," *Critical Inquiry* 18, no. 4 (1992), 804–20. Even more explicitly, see also Revathi Krishnaswamy, *Effeminism: An Alternative Paradigm of Colonial Erotics* (unpublished manuscript, 1994).

36. Gordon Lewis, *Main Currents in Caribbean Thought: The Historical Evolution of Caribbean Society in Its Ideological Aspects, 1492–1900* (Baltimore: Johns Hopkins UP, 1983), 66.

37. Pico Iyer, *Falling Off the Map: Some Lonely Places of the World* (London: Jonathan Cape, 1993).

38. The novel is entitled *Cuba and the Night.* For Iyer in a more explicitly political mode, although it is only a minor variation, see his essay "Castro's Resilient Masses," *New York Times,* August 31, 1994, A-19.

39. Iyer, *Falling Off the Map,* 6.

40. Pico Iyer, "Strangers in a Small World," *Harper's* 289, no. 1732 (September 1994), 13.

41. Iyer, *Falling Off the Map,* 114.

42. See Caryl Phillips, *The European Tribe* (New York: Farrar Straus and Giroux, 1987). Eduardo Galeano has been among those who angrily resist this parallelism: "If Lech Walesa had been born in Guatemala, he would have been disemboweled during the first strike, and . . . his murder wouldn't have merited a fraction of an inch in the world's major dailies," *We Say No: Chronicles 1963–1991* (New York: Norton, 1992), 210.

43. See, for example, *Grand Street* 43, no. 11, 3 (1992) and *The Best of Granta Travel Writing* (London: Granta Books, 1991).

44. Ryszard Kapuscinski, *The Soccer War* (New York: Knopf, 1991); Witold Gombrowicz, *Diary,* Jan Kott, ed., Lillian Vallee, trans., vol. 1 (Evanston, Ill.: Northwestern UP, 1988; orig. pub. 1957).

45. Contrast this, though, with Elena Poniatowska's epistolary novel *Querido Diego, te abrazo, Quiela* (Dear Diego, with love, Quiela) (Mexico: Biblioteca Ero, 1978) where Europe and the third world actually change places. Poniatwoska, another immigrant to Latin America, was born in Paris to a Polish father and a Mexican mother.

46. Gombrowicz, *Diary,* 167.

47. Vaclav Havel, "The New Measure of Man," *New York Times,* July 8, 1994, A-27. Subsequent quotes from Havel's speech are ibid.

48. Julio Cortázar, *Around the Day in Eighty Worlds,* Thomas Christiansen, trans. (San Francisco: North Point Press, 1986; orig. pub. 1967). This is a selection, chosen by Cortázar, of parts of both *La Vuelta el dìa en ochenta mundos* and *Ultimo round* (1969).

49. See the discussion on Cortázar in Paris in Santiago Colás, *Postmodernity in Latin America: The Argentine Paradigm* (Durham, N.C.: Duke UP, 1994).

50. Julio Cortázar, *Nicaraguan Sketches,* Kathleen Weaver, trans. (New York: W. W. Norton, 1989), 86.

51. Julio Cortázar, *Nicaragua, tan violentamente dulce* (Buenos Aires: Muchnik, 1984), 11, 16. My translation.

52. Julio Cortázar, *Los Autonautas de la cosmopista: Un viaje atemporal París–Marsella* (Buenos Aires: Muchnik, 1983). My translations.

53. Margaret Randall, *Albuquerque: Coming Back to the U.S.A.* (Vancouver:

New Star Books, 1986); Richard Rodriguez, *Days of Obligation: An Argument with My Mexican Father* (New York: Viking, 1992).

54. Suzanne Ruta called him, for example the "mysterious subcomandante Marcos, tall, pale, well read, politically sophisticated, and probably not from the region" (Suzanne Ruta, "Chiapas es Mexico," *Grand Street* 50, vol. 13, no. 2 [Fall 1994], 181).

55. Subcomandante Marcos, "Chiapas: The Southeast in Two Winds, a Storm and a Prophecy," in "The Complete Communiqués from the Lacandon between January–August 1994," *Anderson Valley Advertiser* (Boonville, Calif.), August 3, 1994.

56. Pursuing his contacts with the press, Marcos tells the editors at the small, San Cristóbal–based paper *Tiempo* to "say hello to everyone . . . pay my respects," singling out *Tiempo* for having had the courage to cover the events honestly despite the *federales'* threats. About *La Jornada,* he writes encouragingly and as a friend, "I think the mosaic of editorial currents is an important part of the paper's success" (11), and adds similar greetings to *Proceso.*

57. Marcos, "Chiapas," 8.

58. See John Ross, *Rebellion from the Roots: Indian Uprising in Chiapas* (Monroe, Maine: Common Courage, 1995), 19.

59. Marcos, "Chiapas," 10.

60. Since 1982, only five recipients of the Nobel Prize in literature have been from European countries: William Golding (Britain), 1983; Jaroslav Siefert (Czechoslavakia), 1984; Claude Simon (France), 1985; Joseph Brodsky (USSR-United States), 1987; and Camilo José Cela (Spain), 1989. The others have been Gabriel García Márquez (Colombia), 1982; Wole Soyinka (Nigeria), 1986; Naguib Mahfouz (Egypt), 1988; Octavio Paz (Mexico), 1990; Nadine Gordimer (South Africa), 1991; Derek Walcott (Saint Lucia), 1992; and Toni Morrison (Afro-America), 1993. By contrast, between 1945 and 1982, only four were from countries traditionally considered part of the third world. Gabriela Mistral (Chile), 1945; Juan Ramon Jimenez (Puerto Rico-Spain), 1956; Miguel Asturias (Guatemala), 1967; and Pablo Neruda (Chile), 1971.

61. James Atlas, "Constructing Modern Idiom on a Base of Tradition," *New York Times,* October 9, 1992, C-30.

62. Derek Walcott, "A Map of Europe" and "The Sea Is History," *Collected Poems 1948–1984* (New York: Farrar, Straus and Giroux, 1986), 66, 364; *Ti-Jean and His Brothers,* in *"Dream on Monkey Mountain" and Other Plays* (New York: Farrar, Straus and Giroux, 1970), 85–166; *"The Joker of Seville" and "O, Babylon!": Two Plays* (New York: Farrar, Straus and Giroux, 1978); *"Remembrance" and "Pantomime": Two Plays* (New York: Farrar, Straus and Giroux, 1980).

63. Derek Walcott, "Nobel Acceptance Speech," *New Republic* 207, December 28, 1992, 26.

64. John Darnton, "In Sweden, Proof of the Power of Words," *New York Times,* December 8, 1993, C-17.

65. Toni Morrison, "Nobel Lecture 1993," *World Literature Today,* 68, no. 1 (Winter 1994), 7.

66. See Renee Winegarten, "The Nobel Prize for Literature," *American Scholar,* 63, no. 1 (Winter 1994); also, *Library Journal* 116, no. 1 (January 1991), and "The Generalist: Winners of Nobel Prizes in Literature," *Stamp,* October 26, 1991.

67. Aware of the importance of Latin America in the concept, for example, Ilan Stavans has written with barely concealed hostility about Mario Vargas Llosa as "Peru's favorite son, but stationed, like a diplomat, in Europe," and as a champion of "democracy in international forums" while writing "stylish novels and plays, which were frequently set in Piura, Lima, and Arequipa" (Ilan Stavans, "Two Peruvians: How a Novelist and a Terrorist Came to Represent Peru's Divided Soul," *Transition* 61 (1993), 26).

68. One such display case in New York University's Tisch Library, for example, grouped the following titles in 1992: Faye Myenne Ng's *Bone,* David Wong Lou're's *Pangs of Love,* Gina Barkhordar Nahai's *Cry of the Peacock,* Karen Tei Yamashita's *Through the Arc of the Rainforest,* Cristina García's *Dreaming in Cuban,* J. Joaquin Fraxedas's *Lonely Crossing of Juan Cabrera,* and Sashi Tharoor's *Great Indian Novel.* Although placed under a heading that drew attention to a common "minority" vision, these disparate authors actually share only a single community: an Anglo-American community of reception.

69. See, for example, Nawal El-Saadawi, *Woman at Point Zero,* Sherif Hetata, trans. (London: Zed, 1983); Hanan al-Shaykh, *Women of Sand and Myrrh,* Catherine Cobham, trans. (London: Quartet, 1989); Etel Adnan, *Sitt Marie Rose: A Novel,* Georgina Kleege, trans. (Sausalito, Calif.: Post-Apollo, 1982); Andrée Chedid, *The Return to Beirut* (London: Serpents Tail, 1989; orig. pub. 1985); and Assia Djebar, *Women of Algiers in Their Apartment* (Charlottesville: UP of Virginia, 1992; orig. pub. 1980). Also see Naguib Mahfouz, *Palace Walk,* William M. Hutchins and Olive E. Kenny, trans. (New York: Doubleday, 1989; orig. pub. 1956) and Tayeb Salih, *Season of Migration to the North,* Denys Johnson-Davis, trans. (London: Heinemann, 1969). The pervasiveness of the theme is implied by the Moroccan writer Tahar Ben Jelloun's small masterpiece *L'enfant de sable*—about a father so insanely eager for a male heir after having seven daughters that he gives his next child (a daughter) a male name and refuses to let anyone acknowledge she is not a boy (Tahar Ben Jelloun, *L'enfant de sable* [Paris: Èditions de Seuil, 1985]).

70. Otto René Castillo, "Intelectuales apolíticos," *Let's Go! Vamonos Patria a Caminar,* Margaret Randall, trans. (New York: Cape Goliard, 1971), n.p. My translation.

71. The lyrics of this moving song consist entirely of two lines, repeated over and over again: "Independence or Death / We Got to Win."

72. One could turn, for example, to the Haitian poet René Depestre's wildly experimental voodoo poem *Un arc-en-ciel pour l'occident chrétien (A Rainbow for the Christian West),* whose sheer stylistic variety—from ritual invocation to delicate lyricism—suggest any number of canonical analogies (René Depestre, *A Rainbow for the Christian West,* Joan Dayan, trans. [Amherst: U of Massachusetts P, 1977]). But given that that lyricism partakes of a passionate sides-taking on behalf of a communism seen as familialy allied to Black resistance, it may well appear tasteless (if not actually frightening) to many readers—one reason perhaps that it has not enjoyed the success of its nearest relative, Aimé Césaire's *Cahier d'un retour au pays natal (Notebook on the Return to My Native Land).* Césaire himself was a former Communist, of course, but with much less clear affiliations than reflected in the poem for which he is best known

73. Clarice Lispector, *The Stream of Life,* Elizabeth Lowe and Earl Fitz, trans. (Minneapolis: U of Minnesota P, 1989); Dambudzo Marechera, *The House of Hunger: A Novella and Short Stories* (New York: Pantheon, 1978).

5. Cosmopolitanism's American Base

The Jean Baudrillard quote is from *America* (London: Verso, 1988; orig. pub. 1986), 75–6. Baudrillard goes on, however, to write: "*Utopia has been achieved here and anti-utopia is being achieved:* the anti-utopia of unreason, of deterritorialization, of the indeterminacy of language and the subject, of the neutralization of all values, of the death of culture" (97, Baudrillard's emphasis).

1. Judith Williamson, *Consuming Passions: The Dynamics of Popular Culture* (London: M. Boyars, 1986), 3.

2. Leo Löwenthal, "Historical Perspectives of Popular Culture," in *Mass Culture: The Popular Arts in America,* Bernard Rosenberg and David Manning White, eds. (Glencoe, Ill.: Free Press, 1957), 54.

3. Ernst Bloch, *The Principle of Hope,* Neville Plaice, Stephen Plaice, and Paul Knight, trans. (Cambridge, Mass.: MIT P, 1986; orig. pub. 1959), vol. 1, xxxi.

4. Bloch remained hostile to psychoanalysis as such, however, believing that it had "developed in a class which was superannuated even then" (ibid., 137).

5. Jean-François Lyotard, "The Wall, the Gulf, and the Sun: A Fable," in

Politics, Theory, and Contemporary Culture, Mark Poster, ed. (New York: Columbia UP, 1993), 261–275 (264–5 quoted).

6. For a fuller discussion of this turn, see Tim Brennan, "Black Theorists and Left Antagonists," *Minnesota Review,* n.s. 37 (Fall 1991), 89–113.

7. Henri Lefebvre, *Critique of Everyday Life,* John Moore, trans. (London: Verso, 1991; orig. pub. 1947), vol. 1, 49 51.

8. Bloch, *Principle of Hope,* 201.

9. Fredric Jameson, *Marxism and Form: Twentieth-Century Dialectical Theories of Literature* (Princeton, N.J.: Princeton UP, 1971), 153.

10. James K. Lyon, *Bertolt Brecht in America* (Princeton: Princeton UP, 1980), 37.

11. Bloch, *Principle of Hope,* 74, 171.

12. To the *Village Voice,* Shevardnadze's resignation in late 1990 was "one of the most courageous acts by a statesman in the history of 20th century politics"; in *The Nation,* one read that Boris Yeltsin "deserves our support"; in *Socialist Review,* one found a direct link made between the "recently liberated mass populations of Eastern Europe" and the "exhaustion of narratives of progressive futurism."

13. Fredric Jameson, "Conversations on the New World Order," *After the Fall: The Failure of Communism and the Future of Socialism* (London: Verso, 1991), 255–73 (265 quoted).

14. Ernesto Laclau and Chantal Mouffe, "Postmarxism without Apologies," *New Left Review* 166 (November-December 1987), 79–106.

15. C. L. R. James, *American Civilization,* Anna Grimshaw and Keith Hart, ed. (Cambridge, Mass.: Basil Blackwell, 1993). In their pre-publication writings (see n. 16 below), Grimshaw and Hart make a convincing case for referring to the book not as "Notes on American Civilization" (James's only title) but "The Struggle for Happiness"—the original title of his sixth chapter. Differences between James's original typescript and the book published as *American Civilization* are, nevertheless, insignificant, being limited mainly to the supplying of titles to those chapters left untitled in the original and to the addition of endnotes. For convenience, I therefore give citations using the page numbers of the published book (hereafter cited as *AC*). Also, following James's own usage in 1950, the adjective "American"—instead of "North American" or simply "U.S."—will with a few exceptions be used here to refer to the culture and society of the United States.

16. See Anna Grimshaw and Keith Hart, *C. L. R. James and "The Struggle for Happiness"* (New York: Desktop Publishing by Jim Murray of *Cultural Correspondence,* 1991), and Kent Worcester, "C. L. R. James and the American Century: 1938–1953," in *C. L. R. James and His Intellectual Legacies,* Selwyn R. Cudjoe and William E. Cain, eds., (Amherst: U of Massachusetts P, 1995).

17. Included in the recent revival are Sylvia Wynter, "Beyond the Categories

of the Master Conception: the Counterdoctrine of the Jamesian Poeisis," in *C. L. R. James's Caribbean*, Paget Henry and Paul Buhle, eds. (Durham, N.C.: Duke UP, 1992), 63–91; Cedric Robinson, *Black Marxism: The Making of the Black Radical Tradition* (London: Zed Books, 1983); Anna Grimshaw, *C. L. R. James: A Revolutionary Vision for the 20th Century* (New York: C. L. R. James Institute, 1991); Paul Buhle, *C.L.R. James: the Artist as Revolutionary* (London: Verso, 1988); Kent Worcester, "C. L. R. James: A Political Biography" (unpublished manuscript, 1993); Scott McLemee, "Afterword," in Scott McLemee and Paul Le Blanc, *C. L. R. James and Revolutionary Marxism: Selected Writings, 1939–1949,* (New York: Humanities Press, 1993).

18. For its part, *Beyond a Boundary* might be seen as the autobiography James never wrote.

19. See Paul Buhle, "The C. L. R. James Conference: One Participant's Observations" (unpublished, undated open letter to participants in the C. L. R. James Conference at Wellesley College, April 19–21, 1991), 2.

20. James to Webb, September 1, 1943, C. L. R. James Letters to Constance Webb, Schomburg Center for the Study of Black Culture, (hereafter cited as New York Webb Letters). For an opposing emphasis, see Scott McLemee, "In the American Tradition: A Provocation regarding the *Ecole Grimshaw* and Related Matters" (unpublished essay, 1992): "Every significant line of thought in the 1950 document had been anticipated in the pages of James's literary productions for the Trotskyist press over the decade previously" (2). For another dimension of the personal, see Stanley Weir, who writes of James's "need to be in a major industrial society which contained a significant Black population" (Stanley Weir, "Revolutionary Artist," in *C. L. R. James: His Life and Work,* Paul Buhle, ed. (London: Allison and Busby, 1986), 180–4 (180 quoted).

21. Leo Löwenthal, "Historical Perspectives," 52.

22. James's productivity in these years is recorded best in Robert A. Hill, "In England, 1932–1938," in *Life and Work* 69–80. The best short account of James's career can be found in Selwyn Cudjoe, "For Ever, Mellow: Selected Treasures of C. L. R. James's Intellectual Legacy," *C. L. R. James Journal,* Winter 1992, 17–35, and "C. L. R. James Misbound," *Transition,* 58: 124–36.

23. James's political activism might be summarized as follows: chairman, International Friends of Abyssinia (1934–1936); member, Independent Labour Party; cofounder, International African Service Bureau; editor, *International African Opinion* (journal of the Pan African Federation); participant, biracial Southestern Missouri Sharecroppers strike (1941); member, Workers Party, Socialist Workers Party, and other small Leninist organizations; regular contributor, *Socialist Appeal, New International, Labor Action, Correspondence, Militant,* and other interventionist-organizing publications in the United States; member, People's National Movement, Trinidad, and ed-

itor, *The Nation* (its official organ); member and consultant, *Race Today* collective, England.

24. Robinson goes so far as to call James and his group (in the late 1930s and 1940s) "essentially contemplative didactics coupled with revolutionary action" (Robinson, *Black Marxism,* 391).

25. Martin Glaberman, James's longtime comrade based in Detroit, and a member of the Johnson-Forrest tendency of which James was a founding member, kept "A Natural but Necessary Conclusion" out of the edition of *Mariners* whose publication he oversaw. That this was a "suppression" of the material is my interpretation, not his admission, although the interpretation is neither unique nor unfair.

26. C. L. R. James, "Essays and Lectures by C. L. R. James: A Tribute," *Caribbean Quarterly,* 35, no. 4 (December 1989), 29.

27. See Grimshaw, *Revolutionary Vision,* McLemee, "American Tradition," and Worcester, "American Century."

28. James to Webb, March 1, 1946, Webb Letters.

29. C. L. R. James, *The Black Jacobins: Toussaint L'Ouverture and the San Domingo Revolution* (New York: Vintage, 1963; orig. pub., 1938), 41.

30. The semipoetic, apocalyptic snapshots of Jean Baudrillard's *America* and the chatty arcana of U.S. "underground" technocultures in Andrew Ross's *Strange Weather* (London: Verso, 1992) are very different sorts of examples of current nonnative hypostatizations of U.S. popular culture—the U.S. as a European myth. Because the authority of both writers derives in part from their European backgrounds, they are (in this sense) quite unlike James. Baudrillard in particular gives voice to the current clichés of the cosmopolitan moment: "The fifties were the real high spot for the US . . . and you can still feel the nostalgia for those years, for the ecstasy of power, when power held power. . . But if America is now no longer the monopolistic centre of world power, this is not because it has lost power, but simply because there is no centre anymore. It has, rather, become the orbit of an imaginary power to which everyone now refers" (107).

31. For the argument that James shares the views of deconstruction, see Wynter, "Beyond the Categories"; for the view of his independence from traditional Marxism, see Robinson, *Black Marxism.*

32. Robinson, *Black Marxism,* 386.

33. James to Webb, December 15, 1943, Webb Letters.

34. James to "G. W.," August 12, 1953, C. L. R. James Archives, New York (hereafter cited as James Archives).

35. C. L. R. James, "A Natural but Necessary Conclusion," *Mariners, Renegades, and Castaways,* as quoted in "Notes on American Civilization" (typescript version of *American Civilization*), 3.

36. C. L. R. James, *The C. L. R. James Reader,* Anna Grimsaw, ed. (Oxford: Blackwell, 1992), 231.

37. Lefebvre, *Critique of Everyday Life,* 43.

38. For Brecht's early comments on the popular aesthetics of sport, see Bertolt Brecht, "Emphasis on Sport," *Brecht on Theatre,* John Willett, trans. (London: Methuen, 1982; orig. pub. 1926), 6–8: "We have our eye on those huge concrete pans, filled with 15,000 men and women of every variety of class and physiognomy, the fairest and shrewdest audience in the world."

39. According to Walton Look Lai, when James found himself with actual governmental authority for the first time, in Trinidad under Eric Williams, his positions on workers control were much more guarded and conservative; see Walton Look Lai, "C. L. R. James and Trinidadian Nationalism," in Henry and Buhle, *C. L. R. James's Caribbean,* 174–209 (196 quoted).

40. The following passage is typical: "Today in the 'cold war' the picture of America which is being presented to the world by the rulers of America is Whitman's picture. Free individuals, free enterprise, science, industry, democracy—that is the Voice of America and this at a time when every thinking mind in America is pondering over the outcome of precisely what these terms signify for American and human civilization. . . . His 'body beautiful' and 'body electric' and 'seminal wetness' are the reservoir from which advertisers of foods, toothpaste, vitamins, deodorants draw an unending source of inspirations by which to cheat and corrupt the American people" (*AC,* 46).

41. See, for example, James to Webb, February 4, 1944, Webb Letters.

42. C. L. R. James, *Notes on Dialectics: Hegel, Marx, Lenin* (London: Allison and Busby, 1980; orig. pub. 1948), 118.

43. Lefebvre, *Critique of Everyday Life,* 35.

44. C. L. R. James, "Popular Art and the Cultural Tradition," *C.L.R. James Reader,* 247.

45. Cedric Robinson, *Black Marxism,* 374; Darcus Howe, "Interview," in Buhle, *Life and Work,* 146.

46. George Lamming, "Interview," in Henry and Buhle, *C. L. R. James's Caribbean,* 29.

47. James, *C. L. R. James Reader,* 258.

48. C. L. R. James, "Lincoln, Carnival, George Padmore: Writings from the *Nation,*" ibid., 284.

49. James, *C. L. R. James Reader,* 151.

50. James, *Black Jacobins,* 271.

51. James, *C. L. R. James Reader,* 152.

52. C. L. R. James, "Lenin and the Problem," 332.

53. James's comments on George Padmore (288–95) and Kwame Nkrumah (331–46) in *The C. L. R. James Reader* seem to be an appropriate

first response to the widespread notion that Marxism, by being Eurocentric, actually abetted imperialism.

54. Worcester, "James and the American Century," 37.

55. Lyon, *Bertolt Brecht in America,* 37, 39.

56. See Clement Greenberg, *The Collected Essays and Criticism* vol. 2 (Chicago: U of Chicago P, 1986), 64: "The fact is that most people in our society lack the security, leisure, and comfort indispensable to the cultivation of taste; and only a socialist society can provide security, leisure, and comfort."

57. Edmund Wilson, "Who Cares Who Killed Roger Ackroyd?" in Rosenberg and Manning White, *Mass Culture,* 149–5.

58. Bloch, *Principle of Hope,* vol. 1, 35.

59. Marcus Garvey, *Marcus Garvey and the Vision of Africa,* John Henrik Clarke, ed. (New York: Vintage, 1974), 89.

60. See C. L. R. James, "Black Power," *C. L. R. James Reader,* 367 ff., and "The People of the Gold Coast," ibid., 352.

61. James to Webb, March 1, 1946: "I feel that by bringing my full powers to bear on you, I can illuminate you and develop you. Because a genuine exploration and adventure develops both the explorer and the territory."

62. Ibid.

63. Jackson Lears, "A Matter of Taste: Corporate Cultural Hegemony in a Mass-Consumption Society," in *Recasting America: Culture and Politics in the Age of the Cold War,* Lary May, ed. (Chicago: U of Chicago P, 1989), 41.

64. Warren Susman, "'Personality' and the Making of Twentieth-Century Culture," in *New Directions in American Intellectual History,* John Higham and Paul K. Conkin, eds. (Racine, Wis.: Wingspread Conference on New Directions in American Intellectual History, 1977).

65. Lears, "A Matter of Taste," 49, 36, 39.

66. The sort of startled encomiums to the effect that American cinema "giants" were the century's religious idols were already standard discourse in the 1920s—as in César Vallejo's articles, written from Paris for a Peruvian newspaper. "Who is it that has denied the divinity of [Josephine] Baker, of Einstein, of Douglas Fairbanks or of Dempsey? No one" (César Vallejo, "Los Idolos de la vida contemporánea," *Mundial* 358, Lima, April 22, 1927, in *Crónicas,* bk. 2, 1927–1939 [México: Universidad Nacional Autónoma de México, 1985], 108–9; my translation).

67. Carl J. Friedrich, *The New Image of the Common Man* (Boston: Beacon Press, 1950); Geoffrey Gorer, *The American People: A Study in National Character* (New York: Norton, 1948); Henry Steele Commager, *The American Mind* (New Haven, Conn.: Yale UP, 1950).

68. Friedrich, *New Image,* 8.

69. In *Mariners, Renegades, and Castaways* James notes how much Melville

based his ideas on Anacharsis Cloots, a Prussian advocate of the "Universal Republic" based on liberty and brotherhood. This utopian socialism forms the basis, James argued, for the portrayal by Melville of a whaling ship as a microcosm of a polycultural world.

70. Friedrich, *New Image,* 303.

71. Alexis de Tocqueville, *Democracy in America* (New York: Signet, 1956; orig. pub. 1835), 314–5.

72. James Bryce, *The American Commonwealth,* (London: Macmillan, 1889), 452.

73. C. L. R. James, "Letters to Literary Critics," *The C. L. R. James Reader,* 220.

74. Rosenberg and Manning White, *Mass Culture,* 53, 49.

75. It is interesting in this connection to compare James's project with the almost contemporaneous one in England of Raymond Williams, who was also fundamentally literary in his Marxist effort to account theoretically for mass culture. In a little known public lecture, James reviewed William's books *Culture and Society* (1958) and *The Long Revolution* (1960) and later published his remarks pseudonymously as the pamphlet *Marxism and the Intellectuals* by J. R. Johnson (Detroit: Facing Reality Publishing Committee, 1962). Under a heading that reads "The Creative Power of the Working Class," he says that "Mr. Williams is the most remarkable writer that the socialist movement in England has produced for ten years or perhaps twenty . . . of working class origin but with a university education . . . He has developed the idea of culture from an exclusive possession of the educated and intellectuals and shown that the only meaning the word has for today is a *total way of life of the whole people*" (5, his emphasis). Nevertheless, he goes on to add, "Marxists have to show large and grave gaps in Mr. Williams' work, and in his thinking" (5). What makes a worker a worker, says James, is work itself, the labor process. Socialism, then, is primarily about the reorganization of work. "It plays a very small part in Mr. Williams' two books" (11).

76. Leo Löwenthal, "Historical Perspectives," 55.

77. Worcester, "James and the American Century," 29.

78. James to Geismar, April 11, 1961, 1.

6. The World Cuban

The Mayra Vilasis quote is from my interview with her at the Unión de escritores y artistas de Cuba, Havana, January 5, 1993. Vilasis is a well-known film director. The Alejo Carpentier quote is from Salvador Bueno, "The Black and White in the Narrative of Alejo Carpentier," in *AfroCuba: An Anthology of Cuban Writing on Race, Politics, and Culture,* Pedro Pérez Sarduy and Jean Stubbs, eds. (Melbourne: Ocean, in association with the Center for Cuban Studies [New York], 1993), 219.

1. Fernando Ortiz, *La Africanía de la música folklórica de Cuba* (Havana: Editora Universitaria, 1965), 105.

2. Alejo Carpentier, *La Música en Cuba* (Mexico: Fondo de Cultura Economica, 1946), preface.

3. This chapter is largely based on my interviews with practicing New York salsa musicians in 1994 and 1995 and on a research trip to Havana and Matanzas I took in the winter of 1993. I am particularly grateful for the advice and instruction given me by Mario García Joya and other recent Cuban exiles to the United States.

4. Alejo Carpentier, *Entrevistas, Alejo Carpentier,* Virgilio López Lemus, ed. (Havana: Editorial Letras Cubanas, 1985), 72. My translations.

5. By far the best account of Carpentier's intellectual background and literary sources can be found in Roberto González Echevarría's definitive study *Alejo Carpentier: The Pilgrim at Home* (Ithaca, N.Y.: Cornell UP, 1977).

6. Fernando Ortiz, *Los Instrumentos de la música afrocubana* (Havana: Editorial Letras Cubanas, 1952–1955 reissued, 1993–1995); Lydia Cabrera, *Yemayá y ochún: kariocha, iyalorichas, y olorichas* (Eastchester, N.Y.: Eliseo Torres, 1980; orig. pub. 1974). Cabrera was Ortiz's sister-in-law.

7. He poses this paradox in the prologue to a late edition of *¡Écue-Yamba-Ó!;* see Alejo Carpentier, *Obras completas,* vol. 1 (Mexico City: Siglo Veintiuno Editores, 1983), 26.

8. For a particularly uncharitable account of Carpentier's French accent and the supposed inauthenticity it suggests for his later political sympathies, see Guillermo Cabrera Infante, "Alejo Carpentier: A Shotgun Cuban," *Mea Cuba,* Kenneth Hall, trans. (New York: Faber & Faber, 1994), 383–99.

9. Lydia Cabrera, however—an almost exact contemporary of Carpentier—spent precisely the same years in Paris (1926–1939) taking courses in Oriental art and religion. It was the experience of observing similarities between the cultures of Oriental people and Afro-Cubans, she said, that moved her to "devote her entire life to the rich cultural inheritance of the Cuban Negro" (José R. de Armas and Charles W. Steele, *Cuban Consciousness in Literature: 1923–1974* [Miami: Ediciones Universal, 1978], 117).

10. Carpentier, *Entrevistas,* 85.

11. The term *cubanismos* ("cubanisms"), dealt with below in my discussion of Carpentier's journalism from Paris, has its origins in the Afro-Cuban recovery work of *negrismo*—as in Fernando Ortiz's study *Un Catauro de cubanismos* (1923). In this sense the term refers specifically to Cuban Black culture.

12. Carpentier, *Entrevistas,* 63.

13. José Lezama Lima, "La curiosidad barroca," *La Expresión americana* (Santiago de Chile: Editorial Universitaria, 1969), 33–57; Gustavo Pérez Firmat, *Do the Americas Have a Common Literature?* (Durham: Duke UP, 1990), 318, 320.

14. Alejo Carpentier, "Problemática de la actual novela latinoamericana," *Tientos y diferencias* (Barcelona: Plaza and Janes Editores, 1987), 11, 13.

15. Alejo Carpentier, *The Lost Steps,* Harriet de Onís, trans. (New York: Farrar, Straus, and Giroux, 1989; orig. pub., 1953), 44; *La Consagración de la primavera* (Havana: Editorial Letras Cubanas, 1987).

16. And yet, as Ricardo Alarcón, the head of Cuba's National Assembly, recently put it: "We no longer have a centrally planned state monopoly economy any longer and every day things are moving further away from that direction" (*New York Times,* September 30, 1993, A-4).

17. Among the exceptions, see *Contemporary Cuban Culture,* the pioneering special issue of *Social Text,* 15, Fall 1986; *Cuba,* the bilingual special issue of *Third Text,* 20, Autumn 1992; and "Bridges to Cuba/*Puentes a Cuba,*" *Michigan Quarterly Review,* 33, no. 1 (Fall 1994). Cuban-American scholars who have turned their attentions to contemporary culture in Cuba include José Piedra, "Poetics for the Hip," *New Literary History,* 22 (1991), 633–75; Roman de la Campa, "The Latino Diaspora in the United States: Sojourns from a Cuban Past," *Public Culture,* 6, no. 2 (Winter 1994); and Lillian Manzor-Coats, "Marginality Beyond Return: Gender, Racial and Linguistic Politics in U.S. Cuban Theater" unpublished manuscript, 1994. Even here, however, as the titles suggest, the focus is on Cubans in the United States. In this respect, see also Gustavo Pérez Firmat, *Life on the Hyphen: The Cuban-American Way* (Austin: U of Texas P, 1994).

18. Carpentier, *Obras completas,* vol. 1, 23. My translations.

19. Walter Raleigh, *The Discoverie of the Large, Rich, and Beutiful Empire of Guiana* (New York: Da Capo Press, Theatrum Orbis Terrarum, 1968; orig pub., 1596); Wilson Harris, *Palace of the Peacock* (London: Faber and Faber, 1968).

20. Peter Bürger, *Theory of the Avant-Garde* (Minneapolis: U of Minnesota P).

21. Vicky Unruh, *Latin American Vanguards: The Art of Contentious Encounters* (Berkeley: U of California P, 1994).

22. Hal Foster, "The 'Primitive' Unconscious of Modern Art," *October,* 34 (Fall 1985), 58.

23. James Clifford, "On Ethnographic Surrealism," *The Predicament of Culture* (Cambridge: Harvard UP, 1988); Michael Taussig, *The Nervous System* (New York: Routledge, 1992).

24. Clifford, "Ethnographic Surrealism," 132.

25. James Clifford, "Histories of the Tribal and the Modern," *The Predicament of Culture: Twentieth-Century Ethnography, Literature, and Art* (Cambridge: Harvard UP, 1988), 189–214.

26. In his posthumous study, *The Politics of Modernism* Raymond Williams similarly turns to the interwar avant-garde, and once there discovers re-

sources for studying imperialism's impact on the urban artist. (London: Verso, 1989), 37–80.

27. Eduardo Galeano, *The Book of Embraces,* Cedric Belfrage, trans. (New York: W. W. Norton, 1991), 135.

28. Because of its incorporation of French theory, perhaps the most poignant example in this respect is that of Edouard Glissant, *Caribbean Discourse: Selected Essays,* J. Michael Dash, trans. (Charlottesville: U Press of Virginia, 1989).

29. González Echevarría, *Alejo Carpentier,* 39.

30. Carpentier, *Obras completas,* vol. 8 (Mexico: Siglo Veintiuno Editores, 1985), 240.

31. Carpentier, *Entrevistas,* 19.

32. Carpentier, *The Lost Steps,* 25.

33. Alejo Carpentier, *Obras completas,* vol. 8, 320–1.

34. Carpentier, *Entrevistas,* 355–6.

35. Carpentier, *Obras completas,* vol. 8, 251.

36. Carpentier, *Entrevistas,* 99. Carpentier is writing these words in 1963, not the 1930s—that is, after the Cuban Revolution and after his implicit predictions of the 1930s had been realized.

37. Clifford, "Ethnographic Surrealism," 118.

38. Georges Bataille, "The 'Old Mole' and the Prefix *Sur* in the Words *Surhomme* and *Surrealist,*" *Visions of Excess: Selected Writings, 1927–1939* (Minneapolis: U of Minnesota P), 34–5.

39. James Miller handles Bataille in a similar mode, speaking as though the Marxism and more organized socialism hanging so thickly in the air in the 1930s, simply did not exist or existed only as a quirk of Bataille's odd mind. He refers there with startling brevity to his "bizarre kind of Marxism" (James Miller, *The Passion of Michel Foucault* [New York: Doubleday, 1993], 87).

40. Taussig, *The Nervous System,* 6, 153, 162.

41. Walter Benjamin, "Surrealism," *Reflections: Essays, Aphorisms, Autobiographical Writings,* Peter Demetz, ed. (New York: Harcourt Brace Jovanovich, 1978), 179.

42. Taussig, *Nervous System,* 163.

43. For exceptions to this trend, and for that reason more reliable studies, see Susan Buck-Morss, *The Origins of Negative Dialectics: Theodor W. Adorno, Walter Benjamin, and the Frankfurt Institute* (New York: Free Press, 1979), and the preface to Walter Benjamin, *"One-Way Street" and Other Writings,* Edmund Jephcott, ed., Kingsley Shorter, trans. (London: New Left Books, 1979).

44. Peter Osborne, *The Politics of Time: Modernity and Avant-Garde* (New York: Verso, 1995), 189. Margaret Cohen's *Profane Illumination* (Berkeley: U of Cali-

fornia P, 1992) expands Osborne's reading to book-length dimensions, inventing a Benjamin for use while disregarding views expressed in many places, including his correspondence—namely, that "an all too ostentatious proximity to the surrealist movement" would prove "fatal" to the *Arcades* project (for which the surrealism essay was to have served as an "opaque screen"). That Benjamin found much of the intellectual work flowing from communist circles boring or noxious is certainly true. But it did not prevent him from seriously considering joining the Communist Party. He insisted that one should act "in concert rather than against it." In both his artistic preferences and (as above) his dislikes, Benjamin believed himself a "materialist," preferring the "clumsy and caddish analyses of a Franz Mehring . . . to the most profound paraphrases of the realm of ideas emanating today from Heidegger's school." The point is not so much one's own political sympathies as it is the accuracy of scholarship, for Benjamin (and surrealism) cannot be understood in these contemporary readings. Little of the Benjamin revealed in this passage finds its way into current treatments of his work: "[A]nyone of our generation who feels and understands the historical moment in which he exists in this world, not as mere words, but as a battle, cannot renounce the study and the practice of the mechanism through which things (and conditions) and the masses interact." Walter Benjamin, *The Correspondence of Walter Benjamin, 1910–1940,* Gershom Scholem and Theodor W. Adorno, eds., Manfred R. Jacobson and Evelyn M. Jacobson, trans. [Chicago: U of Chicago P, 1994], 342, 372, 300.)

45. Carpentier, *Obras completas,* vol. 8, 334, 336. For Benjamin's appreciative view of Meyerhold, see Benjamin to Julia Radt, December 26, 1926, in Benjamin, *Correspondence,* 311.

46. González Echevarría, *Alejo Carpentier,* 200.

47. Carpentier, *The Lost Steps,* 22.

48. As Mary Louise Pratt has pointed out, Sarmiento "introduced himself in Paris in the role of the flaneur . . . the privileged observer of the city: '*Flaner* is a thing so holy and respectable in Paris, it is a function so privileged that no one dares interrupt it. The flaneur has the right to stick his nose everywhere . . .'" (Mary Louise Pratt, *Imperial Eyes: Travel Writing and Transculturation* [London: Routledge, 1992], 192).

49. Michael Taussig, *Mimesis and Alterity: A Particular History of the Senses* (New York: Routledge, 1993), 219.

50. Yvonne Daniel, *Rumba: Dance and Social Change in Contemporary Cuba* (Bloomington: Indiana UP, 1995), 70.

51. Alejo Carpentier, *La Música en Cuba* 119, 220–1.

52. André Breton, *Les pas perdus* (Paris: Èditions Gallimard, 1969; orig. publ.1924), 8, 114. My translations.

53. For example, Gene Santoro, *Dancing in Your Head: Jazz, Blues, Rock &*

Beyond (1994); Greil Marcus, *Ranters and Crowd Pleasers: Punk in Pop Music 1977–1992* (1993); Nelson George, *The Death of Rhythm and Blues* (1988); Robert Christgau, *Christgau's Record Guide: The '80s* (1990); and Andrew Ross and Tricia Rose, eds., *Microphone Fiends: Youth Music and Youth Culture* (1994). The last two, for being surveys, are particularly marked by having almost nothing to say about salsa or other popular Latin musics. Two of the contributors to *Microphone Fiends,* however—George Yúdice and Juan Flores—have elsewhere been honorable exceptions to the trend. See, for example, their jointly written essay "Living Borders/Buscando America: Languages of Latino Self-Formation," *Social Text,* 24 (1990), 57–84.

54. See, particularly, Vernon W. Boggs, ed., *Salsiology: Afro-Cuban Music and the Evolution of Salsa in New York City* (New York: Excelsior Music Publishing, 1992); Charley Gerard and Marty Sheller, *¡Salsa!: The Rhythm of Latin Music* (Crown Point, Ind.: White Cliffs Media, 1989); Rebeca Mauleón, *Salsa Guidebook for Piano and Ensemble* (Petaluma, Calif.: Sher Music, 1993); Hernando Calvo Ospina, *¡Salsa! Havana Heat, Bronx Beat* (London: Latin America Bureau, 1995); Jahnheinz Jahn, "Rumba," in *Muntu: African Culture and the Western World* (New York: Grove Weidenfeld, 1961), 62–95; and Daniel, *Rumba.*

55. Yvonne Daniel, *Rumba,* 19.

56. The immigration of Mexican labor to the United States, for example, has created important musical subcultures in a number of American cities—perhaps most prominently (outside the Southwest) in Chicago, where traditional *cumbia* and mariachi—alongside pop variants of the Selena variety—dominate three major radio stations. In New York, where Dominican immigration has exploded in recent decades, the distinctive (and non-Cuban) salsa of merengue is hugely evident in radio, dance hall, and street celebrations, as is Colombian salsa (along with the rural music of *vallenato)* through Polito Vargas's popular Sunday-evening program on WSKQ, 97.9 FM.

57. See, however, the excellent treatment of the topic in María de Los Angeles Torres, "Encuentros y Encontronazos: Homeland in the Politics and Identity of the Cuban Diaspora," *Diaspora,* 4, no. 2 (Fall 1995), 211–38.

58. Gerard and Sheller, *¡Salsa!* 4.

59. Calvo Ospina, *¡Salsa!* 76.

60. Gerard and Sheller, *¡Salsa!* 6–7.

61. NG La Banda, "La expresiva," *En la calle,* QB 9002 (New York: Qbadisc, 1992).

62. Fernando Ortiz, *Cuban Counterpoint: Tobacco and Sugar,* Harriet de Onís, trans. (New York: Alfred A. Knopf, 1947), 103. What is often not appreciated in current invocations of transculturation, similarly, is the fact that Ortiz's famous book was concerned not with the creative assimilation of

European imports but with just the opposite: the complete transformation of European civilization by the export of the New World—and primarily Cuban—culture of tobacco.

63. María Teresa Vélez, "Eya Aranla: Overlapping Perspectives on a Santería Group," *Diaspora,* 3, no. 3 (Winter 1994), 294.

64. Calvo Ospina, *¡Salsa!* 103.

65. Leonardo Acosta, *Del tambor al sintetizador* (Havana: Editorial Letras Cubanas, 1983), 78, 83. (Emphases added.)

66. See, for example, Douglas Kahn and Diane Neumaier, eds., *Cultures of Contention* (Seattle: Real Comet, 1985); Elizabeth Ruf, "Teatro del Pueblo, Por el Pueblo, y Para el Pueblo: An Interview with Alan Bolt," *Drama Review,* 31, 4 (Winter 1987), 77–90. My own research in Nicaragua in 1986 also suggested the degree to which pre-existing folk song forms with an explicitly Sandinista content were greeted enthusiastically at concerts and local gatherings by ordinary people. One of the clearest examples is that of Carlos Mejía Godoy in a typical act of sympathetic spokesmanship for the Nicaraguan youth who largely made up the ranks of the FSLN.

67. Putting the same issue in the form of a commentary on the commodification of third-world cultural riches, Argeliers León writes that "music has developed into being the merchandise that nourishes an immense arsenal within the underdeveloped countries of the capitalist formations." He goes on to explore the tension between music's role as liberatory Latin American self-expression and *the* definitive form of a self-alienating bulk-commodity export. Argeliers León, "La música como mercancía," in *Musicología en Latinoamerica,* Gómez Garcìa, ed. (Havana: Editorial Arte Y Literatura, 1985), 407.

68. For the unprecedented scale of post-1959 scholarship dedicated to solidifying the dignity and influence of Afro-Cuban musics, see Yvonne Daniel's bibliography in *Rumba,* 178–91.

69. Ortiz, *La Africanía,* 160.

70. "In 1875, he was called urgently by the Captain General who admitted to admiring him: 'Ignacio Cervantes . . . we are certain now that the money you have earned as a concert performer has found its way into the hands of the insurrectionists. Stop this before we have to imprison you . . . Which way are you going to go?' . . . 'To the United States,' the musician answered. 'It is the closest country to Cuba, and there I will be able to continue doing what I've been doing here.' Stupefied, the General let him go." (Helio Orovio, *Diccionario de la música cubana* [Havana: Editorial Letras Cubanas, 1981], 82.)

71. Wyatt MacGaffey and Clifford R. Barnett in collaboration with Jean Haiken and Mildred Vreeland, *Twentieth-Century Cuba: The Background of the Castro Revolution* (Garden City, N.Y.: Anchor, 1965), 38–9.

72. Pedro Pérez Sarduy and Jean Stubbs, *AfroCuba,* 5, 9.

73. Santiago Colás, "Of Creole Symptoms, Cuban Fantasies, and Other Latin American Postcolonial Ideologies," *PMLA* 110, 3 (May 1995), 389.

74. Daniel, *Rumba,* 13.

75. See, for example, Radamés Giró, "Todo lo que usted quiso saber sobre el mambo . . ." ("Everything You Wanted to Know about Mambo") *La Gaceta,* November–December 1992, 13–17. Note also the international rumba festival in Matanzas in December of 1992, or the Havana '94 *encuentro* that brought together musicians and aficionados from around the world to celebrate Afro-Cuban music.

76. Sarduy and Stubbs, *AfroCuba,* 3, 10.

77. Rafael Duharte Jiménez, "The 19th Century Black Fear," in Sarduy and Stubbs, *AfroCuba,* 40.

78. Pedro Serviat, "Solutions to the Black Problem," in Sarduy and Stubbs, *AfroCuba,* 89.

79. Sarduy and Stubbs, *AfroCuba,* 12.

80. Rogelio Martínez Furé, "Imaginary Dialogue on Folklore," in *AfroCuba,* 116.

81. Anne Walmsley, *The Caribbean Artists Movement, 1966–1972* (London: New Beacon Books, 1992), 145.

82. Jacques Derrida, "Back from Moscow, in the U.S.S.R.," in *Politics, Theory, and Contemporary Culture,* Mark Poster, ed. (New York: Columbia UP, 1993), 197–236 (212 quoted). The distinction I will be making between "mass" and "popular" culture is the one used by Theodor Adorno and Horkheimer and, later, by Stuart Hall and Paddy Whannel: that is, between a corporatist "culture industry," on the one hand, and a culture that "arises spontaneously from the masses themselves," on the other (Theodor Adorno, "Culture Industry Reconsidered," *New German Critique,* 6 (Fall 1975), 12).

83. Dick Hebdige, *Subculture: The Meaning of Style* (London: Methuen, 1979); Lawrence Grossberg, "I'd Rather Feel Bad Than Not Feel Anything: Rock and Roll, Pleasure, and Power," *Enclitic* (Spring-Fall 1984), 94–111; Andrew Ross, *Universal Abandon? The Politics of Postmodernism* (Minneapolis: U of Minnesota P, 1988), xii.

84. John Beverley, "Testimonio, Sendero, Representation, and the New Political Logics," *Mediations,* 17, no. 2 (November 1993), 50. For other arguments that a socialist mass culture has failed, see Jesse Lemisch, "I Dreamed I Saw MTV Last Night," *The Nation,* October 18, 1986, 361, 374–6, and Laura Kipnis, *Ecstasy Unlimited* (New York: Routledge, 1992), 2–32, 102–16. Kipnis's book contains a perceptive chapter linking the (false) assumption that Cuban art is flat and "political" in the bad sense to U.S. foreign policy: "Aesthetics and Foreign Policy," 208–17.

85. John Beverley, *Against Literature* (Minneapolis: U of Minnesota P, 1993), 5.

86. Marc Cooper, "Roll Over Che Guevara," *Village Voice,* July 16, 1991, 29–35.

87. Jay Murphy, "The Young and Restless in Habana," in *Cuba,* special issue of *Third Text,* 20 (Autumn 1992), 115–32.

88. The comments that follow are not meant as a general defense of mass culture experiments in all socialist countries—the so-called "fakelore" of Eastern Europe, for example. I am limiting myself to the Cuban case. Because of the sweeping nature of Beverley's statement, that alone would be sufficient to question it.

89. Beverley, *Against Literature,* 9.

90. Julio García Espinosa, "For an Imperfect Cinema," in *Communication and Class Struggle,* Armand Mattelart and Seth Siegelaub, eds., vol. 2 (New York: Institute for Mass Media Research Council, 1982), 62–66.

91. Acosta, *Del tambor,* 108.

92. Many of these observations on testimonial can be found in Beverley's own work; see Beverley, *Against Literature,* 69–102.

93. Van Gosse, *Where the Boys Are: Cuba, Cold War America and the Making of a New Left* (London: Verso, 1993), 7.

94. Rigo Vásquez, "La Nueva Trova: Written and Sung Poetry in Cuba," *Third Text,* 20 (Autumn 1992), 110.

95. Gosse, *Where the Boys Are,* 5.

96. Yociel Marrero Baez to the author, December 15, 1993.

Conclusion

1. Rudolf Kayser, "Americanism," in *The Weimar Republic Sourcebook,* Anton Kaes, Martin Jay, and Edward Dimendberg, eds. (Berkeley: U of California P, 1994), 395.

2. Apart from the well-known writing on translation by Martin Heidegger and Walter Benjamin and less well-known work like that of Samia Mehrez, I would take as my example here George Steiner, *After Babel: Aspects of Language and Translation* (London: Oxford UP, 1975).

3. Nicolás Guillén, "Tú no sabe inglé," in *Sóngoro consongo y otros poemas: selección del autor* (Madrid: Alianza, 1981), 11–12. My translation.

4. The prevailing mood remains, via French poststucturalist conveyances, Nietzsche's from *The Dawn: "As little state as possible.* All political and economic arrangements are not worth it, that precisely the most gifted spirits should be permitted, or even obliged, to manage them: such a waste of spirit is really worse than an extremity . . . At such a price, one pays far too dearly for the 'general security.'" Walter Kaufmann, ed., *The Portable Nietzsche* (New York & London: Penguin, 1982), 82.

5. Anthony Appiah, "Loyalty to Humanity," *Boston Review,* 19, no. 5 (October/November 1994), 7.

Index

Other books in the *Convergences* series:

Jeffrey Kallberg, *Chopin at the Boundaries: Sex, History, and Musical Genre*
Declan Kiberd, *Inventing Ireland*
Jane Miller, *Seductions: Studies in Reading and Culture*
Masao Miyoshi, *Off Center: Power and Culture Relations between Japan and the United States*
Tom Paulin, *Minotaur: Poetry and the Nation State*
Richard Poirier, *Poetry and Pragmatism*
Jacqueline Rose, *The Haunting of Sylvia Plath*
Tony Tanner, *Venice Desired*
Tzvetan Todorov, *On Human Diversity: Nationalism, Racism, and Exoticism in French Thought*